Radical Cataloging: Essays at the Front

Radical Cataloging

Essays at the Front

edited by K. R. Roberto

INTRODUCTION BY SANFORD BERMAN

McFarland & Company, Inc., Publishers

Jefferson, North Carolina, and London

ALSO OF INTEREST

Revolting Librarians Redux:
Radical Librarians Speak Out,
by K. R. Roberto and Jessamyn West
(McFarland, 2003)

ALTERNATIVE CATALOGING-IN-PUBLICATION DATA

Roberto, K. R. (Keller R.), 1975–, editor.
Radical cataloging: essays at the front. Edited by K.R. Roberto.
Introduction by Sanford Berman.— Jefferson, North Carolina:
McFarland & Company, Inc., Publishers, copyright 2008.

Includes criticisms of traditional Library of Congress cataloging
and subject headings, discussion of how cataloging practices affect
front-line library workers, and suggestions for methods to make
cataloging more inclusive and helpful to library users.

PARTIAL CONTENTS: 1. Cataloging in context —
2. We criticize because we care — 3. Innovative practices.
1. Critical cataloging.   2. Catalogers — Social responsibility.
3. Library of Congress cataloging.   4. Cataloging — Anecdotes.
I. Title: Rad cataloging.   II. Title: Essays at the front.   III. Title: Frontline essays.
Z693 .R63 2008

LIBRARY OF CONGRESS CATALOGUING-IN-PUBLICATION DATA

Radical cataloging : essays at the front / edited by K. R. Roberto ;
introduction by Sanford Berman.
p.   cm.
Includes bibliographical references and index.

ISBN 978-0-7864-3543-2
softcover : 50# alkaline paper ∞

1. Cataloging.   I. Roberto, K. R. (Keller R.), 1975–
Z693.R33   2008   025.3 — dc22   2008007084

British Library cataloguing data are available

Cover photograph ©2007 Shutterstock

Manufactured in the United States of America

McFarland & Company, Inc., Publishers
Box 611, Jefferson, North Carolina 28640
www.mcfarlandpub.com

To Sandy, for leading the way

Table of Contents

III. INNOVATIVE PRACTICES

Preface: What Does "Radical Cataloging" Mean, Anyway?

K. R. Roberto

When I started telling people that I was editing an anthology with the intriguing title of *Radical Cataloging: Essays at the Front*, they always asked what "radical cataloging" meant. Did it mean that I advocated the elimination of AACR2, LCSH, and the MARC format? Did I think that traditional cataloging was dead and we should all become metadata librarians (leaving us with the same problems, more fluctuating standards, but a more glamorous job title)? Was I advocating that we should outsource all cataloging to vendors and to hell with authority control and controlled vocabularies?

The answer to all of the above questions was no, not at all (especially the last one; heaven knows that there are quite enough people in libraryland advocating for such a tragedy already). I soon discovered that, as with many things in my life, I was better at defining what radical cataloging wasn't, as opposed to what it actually was.

I first started using the term sometime in early 2002. After reading a lengthy thread on the AUTOCAT email list about whether political discussions were truly appropriate for the list — the answer, unsurprisingly, was "not especially" — I decided to start an email list where people were welcome to discuss the politics of cataloging, as well as any other relevant topics that came to mind, to their heart's content. For reasons that I can no longer remember, I decided to call it the Radical Cataloging list, or RADCAT for short. If I remember correctly, one of the earliest discussions on the RADCAT list was an attempt to define the term. (Obviously, I have been having some trouble in this area for a while.)

Part of the problem is that the word "radical" can have wildly divergent connotations: think of "radical leftist" and "radical surgery," for example. Radical cataloging is much closer to the former than the latter, fortunately. To avoid this confusion, I usually offer a brief explanation about how the term refers to cataloging from a progressive perspective. So why not just call it "progressive cataloging"? There is a decades-long tradition of referring to progressive and socially responsible library work as "radical librarianship," and using the same adjective allows for a nearly automatic association between the two; additionally, as it happens, the term has recently been co-opted to describe a joint venture between a cataloging vendor and Amazon.com, showing that "progressive" is just as confusing. All things considered, we're probably better off sticking with "radical cataloging."

Many catalogers are radical without even being aware of it. Here are some behaviors and traits that mark the radical cataloger:

• being user-focused with regard to *your* library's users (who may or may not have anything in common with the technophiliac users found in the currently popular Library 2.0 model)

• having a healthy dose of skepticism about the quality of readily available bibliographic records, but choosing to improve their quality and usefulness instead of dismissing them entirely

• realizing that copy cataloging can be just as difficult and complicated as original cataloging, if not occasionally more so, and valuing it accordingly

• knowing when and how to make cataloging decisions that may be in conflict with traditional cataloging standards — or, failing that, since not every cataloger is in a position to make such decisions, recognizing when the rules aren't working and why

• genuinely appreciating traditional cataloging models while examining ways to integrate new and useful ideas into this framework without abandoning what already works

• wanting library OPACs to make better use of the rich MARC data supplied by catalogers

• feeling passionate about cataloging and its benefits, and being willing to discuss this with other library workers without boring them half to death

None of these ideas are new, or shockingly radical, but they are infrequently addressed in much contemporary writing in the field of librarianship. These days, being "user-centered" often involves assuming that all library users have the same needs, and that those needs are perfectly expressed by making library catalogs resemble Google as closely as possible. Libraries outsource and buy catalog records in bulk because we're discouraged from having the time and resources to examine each record by hand; any concerns about the quality of said records are dismissed by saying they're "good enough" and that users, that mythical homogenous group, don't care about MARC records anyway (which begs the question of why we're buying records in the first place, but don't let's go too far down that path). The emphasis is on speed, not quality; it's cataloging by fast-food model.

Cataloging is under attack right now. Admittedly, it probably always has been, since administrators have always been concerned with cutting costs and anything quantifiable is quick to go, but the threats seem to carry more weight these days. Consultants write reports about "the future of the catalog" that recommend heartily embracing the current technological trends and streamlining current practices, if not eliminating them entirely. When those trends are superseded by new forms of technology, then you hire new consultants to make the same recommendations, substituting new buzzwords for the old. It's excellent job security for consultants, but open season on everyone else.

This is not to say that traditional cataloging in the United States using AACR2 and the Library of Congress subject headings doesn't warrant any criticism, because it undoubtedly does. Cataloging rules and procedures can be decidedly cryptic — not just to users and public services staff, but to people who are actually cataloging. There is an excellent body of work, much of which is discussed later in this volume, detailing LCSH's decided lack of appropriate and intuitive language. When we do manage to create excellent bibliographic records, library catalogs don't usually do a good job of successfully displaying the information they contain. There is definitely room for improvement in the field.

The purpose of this anthology is to serve as a tool for catalogers and cataloging advocates. The book is divided into three sections: Cataloging in Context; We Criticize Because We Care; and Innovative Practices. Cataloging in Context offers personal reflections from front-line staff, historical overviews, and theoretical essays. We Criticize Because We Care, as you may have guessed from the title, criticizes the current state of cataloging, including subject thesauri, library vendors, and consultants. Innovative Practices details projects in various types of libraries that make cataloging more useful. Some of the pieces are more radical than others, and I'm not at all sure that all of the contributors would work well together if they had to, but having room to explore different viewpoints and possibilities is part of what makes library work so compelling.

Cataloging may be under siege, but it's not too late to fight back. I hope you find some reasons to do so in the following pages.

Introduction:
Cataloging Reform, LC, and Me

Sanford Berman

In response to a *Bottom Line* interviewer's query, "What do you consider your greatest achievement?" (v. 16, no. 4, 2003, p. 166), I said, in part:

Rescuing the full run of *I.F. Stone's Weekly* from the dumpster in 1968. That's where the hugely influential muckraking newsletter was destined, a victim of reckless weeding by my boss at the UCLA Research Library. More broadly, my professional mission — and perhaps career achievement — has been rescue, or liberation. Maudlin as it may sound, I actually felt almost every day, as a cataloger, that I was liberating library books and audiovisual materials, as well as the information and ideas they contained, by crafting bibliographic records that included clarifying (and searchable) notes, generous topical and other access points (among them tracings for illustrators, translators, eminent foreword and preface contributors, permuted and sub-titles, and small, regional, and specialty presses), no arcane or intimidating abbreviations, and subject headings formulated in both familiar and unbiased language, and representing contemporary themes and events in a timely way. This constructively critical cataloging approach also involved correcting and expanding "outside copy" — typically Library of Congress (LC) records — in order to repair classification and subject analysis mistakes, together with frequent "under-cataloging." That activity, largely conducted at Hennepin County Library in Minnesota, directly triggered the reform or creation of hundreds of LC subject headings, promoted more extensive note-making as general practice, and by precedent and advocacy encouraged full and equitable cataloging treatment for all formats and genres, most notably audiovisual, fiction, and juvenilia. [Reprinted with permission from "If you want my 2¢ worth" by Kent C. Boese. *The Bottom Line,* Vol. 16, Issue 4, Emerald Group Publishing Company.]

The August 9, 2006, *Library Juice* (<http://www.libraryjuicepress.com/blog>) featured an extensive interview with Barbara Tillett, Chief of the Library of Congress Cataloging Policy and Support Office, conducted by Rory Litwin. The conversation centered on how LC creates and changes subject headings and particularly on the issue of "subject heading reform" and "Sanford Berman's activism."

Since Tillett's remarks seriously mischaracterized my "reform" efforts and sugarcoated LC's own practices, I immediately prepared five pages of "random notes" in response. That was on August 12. Although distributed to *Library Juice*, together with massive documentation, nothing has since appeared in Litwin's blog. So here they are.

In a Fall 2004 *Counterpoise* interview, I was asked, "How would you update your comments in 'Jackdaws Strut in Peacock's Feathers,' which appeared in *Librarians at Liberty*, six years later?" I replied:

Of course, some specific examples might be dropped or revised, but I'd retain the overall complaint and indictment. Let me stipulate the continuing problem in a few pithy observations:

• Cataloging should unmistakably identify a given work, convey its nature, content, and thrust, and specify how it can be accessed: e.g., by subject headings and various added entries for title variations, editors, illustrators, notable contributors, translators, associated groups or agencies, and local, specialty, and alternative presses.

• Electronic tinkering and keyword searching do not compensate for rigorous, accurate, fulsome, and fair cataloging at the start: that is, the crafting of a functional bibliographic record.

• Most U.S. libraries rely on Library of Congress cataloging for the bib-records that will appear in their local OPACs. This is especially so for U.S. trade publications, which constitute the bulk of new acquisitions by public, school, and some college libraries.

• Increasingly, most libraries do not review "outside copy" (i.e., the LC or network-supplied data) in a constructively critical fashion. Too often, paraprofessionals or clerks may be assigned merely to check on call number suitability and verify such basic elements as main entry and title, nothing more.

• As demonstrated in "Jackdaws" and numerous other sources, LC-originated copy is often deficient in notes, subject tracings, and other access points. Further, despite some fairly recent improvement in the liberality of heading assignment and the topical and genre treatment of literary works, such assignments remain inconsistent and spotty. Moreover, much subject heading vocabulary is still biased, awkward, or absent.

The dilemma persists: Libraries accept LC-like products and tools with an almost infantile faith that they're really useful. In fact, they are frequently imperfect and dysfunctional. What to do? Undertake more local enhancement and revision, realizing that poor cataloging may undo the considerable effort and expense of selecting and processing material. If the items can't be found, what's the point? Also, support LC's future requests for greater funding and staffing, providing they acknowledge what particularly needs repair, like the more timely establishment of topical headings and the accelerated inclusion of content-clarifying and keyword-searchable notes.

For recent examples of LC cataloging infelicities, see my column, "Berman's Bag," in *The U*N*A*B*A*S*H*E*D Librarian*, no. 132. Last week, I received a gift from students at the College of St. Catherine in St. Paul: *Shut Up Shut Down: Poems* (Minneapolis, MN: Coffee House Press, 2004). It's by Mark Nowak, with an Afterword by Amiri Baraka. It consists largely of poems about work, workers, and the labor movement, punctuated by black-and-white photos, quotations, and reading lists. Coincidentally, it is a case study in what's wrong with standard cataloging. LC assigned a generous four headings: CORPORATE CULTURE, CORPORATIONS—CORRUPT PRACTICES, BUSINESS ETHICS, and GREED, all subdivided by —LITERARY COLLECTIONS. The sole added entry: I. Title. So what's amiss? No added entry (access point) for notable contributor Amiri Baraka. No turnaround title added entry for "Shut down shut up." No tracing for the alternative publisher: Coffee House Press. No note indicating the graphic dimension, the photodocumentary aspect. No genre heading for WORKING CLASS POETRY. No topical headings for plant closings, downsizing, and labor movement. Nor for, say, EMPLOYEE RESISTANCE AND REVOLTS. And GREED is way too broad. This is emphatically about corporate greed, which demands an appropriate new heading. Also needed: AMERICAN POETRY— 21ST CENTURY. Finally, Dewey classifiers placed this essentially verse collection in "American fiction." Not quite bibliocide-by-cataloging, but close. [Copyright 2004, the *U*N*A*B*A*S*H*E*D*™ Library, the "How I Run My Library Good" Letter^sm, PO Box 325, Mount Kisco, NY 10549; reprinted with permission from Issue 132.]

For the record, over two years or longer I submitted suggestions and documentation regarding cataloging improvements and possible new or substitute headings to LC's Cataloging Policy and Support Office. No replies. Then, finally, after some 40 or 50 submissions, came a response, which I believe materialized only because the CPSO chief was ordered to do so by her superior. Since that December 16, 2004 letter, more have arrived. I would dearly like to report that the "thaw" betokens a genuine responsiveness, manifest in concrete reforms or new-heading creation. Alas, that hasn't quite happened. Mostly, it's been perfunctory acknowledgments or tortured explanations about why they won't do what they should do.

Among other things, I've been trying to get them to introduce subject headings for CULTURE WARS, INFOSHOPS, STUDENT ANTI-SWEATSHOP MOVEMENT, PLUTOCRACY, and NATIVE AMERICAN HOLOCAUST, as well as either replacing FANZINES with ZINES or creating ZINES as a complementary descriptor. The latest LC communication was a full-page rebuke, dated 2-10-05, for daring to mention the inadequate Cataloging-in-Publication entry for Nan Levinson's *Outspoken: Free Speech Stories* in my upcoming *College & Research Libraries* review.

Since that interview, both PLUTOCRACY and ZINES have been established as new headings. They are most welcome, although woefully tardy. And such suggested "Zine" permutations as ZINE DISTRIBUTORS, ZINE LIBRARIES, FEMINIST ZINES, and QUEER ZINES still await creation.

Adding "Culture wars" as a UF (unused form/"see" reference) under CULTURE CONFLICT effectively buries the considerable literature on that topic, which particularly refers to contention in the U.S. over public morality. In a 12-26-04 missive to LC, I wrote: "Hennepin County Library established this form in late 1996, initially applying it to 13 titles in the collection. This is HCL's new-heading report in *Cataloging Bulletin* 145:

Culture wars.
cn　HCL form. Assignment: Mark Gerson's *Neoconservative vision: from the Cold War to the culture wars* (1996); Ira Shor's *Culture wars: school and society in the conservative restoration, 1969–1984* (1986); James Davison Hunter's *Culture wars: the struggle to define America* (1991); Gerald Graff's *Beyond the culture wars: how teaching the conflicts can revitalize American education* (1992); Richard Bolton's *Culture wars: documents from the recent controversies in the arts* (1992); Fred Whitehead's *Culture wars: opposing viewpoints* (1994); Russell Jacoby's *Dogmatic*

wisdom: how the culture wars divert education and distract America (1994); Tom Sine's *Cease fire: searching for sanity in America's culture wars* (1995); William J. Bennett's *De-valuing of America: the fight for our culture and our children* (1992), which includes "Culture wars"; Camille Paglia's *Vamps and tramps* (1994), which includes "Culture wars"; Daniel Starer's *Hot topics: everything you wanted to know about the 50 major controversies* (1995), which includes "Culture wars"; Chip Berlet's *Eyes right: challenging the right-wing backlash* (1995), which includes "Culture wars and freedom of expression."

sf   Cultural wars
     Wars, Culture
xx   Cultural policy
     Culture conflict
     Educational policy

This innovation was formally recommended to LC. The original cross-reference structure should be augmented with these additional BTs:

xx   Church and state
     Popular culture
     Religion and politics
     Social policy
     United States — Politics and government —1980–

And this is a possible scope note, derived in part from the myriad "Culture wars" entries presently available (even, I suspect, to LC catalogers) on the Web:

pn   Here are entered materials on disputes and confrontations in American public policy and culture dating from the early 1980s and typically involving such ideologically and religiously-based issues as abortion, gun control, censorship, church-state separation (including school prayer, the Pledge of Allegiance, teaching evolution, and faith-based government programs), and homosexuality.

That model scope note also appeared in a *Library Resources & Technical Services* letter to the editor, Jan. 2006, p. 4.

• Yes, "Mr. Berman" does occasionally submit "news clippings," strictly to further document term-usage for a recommended heading, not as assignment-candidates. (Occasionally, however, a clipping or journal article explicitly mentions books, periodicals, films, or Web sites dealing with the subject, in which case I highlight them for possible application.)

• Finally transforming "Vietnamese Conflict" to "Vietnam War" in *2006* should be cause for embarrassment, not exultation.

• "Lobbying members of Congress" is something I've rarely done. However, if I hadn't prompted the late Senator Paul Wellstone to ask LC why they hadn't yet created a heading for NATIONAL HEALTH INSURANCE, that rubric wouldn't have entered LCSH. (Nothing else had worked.) Similarly, copying my Minnesota senators and congressman recently when querying Librarian of Congress James H. Billington why ARMENIAN MASSACRES hadn't been converted to ARMENIAN GENOCIDE and how come no one at CPSO would respond to my concern at least produced a reply from Deanna Marcum, Associate Librarian for Library Services (reproduced in *The U*N*A*B*A*S*H*E*D Librarian*, no. 139, p. 15–18).

• It's too bad that anyone needs to resort to "grandstanding" to prompt obviously desirable changes. I plead guilty to the charge. Publicly ridiculing the heading WATER CLOSETS at an ALA program later that day translated into a conversion to TOILETS. And repeatedly displaying a light bulb during talks and asking the audience what that item was termed in their catalogs eventually spawned a discrete rubric for LIGHT BULBS (which had previously been termed "Electric lamps, Incandescent"). Too bad, but that's what it took to do the sensible thing.

• I had recommended replacement or dissolution of JEWISH QUESTION as early as 1971 (*Prejudices and Antipathies*, p. 22–26). I (and others) repeated that suggestion for the next many years. Nothing happened. Then, as I reported in *Technical Services Quarterly*, Fall/Winter 1984, p. 188–89: "Finally, in June 1983, nearly 13 years after that heading had been publicly and thoroughly denounced, LC agreed to scrap JEWISH QUESTION. Marjorie Greenfield, an irate Jewish-American librarian, persuaded the Anti-Defamation League to intercede. And that did it."

• Introducing GOD (CHRISTIANITY) was likewise proposed in *Prejudices* (p. 56–57), and has often been repeated by me in print and public speech. There is no compelling reason for not having established the more accurate and fairer form long ago. (This doesn't involve replacing anything, merely creating a new rubric and assigning it consistently to material that treats God from a Christian perspective, instead of indigestibly mish-mashing such works with material that deals in general or from a multifaith viewpoint with the idea of God. The longer the wait for the new heading, the greater the bibliographic pollution and irretrievability of desired items.)

• Incidentally, the trouble with the "God" treatment simply represents a much larger deficiency regarding a host of other religion-related headings (for more examples, see the "Christocentric headings" index entries in the 1993 *Prejudices* reprint).

• "Before we made the change from 'Gypsies' to 'Romanies,' staff members from CPSO ... consulted closely with a renowned expert and advocate in this field." That expert/advocate was doubtless Ian F. Hancock, linguistics professor at the University of Texas–Austin and himself an English Romani. Writings and correspondence by Hancock years before had led Hennepin County Library to make the ethnonym-switch. And those Hancock sources (as well as HCL's treatment details) had been regularly forwarded to LC — with no positive result.

• No explanation is given for continuing to cling to "Lepers" and "Leprosy," except for a reference to MeSH as an authority for such forms. Well, what about the U.S. Public Health Service as a suitable authority? USPHS has favored "Hansen's Disease" and "Hansen's Disease patients" for decades. And they actually *deal* with HD patients and medical personnel. (For more on this terminological dispute, see Fall/Winter 1984 *TSQ*, p. 155–60, and "Hansen's Disease, not Leprosy," *Librarians at Liberty*, December 2000, p. 27–28.)

• "Most of our correspondence contains helpful and constructive suggestions." The clear implication: my correspondence is not either helpful or constructive. Yet for 26 years, I duly forwarded to LC copies of HCL's bimonthly *Cataloging Bulletin*, replete with full syndetic workups for new and changed headings, assignment citations, and quoted usage examples. Lately, in retirement, I have privately recommended dozens of new headings and changes, accompanying each with backup documentation and proposed scope notes and cross-references. (I'll gladly supply photocopies to anyone. Topics range from EROTOPHOBIA and RECOVERED FACTORY MOVEMENT to MORAL PANICS and GENDERQUEERS. Also available: two installments of "Who did it when?," dating from 1990 and 1992, which compare LC and HCL heading establishment by date and language.)

• One unstated reason for why headings aren't created or corrected in a timely fashion is that catalogers may be discouraged from doing so. This is from my column in *The U*N*A*B*A*S*H*E*D Librarian*, no. 137, p. 25:

> As exemplified by the 12-year (or longer) delay in establishing a ZINES heading, I've repeatedly lamented LC's failure to create needed subject descriptors and also Dewey numbers in a timely, responsive, and even proactive fashion. Invariably, the question arises in talks and conversations: Why? How come the laggardliness? Surely, some of the several plausible reasons include underfunding, insufficient staff, and unending backlogs. But there's another reason, too: Attitudes or management priorities, which currently seem to regard digitization as a panacea for space problems, preservation, and searching. (An older and probably continuing mindset is basically conservative and bureaucratic, hesitant to innovate until somehow shamed or otherwise pressured to do so.) These are not merely the speculations of a jaundiced and frustrated outsider. Lately, when a high-ranking member of the LC cataloging establishment was asked how LC creates new subject headings and whether individual catalogers propose them, she replied: "Yes, catalogers are responsible for setting up new subject headings when needed for a work they're cataloging. However, our catalogers are under a lot of pressure to produce widgets. Since they don't get any credit for setting up new subject headings or classification numbers, this work takes a definite back seat to cranking out cataloging." [Copyright 2005, the *U*N*A*B*A*S*H*E*D*™ Library, the "How I Run My Library Good" Letter^sm, PO Box 325, Mount Kisco, NY 10549; reprinted with permission from Issue 137.]

Last Words

Since I composed those "random notes" in mid–August 2006, I'm extremely pleased to report that LC established MORAL PANICS within four or five months of my initial suggestion. Ditto for WICCA, established in late August. And GOD (CHRISTIANITY) finally entered LCSH, albeit some 35 years after having been first suggested. So there's some hope. However, such rubrics as ANARCHA-FEMINISM, ANARCHO-PRIMITIVISM, ANTI-ARABISM, BUTCH AND FEMME, DRAG QUEENS, GI MOVEMENT, GENDERQUEERS, INTERSEXUALS, REPARTIVE THERAPY (SEXUAL ORIENTATION), SECOND-WAVE FEMINISM, SLOW MOVEMENT, and THIRD-WAVE FEMINISM—all proposed between 2003 and 2006—have yet to be sanctified. Further, necessary corrections—like extending the scope of the new TWO-SPIRIT PEOPLE to include all GLBT Native Americans, replacing ARMENIAN MASSACRE with ARMENIAN GENOCIDE, substituting INTERSEXUALITY for HERMAPHRODITISM, and making TRANSGENDER PEOPLE a primary heading rather than an erroneous "see" reference to TRANSSEXUALS—still await attention. Also, while literary works now enjoy much more topical access than they did about 20 years ago, the treatment could be fuller and better. (For instance, John LeCarré's *Mission Song* got tracings for INTELLIGENCE OFFICERS—FICTION and WORLD POLITICS—FICTION, but nothing to represent the occupation of the lead character, an interracial Congolese interpreter, nor any thematic access points for Congo, coups d'état, and mineral resources. Similarly missing: a genre heading, perhaps SPY FIC-TION, ENGLISH.)

The actual "last words" go to David Lesniaski, a cataloging teacher at the College of St. Catherine in St. Paul, Minnesota. In an unsolicited letter, he wrote:

> I couldn't tell whether Tillett was a witness for the prosecution or the defense. Forty years to come up with "Vietnam War"? Insistence on taking submissions only through their forms and their process (not realizing that making those requirements, along with the others — such as the need for "expert" opinion and the reluctance to establish "ephemeral" terms — effectively torpedoes precisely the sorts of headings LC is most deficient in).
>
> Aside from the problems with actual headings and with the process to submit headings/changes, the interview, along with other evidence, suggested to me that LC is the problem, and until the cataloging community finds a way to create its own list (thesaurus, etc.) of headings to make up for the ones LC won't do, or does badly, neither we nor our public are going to see any significant positive changes anytime soon. "Cooperative" is hardly the term for the subject heading situation, for cooperation implies some sort of joint give-and-take, and the evidence is overwhelming that LC doesn't think that way. I think of the series authority debacle last spring, or the Calhoun report, commissioned by LC, that (among other things) talked about a business model and the virtue of cutting back on subject & descriptive cataloging in order to get things through faster — these hardly seem like overtures for the betterment of cataloging through cooperation.
>
> I do wish librarians, and catalogers in particular, were less passive, prone to accept authority, and more willing to do what they know is right. While creating/maintaining headings takes some thought, the mechanics are so simple in any decent online system that the old complaint about time just doesn't hold water any longer [David Lesniaski to Sanford Berman, September 13, 2006].

To which I add only a heartfelt AMEN!

The Existential Crisis of a Cataloger

Beth Thornton

I used to joke about my existential crisis. But it was always a smug sort of joking — poking fun at myself using the same old fodder that people have always used to make fun of catalogers. Yes, I'm a big nerd. I love solving bibliographic problems and I speak MARC. I can spot a typo with the best of 'em, and am actually proud of that fact. Joking aside, I always knew that cataloging is a crucial operation. Without my work, patrons wouldn't be able to find what they need in the catalog or in the library.

Lately I've stopped joking about my existential crisis. It's hitting a little too close to home. My initial "crisis" centered on how other people saw my chosen discipline. It's not hip enough. Nowhere in my job title do the words "electronic" or "metadata" appear, and the image of a cataloger is still some poor freak chained to a desk in a deep, dark basement. Now, though, it's become a true crisis in that I myself wonder about the value of an art that I have spent many years learning. Cataloging and cataloging operations are under threat right now. People are questioning traditional practices, the expense of cataloging operations, and the usefulness of library catalogs themselves. This is our current environment.

In March 2006, a report written by Karen Calhoun for the Library of Congress was made public. This report was extremely controversial in that it questioned the value of library catalogs, saying that a large and growing number of students and scholars routinely bypass library catalogs in favor of other discovery tools (Calhoun 2006). The ever-popular Google, Amazon, and other online search engines are becoming more and more powerful. Reading Calhoun and others would have one believe that the simplicity and guaranteed results of Google make the catalog obsolete, regardless of the fact that a Google search may return many irrelevant hits. The University of California System Bibliographic Services Task Force report states that catalog "users expect simplicity and immediate reward, and Amazon, Google and iTunes are the standards against which we are judged. Our current systems pale beside them" (University of California Libraries, Bibliographic Services Task Force, 2005). In his blog entry "Burn the Catalog," Timothy Burke says that he is not the first to note that Amazon as a catalog or research tool is easier to use and more productive than conventional academic library catalogs (Burke 2004). So why not just collect publisher-supplied metadata ("A great read!" "The number one source for information on...!" "Any collection about ... will need this important memoir!"), make it keyword searchable, et voila. Who needs us?

Speaking of keyword searching, there is even talk of doing away with controlled vocabulary for subjects. Calhoun, in her key findings from her interviews and literature review, says, "Opinions [of LCSH] ranged from the strongly critical to an attitude akin to quiet resignation. There were no strong endorsements for LCSH" (Calhoun 2006). The UC System report also suggested considering the abandonment of "controlled vocabularies (LCSH, MeSH, etc.) for topical subjects in bibliographic records. Consider whether automated enrichment metadata such as TOC and indexes can become surrogates for subject headings and classification for retrieval" (University of California Libraries, Bibliographic Services Task Force, 2005).

Cataloging is an expensive operation. Now, it seems, there are rumblings about whether or not the expense is justifiable. Calhoun in her key findings said that "there was some consensus around the position that cataloging needs to be simpler, faster, and less expensive" (Calhoun 2006). I didn't read any mention of the catalog needing to be better or more accurate, though. Another kick in the gut to catalogers and friends everywhere was the Library of Congress's decision, implemented in late spring 2006, not to create, modify, follow decisions in, or even consult series authority records. The rationale for this was largely to eliminate expense, and it was justified by the fact that there will still be an uncontrolled access point in the record available for keyword searching. In discussions that followed at various meetings, it was even said that other libraries might want to follow LC's lead. To make matters worse, Association of Research Libraries library directors endorsed LC's decision. I know for a fact that there are administrators out there who were catalogers, once upon a time. Did they forget the value of controlled access for series? Or do they remember and just not think it's important anymore?

Similarly, in my own backyard, the price tag of authority control is seen as high and is questioned. We are in a union catalog environment, and the university system foots the bill for each institution's subscription to an authority control service. In the past couple years, the person who writes the checks has wondered whether this money might better be spent elsewhere. Granted, this is a lot of money, and many of the libraries are not cleaning up their databases using the authority reports. But why are they not cleaning up the databases? Could it be that they don't have staff to do so? And why don't they have staff to do so? Could it be due to administrative priorities?

All of this is disheartening, to say the least. I have days where I feel frustrated and powerless. In discussions with colleagues over the last couple of years, at least two have said to me that they're not overly worried because they will soon be retiring. Fine. Run across those ropes off this ship. It strikes me as sad that people who have dedicated entire careers to cataloging are so easily willing to cover their ears and turn away. I suspect that many of us feel a certain amount of powerlessness over the future of our discipline, and maybe if I were close to retirement I'd react the same way. But me, I have many years left. I'm not fresh out of graduate school. My enthusiasm has been somewhat tempered by the reality of production quotas, supervision, and the constraints of the institution in which I work.

In order to stay committed to doing my job, I need to find meaning in it (or I need to move to another area of the library!). To what extent do I agree with those who state that the catalog is obsolete, that keyword searching is all a patron needs, and besides, nobody uses the catalog (and if they do, they don't read but a few lines on the screen)? If I find a part of me that agrees, is there any role, however small, I could play in working towards change? Admittedly, in the section above I have been taking quotations out of context; I hate it when people do that. Many of the same reports and essays from which I took passages threatening the future of cataloging also make suggestions for areas of change. The point of the UC document was to "rethink" the provision of bibliographic services, not "How can we get rid of cataloging?" "Our challenge is to prioritize what work we can continue to do and then do it intelligently, do it once throughout the entire system, and do it as well as if not better than our 'for profit' peers" (University of California Libraries, Bibliographic Services Task Force, 2005). Are we all ready for a challenge?

Perhaps challenges and criticisms aren't something to fear; granted, I think it's okay to feel that initial pissed-off "How could they *say* that?" feeling. That will move us to action. Difficult as criticisms might be to hear, there may some truth to them. There are things we could do better. In a perfect world, we would be empowered by more resources, by time to experiment, and by more continuing education. However, things being what they are, part of the challenge is moving forward with the resources we have. What are these resources?

The first obvious one is catalogers. There are still many of us who are nowhere near retirement. We like what we do. We're intelligent and willing to learn. Also, our jobs don't seem to be going away. Granted, they are changing, but they're still out there. In their 2006 article, Deeken and Thomas wrote about their 2001 study of technical services job ads. They found a large increase in the number of technical services positions. I took an informal look at cataloging jobs posted on SERIALST, an email list on the subject of all things serial-related, during November 2006. Almost every one I saw was looking for a creative, innovative, and energetic person. Many of them asked for a familiarity with metadata schemas other than MARC.

Another existing resource is tradition. We have a system of cataloging rules and practices that has evolved over the years. It will continue to evolve. We know the value of controlled vocabulary. Among other things, it groups synonyms under one term; no matter which one someone is searching, she'll come up with all the works on that subject. It is useful for improving relevancy. No matter how a record is retrieved (using keyword searching, for example), a patron can just search by the controlled terms in the subject field — often by just clicking — and find everything a library holds on that subject. A recent study (Gross and Taylor 2005) found that if subject headings were removed from bibliographic records, a full one-third of the results students currently retrieve would be missed because the keywords came from the subject headings. Not only would you lose the value of controlled vocabulary, but you would also lose many hits that are currently retrieved by keyword searching. Combine this second resource with the first — enthusiastic, creative people who are experts in traditional cataloging — and you have a powerhouse.

A third resource is our cooperative cataloging programs. My library is a CONSER participant, and as a result, I've observed firsthand the innovation and training that comes from that cooperative program. I've seen some of the Program for Cooperative Cataloging's initiatives, and their response to various catastrophes. I think that these programs are where we'll look for support in the future. One initiative coming from CONSER is the proposed CONSER standard record for serials. The goal is access — to simplify and still create a useful record for catalog users. The cataloging practices for creating these records, while still involving judgment, make serials cataloging much easier to teach.

Another possibility in my backyard for cataloging cooperation doesn't involve a cooperative cataloging program. Thinking of the small institutions in my library consortium for which authority control reports are impossible to do, perhaps there might be some sort of cooperation that could help them. This might be impractical, or impossible, but if this idea is further explored, it could have potential.

Finally, we have a great resource in catalog advocates. Soon after Calhoun's report was made public, Thomas Mann wrote a critical review (Mann 2006). He makes some very good points about the entire premise of the report. He overturns her business model premise and retools her "niche model," saying that the actual niche audience served by research libraries is that of scholars, as distinct from quick information seekers (Mann 2006). Even for quick information seekers, however, is something on any topic — found because there are more and more keywords available to search — enough? (Mann 2006).

I have an opinionated colleague who sometimes frets that books will go away someday. I firmly disagree with that statement. I quote Mann's comments on books (remember books?), because I think this is almost poetic:

> Books, by their very nature, are more important to scholarship than to quick information seeking. And scholarship is directly and severely undercut, rather than enhanced, if "getting the books on the shelf quickly" also entails the dismantling of the cataloging structures that provide the best access to them [Mann 2006].

True, catalogers are facing some challenges. There are people who may say that we are on the verge of becoming extinct. We love our rules and their interpretations, we don't believe that keyword searching is the answer, and we don't want to throw away our traditions to chase after shiny things. Maybe we *should* chase after the shiny things, but we still need to bring our cataloging traditions with us. If there are enough of us to carry them, we can do it. There are many bright, young(ish) cataloging types out there. I could make a long list of people I admire in the field. We can face the future while holding on to the important aspects of the past. I believe it.

Notes

Burke, Timothy. (2004, January 20). Burn the catalog. *Easily distracted.* Available: <http://www.swarthmore.edu/SocSci/tburkel/permal2004.html>.

Calhoun, Karen (2006). The changing nature of the catalog and its integration with other discovery tools. Available: <http://www.loc.gov/catdir/calhoun–report–final.pdf>.

Deeken, Jo Anne, and Deborah Thomas. (2006). Technical services job ads: changes since 1995. *College & Research Libraries.* 67(2): 136–145.

Gross, Tina, and Arlene G. Taylor. (2005). "What have we got to lose? The effect of controlled vocabulary on keyword searching results." *College & Research Libraries* 66(3): 212–230.

Mann, Thomas. (2006). The changing nature of the catalog and its integration with other discovery tools. Final Report. March 17, 2006. Prepared for the Library of Congress by Karen Calhoun. A critical review. Available: <http://guild2910.org/AFSCMECalhounReviewREV.pdf>.

University of California Libraries. Bibliographic Services Task Force. (2005). Rethinking how we provide bibliographic services for the University of California. Available: <http://libraries.universityofcalifornia.edu/sopag/BSTF/Final.pdf>.

A Hidden History of Queer Subject Access

Matt Johnson

Sexual minority populations have long been ascribed "hidden histories." This lack of transparency takes on an added significance in library and information science, where the origins of current standards and practices are customarily veiled to information seekers and often obscure to professionals as well. This chapter documents how, over the course of the past four decades, librarians have pursued a variety of strategies to make gay, lesbian, bisexual and transgender people and experiences visible and accessible in library catalogs. Some of those strategies have relied on modifying established cataloging instruments, notably the Library of Congress Subject Headings. Others have involved the adoption of newer technologies, such as information retrieval thesauri. The appraisal of these knowledge domains in the context of their production serves to fill a void in our knowledge about GLBT library history, as well as GLBT history more broadly. It also demonstrates the continued relevance of this type of knowledge production both for information professionals and for those we serve.

Libraries and GLBT Activism

Just as the new generation of gay and lesbian political activism in the United States was an outgrowth of civil rights and anti-war activism which dominated the 1960s and early 1970s, so too was gay and lesbian activism in American librarianship closely allied with a broader activist movement within the profession. Librarians staged a picket of General Maxwell Taylor's speech supporting U.S. involvement in the Vietnam War at the American Library Association (ALA) annual meeting in June 1967. The following year, ALA members presented a petition asking for the formation of a round table on the social responsibilities of libraries. Within six months, the petition was approved and the Social Responsibilities Round Table (SRRT) was incorporated as a unit of ALA (Forsman 1971).

From the outset, the SRRT lacked a centralized mission, instead becoming a platform for a wide spectrum of leftist causes concerning libraries and their relationship to the larger society, as well as some causes which were not library-specific, notably the anti-war movement (Curley 1974). Numerous caucuses and task forces rapidly formed and allied themselves with SRRT; the Task Force on Gay Liberation (TFGL) was one such affiliate group. Convened by Israel Fishman at ALA's 1970 meeting in Detroit and promptly endorsed and allocated funding by SRRT, TFGL's formation came within a year of the riots at New York's Stonewall Inn, a year in which gay and lesbian organizing stepped up considerably and became more public and confrontational in its tenor. The Task Force (now the Gay, Lesbian, Bisexual and Transgender Round Table) has the distinction of being the first-ever professional organization for gay and lesbian people. It wasted no time in advocating for gay librarians, as well as pointing up deficiencies in library services to gay and lesbian patrons (Gittings 1998).

SRRT and its attendant factions inspired considerable (and often justifiable) criticism from their contemporaries, both on the grounds of the groups' lack of a unitary focus (Curley 1974) as well as the danger which such activism posed to intellectual freedom and professional impartiality. Unfortunately, intelligent, reasoned criticisms often also betrayed the very sorts of bias which SRRT sought to eradicate, such as the oblique assertion that "[t]he *raison d'etre* of the ALA is not ... [t]o promote homosexualism as a lifestyle" (Berninghausen 1972, 3675). SRRT activism of the 1960s and 1970s was no doubt a hallmark of a turbulent period in the history of the profession in the United States, but the enthusiasm with which its adherents have sought to engender professional and social change have yielded positive long-term developments. Among the most significant of these is the ongoing drive to improve intellectual access to materials about socially marginalized people generally and about gay, lesbian, bisexual, and transgender people in particular.

Subject Access: Efforts at Reform

In a series of letters in the library press, the first of which appeared in *Library Journal* in February 1969, Sanford Berman commenced a campaign of protest against "chauvinistic headings" employed by the Library of Congress as subject descriptors — a campaign which came to define his entire professional career (Berman 1969). Berman's suspicion that the Library of Congress Subject Headings (LCSH) contained an implicit and pervasive Euro-American bias was confirmed by his work with African materials, for which LCSH descriptors were often wholly inappropriate. Berman was commissioned by ALA to produce a book manuscript substantiating these claims. The result was *Prejudices and Antipathies: A Tract on the LC Subject Heads Concerning People* (Berman 1971), published by Scarecrow Press after ALA balked at publishing the book without significant cuts.

Berman's energetic correspondence had already fueled similar speculations by others in the profession (Foskett 1971; Yeh 1971), but the appearance of *Prejudices and Antipathies* effectively threw gasoline on the smoldering question of bias in library resource description. The scope of the little book was vast, encompassing dozens of heading denoting racial, ethnic, religious, and sexual minorities as well as women, youth, disabled people, and champions of progressive and leftist political causes. Berman was unsparing in his characterizations of how each heading documented exhibited the eponymous "prejudices and antipathies" of mainstream American society; his copious and detailed documentation provided support for the alternative headings he proposed in place of each objectionable one. Paramount was the belief that in order to avoid misleading or pejorative language, subject descriptors concerning people should reflect the terminology employed by the population in question to describe themselves (e.g., "Blacks" instead of "Negroes"). The sheer outrageousness of some descriptors employed by LCSH at the time (e.g., "Yellow Peril," "Mammies," "Incorrigibles"), as highlighted by Berman, did much to promote wide discussion of his "tract" among librarians already primed for its appearance by several years of social responsibility activism.

Unbiased subject access was an early concern of both TFGL and the SRRT Task Force on Women in particular. TFGL's first-ever sponsored program at the 1971 ALA annual meeting was a panel entitled "Sex and the Single Cataloger" (Gittings 1998). Panelists Steve Wolf and Joan Marshall advanced the idea that not only LCSH but also Library of Congress Classification (LCC) and Dewey Decimal Classification (DDC) were riddled with anti-gay and anti-feminist bias and should be overhauled. Their remarks appeared in the 1972 collection *Revolting Librarians* (Marshall 1972; Wolf 1972); both contained high praise for Berman's *Prejudices and Antipathies*, notably his recommendation that the "see" reference to "Sexual perversion" be deleted from the headings "Homosexuality" and "Lesbianism." Its deletion in 1972 anticipated the eventual depathologization of homosexuality by the American Psychological Association in 1974 (Greenblatt 1990). Also in 1974, the SRRT Task Force on Women convened the Committee on Sexism in Subject Headings, which included Marshall. The report which the committee prepared for ALA's Resources and Technical Services Division that year recommended limited changes to LCSH (the substitution of "Women" for the generic "Woman," and the deletion of "as" forms relating to occupations — "Women as librarians" became "Women librarians," among others) which were quickly implemented.

While many in the profession were eager to point up the biases and inadequacies betrayed by LCSH, fewer were inclined to systematically investigate how LCSH descriptors were applied (or misapplied) to library materials. A contemporary study undertaken at UCLA and Florida State University (Milstead, Harris and Clack 1979) validated many claims made by Berman concerning how LCSH heads inadequately described materials in many collections. However, the study also emphasized how recommendations made by Berman, Marshall and others positively influenced the Library of Congress to make changes to descriptors within a comparatively short time span. These changes included a number of those first outlined by the Task Force on Women and the Task Force on Gay Liberation. It was not until the 1990s, however, that the Program for Cooperative Cataloging began its Subject Authority Cooperative Program (SACO), which allowed specially trained catalogers outside the Library of Congress to propose new LCSH headings "based on their libraries' new acquisitions or their users' needs" (Stone 2000, 7). This effort at including more voices in the process of growing and revising the LCSH vocabulary has met with criticism on the part of some librarians for being an unduly cumbersome process, but it has done a good deal to address numerous complaints which had lingered since the 1970s (Litwin 2006), and it has augmented the vocabulary with numerous headings pertaining to GLBT people and human sexuality more broadly which would likely not have appeared otherwise.

As the Library of Congress has commenced a measured response to criticism of its subject descriptors, activist interventions into intellectual access to material pertaining to socially marginalized groups have spurred much discussion on the history and future of LCSH as a bibliographic tool (Chan 1978; Miksa 1983; Studwell 1990). Hope Olson (1998; 2001) has made the compelling argument that, despite revisions, LCSH still does not adequately accommodate socially marginalized knowledge bases, particularly material on gender and sexuality. Many writers have noted the perennial and fundamental inexactitude of the construction and deployment of subject heads generally, conceding that subject cataloging "is at least as much an art as it is a science" (Studwell 1990, 8). Whatever these authors' misgivings, the retention and revision of LCSH as a standard is generally recommended; its usage is already so widespread and entrenched as to render its substitution generally impracticable. The prevailing theory of subject cataloging at the Library of Congress was established by Charles Ammi Cutter's *Rules for a Dictionary Catalog* in 1876, and was further entrenched in the mid-twentieth century by the publication and dissemination of Library of Congress catalog cards (incorporating Library of Congress Subject Headings) to libraries across the United States and, increasingly, outside of it as well. Moreover, new technologies introduced around 1970, including Machine-Readable Cataloging (MARC) and networked bibliographic databases such as OCLC, adopted LCSH as a standard, further militating against the adoption of alternate modes of subject description in all but the most specialized library collections.

A notable exception to this rule was the Hennepin County Library, which between 1973 and 1999 developed its own subject authority file under Sanford Berman's leadership. The development of the authority file was documented in the *Hennepin County Library Cataloging Bulletin*, a publication which circulated widely among technical services professionals. Many other libraries began to adopt Hennepin subject heads, including a number which addressed GLBT topics (Elrod 1977; White 1977), to address inadequacies in LCSH, and over time LC incorporated numerous heads established by Hennepin. In 1999, however, with imminent plans to join OCLC, the Hennepin County Library administration insisted that the subject authority file be replaced with LCSH terms in order to ensure compatibility with the shared database, an action which Berman protested (Eichenlaub 2003).

Information Retrieval Thesauri: An Alternative Approach

Early railings against LCSH were contemporaneous with an innovation in subject access which was growing in currency and significance: the information retrieval thesaurus. In the post–World War II period, various researchers in engineering and the sciences grappled with the problem of organizing an ever-increasing number of scientific publications and making them accessible. Solving this problem was viewed as critical to the continued, unhindered advance of human knowledge. The concept of the information retrieval thesaurus — a standardized associative indexing vocabulary — was quickly seized upon by these researchers as "a secondary, supplementary indexing aid" (Roberts 1984, 282) for manual indexers in industrial research settings in the United States and the United Kingdom. The first completed information retrieval thesaurus in use was that of the E. I. du Pont de Nemours and Company, published in 1959. Only a few years after the introduction of the term, "thesaurus" had become a buzzword in documentation studies, and attempts were being made to codify as well as historicize its usage (Vickery 1960). By 1967, with the publication of *Thesaurus of Engineering and Scientific Terms*, standards for thesaurus construction as well as prescribed syndetic relationships had been largely agreed upon by practitioners (Krooks and Lancaster 1993). In 1974 the American National Standards Institute produced the first edition of its *Guidelines for Thesaurus Structure, Construction, and Use*, using the *Thesaurus of Engineering and Scientific Terms* as a model (Roe and Thomas 2004).

The two decades from the mid–1960s to the mid–1980s might well be called the golden age of information retrieval thesauri. Thousands of these domain-specific controlled vocabularies were independently developed in academic, industrial, military, government and nonprofit sectors. Unsurprisingly, given the factors outlined above, this standard enjoyed little currency in libraries. However, the Library of Congress was persuaded to adopt some of the conventions of the thesaurus. In 1985, LCSH imported the vocabulary of the ANSI standard to describe relationships among terms on the list, though syndetic "see" and "see also" references had appeared as early as the fourth (1943) and fifth (1948) editions (Stone 2000). Yet LCSH cannot be said to conform entirely to the standard because of its continued use of faceted subdivisions.

Thesauri had admittedly proven most useful in highly particularized knowledge domains, where vocabulary sets were already more limited and more standardized given the formality of scientific discourse and the limited number of people deploying the concepts described by thesaurus terms. Despite the growth of networked electronic information retrieval systems in the 1980s (including online library catalogs and their new dynamic keyword searching utility), the development of "open-world" meta-thesauri through the union of various established vocabularies — the universal knowledge domain ideally encompassed by the library catalog and tools such as LCSH and Dewey Decimal Classification — remained prohibitive (Lancaster 1986; Bates 1989; Jantz 1999). Also, thesauri did not escape the issue confronted by LCSH of requiring continual expansion and revision in order to retain their utility.

Antecedents to GLBT Thesauri

A feeling that more thoroughgoing changes were needed to better describe library resources pertaining to women inspired the SRRT Committee on Sexism in Subject Headings to apply for a Council on Library Resources grant to develop a thesaurus utilizing nonsexist language. The grant was awarded and the thesaurus completed by Joan Marshall with the coordination of the committee; it was published as *On Equal Terms: A Thesaurus for Nonsexist Indexing and Cataloging* (Marshall 1977). Rather than attempting a formal innovation, Marshall's thesaurus opts for pragmatism, mapping terms exactly to the LCSH format using an updated vocabulary. Meanwhile, *A Women's Thesaurus* (Capek 1987) was beginning to be developed by the Business and Professional Women's Foundation in conjunction with Marshall and many academic women's studies research centers around the U.S. This was a unique project which resulted in a list of descriptors novel in both form and content. It was tested in many libraries and other information retrieval settings (the California State University system, the Educational Resources Information Center, and the United Nations, among others), but appears to have been adopted by few. No revision of either Marshall's or Capek's thesaurus has been subsequently published. The development of both these thesauri, characterized by an initial flurry of enthusiastic activity, followed by the decline of the completed work into disuse, obsolescence, and obscurity, is also characteristic of the GLBT thesauri and classification schemes which are discussed below.

One thesaurus in a related subject area is that of the Kinsey Institute for Research in Sex, Gender and Reproduction at Indiana University (Brooks and Hofer 1976). In 1970, the Institute for Sex Research (as it was then known) received a grant from the National Institute of Mental Health to organize its extensive holdings; as a component of this, a controlled vocabulary was developed to provide access to the periodical collection. This vocabulary served as a template for the thesaurus developed by the Sexuality Information and Education Council of the United States (SIECUS), but relies heavily on clinical terminology. (For example, the term "gay" appears nowhere in the Kinsey thesaurus.) While it remains in use, it is overdue for a major revision, and is not easily applicable to women's studies or GLBT studies collections.

GLBT Thesauri: An Overview

A number of GLBT collections adopted the strategy pursued by *On Equal Terms* and *A Women's Thesaurus*, developing their own lists of contextually relevant subject descriptors. As was true of the many women's studies centers whose subject lists Capek drew on to build *A Women's Thesaurus*, most gay and lesbian collections created lists independently of one another to describe their own particular holdings. Between the mid–1970s and the mid–1990s, as many as a dozen distinct, identifiable gay and lesbian thesauri, lists of headings, and classification schemes were developed. Concurrent with the production of gay and lesbian thesauri in this period was the production of indexes to gay and lesbian periodicals, as well as initiatives to ensure that gay and lesbian periodicals would appear in more general periodical indexes and directories (Potter 1986; Garber 1993; Ridinger 1997; Gough 1998). Unfortunately, no comparable effort was made to coordinate all these instruments until the mid–1980s, when the Gay and Lesbian Task Force convened a thesaurus committee to synthesize a number of extant indexes and other vocabularies and produce something approaching a uniform standard, *International Thesaurus of Gay and Lesbian Index Terms* (Gregg and Ridinger 1988). Yet the Gregg and Ridinger thesaurus has enjoyed little circulation or application among gay and lesbian collections. This is likely due to the fact that it does not conform to the conventions of the information retrieval thesaurus; Gregg died of AIDS before the project could be completed per its original specifications.

One notable early GLBT thesaurus (Michel 1990) was developed by Dee Michel while he was an MLIS student at the University of Illinois in 1983. Unlike most thesauri, it was not developed to describe a particular collection of materials; Michel used various print resources which he had to hand — periodicals, as well as Jonathan Ned Katz's seminal collection of primary source documents *Gay American History* (Katz 1976) to develop the vocabulary. The thesaurus was later included in a kit containing a cataloging manual and a decimal classification system for GLBT materials, both also developed by Michel and available for sale. This kit became the tool used for cataloging and classification at the library of the ONE Institute in Los Angeles. This library is now overseen by the University of Southern California; it is unclear if Michel's schemes are still in use to describe the collection. The Michel thesaurus has not been revised since 1990; given its knowledge base, coverage of women, bisexual and transgender people, non–U.S. topics and ethnic minorities within the U.S. is also limited. It nonetheless retains the distinction of being the first widely known GLBT thesaurus; though not widely applied, its influence is apparent in that many of its terms as well as relationships have been incorporated into subsequent GLBT thesauri.

The thesaurus of the Internationale Homo en Lesbisch Informatiecentrum en Archief (International Gay and Lesbian Information Center and Archive, or IHLIA) was developed in 1993 by combining the subject lists of two important GLBT collections in the Netherlands (Amsterdam's Homodok and Leeuwarden's Anna Blaman Huis) and adding a syndetic structure (Van Staalduinen et al. 1997). It is available in English and Dutch. Since the original subject lists were developed to describe the holdings of these institutions, the terminology is largely specific to the Netherlands and the European Union, although there is global coverage extending to North America and former Dutch colonies. It also incorporates numerous format and genre descriptors, as well as separate lists of geographical and chronological subdivisions. This last is not customary for a thesaurus, but rather parallels the structure of LCSH. The IHLIA thesaurus continues to be used to describe these collections; it was published but has not been revised since 1997. Like the Michel thesaurus, the IHLIA vocabulary has not been widely applied elsewhere, but later GLBT vocabularies have been derived from it.

Conclusion: GLBT Thesauri Now

The majority of GLBT thesauri, classification schemes and other cataloging tools documented below are identifiable only from bibliographies. Unlike periodical indexes, thesauri were traditionally not intended as reference tools for the general user, and consequently were not generally published or disseminated. Hence in the case of many it is difficult to verify whether or not a given "thesaurus" indeed had the requisite syndetic structure or whether or not it is still (or was ever) used to describe a collection. Meanwhile, more and more GLBT collections have adopted LCSH heads (often somewhat modified) for greater ease of description, retrieval, and record sharing (Michel 2006). As LCSH has incorporated a greater variety of headings, notably through the SACO program described above, this approach has become more practicable; lists of GLBT-related LCSH headings are in circulation as cataloging aids (DeSantis 2000).

Yet even given all this, the information retrieval thesaurus remains a relevant tool for GLBT collections in networked electronic environments. Librarians, information architects, web taxonomists and other professionals continue to develop controlled vocabularies to better describe these electronic resources, particularly web-based resources, and improve both precision and recall in information retrieval. Information retrieval thesauri are strongly recommended as a model for this purpose, preferred to precoordinated subject headings for ease of mapping onto user query terms (Bates 1989; Roe and Thomas 2004).

In 2004, EBSCO Information Services launched *GLBT Life*, a full-text database product available to libraries by subscription. *GLBT Life* incorporates a thesaurus specifically developed to index the contents the database. These include mostly English-language GLBT periodicals, both scholarly and non-scholarly, as well as a number of edited volumes and monographs. With a total of approximately 6,500 terms, it far outstrips any prior GLBT thesaurus in terms of scope. In addition to relying on content from the sources being indexed, the *GLBT Life* thesaurus also incorporates LCSH headings wholesale as terms, many of which are precoordinated with subheads. The *GLBT Life* thesaurus is a proprietary vocabulary and hence has not been applied to local collections.

The International Resource Network (IRN; online at irnweb.org), a Ford Foundation–funded initiative of the Center for Lesbian and Gay Studies, is a social networking website where GLBT studies academics and other professionals may exchange information and research (Johnson 2006). The site is designed to allow users to upload their own content and append relevant metadata themselves upon upload, including subject tags selected from the IRN thesaurus. (As of November 2007, the IRN is still in development.) It merits noting that the design and vocabulary of both the IRN and *GLBT Life* thesauri are both heavily dependent on earlier generations of GLBT thesauri, attesting to the ongoing value of subject-specific thesauri which predate the web environment to the description and organization of digital collections. They are heirs to a tradition of queer knowledge domain-building which extends back nearly forty years.

Selected GLBT Thesauri, Subject Headings Lists, and Classification Schemes

This list is derived in large part from two web pages maintained by the GLBT Round Table and its affiliate members: "Classification schemes for lesbian/gay materials," <http://isd.usc.edu/~trimmer/glbtrt/bibresources.htm> and "GLBTRT Clearinghouse inventory" <http://www.niulib.niu.edu/lgbt/inventory.html>.

Colfax, Leslie, ed. (1974). *Homosexual Subject Heading Schemes*. Bossier City, LA: Homosexual Information Center.

DeSantis, John, ed. [2000]. Library of Congress queer subject headings. Available: <http://www.dartmouth.edu/~jcd/qsubj.html>.

Elrod, J. McRee. (1977). Sexuality: suggested subject headings. *Hennepin County Library Cataloging Bulletin* 30: 28–30.

Gregg, Joseph, and Robert B. Marks Ridinger, eds. (1988). *International Thesaurus of Gay and Lesbian Index Terms*. [Chicago]: Thesaurus Committee, Gay and Lesbian Task Force, American Library Association.

Hoffmeier, Kurt. (1979). *William Way Community Center Library Classification Scheme*. [Philadelphia: s.n.].

List of Subject Headings for Use in Cataloging the Sexual Literature of Libraries. (1974). Rev. ed. Bossier City, LA: Homosexual Information Center.

Michel, Dee. (1990). *Cataloging Manual.* Rev. ed.
Michel, Dee, ed. (1985). *Gay Studies Thesaurus.* Rev. ed.
Michel, Dee, and David Moore. (1990). *Michel/Moore Classification Scheme for Books in Lesbian/Gay Collections.* Rev. ed.
Moore, David, with Walter Williams and Jim Kepner, eds. (1985). *International Gay & Lesbian Archives Classification System.* Rev. ed.
Parkinson, Phil, ed. (1984a). *Thesaurus of Subject Headings.* Wellington, N.Z.: Lesbian and Gay Rights Resource Centre.
Parkinson, Phil, ed. (1984b). *GDC: Gay Decimal Classification.* Wellington, N.Z.: Lesbian and Gay Rights Resource Centre.
Sipe, Lynn, ed. (1980). *National Gay Archives Library Classification System.* [Los Angeles]: Library Committee, National Gay Archives.
Van Staalduinen, Ko, et al., eds. (1997). *A Queer Thesaurus: An International Thesaurus of Gay and Lesbian Index Terms.* [Amsterdam: Homodok; Leeuwarden: Anna Blaman Huis].
White, David Allen. (1977). Homosexuality and gay liberation: an expansion of the Library of Congress Classification Schedule. *Hennepin County Library Cataloging Bulletin* 28: 35–38.

Works Cited

American National Standard Guidelines for Thesaurus Structure, Construction, And Use. (1974). New York: American National Standards Institute.
Bates, Marcia J. (1989). Rethinking subject cataloging in the online environment. *Library Resources & Technical Services* 33 (4): 400–12.
Berman, Sanford. (1969). Chauvinistic headings. *Library Journal* 94: 695.
Berman, Sanford. (1971). *Prejudices and Antipathies: A Tract on the LC Subject Heads Concerning People.* Metuchen, NJ: Scarecrow Press.
Berninghausen, David. (1972). Antithesis in librarianship: social responsibility vs. the Library Bill of Rights. *Library Journal* 97: 3675–3681.
Brooks, JoAnn, and Helen C. Hofer, eds. (1976). *Sexual Nomenclature: A Thesaurus.* Boston: G. K. Hall.
Capek, Mary Ellen S., ed. (1987). *A Women's Thesaurus: An Index of Language Used to Describe and Locate Information About Women.* New York: Harper & Row.
Chan, Lois Mai. (1978). *Library of Congress Subject Headings: Principles and Application.* Littleton, CO: Libraries Unlimited.
Curley, Arthur. (1974). Social responsibility and libraries. *Advances in Librarianship* 4: 77–101.
Eichenlaub, Naomi. (2003). Silencing Sandy: the censoring of libraries' foremost activist. In *Revolting Librarians Redux: Radical Librarians Speak Out,* edited by Katia Roberto and Jessamyn West. Jefferson, NC: McFarland.
Forsman, C. (1971). Up against the stacks: the liberated librarian's guide to activism. In *Library Lit: The Best of 1970,* edited by Joel J. Schwartz and William A. Katz. Metuchen, NJ: Scarecrow Press.
Foskett, A. C. (1971). Misogynists all: A study in critical classification. *Library Resources & Technical Services* 15 (2): 117–21.
Garber, Linda, ed. (1993). *Lesbian Sources: A Bibliography of Periodical Articles, 1970–1990.* New York: Garland.
Gittings, Barbara. (1998). Gays in library land: the Gay and Lesbian Task Force of the American Library Association: the first fifteen years. In *Daring to Find Our Names: The Search for Lesbigay Library History,* edited by James V. Carmichael. Westport, CT: Greenwood Press.
Gough, Cal. (1998). The Gay, Lesbian, and Bisexual Task Force of the American Library Association: a chronology of activities, 1970–1995. In *Daring to Find Our Names: The Search for Lesbigay Library History,* edited by James V. Carmichael. Westport, CT: Greenwood Press.
Greenblatt, Ellen. (1990) Homosexuality: the evolution of a concept in the *Library of Congress Subject Headings.* In *Gay and Lesbian Library Service,* edited by Cal Gough and Ellen Greenblatt. Jefferson, NC: McFarland.
Jantz, Ronald C. (1999). An approach to managing vocabulary for databases on the web. *Cataloging & Classification Quarterly* 28(3): 55–66.
Johnson, Matt. (2006). International Resource Network. *GLBTRT Newsletter* 18 (2): 6.
Krooks, D. A., and F. W. Lancaster. (1993). The evolution of guidelines for thesaurus construction. *Libri* 43 (4): 326–42.

Lancaster, F. W. (1986). *Vocabulary Control for Information Retrieval.* 2d ed. Arlington, VA: Information Resources Press.

Litwin, Rory. (2006, 6 August). Interview with Barbara Tillett. *Library Juice.* Available: <http://libraryjuice press.com/blog/?p=115>.

Marshall, Joan. (1972). LC labeling: an indictment. In *Revolting Librarians*, edited by Celeste West, et al. San Francisco: Booklegger Press.

Marshall, Joan. (1977). *On Equal Terms: A Thesaurus for Nonsexist Indexing and Cataloging.* New York: Neal-Schuman.

Michel, Dee. (2006). Standard cataloging systems and innovation in GLBT community libraries. Paper presented at the GLBT ALMS 2006 Archives, Libraries, Museums and Special Collections Conference, University of Minnesota, 19 May.

Miksa, Francis. (1983). *The Subject in the Dictionary Catalog from Cutter to the Present.* Chicago: American Library Association.

Milstead Harris, Jessica L., and Doris H. Clack. (1979). Treatment of people and peoples in subject analysis. *Library Resources & Technical Services* 23 (4): 374–90.

Olson, Hope A. (1998). Mapping beyond Dewey's boundaries: Constructing classificatory space for marginalized knowledge domains. *Library Trends* 47 (2): 233–54.

Olson, Hope A. (2001). The power to name: representation in library catalogs. *Signs* 26 (3): 639–68.

Parkinson, Phil, and Chris Parkin. (1998). Safe harbour: The origin and growth of the Lesbian and Gay Archives of New Zealand. In *Daring to Find Our Names: The Search for Lesbigay Library History*, edited by James V. Carmichael. Westport, CT: Greenwood Press.

Potter, Claire, ed. (1986). *The Lesbian Periodicals Index.* Tallahassee, FL: Naiad Press.

Ridinger, Robert B. Marks. (1997). Playing in the attic: indexing and preserving the gay press. In Kester, N. G. (ed.), *Liberating Minds: The Stories and Professional Lives of Gay, Lesbian, and Bisexual Librarians and Their Advocates.* Jefferson, NC: McFarland.

Ridinger, Robert B. Marks, ed. (1985). *Index to* The Advocate, *1967–1982.*

Roberts, Norman. (1984). The pre-history of the information retrieval thesaurus. *Journal of Documentation* 40 (4): 271–85.

Roe, Sandra K., and Alan R. Thomas, eds. (2004). *The Thesaurus: Review, Renaissance, and Revision.* New York: Haworth.

SIECUS thesaurus. [n.d.] New York: Sexuality Information and Education Council of the United States.

Stone, Alva T. (2000). The *LCSH* century: a brief history of the *Library of Congress Subject Headings*, and introduction to the centennial essays. In *The LCSH Century: One Hundred Years with the Library of Congress Subject Headings System*, edited by Alva T. Stone. New York: Haworth.

Studwell, William E. (1990). *Library of Congress Subject Headings: Philosophy, Practice, and Prospects.* New York: Haworth.

Vickery, B. C. (1960). Thesaurus — a new word in documentation. *Journal of Documentation* 16 (4): 181–89.

Wolf, Steve. (1972). Sex and the single cataloger: new thoughts on some unthinkable subjects. In *Revolting Librarians*, edited by Celeste West, et al. San Francisco: Booklegger Press.

Yeh, Thomas Yen-Ran. (1971). The treatment of the American Indian in the Library of Congress E-F Schedule. *Library Resources & Technical Services* 15 (2): 122–28.

Cataloging in Non-Roman Scripts: From Radical to Mainstream Practice

Bella Hass Weinberg

Introduction

In the United States, maintaining catalogs in non–Roman scripts (writing systems other than the Latin alphabet) was, until recently, considered a radical cataloging practice. The mainstream practice was to Romanize (convert to the Latin alphabet) all bibliographic data. In 1974 I published a paper arguing that from both the cataloger's and the user's perspectives, Romanization of bibliographic data is not good practice (Weinberg 1974). The cataloger who can handle non–Roman scripts must master a complex set of rules for converting these to the Latin alphabet. The user interested in reading library materials in non–Roman scripts knows the foreign writing systems but not necessarily the library's rules for converting non–Roman scripts to the Latin alphabet.

Three years after my paper appeared, Sumner Spalding, the editor of *Anglo-American Cataloging Rules* (1967), published a paper (Spalding 1977a) with similar arguments, but he neglected to cite his earlier paper making the case *for* Romanization: it provides an integrated catalog with all the works of an author, in all languages and scripts, filed under a single Roman-alphabet heading (Spalding 1960). He cited that paper in a letter acknowledging the priority of my arguments (Spalding 1977b, 303).

Why the reversal? In the 1970s computers were being applied to the production of library catalogs in card and book form. OCLC (initially the Ohio College Library Center, later the Online Computer Library Center) was promising non–Roman scripts, and the New York Public Library (NYPL) was developing them for its book catalog (Malinconico et al. 1977). The thesis of this chapter is that technology turned cataloging in non–Roman scripts into mainstream practice.

Scope of the Chapter and Extent of the Literature

While I am most familiar with the literature on the use of the Hebrew alphabet in cataloging, the focus of this chapter is on general principles and practices relating to the inclusion of non–Roman scripts in bibliographic and authority records. This paper does not cover the "how" of Romanization; *ALA-LC Romanization Tables* (1997) is a useful reference work for catalogers working with non–Roman scripts. This paper also does not deal with changes in Romanization schemes, such as the shift from Wade-Giles to Pinyin for Chinese bibliographic records.

Aside from Romanization tables, the literature on transliteration is vast, as is evident from Hans Wellisch's (1975a) book-length bibliography on this subject. Prior to the publication of his dissertation, *The Conversion of Scripts* (Wellisch 1978), Wellisch published a series of articles on non–Roman scripts. "The relative importance of the world's major scripts" (Wellisch 1975b) may have provided guidance to those developing non–Roman scripts for bibliographic utilities and integrated library systems, although financial considerations and political pressure were factors in the sequence of development in the 1980s of non–Roman character sets by RLIN (the Research Libraries Information Network) and subsequently by OCLC. The newsletters of these bibliographic utilities contain many progress reports relating to the implementation of non–Roman scripts.

A collection entitled *Cataloging and Classification of Non-Western Material* (Aman 1980) contains many chapters on non–Roman scripts, all of which discuss the problems of Romanization, and some of which argue for original-alphabet access.

Prior to the implementation of non–Roman scripts by the bibliographic utilities, there were many homegrown automated library systems with selected non–Roman scripts, just as there were word processing packages with alphabets other than the Latin one. Descriptions of such systems are not all cited here. An important general point was made by Kuperman (1987) that the key issue is standardization of the coding of the character set. A bibliography, *Computational Linguistics in Information Science* (Sabourin 1994) contains many index entries relating to non–Roman scripts under the heading "character coding" (vol. 2, 594–95). Those articles are not cited here.

In the last decade of the 20th century and the first one of the 21st century, the nature of publications relating to non–Roman scripts in cataloging changed: a few papers continued to make the case against complete Romanization of bibliographic data, but there were hardly any homegrown systems, as everyone realized that character sets had to be standardized to facilitate exchange of bibliographic data. The literature became more technical, focusing on the details of input and tagging of vernacular bibliographic data.

The sections that follow treat vernacular cataloging in the pre-computer era, the philosophy of Anglocentricity vs. multiculturalism, vernacular cataloging with machine-readable character sets, non–Roman authority files, reversal of Romanization, obliteration of the works of early writers on vernacular cataloging, and reinvention of the software for this application.

Vernacular Cataloging in the Pre-Computer Era

In the field of linguistics, the term *vernacular* means spoken language (Crystal 1997, 410–11), but in library science, the phrase *vernacular scripts* refers to writing systems other than the Latin alphabet. "Cataloging in the vernacular" means recording bibliographic data in the original script rather than Romanizing it — or in addition to Romanizing it.

The term *vernacular* is not defined in this sense in Harrod's (2005, 725) dictionary of library science terminology, and it is not clear how the "semantic drift" from linguistics occurred. I am not sure when the term *vernacular scripts* was first used in the literature of our field, but it is found in the title of a pioneering paper on the use of non–Roman scripts in an automated library catalog (Malinconico et al. 1977).

In countries whose national languages employ scripts other than the Latin alphabet, vernacular cataloging — without Romanization — has always been the norm. In Russia, for example, catalogs feature the Cyrillic alphabet; in Israel, the Hebrew alphabet is employed in cataloging works printed in that script (records for English-language works are not Hebraized). From visits to the Jewish National and University Library in Jerusalem, I know that before automating, the JNUL had card catalogs in the Arabic and Cyrillic alphabets in addition to those in the Hebrew and Latin alphabets.

In the U.S. in the pre-computer era, vernacular cataloging was done primarily for ideographic scripts, such as Chinese, and for consonantal alphabets, such as Arabic and Hebrew. The Library of Congress (LC) acronym for such scripts is JACKPHY (Japanese, Arabic, Chinese, Korean, Persian, Hebrew, and Yiddish). The reason these scripts receive special processing is that Romanization of such writing systems is complex and often indeterminate, and library users have great difficulty searching in Romanized catalogs. The systems used by the Library of Congress for Romanizing Hebrew and Arabic employ phonetic transcription; the vowels must be supplied by the cataloger (Vernon 1996, 2). Chinese is an ideographic script, and the cataloger must know how the characters are pronounced. Besides the difficulties of Romanization, there are religious and cultural reasons for preserving original scripts.

Dunkle (1993, 216), in writing about East Asian materials, presents the following alternative: "The issue is access: romanized access through a Latin script library catalog or nonromanized access through a browsing collection." She seems to accept that there will be Romanized access only, and advocates a separate physical collection of East Asian materials to compensate for this.

Library of Congress printed cards produced throughout most of the 20th century included descriptive bibliographic data in vernacular scripts, but the main entry heading and all other access points were Romanized. (OCLC did not have the capability to print non–Roman script data on its computer-produced cards.) As I pointed out in my survey of Anglo-American practices in Hebraica cataloging (Weinberg 1992, 14), LC omitted the author statement in the original script, presumably on the assumption that the vernacular form of the author's name was redundant with the Romanized heading. Some American libraries maintained author headings in vernacular scripts, but this was considered radical. (See section on non–Roman authority files below.) Opinions condemning (or mocking) non–Roman headings were usually expressed orally.

The Library of Congress provided the Romanization of non–Roman script titles on its printed cards, but in its Hebraic section, a card catalog arranged by title in Hebrew script was maintained. Most Judaica collections in the U.S. followed this practice: Romanized author headings and vernacular title access. General libraries often provided only

Romanized access points. Zipin (1984) observed that when records for works in non–Roman scripts were left out of OPACs (online public access catalogs), users — who assumed that all of the library's holdings were represented in the computerized catalog — did not know of the existence of these materials, and they remained unused.

The International Standard Bibliographic Description (ISBD) validated the use of vernacular scripts in cataloging, but this standard was limited to description and said nothing about access points. ISBD(M) (International Federation of Library Associations 1974) was incorporated into *Anglo-American Cataloging Rules*, Chapter 6 (1974), and subsequently into AACR2 (*Anglo-American Cataloguing Rules*, 1978). Rule 1.0E of AACR2, however, requires that original scripts be used for bibliographic description only "if practicable."

Anglocentricity vs. Multiculturalism

Fully Romanized bibliographic records coincide with *Anglocentricity* in the United States — the view that everyone throughout the world should learn to speak the English language and master the alphabet in which it is written.

In contrast, ISBD coincided with a philosophy of *multiculturalism* — cultures other than the American one deserve respect. Not all users of American libraries know English, and these users deserve to have access to library materials in their native languages and scripts. Translation of Library of Congress subject headings into Spanish (e.g., *Bilindex* 1984) reflects this philosophy.

Software producers currently produce manuals and interfaces in multiple languages and scripts, and developers of integrated library systems are doing the same. The Queens Borough Public Library, in New York City, was a pioneer in developing a multiscript interface for its OPAC to serve its diverse community (Strong 2000). NetLibrary (2006) allows the user to select an interface language to search its catalog of e-books. The options are English, Spanish, French, German, Chinese, Japanese, Korean, and Thai.

Vernacular Cataloging with Machine-Readable Character Sets

The New York Public Library employed reversible Romanization of Hebrew, i.e., the substitution of a Latin-alphabet letter for each Hebrew letter, for its book catalog (New York Public Library 1972–81); this Romanized data was converted to the original script at the printing stage. The handling of these NYPL records on RLIN is discussed in the section below entitled "Reversal of Romanization."

While RLIN was developing non–Roman scripts, the Library of Congress did double processing of non–Roman records: entering fully Romanized records into its automated system and printing cards with non–Roman data. Maher (1987, 42) details the exceptions to this practice; for example, CIP (Cataloging-in-Publication) items received Roman-only cataloging.

After RLIN made its first non–Roman character set available, the MARC (machine-

100	0		‡6 880-01 ‡a Shengyan.
245	1	0	‡6 880-02 ‡a Zheng xin Fo jiao, Han Zang fo xue / ‡c Shi Shengyan zhu.
250			‡6 880-03 ‡a Chu ban.
260			‡6 880-04 ‡a Taibei Shi : ‡b Dong chu chu ban she, ‡c Minguo 82 [1993]
300			‡a 3, 5, 165, 101 p. ; ‡c 22 cm.
490	1		‡6 880-05 ‡a Fa gu quan ji. Di 5 ji ; ‡v di 2 ce
504			‡a Includes bibliographical references.
505	0		‡6 880-06 ‡a Zheng xin di Fo jiao — Han Zang fo xue tong yi da wen.
650		0	‡a Buddhism ‡x Doctrines ‡x Introductions.
650		0	‡a Buddhism ‡z China ‡x Miscellanea.
650		0	‡a Buddhism ‡z China ‡z Tibet ‡x Miscellanea.
700	0	2	‡6 880-07 ‡a Shengyan. ‡t Zheng xin di Fo jiao. ‡f 1993.
700	0	2	‡6 880-08 ‡a Shengyan. ‡t Han Zang fo xue tong yi da wen. ‡f 1993.
800	0		‡6 880-09 ‡a Shengyan. ‡t Fa gu quan ji. ‡n Di 5 ji ; ‡v di 2 ce
880	3	0	‡6 246-00 ‡a 漢藏佛學
880			‡6 250-03 ‡a 初版.
880			‡6 260-04 ‡a 台北市 : ‡b 東初出版社, ‡c 民國82 [1993]
880	1		‡6 490-05 ‡a 法鼓全集. 第5輯 ; ‡v 第2冊
880	0		‡6 505-06 ‡a 正信的佛教 — 漢藏佛学同異答問.
880	0	2	‡6 700-07 ‡a 里嚴. ‡t 正信的佛教. ‡f 1993.
880	0	2	‡6 700-08 ‡a 里嚴. ‡t 漢藏佛学同異答問. ‡f 1993.
880	0		‡6 800-09 ‡a 里嚴. ‡t 法鼓全集. ‡n 第5輯 ; ‡v 第2冊
987			‡a PINYIN ‡b OCoLC ‡c 20010608 ‡d c ‡e 04.15.2001

Figure 1: OCLC record with East Asian script. All non–Roman data are in 880 fields, grouped at the end of Latin-character fields. Image taken from OCLC's WorldCat® database and used with permission. WorldCat® is a registered trademark of OCLC Online Computer Library Center, Inc.

readable cataloging) format was amplified with an 880 field, called "Alternate Graphic Representation," into which non–Roman characters could be input (Aliprand 1992). The label for the MARC tag always bothered me: the non–Roman data is not an *alternate* representation; it's the *primary* one! Romanized data is the alternate. In OCLC, 880 fields with data in many non–Roman scripts are now available. Figure 1 contains an OCLC record with East Asian characters in the 880 fields.

RLIN's work in coding character sets fed into Unicode, a universal character set developed by an industry consortium. Integrated library systems currently offering non–Roman capabilities are generally Unicode-based. In a two-part article, Coyle (2005, 2006) describes the Unicode character set and its use in library systems.

The Library of Congress did vernacular cataloging on RLIN long before LC's OPAC was able to display non–Roman scripts. (OCLC did not have this capability for several years after RLIN implemented it.) From personal communications, I know that non–Roman capability was specified in the RFP (request for proposal) for LC's commercial integrated library system, but the scripts could not be displayed at the time of the implementation of the system. LC's OPAC now includes instructions for displaying and searching non–Roman scripts. Pearlstein (2006) provides hints for search and display of Hebrew script in LC's OPAC, indicating that these processes are not transparent. It is well known that users do not consult help files, and search failure with non–Roman data may result from the lack of such consultation.

In the early days of development of machine-readable character sets for non–Roman scripts, vernacular characters were used for bibliographic description, while the Roman alphabet was used for headings — mirroring the pattern on catalog cards. Later, interest developed in providing vernacular access points on RLIN. The question then arose whether these access points should be standardized. This led to an explosion of interest in non–Roman authority files, which are discussed in the following section.

Non-Roman Authority Files

In libraries that maintain separate catalogs by script, authority files on cards with headings in non–Roman scripts have long been maintained. An example of such an institution is the Jewish National and University Library (JNUL) in Jerusalem. From team-teaching a course on Hebrew cataloging at the Jewish Theological Seminary in the mid–1970s with a representative from the Library of Congress, I know that LC recorded the Hebrew forms of names on authority cards, but provided no cross-references from these forms to Latin-alphabet headings.

The JNUL staff worked on developing the ALEPH integrated library system in the early 1980s. (I was then a guest lecturer in the library school of the Hebrew University and was occasionally consulted by the systems people.) The ALEPH system had an authority module and the ability to make global changes (Levi 1984). (*Global change* means that if a heading is changed in an authority file, the corresponding access points on all bibliographic records containing that heading are automatically revised.) The ALEPH system, now owned by Ex Libris, has gone through many versions and has been acquired by large library systems throughout the world. Many of its customers are Judaica libraries interested in Hebrew script.

RLIN allowed libraries to input added entries in non–Roman scripts. Aliprand (1993) provides a technical analysis of the linkage between non–Roman forms of name and their Latin-alphabet counterparts. Some libraries just input the vernacular form found in the work rather than establishing a non–Roman heading according to AACR2 principles.

Figure 2, which includes Hebrew script, contains parallel headings for an author main entry and two added entries. None of these pairs is semantically equivalent. The Hebrew surname of the primary author consists of a single letter, but the Roman heading has the spelled-out form *Aleph*. Both added entries in the Latin alphabet are based on the spellings found on added title pages rather than being systematic Romanizations of the Hebrew forms. These headings were established in accordance with an alternative rule from AACR2R (*Anglo-American Cataloguing Rules* 1988, rule 22.3C2) for which the Judaica library community argued.

Discussion in the cataloging community of the machine-readable format of authority files predates the acquisition by the Library of Congress of a commercial integrated library system with non–Roman capability. Discussion papers on this question, drafted by LC, followed RLIN's implementation of non–Roman scripts. (I commented on some of these discussion papers.) With Joan Aliprand, I presented a paper at the 2001 IFLA (International Federation of Library Associations) conference that analyzed the structural issues of multi-script authority files (Weinberg and Aliprand 2002). The focus of the paper was on establishing non–Roman headings on the script level or the language level; we argued for the latter.

Tag	Ind	Ind	Content
040			CU ǂc CUY ǂd DLC ǂd OSU
066			ǂc (2
020			9654076098
020			9789654076098
024	8		0024900016671
042			lccopycat
050	0	0	PJ5055.12.L54 ǂb O68 2006
090			ǂb
049			DVPP
100	1		‏.א ,אריק‎
100	1		Aleph, Arik.
245	1	0	‏משוררים 2 אופציה פואטית / ǂc אריק א., עמוס אדלהייט ; ערך והקדים מבוא גבריאל מוקד.‎
245	1	0	Optsyah po'etit 2 meshorerim / ǂc Arik A., 'Amos Edelhait ; 'arakh ve-hiḳdim mavo Gavri'el Moḳed.
246	3		‏אופציה פואטית שני משוררים‎
246	3		Optsyah po'etit shene meshorerim
246	1		ǂi Title on t.p. verso: ǂa Poetic option 2 poets
260			‏ירושלים : ǂb עמדה/כרמל, ǂc 2006.‎
260			Yerushalayim : ǂb Emdah/Karmel, ǂc 2006.
300			136 p. ; ǂc 23 cm.
440		0	‏סדרה לספרות עברית‎
440		0	Sidrah le-sifrut 'Ivrit
490	0		‏סדרה לספרות עברית‎
700	1		‏אדלהייט, עמוס.‎
700	1		Edelheit, Amos.
700	1		‏מוקד, גבריאל.‎
700	1		Moḳed, Gabriel.

Figure 2. OCLC record with Hebrew script. Corresponding Roman and non–Roman data elements are juxtaposed. Image taken from OCLC's WorldCat® database and used with permission. WorldCat® is a registered trademark of OCLC Online Computer Library Center, Inc.

Non-Roman headings and the structure of authority files are now discussed in the major American journals devoted to cataloging, *Library Resources & Technical Services* (Aliprand 2005; Agenbroad and Aliprand 2006; Lerner 2006) and *Cataloging & Classification Quarterly* (Agenbroad 2006). The head of LC's Cataloging Policy and Support Office, Dr. Barbara Tillett, frequently discusses non–Roman headings in her papers and presentations on *access control* (a neologism for *authority control*). Cazabon (2002) discusses multiscript authority files in a French paper.

Tillett chairs the Planning Committee of the IFLA Meeting of Experts on an International Cataloging Code. Her report of the first meeting, held in 2003, notes that Working Group 1, on Personal Names, discussed parallel headings in different scripts (Tillett

2004). The draft of *Functional Requirements for Authority Records* (IFLA 2005) includes examples of such pairs. The notes of a strategic directions meeting of the Program for Cooperative Cataloging of the Library of Congress (2006), under the rubric "International Authority File," state: "Consider multiple, equal 1XX fields for multilingual and multi-script data." Thus, the radical cataloging practice of providing author headings in non–Roman scripts has become mainstream.

Reversal of Romanization

The New York Public Library's automated book catalog used the reversible transliteration table of the *American National Standard Romanization of Hebrew* (American National Standards Institute 1975), a letter-for-letter substitution proposed by Herbert Zafren (1969), to input bibliographic data in that script. At the printing stage, the transliteration was converted to Hebrew script (New York Public Library 1972–81).

NYPL's transliterated records were loaded on RLIN and eventually converted to Hebrew script. The transliteration was incompatible with the transcription done by other libraries in accordance with the ALA/LC system for the Romanization of Hebrew (Maher 1987), and the latter system was used for clustering of records.

The Cyrillic character set of RLIN was hardly employed because systematic Romanization of that alphabet was relatively easy. (For a paper presented at Brandeis University in 1996, I requested from the Research Libraries Group statistics on the number of records available for each of its non–Roman character sets.) Languages employing the Cyrillic alphabet have vowels, and the Romanization is pronounceable. A recent article (Jacobs et al. 2004) discusses the "de-transliteration" of Romanized Cyrillic, i.e., reversing such data to the original script. The project was developed at the Queens Borough Public Library, which has a multi-ethnic audience, including many Russian speakers. The authors of the paper did not cite a similar one published a dozen years earlier (Aissing 1992).

It has been demonstrated that some Romanized bibliographic data can be flipped to the original script. The cataloging policy question is: Will the vernacular data be considered primary for the purposes of clustering in the OCLC/RLIN bibliographic utility, or will Romanized data still be required? The rationale for requiring Romanization after RLIN developed vernacular scripts was that not all libraries had non–Roman capability in their OPACs. The Library of Congress (2005) has considered a non–Roman core record in which not all bibliographic data is Romanized.

It is hard to predict how long it will take until non–Roman scripts in integrated library systems become standard. The predictor of the paperless society (Lancaster 1978) had to write "The Paperless Society revisited" (Lancaster 1985) when his predictions did not all come true. In rereading the predictions at the end of my review of Judaica library automation (Weinberg 1991), I'm pleased to note that most of my prognostications are facts today.

Most integrated library systems with non–Roman capability are Unicode-based, but Goundry (2001) has written about the limitations of this character set. Modifying standard character sets is a complicated business with implications for integrated library systems.

The situation at St. John's University Libraries as of February 2007 may be typical of the state of diffusion of non–Roman technology: the University Library is a member of OCLC, into which one can input non–Roman data. The library has the Voyager integrated library system (ILS), which is Unicode-compliant and can display non–Roman bibliographic data. End-users cannot input non–Roman search arguments, however, unless foreign-language settings are changed in the public computers that access the ILS, and students do not have the authority to change language settings on these computers. The university has issued laptops to the entire undergraduate population, and students can customize settings on laptops issued to them, as they see fit (John Garino, personal communication, Feb. 1, 2007).

Obliteration and Reinvention

Many American publications on cataloging in non–Roman scripts in the electronic environment obliterate the writings of those who articulated the principles of vernacular cataloging before the technology became available. This is comparable to the publications on organizing the Internet, e.g., proposals for the "semantic Web," that fail to cite the sophisticated writings of librarians and information scientists on thesauri and classification. Garfield (1975) wrote about the "obliteration phenomenon" in the hard sciences, but it is found in library and information science as well.

For decades I have observed that catalogers who have published papers about the writing system of a single language family do not cite the literature relating to other language groups. But as has been demonstrated for one script — Cyrillic — those in the post–Internet era are unfamiliar with the publications of the pre–Internet era. While it is not surprising that computer scientists fail to consult indexes to the literature, one would expect librarians to do literature searches before publishing papers on "innovations." Regardless of who gets the credit, however, cataloging in non–Roman scripts greatly benefits the users of materials written in such scripts.

Librarians' failure to search the prior literature has resulted in duplicative analyses of the issues inherent in cataloging with non–Roman scripts. A related phenomenon is the redundant development of non–Roman script capabilities by integrated library systems. The character sets developed by RLIN became national standards, but the logic of the directionality of right-to-left scripts in multi-script cataloging records was proprietary. Thus several vendors developed software for this purpose independently of each other. Libraries that purchased such systems in some cases had to request corrections to the logic of the display of multiple scripts, and such corrections were time-consuming and expensive to implement. (As a consultant, I have personal knowledge of this.) In the domain of cataloging with-non Roman scripts, we thus had reinvention of software as well as principles.

Conclusion

The use of non–Roman scripts in cataloging constitutes a case of the tail (technology) wagging the dog (cataloging principles). As Holmes (1996) wrote, "The Committee on

East Asian Libraries of the Association for Asian Studies has argued for vernacular records for many years, but this was not feasible on a large scale until the development of automation" [p. 69]. Maintaining catalogs and authority files in non–Roman scripts was considered a radical practice in the U.S. when typewriters with non–Roman scripts were hard to find and computers had only a Latin-alphabet character set. The development of non–Roman character sets by RLIN and integrated library systems made cataloging in vernacular scripts a mainstream activity and led to a rethinking of cataloging principles as they relate to languages other than English and scripts other than the Latin alphabet.

Acknowledgments

The author acknowledges the help of her former graduate assistant Betty Ann Derbentli with the literature search for this chapter. Prof. Cynthia D. Chambers, Head, Information Management, St. John's University Library, demonstrated OCLC Connexion and provided sample records. John Garino, Assistant Director, Systems, St. John's University Libraries, explained the relationship among the non–Roman capabilities of OCLC, Voyager, and public computers in the University Library. Several student assistants in the Division of Library and Information Science word-processed many drafts of this chapter.

This chapter contains information taken from OCLC's WorldCat® database; the information is used with OCLC's permission. WorldCat® is a registered trademark of OCLC Online Computer Library Center, Inc.

References

Agenbroad, James E. (2006). Romanization is not enough. *Cataloging & Classification Quarterly* 42(2): 21–34.

Agenbroad, James E., and Joan Aliprand. (2006). Letters to the Editor. *Library Resources & Technical Services* 50(4):227–30.

Aissing, Alena L. (1992). Computer-oriented bibliographic control for Cyrillic documents with or without script conversion. *Information Technology and Libraries* 11(4):340–44. Also available on ProQuest.

ALA-LC Romanization Tables: Transliteration Schemes for Non-Roman Scripts. (1997). Approved by the Library of Congress and the American Library Association. Tables compiled and edited by Randall K. Barry. Washington: Library of Congress, Cataloging Distribution Service.

Aliprand, Joan M. (1992). Nonroman scripts in the bibliographic environment. *Information Technology and Libraries* 11(2):105–19. Also available on ProQuest.

Aliprand, Joan M. (1993). Linkage in USMARC bibliographic records. *Cataloging & Classification Quarterly* 16(1):5–37.

Aliprand, Joan M. (2005). Scripts, languages, and authority control. *Library Resources & Technical Services* 49(4):243–49.

Aman, Mohammed M., ed. (1980). *Cataloging and Classification of Non-Western Material: Concerns, Issues and Practices.* Phoenix, AZ: Oryx Press.

American National Standards Institute. (1975). *American National Standard Romanization of Hebrew.* New York: ANSI. (ANSI Z39.25 —1975). Table 4: Keypunch-compatible transliteration style.

Anglo-American Cataloging Rules, North American Text. (1967). Chicago: American Library Association.

Anglo-American Cataloging Rules, North American Text. (1974). Chapter 6: Separately published monographs. Chicago: American Library Association.

Anglo-American Cataloguing Rules. (1978). 2nd ed. Ed. by Michael Gorman and Paul W. Winkler. Chicago: American Library Association.

Anglo-American Cataloguing Rules. (1988). 2nd ed. 1988 revision. Chicago: American Library Association.

Bilindex: A Bilingual Spanish-English Subject Heading List: Spanish Equivalents to Library of Congress Subject Headings. (1984). Oakland, CA: California Spanish Language Data Base.

Cazabon, Marie-Renée. (2002). Multilinguisme et multiscripts: l'avenir informatique. *Bulletin des Bibliothèques de France* 47(6):106–07.

Coyle, Karen. (2005). Unicode: the universal character set. Part 1: The computer and language. *The Journal of Academic Librarianship* 31(6):590–92.

Coyle, Karen. (2006). Unicode: the universal character set. Part 2: Unicode in library systems. *The Journal of Academic Librarianship* 32(1):101–03.

Crystal, David. (1997). *A Dictionary of Linguistics and Phonetics.* 4th ed. Oxford, UK: Blackwell Publishers.

Dunkle, Clare B. (1993). Why put East Asian materials in a separate collection?: The issue of access. *The Journal of Academic Librarianship* 19(4):216–19. Also available on EBSCO.

Garfield, Eugene. (1975, December 22). The "obliteration phenomenon" in science — and the advantage of being obliterated. "Current Comments" in *Current Contents* 51/52. Reprinted in: *Essays of an Information Scientist*, vol. 2, 1974–76. Philadelphia, PA: ISI Press, 1977, 396–98.

Goundry, Norman. (2001). Why Unicode won't work on the Internet: linguistic, political, and technical limitations. Available: <http://www.hastingsresearch.com/net/04-unicode-limitations.shtml>.

Harrod's Librarians' Glossary and Reference Book. (2005). 10th ed., compiled by Ray Prytherch. Aldershot, England; Burlington, VT: Ashgate.

Holmes, Anne Wyman. (1996). Non-Roman scripts: the problems of small libraries. *Public & Access Services Quarterly* 2(1):65–74.

IFLA UBCIM Working Group on Functional Requirements and Numbering of Authority Records (FRANAR). (2005). *Functional requirements for authority records: a conceptual model.* Draft. Available: <http://www.ifla.org/VII/d4/wg-franar.htm>.

International Federation of Library Associations. (1974). *ISBD(M): International Standard Bibliographic Description for Monographic Publications.* First standard edition. London: IFLA Committee on Cataloging.

Jacobs, Jane W., Ed Summers, and Elizabeth Ankersen. (2004). Cyril: expanding the horizons of MARC21. *Library Hi Tech* 22(1):8–17.

Kuperman, Aaron Wolfe. (1987). Hebrew word processing. *Judaica Librarianship* 3:17–20.

Lancaster, F. W. (1978). *Toward Paperless Information Systems.* New York: Academic Press.

Lancaster, F. W. (1985). The paperless society revisited. *American Libraries* 16:553–55.

Lerner, Heidi. (2006). Anticipating the use of Hebrew script in the LC/NACO authority file. *Library Resources & Technical Services* 50(4):252–63.

Levi, Judith. (1984). ALEPH: An online real-time integrated library system. *Judaica Librarianship* 1:58–63, 69.

Library of Congress. (2005). *Non-Roman Core Record Task Group: Final Report.* Available: <http://www.loc.gov/catdir/pcc/archive/jackphy.html>.

Library of Congress. (2006, April 27). *Strategic directions 2010 for the Program for Cooperative Cataloging (PCC). Strategic direction (SD) 4: Pursue globalization.* Brainstorming session at PCC OpCo. Available: <http://www.loc.gov/catdir/pcc/bibco/SD_4.pdf>.

Library of Congress Online Catalog. (2006). Help page: displaying and searching non–Roman characters in the online catalog (Unicode). Available: <http://catalog.loc.gov/help/unicode.htm>.

Maher, Paul. (1987). *Hebraica Cataloging: A Guide to ALA/LC Romanization and Descriptive Cataloging.* Washington, D.C.: Cataloging Distribution Service, Library of Congress. Online edition, slightly revised, 2005. Available: <http://www.library.yale.edu/cataloging/hebraicateam/>.

Malinconico, S. Michael, Walter R. Grutchfield, and Erik J. Steiner. (1977). Vernacular scripts in the NYPL automated bibliographic control system. *Journal of Library Automation* 10(3):205–25.

NetLibrary. (2006). eBook Details. Available: <http://www.netlibrary.com/>.

New York Public Library. Research Libraries. (1972–81). *Dictionary Catalog of the Research Libraries.* New York: NYPL.

OCLC. n.d. International cataloging: use non–Latin scripts. Available: <http://www.oclc.org/support/documentation/connexion/client/international>.

Pearlstein, Peggy. (2006). Searching the Library of Congress Online Catalog using Hebrew script: search and display hints. *Association of Jewish Libraries Newsletter* XXV(4):35.

Sabourin, Conrad F. (1994). *Computational Linguistics in Information Science: Bibliography.* Montreal: Infolingua. (Infolingua 16.1–2).

Spalding, Sumner. (1960). Transliteration of vernacular alphabets, cooperative cataloging of vernacular materials, and cataloging treatment of pamphlet materials. (Conference on American library resources on Southern Asia, Working Paper No. 8). *Journal of the Oriental Institute* X(2):[184]–203.

Spalding, Sumner. (1977a). Romanization reexamined. *Library Resources & Technical Services* 21:3–12.

Spalding, Sumner. (1977b). In the mail: Romanization. *Library Resources & Technical Services* 21:303–05.

Strong, Gary E. (2000). LinQing the world to Queens — and Queens to the world. *American Libraries* 31(9):44–46.

Tillett, Barbara B. (2004, June 26). IME ICC: Report of 1st meeting, Frankfurt, Germany, July 28–30, 2003. PowerPoint presentation to ALA/CC:DA. Available: <http://www.libraries.psu.edu/tas/jca/ccda/docs/imeicc-ccda.pdf>.

Vernon, Elizabeth. (1996). *Decision-making for Automation: Hebrew and Arabic Script Materials in the Automated Library.* Urbana-Champaign, IL: Graduate School of Library and Information Science. (Occasional Papers, no. 205).

Weinberg, Bella. (1974). Transliteration in documentation. *Journal of Documentation* 30:18–31.

Weinberg, Bella. (1991). Automation and the American Judaica library during the first quarter century of the Association of Jewish Libraries, 1965–1990. *Judaica Librarianship* 5:167–76.

Weinberg, Bella. (1992). Judaica and Hebraica cataloging: Anglo-American traditions. *Judaica Librarianship* 6:13–23.

Weinberg, Bella Hass, and Joan M. Aliprand. (2002). Closing the circle: automated authority control and the multiscript YIVO catalog. *International Cataloging and Bibliographic Control* 31(3):44–48.

Wellisch, Hans H. (1975a). *Transcription and Transliteration: An Annotated Bibliography on Conversion of Scripts.* Silver Spring, MD: Institute of Modern Languages.

Wellisch, Hans H. (1975b). The relative importance of the world's major scripts. *Libri* 25:238–50.

Wellisch, Hans H. (1978). *The Conversion of Scripts: Its Nature, History and Utilization.* New York: Wiley. (*Library Literature,* 1976–77, p. 1314, notes the title of the thesis on which this book is based: *Conversion of Scripts: Its Nature, History and Utilization, with Particular Reference to Bibliographic Control.* Thesis (Ph.D.), University of Maryland, 1975.

Zafren, Herbert C. (1969). Computers, transliterations, and related things. *Proceedings of the 4th Annual* [Association of Jewish Libraries] *Convention,* p. 55–56.

Zipin, Amnon. (1984). Romanized Hebrew script in the online catalog at the Ohio State University Libraries. *Judaica Librarianship* 1:53–57.

Ubiquitous Cataloging

Bradley Dilger and William Thompson

Cataloging Becomes Ubiquitous

Ask library users to describe their Online Public Access Catalog (OPAC), and then to describe Google, and most will give indistinguishable answers. This is no surprise. In many libraries, the stand-alone, single-function card catalog, designed to find books on nearby shelves, has been all but replaced by integrated multifunction catalogs which not only search local holdings, but can also search the holdings of other libraries — and can request and check out items from afar. However, library users' conflation of OPACs and other entities also exists because Amazon.com, Google Books, and similar sites are in fact the primary catalogs for many people. In fact, LibraryThing, a popular social network and book catalog, uses either Amazon.com or the Library of Congress as its two main default sources for gathering book information, suggesting an equivalence between the two. Further blurring long-established boundaries, as more content becomes available online in alternative catalogs and other databases, catalogs are not only a pathway to texts, but also a final destination. Users rely on OPACs not only to locate netLibrary books or government documents, but to retrieve them as well — if they are not already bypassing local catalogs in favor of Google Books.

Most importantly, as we enter the dawning age of ubiquitous computing, what Adam Greenfield calls "everyware," we are also entering the dawning age of ubiquitous cataloging. Indeed, we live in the golden age of catalogs, because cataloging, once the province of scholars armed with pen and paper, has become one of the core skills of computing — a "unit operation," to use the framework proposed by Ian Bogost (2006, 3). More and more of our daily activities involve cataloging, which we believe must be considered in five ways. The first is the traditional sense: categorization and/or classification by trained ontologists guided by established standards. Librarians all over the world participate in this work every day. The second is categorization and/or classification by people without professional training, likely using no formal guidelines. Numerous web sites considered part of "Web 2.0," which revolves around network-based applications and user input, as opposed to more traditional web sites that broadcast information, facilitate this type of cataloging. LibraryThing and Amazon.com fit this bill, as do bookmark managers like del.icio.us and photography-sharing sites such as Flickr. The third might be called "catalog-networking": the act of browsing catalogs, comparing them, and connecting all kinds of information systems. In the age of Google, this activity happens continuously, at the hands of both professional ontologists and those who catalog-network for fun, at school, or on the job (often through the same Web 2.0 sites). The fourth is the design of catalogs and cataloging interfaces, whether OPACs, less traditional systems like LibraryThing, or even search functionalities like Apple's Spotlight for Mac OS X. Obviously, as information systems proliferate, so does the need to manage the information they contain and thus this manner of cataloging as well. The fifth and final type is cataloging of catalog users: the collection, storage, and retrieval of information about catalog users, in both contexts immediately connected to, and seemingly far from, traditional cataloging. Today, a trip to the market can initiate this kind of cataloging: as customers swipe a key fob required for a discount, databases quietly plan restocking of inventories and accumulate information about purchases that can be articulated to consumer demographics. (In library terms, the grocery store "engages in collection development programs appropriate to its user community.")

A brief case study of LibraryThing illustrates the importance and interconnectedness of these five senses of cataloging. The primary purpose of the site is building a personal catalog: one's own searchable and sortable database of books, accessible from any device with a web browser. What if the patrons of a library could voluntarily make these off-site catalogs visible to other interested readers? Then library catalogs would create connections between patrons — user communities. LibraryThing is designed this way: it allows readers to share their lists of books they have purchased or read and to discover others who have read the same texts. Readers can import records from several sources of bibliographic information; as noted above, they are Amazon.com, the Library of Congress, and numerous other sources. Once they have imported a record, readers can add subject headings of their own, called "tags," which can be matched against those of other LibraryThing users — providing another way to discover texts. Additionally, readers can quickly link via author or title to public records in any individual's personal collection. This double functionality enables readers to create a private catalog of their own reading, while simultaneously creating a "union catalog" linking all readers. The site also allows users to review books, comment on the reviews of other readers and facilitates intra-reader communication via email or online groups. In other words, site designer Tim Spalding and the community of LibraryThing users who have contributed to its development have covered all five senses of cataloging as we've defined it: integrating (1) established, formal cataloging protocols and catalogs with (2) user-contributed data, while (3) facilitating comparisons between wide varieties of formal and informal cataloging systems. Also, LibraryThing (4) constantly updates its design and functionality to meet user needs, while (5) allowing users to see each other yet still control their own privacy.

LibraryThing and similar Web 2.0 sites provide models of cataloging to be carefully studied and emulated by all kinds of libraries (Miller 2005). The OPAC monopoly on cataloging is dead, thanks to Google, LibraryThing and a host of other web-based systems that facilitate one or more of our five kinds of cataloging. While OPACs are far from dead, unless they change, library catalogs and the work of catalogers will be downgraded to a finding aid, a quick stop in a circuit that begins with and returns to Amazon.com or Google Books. Indeed, Google's massive text digitization project is changing the way people locate information in and about books, and could do even more: as a recent *New Yorker* article estimated, digitizing all 32 million books in WorldCat would cost about $800 million — well within the reach of a company capitalized at $150 billion (Toobin 2007, 33). In this essay, we join those arguing for expanding the functions of library catalogs and calling on cataloging vendors to do the same (Byrum 2005, Lossau 2004). In this way, libraries can maintain their commitment to user-centered technology while keeping the catalog centered in the library — no longer a given, as D. Grant Campbell and Karl V. Fast point out (Campbell and Fast 2004, 26). This work would simultaneously enhance libraries' position as the center of community information networks. Imagine a map that merged Library-Thing data and Google Maps to show the distribution of local readers of Agatha Christie mysteries; that would provide an entirely new kind of community analysis. Libraries can enable these new kinds of information resources while answering their core missions and continuing to defend the privacy rights of their patrons. To these ends, we draw upon network theory to show why and how librarians should consider cataloging broadly, as we do, and to outline methods for answering the implicit challenge of LibraryThing and other alternative catalogs emerging from Web 2.0 — or rather, for seeing these information systems as possible partners, not competitors, in a world of ubiquitous cataloging.

Catalogs and Networks

Most library patrons would agree that library catalogs allow users to locate books and other materials by author, title, and subject. But most librarians would hasten to point out they can do much more. Catalogs allow connections between diverse subjects, provide pathways for researchers to contact each other, etc. To use the terms of network theory, catalogs are simultaneously points of entry into networks, network nodes, and even means for making new nodes and connections. As we note above, we are not the first to apply network theory to library catalogs; they have always had a social component, enabling connections between readers and authors (Campbell and Fast 2004, 35). Traditionally, library catalogs create what Mark Granovetter called a "bridge," the only path between one knowledge network (the library patron) and another (the particular work or works of interest in a library's collections). The catalog allows users to discover, identify, and with the help of the shelf classification system, retrieve specific works new to them, bringing them into their knowledge networks. In this manner, catalogs aid research, discovering knowledge, and findability, locating a particular object or idea (Morville 2005, 4). Arguably, connecting users and the works otherwise unknown to them remains the most critical function of library catalogs. But the connections catalogs facilitate aren't always unique, especially for experienced researchers who are aware of many important authors and texts, even those not in their fields. Granovetter famously called these connections between two otherwise disconnected networks "weak ties." His analogy compares acquaintances and friends (Granovetter 1973, 1366). With friends, we have strong ties; we communicate with them routinely and share quite a bit of their knowledge, which is why so much can go unsaid between friends (Granovetter 1973, 1371–73). With acquaintances (weak ties), we communicate less frequently, perhaps rarely, but they know people and possess information our friends don't. Weak ties are powerful because their weakness provides an entrée into the unknown, into new areas of knowledge where we can make discoveries and extend or even radically change our knowledge networks. While the information redundancy characteristic of strong ties allows close-knit groups to perform complex tasks fairly easily, common knowledge can make new ideas difficult to come by and novel experiences difficult to process (Justesen 2004, 89). People tend to cling to what is familiar. As a result, strong ties can create the informational equivalent of vendor lock-in. Ideally, people and other knowledge-gathering systems need *both* sorts of ties: weak ties to provide novelty and encourage innovation, and strong ties to enable complex tasks.

Describing ourselves as "knowledge networks" may seem odd, but is a critical distinction: complex biological and intellectual networks generate what and how we know. Textual knowledge is a dense network of sentences, allusions, metaphors, argumentation, disciplinary knowledge, citations to other works, and the knowledge, desires, motives of other human beings and cultures. While knowledge creation and dissemination has always involved reworking the ideas of others, computer technology's embedding of cut and paste into the heart of its operation foregrounds the interconnectedness of knowledge (Ulmer 1994). More and more often, we are aware of and encourage involvement in networks of all kinds, both the literal social networks forged at home, work, and play, virtual social networks made possible by the Internet, and those which combine the two, like email lists maintained by academic organizations, or, for that matter, MySpace and Facebook — which are now so popular they have become uncool (Vara 2006). Catalogs more than anything should be about the extension of knowledge networks, and we believe the best way is facilitating the creation of weak ties.

This creation need not be carefully planned and orchestrated. Granovetter points out that because weak ties can be made quickly, we can afford to have many of them without expecting rewards on the short or long term. And different types of ties are more amenable to individuals for different reasons. Full text databases provide an excellent example: some provide better access to summaries and analysis, some to bibliographic information. For certain users, such as undergraduate students, citation data will be less valuable than an explanatory preface or a saved trip to the stacks (Serotkin 2005). For all kinds of cataloging, it is difficult to know beforehand what particular connections, or even which kinds of connections, will be the most rewarding on the short and long term. Hence, we believe catalog designers should think carefully about limiting the ways their interfaces function in the name of efficiency or effectiveness, and we suggest emulating the Web 2.0 catalogers who work hard to allow interaction with and integration of networks of all kinds. We'll return to this critical point later in this essay.

Cataloging as Communication

All five definitions of cataloging we identified above involve communication, and in fact, catalogs themselves are communication media through which libraries and users exchange information. Catalogs deliver not only clues to finding texts one is looking for but information about cataloging standards and relevant subject headings. Like a language, the catalog itself is a technological infrastructure whose design shapes what can and cannot be represented, not a transparent entity which passes information to users without value judgments. Sanford Berman and Clay Shirky, among others, have pointed out this ideological work in the Dewey Decimal System, which, for example, allots many times the classification space for texts about Christianity than it does for other religions (Shirky 2005). In a more practical vein, Nicholson Baker argued that conversions of card catalogs to OPACs often excluded highly localized and potentially very valuable metadata that librarians added to catalog cards, often by hand (Baker 1994).

While it's impossible to create any communication system that functions as in Michael Reddy's "conduit metaphor," where meanings are transmitted as if they were objects unaffected by language, catalogers can make their activities public so that users can better understand the decisions they make while entering metadata, designing catalog interfaces, and developing standards. In many ways, the publication of library catalog standards such as the Anglo-American Cataloguing Rules (AACR2) provides far more openness than the online catalog-like services we are considering in this essay. For example, while Google provides some explanation of its "PageRank" algorithm for ranking web pages, the specifics are kept under wraps (Google 2007). OPAC maintainers should strive to keep this openness, and extend it by integrating more accessible versions of cataloging standards into catalogs of all kinds.

Most library catalogs broadcast information largely in one direction, from the library to the user. Users seldom use OPACs to communicate with libraries and *never* for reaching one another — at least not directly. Campbell and Fast argue that traditional catalogs do act as an important avenue of *indirect* communication between readers and writers by allowing scholars to reliably identify specific works, which they may then read and comment upon, with the knowledge that other readers and writers will do the same with identical texts. Further, they argue that catalogs' function as communication media also allows for fostering communities of practice (Campbell and Fast 2004, 34). Using an OPAC, a scholar researching Coleridge's contribution to Romantic theories of the imagination can easily locate and retrieve a copy of John Livingstone Lowes' classic 1927 study, *The Road to Xanadu,* as well as Coleridge's own *Biographia Literaria,* and enter into dialog with both Lowes and Coleridge — and many other scholars through other books and the citations contained within them. Access to many texts allows scholars to emulate or contest evidentiary and citational protocols found in them. In this way, the catalog indirectly fosters a community of scholarly practice among readers and writers.

Though the catalog contributes indirectly to this process, its contribution is powerful: remove the ties generated by the catalog, and many research communities would vanish. Certainly, findability remains crucial to research today, though communities of practice are not necessarily forming around or through "proper" library catalogs. At least now, researchers are creating this infrastructure on their own, demonstrating both their desire for two-way inter-research communication and the ability of catalog-like services to organize it. Publication in many academic scientific communities has changed significantly thanks to sites such as the pre-print server arXiv.org, where articles are posted online in advance of their official publication in print — allowing the information to be used sooner rather than later (Johnson 2004, 5). Without a doubt, LibraryThing provides a second useful example of a communication-enhanced cataloging service, given its integration of forums and facilitation of contact. Furthermore, scholarly databases such as the Association for Computing Machinery (ACM) Digital Library include authors' email addresses as live links in their records, allowing very rapid and direct communication. For us, these and other examples demonstrate network building through facilitation of weak ties, underscoring our claim that traditional catalog designs must recognize their value as well and seek to alter their functionality in ways which allow users to create a wide variety of weak ties through the catalog.

Play and Parody in Cataloging

As cataloging becomes ubiquitous, catalogs need to allow more uses, more contexts of use, and more interoperability with other catalogs and catalog-like systems — in other words, more opportunities for catalogs to be integrated into social, communicative, and educational networks. We have already pointed out some features of catalog-like web sites, which we feel OPACs should consider, and we would like to suggest some more. First, we'd like to note two broad movements that demand special attention.

Play and parody should enter the catalog, for they allow for the creation of unexpected ties to known networks, as well as ties to new networks. The boundary space between the known and unknown is where new knowledge is most easily formed. Play, as Jacques Derrida noted, is the result of the inability of any structure to be complete (1978, 289). This is not simply to say all catalogs will be incomplete because there will always be new books but more fundamentally because the catalog is structured around incompletion and absence. Cataloging assuages an absence, a desire for getting at the knowledge contained in a library's collection and creating new knowledge from it. Catalogs still act as permeable boundaries between people and "real" knowledge and "potential" knowledge contained in the collection, mediating the indeterminacy between what is known (a work's title, author, or subject) and the desire for the unknown (the work's content and, more importantly, its potential use). For example, a reader might know a library has Keith Waldrop's translation of *Les Fleurs du Mal,* and might even know a little about its content. That same reader may have read reviews or other translations of *Les Fleurs du Mal.* But until she gets and reads Waldrop's translation, she can't know what the book knows, or how that knowledge will affect her. The catalog was designed to respond to a desire that will never been fully satisfied because it is insatiable, a form of play.

Of course, catalogs and catalogers have always mediated, even wrestled with, the knowledge boundary. Consider how difficult it has been to establish what seems to be known: an author's name, the correct title, the edition, etc. How much of the unknown to include in the catalog has long been a point of contention. The space constraints of catalog cards (and to a significant degree of Machine-Readable Cataloging (MARC) records after cards), meant that including significantly more information was difficult to do. Not that librarians didn't try, as Baker's argument about handwritten notes on catalog cards reminds us (1994, 76).

But traditional cataloging often functions to reduce play. For example, subject access in a library catalog is determined firstly by committees composed of catalogers who approve the subject headings, and secondly by individual catalogers who employ those same headings. The recently created subject heading CAMP (STYLE) will allow a large group of materials formerly dispersed to be collected together. But camp, as a rhetorical and personal style, has been around for a long time, and the thousands of materials published that could usefully be accumulated under this heading will not be gathered there soon. If catalogs, while retaining their own subject headings, opened their discursive spaces, allowing users to classify works as "camp," and encouraged patrons to share these subject headings with others, a great many items might be quickly identified as "camp." Some of these would be items a professional cataloger might not designate as "camp"— for instance, a catalog user might designate Susan Sontag's "Notes on Camp" as itself a form of camp rather than a description of it. Though seldom admitted into traditional cataloging, these kinds of disagreements are inevitable, interesting, and often fruitful — exactly what we have in mind when we call for the admission of play into the catalog.

Some might argue that changing the boundaries of OPACs in this way would amount to a parody of cataloging, or that it would fail as cataloging. Yes and no. Mikhail Bakhtin points out in *The Dialogic Imagination* that parody is possible because formal discourses, like that of the catalog record, are not complete, not inevitable (1981, 59). Within the limits of their genre (epic poetry, a junior high civics class, or cataloging), such discourses don't say everything. Parody compels a discourse to say things it ordinarily wouldn't — perhaps even certain truths. Bakhtin uses the example of Rabelais's parodies of religion, which say what the church would not say about itself. In our time, *South Park* is a Rabelaisian parody of middle-class America, delivered via the forms of normal childhood. (And in 1994 Baker was, in essence, calling the OPAC a parody of the card catalog.) As Bakhtin says, "Parodic travestying literature introduces the permanent corrective of laughter, of a critique on the one-sided seriousness of the lofty direct word, the corrective of a reality that is always richer, more fundamental, and, most importantly, too contradictory and heteroglot to be fit into a high and straightforward genre" (1981, 55). While it might be difficult to accept the notion that parody should be integrated into the texts it refigures, or at the least presented as complementary, we think its power as critique offers a way for catalogs to simultaneously create the two-way communications we've called for above, while facilitating both a very formative strong tie to the original being parodied, and valuable weak ties to texts and discourses that would not be connected absent the critique of the parody. Parody can also be an example of allowing play into a system of discourse, another way of telling the truth, of keeping a discourse honest.

Cataloging in Web 2.0

Our call for catalogs to reinvent themselves by becoming better networks, by integrating communication, and by allowing play and parody is motivated in large part by

LibraryThing, del.icio.us, and similar sites that Tim O' Reilly first labeled "Web 2.0" (2005). Fairly new services such as the social bookmarking manager del.icio.us or the photo-sharing site Flickr are joined by comparatively venerable sites like Google and Amazon.com in performing one or more of the five types of cataloging we identify at the start of this essay. Where first-generation web sites used a variety of methods to provide information to users — essentially an update of newspapers or broadcasting — Web 2.0 sites integrate a high degree of user input and interaction. Arguably, that input, whether kept private or made public, whether individual or aggregated, is the core of Web 2.0, and essential to the cataloging functionality of the sites we discuss here. While not all Web 2.0 sites engage in cataloging, many do, and we want to describe why some are so effective, as we continue to draw upon them to suggest methods for rethinking cataloging.

LibraryThing and Amazon.com both allow and even encourage forms of play and parody in several ways. Both allow users to add metadata, usually in the form of keyword-like "tags," which expand upon the subject headings provided when a record is imported into the system. These tags are searchable across personal collections and across the holdings of both systems. Among other things, Amazon.com allows readers to contribute reviews, comment on other reviews, and create lists of books that are keyed to records. Because it is not standardized, this user-contributed content is inherently transdisciplinary, often linking texts in surprising ways. For example, Amazon.com readers' lists are deeply personal and often irreverent — and very useful because they can connect texts in ways catalogs do not. These lists cover subject matter which might be considered esoteric (for example, information visualization in English studies, transsexuals in film, Australian rules football) and use a tremendous variety of approaches for evaluation, collecting items not covered by traditional searches. These resources offer additional ways of envisioning texts cataloged by Amazon — without interfering with the site's own classification systems.

A second example shows the power of parody. LibraryThing's author and title "clouds" reveal that J. K. Rowling and J. R. R. Tolkien are the most heavily collected authors on the site. Rowling and Tolkien are followed by a host of others, many the authors of genre fiction (mysteries, science fiction, and young adult) and, with the notable exception of Jane Austen, few traditionally canonical authors. In other words, the Library-Thing catalog dramatically demonstrates a truth librarians have long known: readers prefer popular fiction to the canon. However, when libraries respond to their users' wishes and make more space for popular fiction, they are often hammered by traditionalists who perceive the library as an institution meant for the betterment of the public, as recently occurred with the Fairfax (Virginia) County Library's weeding program (Hollingsworth 2007). In other words, a catalog designed along the lines of LibraryThing could successfully parody the implied cultural elitist view of libraries and open up the age-old debate about libraries' purposes and clientele. A more participatory catalog would situate this debate between readers themselves, via the catalog (in user groups, for example).

What sites like LibraryThing catalog, and for whom, varies widely, as do the methodologies employed, which is consistent with our call for a diversity of approaches in the name of facilitating weak ties. Del.icio.us focuses on web bookmarks, anything with a uniform resource locator (URL). Flickr allows uploading, organizing, and sharing of photographs and other computer-generated images. The CiteULike citation manager supports sorting, input, and export of citations for academic writing (and, like many Web 2.0 sites, is targeted at a very specific audience: researchers using common databases like JSTOR and bibliographic tools such as BibTeX). While these and other sites differ in the content of cataloging, they all answer the question "for whom" in two identical ways. The content that users identify, annotate, share, and return to is originally intended for the end user doing the work. Bookmark managers like del.icio.us solve a terrible but common problem: how people using multiple computers and web browsers can establish a single source for bookmarks. But there is a critical second audience: anyone using a site which allows users to make their input public can compare her content to individuals who have saved similar items or used similar annotations, as well as to the aggregated display of all site users. In this way, these web services employ what Mike Robinson would call a "double level language."

Double Level Languages

Writing about what is now often called "computer supported collaborative work," Robinson (1991) proposed that applications with a double level language possess a formal language and what he calls a "cultural" language. The formal language structures and organizes the work, providing clarity and the ability to share information at the cost of being rigid. In the case of traditional catalogs, that would be the AACR2 standard; for LibraryThing, del.icio.us, and similar sites, that would be the interface elements which allow users to upload content, add titles and other metadata, and control how it is shared — though we should hasten to note that the sites we've seen have tried to ensure their rigidity enables, rather than constrains, end users. The cultural language allows work to be commented upon and extended in a manner that does not necessarily sacrifice the integrity of the formal language. On the Web, these cultural languages take numerous forms: on- and off-site forums and commentary; patterns in user-contributed information; visualizations of aggregated data; inter-site mash-ups and combinations; and a general reflection of cultural trends into cataloged content (often called "memes").

Double language systems draw from the strength of each language. The cultural language provides the ability to innovate and connect to the "unknown" at the cost of increasing ambiguity or, if you like, semantic entropy. Yet it is this tension between the orderly and chaotic that allows new knowledge to enter into established networks (Robinson 1991, 40, 42–43). Anders Lundquist illustrated this process nicely in a case study of Cisco's use of newsgroups for product support. Newsgroup users created a cultural commentary on Cisco's formal work processes and router products, fueling product innovation and also building expertise in its community of users, some of whom even became official Cisco support personnel (Lundquist 2004, 98–99, 102). Most importantly, double-level languages bring together many of the elements we've argued for in this essay: they boost the creation of weak ties, encourage two-way communication, and allow play and parody to be integrated without sacrificing the original. In this vein, Amazon.com differentiates between user-submitted and "editorial" reviews; similarly, a catalog site could differentiate between metadata supplied by the Library of Congress and that shared by end users.

Furthermore, many Web 2.0 services use rigid formal languages such as Really Simple Syndication (RSS) for information exchange with other web sites, but have few restrictions on the ways these formal languages can be used. This flexibility allows the idea of "double leveling" to become recursive: a list of bookmarks from del.icio.us can be the formal language upon which cultural languages from LibraryThing can build, and so on. Part of this is a matter of attitude: how do site proprietors react when they find their classification systems being used in unintended ways? Those who respond by incorporating users' innovations, as Lundquist documented with Cisco, are far more likely to develop the energetic, devoted user base capable of such surprising work.

Tagging

While this interaction sounds quite complicated, it's actually very simple, thanks to the simple but powerful metadata system called "tagging." Sites that use tags for classification allow users to create multiple tags, which are a kind of keyword, for contributed content. For example, one can use LibraryThing to create an entry for *Moby-Dick* by tagging it in this manner: "melville, literature, long, novel, whale, tech, toread." These tags function like subject headings (in that disparate materials may be linked together through them), and can be shared with other users of the service, who in turn may or may not use them for their own purposes. Many sites allow users to copy items from each other including tags and other metadata, in much the same way the Online Computer Library Center (OCLC) facilitates record sharing. Furthermore, tags don't have to relate to content fixedly — the tag "toread" is almost certainly temporary and indeed specific to a single user (Shirky 2005).

But tags can provide a quick and easy way to traversing multiple sets of metadata. On del.icio.us, for example, users can quickly move between the following views:

- a single item the user dilger has tagged "cataloging"
- all items dilger has tagged "cataloging"
- all items any user has tagged "cataloging"
- a single item tagged "cataloging" by the user wat100
- all items tagged by wat100

This rapid movement facilitates the creation of multiple weak ties: to other users with similar tags, to other texts which one might find useful, or to tag lists which one can return to and monitor for new, interesting items. Notably, allowing a catalog to integrate tagging would foster connections between items and searches — imagine adding "all items tagged fiber in my OPAC" to the list above. Allowing users to add tags to a catalog, whether integrated in the catalog itself or as a double-level language via external connections to sites such as LibraryThing, would make cataloging a more dynamic and open-ended process, a discursive space in which users might create connections or explore connections already made by professional catalogers. It might even be that the professional cataloging community would adopt tags created by users. The catalog could then become a discursive space that allows for the creation of tagging as a form of legitimate peripheral participation in the community of practice of cataloging. Along these lines, del.icio.us automatically suggests tags other users have adopted for similar links. The user can choose to adopt the tags or not. By offering the suggested tags, del.icio.us increases the sociality of the network and fosters the creation of a user-driven descriptive language, thus allowing for standardization and idiosyncrasy alike.

Legitimate peripheral participation is defined by Jean Lave and Etienne Wegner as "the process by which newcomers become part of a community of practice" (Lave and Wegner 1991). Libraries function as communities of practice: newcomers hired into a library learn the "way things are done here," but because they are on the periphery of a library's established practices, they are more likely to do things differently, to bring in new knowledge, to innovate. Yet even though they are peripheral, the library is more apt to adopt the innovations of new librarians as opposed to others, because it views them as legitimate thanks to their MLS degrees. Similarly, users who add tags to a catalog would be participating in a peripheral but legitimate way in the work of the catalog, a large part of which is the identification of information and of the relationships between works. Moreover, because users would not be bound by the limits of a particular collection, their tags could lead out of the collection and into other knowledge domains: the holdings of other libraries, journal literature, websites, weblogs, and out of the typographical domain entirely, to images and to audio and video content. This richness of content is visible in the diversity of Web 2.0 sites, some of which, like those listed here, privilege the crowd; but others, like Ma.gnolia and Citizendium, seek to maintain the discreteness of expertise by user-edited groups and peer review structures (Sanger 2006).

Tagging has its critics — librarians and information architects alike have pointed out some of its limitations (Rosenfeld 2005). For example, given that few if any sites which use tags check users' spelling, using "catalging" for one or more texts will cause those items to disappear from lists made from properly spelled tags. Darlene Fichter has argued that variant forms such as "bunny, bunnies, and rabbit, Easter, or a proper name" can similarly reduce the usefulness of tagging (Fichter 2006, 43). But these problems have been confronted by traditional catalogers for years — and few would propose abandoning subject headings because of variations in spellings of "al-Qaeda." While tagging and its much ballyhooed companion "folksonomy" (classification by amateurs, as opposed to "taxonomy" created by experts) aren't going to automatically revolutionize the art and craft of cataloging, they remain valuable tools for reaching the larger goals we've set out as cataloging moves towards ubiquity.

Interoperability

There are other ways catalogs could foster weak ties. We are used to thinking of the catalog as one thing and items it catalogs as another, but in a digital environment those distinctions are often blurred. Amazon and Google Books provide limited access to the content of many books in their collections, thus approximating Jorge Luis Borges's vision of a map coincident with the geography it describes (Borges 1972). The limited access Amazon.com and Google Books provide is through keyword searches of scanned materials and limited browsing of a few pages of any one book. Users can search all pages of all scanned materials in the Google archive, whereas within Amazon.com this ability is more limited (though books are linked in other ways). These keyword searches make Google Books and Amazon.com powerful research tools. Seeing actual pages from the works, however, leverages this power even further, especially when these pages include a book's bibliography and/or index. Given that information, users can query Open WorldCat from the Google Books record to locate the item in the nearest library, or use a service like Amazon to purchase the book. Amazon supplements keyword searching with lists of "Statistically Improbable Phrases" (SIPs). According to Amazon, these phrases repeat an "improbable" number of times in a book, as determined by an algorithm that compares all books that have been scanned (Amazon.com 2006, #3). SIPs are linked to other books that use them, creating a quantitatively driven form of "subject access" that works rather well, though not like traditional subject headings. Instead of directing people toward similar items, SIPs can establish or reveal connections between books that readers might not have expected.

Imagine the power of these resources if they were made interoperable by the simple method that del.icio.us employs for exchanging information. The web address <http://del.icio.us/dilger/cataloging> provides a reverse chronological list of all items the del.icio.us user dilger has tagged "cataloging." Similar URLs are available for all of the instances we note above, and provide easy access to dynamic metadata sets which are actively maintained. Additionally, one can see recent items *anyone* has tagged "cataloging" with <http://del.icio.us/tag/cataloging/>. Reloading that page every few minutes shows the size of the community of people interested in cataloging — all of whom could become nodes in one's knowledge network. Notably, del.icio.us offers other ways to get lists of tags, such as RSS feeds or JavaScript Object Notation (JSON) objects. Programmers are using these streams of cataloging data to create new ways of organizing the flow of information on the web, drawing upon the double level language capability of many sites to create sophisticated ways of visualizing metadata. We hope for more integration of information from local OPACs into those streams — and for more flow of information to and from the unofficial catalogs of Web 2.0 and the OPACs on whose door they are, ever so quietly, knocking. We hope to see more discussions about all five of the cataloging activities we have discussed here, with participation from academic librarians, programmers working for Silicon Valley startups, and the general public. With the ubiquitous cataloging we hope to see — a matrix of activities performed with a hybrid of traditional OPACs and other online services — a library patron could learn about a book in the library catalog, search its contents via Google Books or Amazon, check a few reviews and make a quick writeup of the text in LibraryThing, and decide whether to purchase the book or retrieve a copy off a nearby shelf.

Bibliography

Amazon.com. (2006). Amazon.com statistically improbable phrases. Available: <http://www.amazon.com/gp/search-inside/sipshelp.html/002–2471746–4597601>.

Baker, Nicholson. (1994, April 4). Discards: card catalogs destroyed as online systems grow. *New Yorker,* 64–70.

Bakhtin, Mikhail M. (1981). *The Dialogic Imagination,* ed. Michael Holquist. Austin: University of Texas Press.

Bogost, Ian. (2006). *Unit Operations: An Approach to Videogame Criticism.* Cambridge: MIT Press.

Borges, Jorge Luis. (1972). Of exactitude in science. In *A Universal History of Infamy.* Trans. Norman Thomas di Giovanni. New York: Dutton.

Byrum, John D., Jr. Recommendations for urgently needed improvement of OPAC and the role of the National Bibliographic Agency in achieving it. World Library and Information Congress: 71st IFLA General Conference and Council, August 14–18, 2005, Oslo, Norway. Available: <http://www.ifla.org/IV/ifla71/papers/124e-Byrum.pdf>.

Campbell, Grant D., and Karl V. Fast. (2004). Panizzi, Lubetzky, and Google: How the modern web environment is reinventing the theory of cataloguing. *Canadian Journal of Information and Library Science* 28 (3): 25–38.

Derrida, Jacques. (1978). Structure, sign, and play in the discourse of the human sciences. In *Writing and Difference.* Chicago: University of Chicago Press.

Fichter, Darlene. (2006). Intranet applications for tagging and folksonomies. *Online* 30 (3): 43–45.

Google. (2007). Corporate information: Technology overview. Available: <http://www.google.com/corporate/tech.html>.

Granovetter, Mark S. (1973). The strength of weak ties. *American Journal of Sociology* 78 (6): 1360–80.

Granovetter, Mark S. (1983). The strength of weak ties: A network theory revisited. *Sociological Theory* 1: 201–33.

Greenfield, Adam. (2006). *Everyware: The Dawning Age of Ubiquitous Computing.* Berkeley: Peachpit Press.

Hollingsworth, Helen C. (2007, January 21). "Fairfax, don't take the culling too far; the public library is one institution that shouldn't be dumbed down." *Washington Post,* B8.

Johnson, Richard K. (2004). The future of scholarly communication in the humanities: adaptation or transformation? Available: <http://www.arl.org/sparc/pubs/docs/SPARC_CELJ.pdf>.

Justesen, Susanne. (2004). Innoversity in communities of practice. In *Knowledge networks: Innovation Through Communities of Practice,* ed. Paul Hildreth and Chris Kimble. London: Idea Group Publishing.

Lave, Jean, and Etienne Wegner. (1991). *Situated Learning: Legitimate Peripheral Participation.* Learning in Doing: Social, Cognitive, and Computational Perspectives. New York: Cambridge University Press.

Lossau, Norbert. (2004, June). Search engine technology and digital libraries: libraries need to discover the academic internet. *D-Lib Magazine* 10 (6). Available: <http://www.dlib.org/dlib/june04/lossau/06lossau.html>.

Lundkvist, Anders. (2004). User networks as sources of innovation. In *Knowledge networks: Innovation Through Communities of Practice,* edited by P. Hildreth and C. Kimble. London: Idea Group Publishing.

Miller, Paul. (2005). Web 2.0: Building the New Library. *Ariadne* 45. Available: <http://www.ariadne.ac.uk/issue45/miller>.

Morville, Peter. (2005). *Ambient Findability.* Cambridge: O'Reilly.

O'Reilly, Tim. (2005). What is Web 2.0?: Design patterns and business models for the next generation of software. Available: <http://www.oreilly.com/go/web2>.

Sanger, Larry. (2006). Toward a new compendium of knowledge. Available: http://citizendium.org/essay.html>.

Serotkin, Patricia B. (2005). If we build it, will they come?: Electronic journals acceptance and usage patterns. *Libraries and the Academy* 5(4): 497–512.

Shirky, Clay. (2005). Ontology is overrated: categories, links, and tags. Available: <http://www.shirky.com/writings/ontology_overrated.html>.

Reddy, Michael J. (1993). The conduit metaphor: a case of frame conflict in our language about language. In *Metaphor and Thought, Second Edition.* Cambridge: Cambridge University Press http://wrecking.org/write/index.php?title=Cataloging_draft_1—_note-23http://wrecking.org/write/index.php?title=Cataloging_draft_1—_note-23.

Robinson, Mike. (1991). Double level languages and co-operative working. *AI and Society* 5 (1): 34–60.

Rosenfeld, Louis. (2005). "Folksonomies? How about metadata ecologies?" Available: <http://louisrosenfeld.com/home/bloug_archive/000330.html>.

Toobin, Jeffrey. (2007). Google's moon shot. *New Yorker* 82 (48): 30–35.

Ulmer, Gregory L. (1994). *Heuretics: The Logic of Invention.* Baltimore: Johns Hopkins University Press.

Vara, Vauhini. (2006, October 26). MySpace, ByeSpace? Some Users Renounce Social Sites As Too Big. *Wall Street Journal.*

The Genre Jungle: Organizing Pop Music Recordings

Michael Summers

Introduction and Methodology

What is pop? What is rock? Is one a subset of the other, or are they independent? Is rock different from rock 'n' roll, and if so, how? How can we differentiate between different kinds of soul music? Is R&B the same as rhythm & blues?

These are the kinds of questions that prompted me to write this paper. As a librarian I am naturally interested in how people describe things — or, to be more precise, what descriptors, or labels, they attach to objects and experiences. And it has always seemed to me that pop music is an area in which people apply descriptors with messy abandon!

Pop music is an enormous subject, and one that I don't pretend to be comprehensively informed about. For this reason, I have adopted a case-study style of research. I start off by looking at five bands/artists and recording how they have been described and classified by a selection of different agencies. These bands have been chosen purely because, listening to them and reading about them, it struck me that they would be hard to classify. In the next section I look at some genre headings and examine how they have been defined, particularly by reference works. Reference works that define pop music genres are hard to come by: the ones I focus on here are Grove Music Online (<http://www.grove music.com>) and Allmusic (<http://www.allmusic.com>), also known as the All Music Guide. Allmusic offers definitions of a wealth of genres and subgenres; Grove, on the other hand, describes relatively few, but often in more detail. After looking at genre definitions, I turn my attention to interactive methods of organizing pop music, as found on some music web sites. These methods usually involve building up profiles of the people who use them, then using software to match up profiles of users with similar tastes. This often turns out to be an effective way of enabling people to discover new music, and is known as "collaborative filtering." Websites that use profile matching as an aid to music discovery are often known as "recommender systems"; I look at one such recommender system, Last.fm (<http://www.last.fm>), in detail.

It should be borne in mind that I am writing from a British perspective, and that the terms and descriptors I use may have different layers of meaning in other regions. Having said this, Allmusic, which is U.S.-based, and Grove, which is U.K.-based, agree on many points. There are regional differences in the way the music industry is structured, too: Simon Frith notes in particular how "the British popular music world doesn't fall into neat pop and rock divisions" and says that it would be "more logical to treat it as a market unity,"[1] a point that should be remembered while reading my discussion of the terms "rock" and "pop."

"Acid-Bonkers-Metal": Uncontrolled Vocabularies for Pop Music

People love to talk about pop music — a healthy indicator of its central position in our culture. But how do they talk about it? Probably not the way librarians do! But why? Librarians like to use controlled vocabularies, bringing items that share characteristics together under some kind of subject heading. This immediately presents a problem for pop music: musicians don't like being pigeonholed, and are keen to produce work that *doesn't* share similarities with other work (otherwise they won't get noticed); likewise, listeners are often intrigued by music that doesn't fit comfortably into an existing genre. Music may often be more commercially successful when it occupies the center ground of a genre, but it is often more musically exciting when it sits on the fence.

Music journalists too get excited about music that's hard to classify, and they talk about it in terms of its distance from known points. Band A sounds a bit like band B, and a lot like band C on some tracks. This can lead to flowery, multi-hyphenated descriptions as the writer alludes to all the known styles that combine to make a new, unknown composite. In a single issue of *NME*, a British pop music magazine, various bands were described as "British post-hardcore," "Nirvana-meets-Suede," "gospel-Latin-samba-house," and, best of all, "booty-rocking, Rolling Stones-y type bluegrass punk rock stripper music."[2] At the other end of the spectrum, most public libraries that I've encountered call all pop music "Rock and Pop." Can the people who organize pop music collections learn something from journalistic flamboyance? Is there a middle ground between *NME* and my public library?

Another area where more instinctive, uncontrolled descriptions of music are to be found is in production music. Production music is something we've all heard a lot of, but rarely given much attention to: it's the anonymous, generic music that's often played in cafés and shops, or which accompanies corporate presentations. Production music is produced by specialist music companies, which license it to other companies to use in their marketing or advertising. Production music is sometimes confusingly called "library music," a term I've avoided here.

Production music companies often have publicly searchable databases on their websites. The headings used to organize the music are often unlike the headings found in other music collections, and reflect the use to which the music may be put: "Holidays," "Industrial," "Science," and "Shopping" are typical categories. However, the headings can also apply to the music itself: there's no point using music for a presentation about industry if it doesn't sound, well, industrial: energetic, focused, rhythmically regular, etc. Music in the "Holidays" category must surely be uplifting, escapist, exciting.

Production music companies also describe their music purely in terms of what it sounds like, and the descriptors they use are often effective at conveying the feel of a piece of music. Audio Network, a U.K. company, allows potential clients to search for music under the headings "Cheese/Kitsch," "Grooves," and "Retro," as well as many others. De Wolfe Music, another British company, offers a list of "suggested keywords" to be used in conjunction with genre searches. These keywords include such tags as "relaxed," "blasé," "cartoon," "assertive," "epic," "fearless"—again, descriptors that are good at conveying an immediate impression of what the piece sounds like, but which would rarely be found in a library catalog.

Bands and Artists

Different agencies put the same music in different categories. To illustrate this, I have chosen five bands/artists and tabulated how they have been categorized by a selection of agencies, then commented on the choice of categories. The first four agencies are online (three vendors plus Allmusic); the next two are real libraries (the libraries of Bowling Green State University and the University of North Texas, chosen because they have recordings of most of the artists studied here); the last two are large CD stores in central London. It could be argued that, since these are very different types of organizations, we can't expect them to use descriptors in the same ways. That, however, is part of the point: a term such as Dance has meanings that vary widely according to context, so we should be cautious about using it as an indication of *what the music actually sounds like.*

A note about capitalization: genres are capitalized when used as labels, but not in the normal flow of text. I describe Level 42 as funk-rock, because that's what they sound like to me, but I would hesitate before assigning them the labels Funk or Rock, or a hybrid of the two. There is, of course, no clear dividing line between the two types of usage.

We start with everyone's favorite disco rockers.

Scissor Sisters

Allmusic	Rock
Napster	Pop
MSN UK	Dance
iTunes	Electronic (used to be Pop)
BGSU	— —
UNT	Rock music — 2001–2010; Alternative rock music
HMV Oxford Street (west)	Rock & Pop
Virgin Megastore, Piccadilly	Rock/Pop

Table 1: How various agencies have categorized the Scissor Sisters

Allmusic describes the Scissor Sisters as "genre– and gender-defying," and the online resources have certainly found them hard to classify. When this paper was first being researched, iTunes classified them as Pop, but at the time of writing this had been changed to Electronic. In their iTunes biography, the Scissor Sisters get three genre headings: Electronic, Dance, Pop/Rock. The Electronic genre in iTunes is populated with titles such as *Pure Bar Lounge Atmosphere* and *The Chill Out Season*, which suggest a more detached method of music-making than the Scissor Sisters' song-oriented get-up-and-dance approach. The Electronic descriptor does make one kind of sense: both Electronic music and the Scissor Sisters refer back to 1970s disco.[3]

The three real-world resources all include Rock in their descriptors (though some would say there is a semantic difference between "alternative" and "popular"). Allmusic, in its description of the genre Rock, says that it "has been defined by its energy, rebellion and catchy hooks." The Scissor Sisters certainly have energy and catchy hooks; it could also be said that they are rebelling against musical and sexual stereotypes. Allmusic goes on to say that the genre Rock "has been fragmented, spinning off new styles and variations every few years." The Scissor Sisters have taken this further, attracting attention with the way in which they regenerate and recombine pre-existing genres and sub-genres.

Level 42

Allmusic	Rock
Napster	Pop
MSN UK	Soul/R'n'B/Funk
iTunes	Rock
BGSU	Rock (aggregate heading)
UNT	Rock (aggregate heading); New wave music
HMV Oxford Street	Rock & Pop
Virgin Megastore	Rock/Pop

Table 2: How various agencies have categorized Level 42. "Aggregate heading" means that a variety of descriptors were assigned, but all included the word "rock."

With Level 42, a British funk-rock group that came to prominence in the 1980s, we again see a split between the divergent classifications of the online resources and the mostly Rock labels handed out by the real-world resources.

Although Level 42 are described by MSN as Soul/R'n'B/Funk, many of their albums are hilariously labeled Folk. This must be an error: browsing the genre headings, the band can only be found under Soul/R'n'B/Funk.

University of North Texas Libraries gives a second genre heading to Level 42: New Wave. In its description of this genre, Allmusic mentions such a diverse array of bands and styles —"post-punk," "nervy power pop," "synth rockers," "rock revivalist," "pop-reggae," "mainstream rockers," "ska revivalists"— that it is hard to see what the term actually means. However, it does say that all New Wave bands "shared a love of pop hooks, modernist, synthesized production, and a fascination for being slightly left of center," and Level 42 certainly do have most of these attributes.

Jamiroquai

Allmusic	Rock
Napster	Pop
MSN UK	Pop
iTunes	Dance
BGSU	*Canned Heat* (song):
	note: Popular dance music
	subjects: Popular music —1991–2000;
	Dance music
	Little L (song):
	note: Dance song
	subjects: Dance music;
	Popular music — 2001–2010
UNT	Popular music —1991–2000
	(2 albums)
HMV Oxford Street	Rock & Pop
Virgin Megastore	Rock/Pop

Table 3: How various agencies have categorized Jamiroquai

Although Jamiroquai are described as Dance by iTunes, all the group's albums are given the descriptor Pop. If browsing by genre heading, the band appears under both Dance and Pop. In the group's biography, they are assigned these labels, in this order:

1. Dance
2. Jazz
3. Rock
4. Electronic
5. Adult Alternative
6. R&B/Soul
7. Bop
8. Pop/Rock
9. Soul

Jamiroquai are an eclectic group, so it would not be inappropriate to give them more than one genre heading. However, for someone who had never heard any of their music, this thicket of genres does not help create an idea of the group's sound.

Where iTunes describes the band as Dance but labels all the albums Pop, Napster labels the band Pop but gives the albums the descriptors Dance/Electronic or Alternative:

		iTunes	*Napster*
Classification of the band:	Jamiroquai	Dance	Pop
Classification of the albums:	Emergency on Planet Earth	Pop	Dance/Electronic
	The Return of the Space Cowboy	Pop	Dance/Electronic
	Traveling Without Moving	Pop	Alternative
	Synchronized	Pop	Alternative
	A Funk Odyssey	Pop	Dance/Electronic
	Dynamite	Pop	Alternative

**Table 4: Comparison of the labeling by iTunes and Napster
of the band Jamiroquai and their albums**

BGSU library also uses the descriptor Dance for its two Jamiroquai tracks. Allmusic describes Dance as a post-disco genre where "the beat is king," and in this sense,

Dance is a better descriptor for Jamiroquai, with their tightly arranged, funk-influenced scores, than Rock. However, Jamiroquai are very much a band, not the creation of a lone studio producer, and Rock has more associations of instrumental and vocal skill than does Dance. This is another example of descriptors having different meanings according to context and the priority given to different musical attributes, leading to the inconsistent application of descriptors.

Pet Shop Boys

Allmusic	Rock
Napster	Pop
MSN UK	Pop
iTunes	Alternative
BGSU	Rock (aggregate heading)

UNT	*One More Chance* (song):
	    note: Club/Dance Music*
	    subject: Rock music—1981–1990

HMV Oxford Street	Rock & Pop
Virgin Megastore	Rock/Pop

Table 5: How various agencies have categorized the Pet Shop Boys.

*UNT's recording of *One More Chance* is followed by a remix, which may explain the Club/Dance descriptor.

The descriptor that stands out here is iTunes' Alternative, which is problematic anyway, as it is not clear what it is alternative to. Looking at the descriptors given to the songs on iTunes, rather than to the band itself, it turns out that only a minority of the songs are labeled Alternative: most are Pop, and a few are Rock or Dance. In the band's biography, ten genre descriptors are given, including the more appropriate Dance, Pop, and Electronic. "Alternative" is the first descriptor in the list: could it be that these ten genres were assigned in no particular order, but that the first was chosen as the one to represent the band?

The other striking thing about the chosen resources' classifications of the Pet Shop Boys is the preponderance of the descriptors Rock and Pop, and the absence of such descriptors as Dance or Electronic (UNT's note of "Club/Dance music" might apply to the remix that shares a carrier with *One More Chance*). Most of the things we associate with Rock — an emphasis on instrumental/vocal skill, spontaneity, expressions of raw emotion, references to older Rock 'n' Roll or Rhythm & Blues styles — are absent or backgrounded in the Pet Shop Boys (see the next section for more exploration of the genre Rock). One reason for the absence of the descriptor Dance in the chosen resources may be the Pet Shop Boys' use of lyrics which are often emotionally detached or cynical, even when surrounded by the lush sounds of synth-pop. Perhaps it is this verbal remove from the hedonism of the dance floor that prevents classifiers from assigning them the Dance label.

Lauryn Hill (*The Miseducation of Lauryn Hill*)

Allmusic	Rap
Napster	Pop
MSN UK	Soul/R'n'B/Funk

iTunes	R'n'B/Soul
BGSU	Rhythm and Blues Music; Soul Music
UNT	Rhythm and Blues Music; Popular Music—1991–2000; Soul Music
HMV Oxford Street	Urban
Virgin Megastore	Urban

Table 6: How various agencies have categorized Lauryn Hill

Lauryn Hill's ground-breaking and wide-ranging 1998 album *The Miseducation of Lauryn Hill* has, not surprisingly, resulted in a diverse range of classifications among the chosen resources. Hill's Allmusic biography points out that she grew up with her parents' multi-genre record collection, and claims that *Miseducation* integrates "rap, soul, reggae and R&B into her own sound."

The two CD stores introduce a new genre, Urban. Allmusic describes Urban as a style with its roots in soul and R&B, consisting mainly of romantic ballads with high production values, but which also makes room for "uptempo, funky dance tracks." It also mentions the "controlled yet soulful vocals" that can often be heard on Urban tracks. This all seems a fair description of *Miseducation*.

MSN, iTunes and both the libraries use the labels R'n'B or Rhythm & Blues. Rhythm & Blues is a genre that goes back to the 1950s — BGSU holds recordings by Rhythm & Blues artists Elmore James and Dave Bartholomew in this category. Lauryn Hill doesn't sound much like a 1950s Rhythm & Blues artist; perhaps R&B is an updated form of the genre? Or perhaps Rhythm & Blues and R&B are the same genre, but with shared characteristics that go beyond the music? When browsing by genre in Napster, Lauryn Hill is found under "R&B/Contemporary R&B," a descriptor that hints at a historical split between two forms of Rhythm & Blues. The problems surrounding these terms are explored at greater length further on.

Napster's description of Hill raises further questions. On her biography page, under the heading "genres," we see: "Hip-Hop: Contemporary R&B, Soul, Underground." The punctuation suggests that R&B, and perhaps Soul too, is a subgenre of Hip-hop. Hip-hop was a late-1970s development, whereas Rhythm & Blues (the old form) goes back to the 1950s, as mentioned above. This presentation of genres and subgenres reinforces the idea that there are old and new forms of Rhythm & Blues. The same might also be true of Soul, as evinced by the use of the term Neo-soul. Indeed, Allmusic claims that the genre Neo-soul is "roughly analogous to contemporary R&B," and lists *The Miseducation of Lauryn Hill* as a Neo-soul album highlight.

When Napster displays the page for *Miseducation*, the "subject path" that appears at the top of the screen is "Home > Pop > Lauryn Hill > The Miseducation of Lauryn Hill." It is unclear where the term "Pop" comes from: it is not among the genres listed on Hill's biography, and when browsing by genre, she is found under R&B, not Pop.

While researching this piece I was fortunate to be able to read Deborah C. Fether's 2006 master's dissertation, *An Investigation into the Classification of Popular Music Genres by Online Organisations, Shops and Libraries*.[4] Fether and I independently arrived at the same research technique: we chose a handful of bands and artists that we thought would be difficult to categorize, then recorded how various agencies did categorize them. In the following paragraphs I want to comment on the results of some of Fether's research.

Fether has indeed chosen artists who have been given widely divergent descriptors by her chosen agencies. As an example, look at the following list of classifications given to the artist Moby, and the type of agency that classified him:

Moby

Soul & Dance	Big CD store, central London
Dance	Small CD store, London suburbs
Ambient	Chain of CD/book stores
Pop	University library
Rock & Pop	Public library, London suburbs
Electronic Rock	Online retailer
Electronica	Online encyclopedia

**Table 7: Descriptors given by various types of agencies
to the artist Moby. Data from Fether.**[5]

Even taking into account the different contexts in which these agencies operate, such a wide variety of descriptors can be of very little use. And even taking account of the way in which labels develop and change their meanings over time, such descriptors as "soul," "dance" and "rock" have substantively different meanings, and arise from recognizably different musical traditions. It is true that Moby hasn't always produced the same style of music — in the 1990s he temporarily introduced heavy rock sounds into his work. But even agencies that classify at album level don't reflect this career change: the online retailer calls the album *Animal Rights*, where Moby strayed into heavy rock territory, "Dance," whereas the suburban public library calls the album *18*, which sees him move back into the world of Electronica, "Rock & Pop."[6]

Another band that Fether looked at was Gorillaz:

Gorillaz

Rock & Pop	Big CD store, central London
Rock & Pop	Small CD store, London suburbs
Rock & Pop	Chain of CD/book/stationery stores
— —	University library
Rock & Pop	Public library, London suburbs
Rock, Hip-hop/Rap	Online retailer
Rock	Online encyclopedia

**Table 8: Descriptors given by various types of agencies
to the band Gorillaz. Data from Fether.**[7]

What is striking about this table is the consistency with which the agencies have described Gorillaz as Rock. Rock is a performer-oriented genre which emphasizes the immediacy and energy of human emotions. Lead singers, individual rock "stars," provide a focus for the musical energy. In Gorillaz, there is more than one vocalist, and the band sounds as if it is held together more by its ideas than by the personality of any one individual. Moreover, Gorillaz go out of their way to avoid presenting a human face to the audience: in the image the band projects, in its posters and album art, the places of the human musicians are taken by Jamie Hewlett's memorable cartoon-book figures. According to Allmusic, Gorillaz was "conceived as the first 'virtual hip-hop group'". Musically, the band is eclectic and inventive, mixing Britpop tunefulness with hip-hop beats. The list of "moods" (sub-subgenres, if you like) suggested by Allmusic includes "trippy," "ironic," "literate," "lush" and "theatrical." "Ironic" is a particularly interesting descriptor to use if the genre is Rock: in his Grove definitions, Richard Middleton notes Rock's perceived "authenticity" and "commitment."[8]

Genres

We now turn our attention from bands and artists, and the multiplicity of genres that have been assigned them, to the genres themselves and the confusing networks of meanings that they have come to acquire. I focus on two groups of genres: Pop, Rock, and Pop/Rock; and Rhythm & Blues, R&B, and Soul.

Pop, Rock, and Pop/Rock

The terms "Pop" and "Rock" continue a "confusing dialogue"; the boundary between them is "fuzzy, moveable and controversial."[9] Richard Middleton, in the introduction to his article on Pop for Grove Music Online, gives caveats to many of his definitions. He does, however, attempt to describe what the two traditions sound like, though the fact that the following quotation appears in parentheses in the original indicates the caution with which it should be applied:

> "Rock" is generally thought of as "harder," more aggressive, more improvisatory and more closely related to black American sources, while "pop" is "softer," more "arranged" and draws more on older popular music patterns.[10]

Rock and Pop can also be described in terms of different approaches to music-making, and musicians' relationships with the music industry, with Pop musicians showing more of a willingness to accommodate the industry's need to make money:

> The governing principles that were felt to underlie these [rock] styles were their seriousness and commitment. These qualities were the basis of a contrast made by rock fans and musicians between their music and contemporary popular music styles considered to be more commercially orientated [*sic*], by now often described pejoratively as "pop."[11]

The distinction between Rock and Pop began to break down in the 1970s, for a variety of reasons. Punk, with its anarchic approach to music and music-making, questioned how far Rock really was from the profit-oriented music industry, showing it to be "knowingly constructed and, moreover, ... frequently the vehicle of commercial calculation and manipulation."[12] Feminists attacked "the masculinist assumptions of rock self-expression."[13] Allmusic states,

It wasn't until the dawn of the '70s — around the time when rock & roll's first generation fans were settling into adulthood — that truly equal pop/rock fusions became the epitome of mainstream music.[14]

This implies that, as rock's first audiences grew out of their youthful rebellious stage, the music followed suit.[15] The ideology of rock was then challenged by the popularity of disco, both musically, as it abandoned strong backbeats in favor of regular eighth-note percussion patterns,[16] and in the way it was created, with the active participation of studio-based producers.[17] MTV, which started broadcasting in 1981, promoted musicians "whose audiences transcended narrow genre boundaries," such as Madonna, Prince, Michael Jackson and Bruce Springsteen[18]: this further eroded the distinction between Rock and Pop. More recently, dance music, like disco, has challenged rock's ethos of the performer as creator:

> Dance music practice suggested that, in the world of collective production that actually obtained in popular music, rock's ideology of self-authorship was a fabrication and also boringly egotistical. New production technology — especially sampling, digital storage of musical data and computer-sequenced assembly of compositions — weakened the connection, insisted on by rock, between musical value on the one hand and instrumental and vocal performance skill on the other.[19]

All these attacks on the ideology of rock are, of course, attacks on the claims made about how it is produced, not attacks on the music itself, which stands or falls on its own merits. When people use the word "rock" to describe a piece of music, they evoke, or used to evoke, associations of musical authenticity, integrity, and the preeminence of the performer as creator. The criticisms of the ideology of rock that I have outlined call into question the validity of the associations that we connect with the word "rock," and, by extension, the term itself: Rock was always more about the way the music was made than about the music itself.

For an entertaining aside to the Pop-Rock argument, readers should look into a debate that took place in the House of Lords (the British upper house of Parliament) in 1990. The U.K. government was ready to license three new commercial national radio stations, and they wanted one to be "other than pop." An organization called Rock FM made a bid for this station, arguing that rock and pop were different. The government took a different view, and changed the conditions attached to the tender so that they excluded music with "''a strong rhythmic element and a reliance on electronic amplification" rather than music from one particular genre.[20]

If Rock is a less valid term now than it was in the 1960s — if the reason for calling something Rock was to distinguish it from Pop, but the perceived distance between the two genres has now diminished — then perhaps Pop/Rock is a valid replacement term. This is, of course, a very broad heading, a "catchall phrase, referring to nearly any pop music made after rock & roll was absorbed into the pop mainstream."[21] The key word here is "mainstream": the use of *either* Pop *or* Rock suggests that there are two mainstreams, each working within a different music aesthetic, whereas they are really both parts of a single, multi-faceted music industry, along with other, more clearly defined genres, such as Hip-hop and Country. Allmusic, Napster and iTunes all have big Pop/Rock categories, and they often describe bands as being Pop/Rock as well as either Pop or Rock, suggesting that neither Pop nor Rock is incompatible with a joint category.

Rhythm & Blues, R&B, and Soul

As with Pop, Rock and Pop/Rock, Rhythm & Blues, R&B and Soul are a loose collection of related genres that have developed at different times in the history of pop music, and now perform another "confusing dialogue."

R&B is obviously an abbreviation of Rhythm & Blues, but are they the same genre? Allmusic makes no distinction between them: Fats Domino, Ray Charles, and Ms. Dynamite, who released her first album in 2002, are all described as R&B artists. There is no genre description for Rhythm & Blues, and R&B is described as a genre that developed in the late 1940s and "laid the groundwork for rock & roll." Allmusic goes on to say that R&B evolved into Soul, "which was funkier and looser than the pile-driving rhythms of R&B." However, R&B cannot have completely disappeared, otherwise Ms. Dynamite and similar artists would not have been able to be described as such. In the 1980s and 90s Urban and Quiet Storm, which Allmusic tells us are R&B subgenres, became popular; through this period, R&B artists also began adding elements of Hip-hop to their work.

The problem for anyone applying labels to pop music — labels that bring together tracks with shared musical characteristics — is that artists grouped together under the Rhythm & Blues/R&B umbrella sound very different. Ms. Dynamite does not sound like a late 1940s Rhythm & Blues artist; neither does Beyoncé (described as R&B by Allmusic and Napster). There is a tendency among some of those who write about music to reserve the Rhythm & Blues label for music from the pre–Soul period. Grove doesn't have an entry for R&B, and in its "Rhythm and Blues" article it concentrates on music created before the 1960s. Peter Gammond in *The Oxford Companion to Popular Music*, published in 1993, also talks about only the older kind of music in his "Rhythm 'n' Blues" article, and there is no entry for R&B.[22] (Gammond is, however, out of touch: Rap and Hip-hop only get nineteen lines between them.)

In other circumstances, Rhythm & Blues has split into (old) Blues and (new) R&B categories. In Allmusic and Napster, Elmore James is described as Blues and Ms. Dynamite as R&B, whereas it will be remembered that Lauryn Hill, a similar artist to Ms. Dynamite, and Elmore James were both described as Rhythm & Blues by the BGSU library.

Beyoncé is described by Allmusic, Napster and iTunes as Contemporary R&B. Allmusic describes "Contemporary R&B" as a development of Urban that sounds "slickly produced," and whose exponents "are obsessed with bringing the grit, spirit, and ambitiousness of classic soul ... back to contemporary soul and R&B" (though Allmusic fails to explain how anything can be both slick and gritty). The use of the term Contemporary R&B makes explicit the split between the two forms of Rhythm & Blues, and Allmusic's genre descriptions suggest a "genre evolution" of Rhythm & Blues > Soul > Urban > Contemporary R&B, with previous forms of the genre cross-pollinating with present ones.

There is also a split between older and newer forms of the genre Soul, with the newer forms sometimes being given the descriptor Neo-soul (as has already been discussed in relation to Lauryn Hill). Neo-soul artists "pay more devotion to the era of classic soul, often seeking a sound and a style of songwriting with few concessions to events in the music world post–1975."[23]

Recommender Systems

It takes no great leap to make the connection between the richly layered meanings attached to genre headings and the wide selection of descriptors applied to some bands, as described above. What is the solution for the pop music cataloger or anyone else interested in the systematic arrangement of pop music recordings?

One solution is to look to the collective intelligence of the internet. Pop music has been one of the internet's favorite subjects from the start. Many websites collect data from and about their users to further enhance the way the website is organized — the "customers who liked that also liked this" phenomenon.

There are two main ways websites can collect information from or about their users: they can ask them directly to input it, or they can gather it passively as the user interacts with the website.[24] Both these methods build up a profile: if information is asked for, it

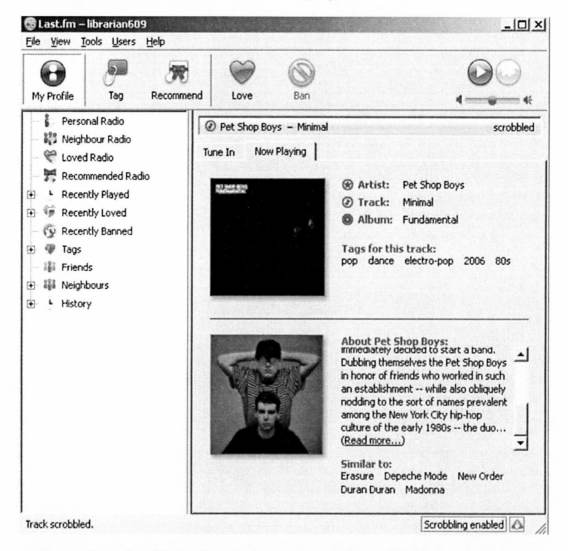

Figure 1: Screenshot of the Pet Shop Boys' song *Minimal* being scrobbled by Last.fm's software.

usually contributes to a demographic profile (age, sex, geographic location, etc.); if information is gathered passively, it usually contributes to a "taste profile" (this user downloaded this track, this one, this one and that one, but expressed a dislike for this one, etc.). Many websites, of course, use both types of profiling.

There are many pop music websites like this, but this paper will focus on one of them, Last.fm, which bills itself as "the social music revolution." Last.fm is unusual in that the mechanism by which the website learns what a user's musical tastes are, rather than staying on the website, invites itself into the user's own computer: when users sign up to Last.fm they get asked to download a specially designed piece of software. This software, called a *scrobbler* (see fig. 1), listens in when the user plays a track on her computer and sends information about that track back to the website.

Last.fm allows — encourages — an extra layer to be added to that information. While a track is playing on the user's computer — and being "scrobbled" back to the website — the user can tag it with a descriptor, either by picking a word or phrase from a list suggested by the scrobbler or by inventing one. The software collects together all the tags that have been attached to a particular track, and calculates which are the most popular; these then form a collectively chosen set of descriptors for the track.

Each track the user's computer scrobbles back to the website contributes to the user's profile. Last.fm then establishes which profiles are "neighbors" (i.e., which users have similar musical tastes), and makes recommendations based on what a user's neighbors are listening to. The system is based on the premise that if I like bands A, B, C, and D and you like bands A, B, and D, then you'll probably like Band C as well.

The result is a powerful and sophisticated music recommender and describer system. Users can log in to their Last.fm account and see who their musical neighbors are and what they've been listening to, and find out how their favorite tracks have been tagged and what other tracks have been attached to those tags.

At the time of writing this paper, I had been a Last.fm member for six weeks, and had scrobbled 72 tracks. I had also listened to a great many tracks without scrobbling them, including on CDs and the radio. Of the 20 bands and artists recommended to me by Last.fm, seven were already in my CD collection, and an impressive nineteen were bands I either already knew well or wanted to get to know better. I had listened to none of them through the scrobbler.

What are the implications of this for the pop music cataloger? Someone looking for unknown music in a style they like is probably going to get much better results using a recommender system such as Last.fm than if they just looked at agency-applied headings.

What of the tags themselves? Do they shed any light on how we might describe the music? Whenever a track is being scrobbled to Last.fm, a selection of tags appears in the window (see fig. 1) — these are the most popular tags chosen by people who have already scrobbled this track. Looking still at figure 1, we can see that the tags for the Pet Shop Boys' song *Minimal* are "pop," "dance," "electro-pop," "2006" and "80s." How can this song warrant the descriptors "2006" *and* "80s"? The song was released in 2006, but the Pet Shop Boys are using a musical language they developed in the 1980s, so both tags are relevant.

A librarian used to applying different kinds of access points in appropriately different ways may be surprised to see different kinds of descriptors presented in the same tag set.

For example, the suggested tags for Prince's "Musicology" are the undeniable "prince" and "2004" (the year the song was released) alongside the more subjective "booty-shaker."

Having "prince" as a tag for Prince shows that the tag system doesn't always work at optimum efficiency. Two of the tags given for another Pet Shop Boys track, "I'm With Stupid," are "synth-pop" and "synthpop." One of the tags given for their "The Sodom and Gomorrah Show" is "erasure," which is in fact the name of another band, who sound not entirely unlike the Pet Shop Boys. Since the scrobbler's window includes a list of similar bands, and when listening to "The Sodom and Gomorrah Show" Erasure appear in this list, this tag would seem to be a waste of space. Or is it? The similar artists list is computed by Last.fm's software; the tag has been chosen by a human listener. This enhances what we know about this track: not only did the software match it up with the work of Erasure one or more humans did too, perhaps because they thought it was *especially* like the work of Erasure, or perhaps they thought the software might not make the connection so they should instead.

The list of tags given for "Flurries," a track by jazz-funk group Soulive, is particularly interesting. The tags are:

favorite jazz
i am a party girl here is my soundtrack
soulnetwork-co-uk
hammond
soulive

The third of these tags is the name of a real website that brings together people who like soul. The fourth is the name of a kind of electric keyboard the band uses. The fifth is obviously the name of the band. This list of tags looks as if it might have been created by only a very small number of scrobblers, if not just one: not enough people have scrobbled and tagged this track for the most generally useful tags to float to the surface. This illustrates a problem that recommender systems have: they don't know where to place new items and new users.[25] In collective intelligence systems, we need to have some collectivity before we get any intelligence. Sensibly, Last.fm didn't offer me any recommendations until I'd been scrobbling for a couple of weeks.

Conclusion

The classification problems outlined so far do not belong uniquely to music. David Jennings notes how three online resources, the Internet Movie Database, Wikipedia and the All Movie Guide, assign different descriptors to the film *The Big Lebowski*:

IMDB	Wikipedia	All Movie Guide
Comedy	Black comedy	Comedy
Crime	Cult films	Crime comedy
Mystery	Neo-noir	Screwball comedy
		Buddy film

**Table 9: Descriptors assigned to the film *The Big Lebowski*
by three internet resources. Data from Jennings.[26]**

In music, categorization is hard because the content is non-verbal: the particular attributes that would link a piece of music with a category are hard to pin down. In film, categorization is hard perhaps because, in the two-hour (or so) span of a feature film, many genres may be alluded to, and every viewer attaches different levels of importance to the allusions. Both pop music and film are part of a fast-moving pop culture with heavy commercial interests: more reasons that make it hard to apply descriptors objectively. The pop music industry often uses genres to sell music to groups of customers who it thinks are divided along genre lines,[27] and it is hard for those trying to objectively describe the music to resist adopting the terminology employed by those trying to sell it.

Perhaps the attempt to organize pop music by genre should be abandoned, at least by collections with online-only access. Well-established agencies, such as iTunes, Napster and Allmusic, come up with wildly different descriptors for the same artists. Websites that employ collaborative filtering techniques, bypassing the work of trained classifiers, are proving to be more efficient aids to discovery. Above all, it is extremely difficult to pin down the links, if there are any, between the meaning of a genre descriptor, and any meaning there may be embedded in the music: a reggae track does not "contain" reggae in the same way that a book on cooking "contains" recipes. The musical characteristics associated with one genre often turn out to be similar to the musical characteristics associated with another. It is the perceived differences between combinations of characteristics that give rise to genres, and those differences, subject to fast-flowing commercial and social currents, are also very hard to pin down.[28]

Some organizations — usually real-world ones with shelves that people can browse — cannot get away with not dividing up pop music by genre. Other collections should concentrate on providing a sufficient number of non-genre access points, differentiating, for example, between release and re-release dates of recordings. There are an increasing number of ways for people to find out about new music — this subject occupies the whole of David Jennings' *Net, Blogs and Rock 'n' roll*— ranging from radio to word-of-mouth to playlists posted on social networking websites — and almost all of them are better than top-down, agency-applied descriptors.

Notes

N.B.: Access to Grove Music Online requires a subscription. If online access is not possible, find your way to the latest print edition: *The New Grove Dictionary of Music and Musicians*, 2nd ed. (New York: Oxford University Press, 2001).

1. Simon Frith, *Performing Rites: Evaluating Popular Music* (Oxford: Oxford University Press, 1996), 83.

2. *NME: New Musical Express*, January 3, 2004. The phrase "acid-bonkers-metal" also comes from this issue.

3. *Allmusic*, s.v. "Electronica." Available: <http://www.allmusic.com/cg/amg.dll?p=amg&token=&sql=73:11605> (accessed January 8, 2007).

4. Deborah C. Fether, *An Investigation into the Classification of Popular Music Genres by Online Organisations, Shops and Libraries* (Master's thesis, City University, London, 2006).

5. Ibid., 34–35.

6. *Allmusic*, s.v. "Moby." Available: <http://www.allmusic.com/cg/amg.dll?p=amg&sql=11:fmdyyl2jxp9b~T1> (accessed January 8, 2007).

7. Fether 34–35.

8. Richard Middleton, "Rock." *Grove Music Online*, s.v. Available: <http://www.grovemusic.com/shared/views/article.html?section=music.49135> (accessed November 10, 2006).

9. Richard Middleton, "Pop, sect. 1: Introduction." G*rove Music Online*, s.v. Available: <http://www.grovemusic.com/shared/views/article.html?section=music.46845.1> (accessed November 13, 2006).

10. Ibid.

11. *Grove Music Online*, s.v. "Rock" (accessed November 10, 2006).

12. Ibid.

13. Ibid.

14. Allmusic, s.v. "Pop/Rock." Available: <http://www.allmusic.com/cg/amg.dll?p=amg&sql=77:4489> (accessed January 8, 2007).

15. See also *Grove Music Online*, s.v. "Pop, sect. IV, 1 (ii): Europe: The British Isles: From Rock to Dance." Available: <http://www.grovemusic.com/shared/views/article.html?section=music.46845.4.1.2> (accessed November 13, 2006).

16. *Grove Music Online*, s.v. "Pop, sect. III, 4: North America: The 1970s." Available: <http://www.grovemusic.com/shared/views/article.html?section=music.46845.3.4> (accessed November 13, 2006).

17. Ibid.; see also *The Penguin Encyclopedia of Popular Music*, ed. Donald Clarke (London: Viking, 1989), s.v. "Rock, Rock 'n' roll, Rockabilly."

18. *Grove Music Online*, s.v. "Pop, sect. III, 5: North America: The 1980s." Available: <http://www.grovemusic.com/shared/views/article.html?section=music.46845.3.5> (accessed November 13, 2006).

19. *Grove Music Online*, s.v. "Rock" (accessed November 10, 2006).

20. Frith, *Performing Rites*, 81–83.

21. *Allmusic*, s.v. "Pop/Rock" (accessed January 8, 2007).

22. Peter Gammond, *The Oxford Companion to Popular Music*, (Oxford: Oxford University Press: 1993).

23. *Allmusic*, s.v. "Neo-Soul." Available: <http://www.allmusic.com/cg/amg.dll?p=amg&sql=77:12955> (accessed January 8, 2007).

24. Juntae Kim, "What Is a Recommender System?" Lecture given at *The Present and Future of Recommender Systems*, Bilbao, 12 September 2006. Available: <http://blog.recommenders06.com/?p=31> (accessed December 3, 2006).

25. Ibid.

26. David Jennings, *Net, Blogs and Rock 'n' roll: The New Era of Digital Discovery and the Download Culture* (London: Nicholas Brealey Publishing, forthcoming), 24.

27. See Frith, *Performing Rites*, 84–86.

28. See also Fether, *An Investigation into the Classification of Popular Music Genres*, especially chapters 4 and 5.

Playing Fast and Loose with the Rules: Metadata Cataloging for Digital Library Projects

Jen Wolfe

"*Funny, you don't look like a librarian.*" As my Gen X and Y colleagues can attest, this is a fairly typical response after coming out to a civilian as a young librarian. "But I am," I always protest. "My closet is full of twin sets, I reread the complete works of Jane Austen more or less annually, and I own no less than three cats. You can't get much more card-carrying than that."

Within my profession, however, I used to encounter a slightly different reaction upon outing myself as a cataloging librarian: "Funny, you don't seem like a cataloger." This observation proved harder to refute, mostly because it was true. As my coworkers noted, I don't fit the (completely false, of course) cataloger stereotype: antisocial, pedantic, and change-averse. But the difference goes even deeper.

I am a rule breaker. Not all the rules, of course — only the bad ones. You know which ones I mean: redundant, archaic, impractical, inefficient and/or anti-user, holdovers from an era when rules were designed to limit the number of drawers required to house a card catalog, so time-consuming as to be unscalable in the face of the Internet Age and its untidy partner, the Information Explosion. While my more virtuous peers sought to reform these rules through legitimate channels such as committee work with standards bodies, I turned rogue. Giving new meaning to the term "naughty librarian," I wantonly included more than two author added entries per record, transcribed from packaging rather than title screens, and generally ignored the parts of cataloging practice that felt like so much rearranging the order of 500 notes on the *Titanic* while on a collision course with Google and Amazon. Worst of all, I didn't even feel guilty.

This attitude quickly got me transferred from technical services to digital library services, where my penchant for rule-breaking could be used for good and not evil. It also earned me a twenty-first-century job title, one that continues to perplex, albeit for a different reason. A common response from those who receive my new business card: "'Metadata Librarian?' What does that even mean?"

Every User, Her Digital Object; Every Digital Object, Its User

Such a career shift to metadata cataloging is becoming more and more common-place, even among non-transgressors; as libraries increasingly move collections online, technical services staff are being called on to adapt print-centric procedures to the digital age. In response to a variety of factors — increased outsourcing of routine cataloging work to vendors; the looming shadow of mass digitization projects such as Google Book and the Open Content Alliance scanning their way through libraries' published holdings; and continuing pressure from patrons for electronic access to everything — local efforts have narrowed in scope to focus sharply on institutions' rare and unique materials. Archives, personal papers, manuscripts, image collections, ephemera — holdings tradi-tionally considered unsuitable for item-level cataloging in MARC format due to their vol-ume and their unbooklike qualities — have become prime candidates for item-level digitization. Enter the metadata cataloger.

"But *all* library cataloging is metadata cataloging," you might point out, and rightly so. Metadata, broadly defined, does indeed encompass such "data about data" as MARC records (as well as catalog cards, phone book entries, the tag on the back of your sweater, et cetera). And on the surface, the primary goal of metadata cataloging for digital library projects is identical to that of traditional cataloging: providing standardized, consistent description and access for library materials, thereby collocating like items, saving the time of the user, and doing other activities that would make Ranganathan proud.

However, the contrast between the two bodies of practice is revealed in the string of buzzwords used to describe post–MARC metadata schemas such as Dublin Core: sim-plicity, interoperability, flexibility, and extensibility. These characteristics promote the overarching goal of producing "data about data" in the form of bibliographic records that are quicker, easier and less expensive to create and share, accommodating a wide variety of formats, systems, uses and reuses: a goal that can be much more challenging with the complicated and inflexible troika of MARC, AACR2, and LCSH.

Six Impossible Things Before Ingest

Since metadata practice for digital library projects was developed in response to the complexity and inflexibility of traditional practice, an examination of some of its char-acteristics and trends reveals core cataloging principles turned upside down. The result is a mixture of the familiar with the strange that can make the uninitiated feel like they're cataloging down the rabbit hole.

Collaboration, not isolation. Building digital library collections is by nature a collabo-rative activity, one that involves cooperation among a variety of people. These can include library staff members from departments such as digital initiatives, technical services, col-lection development, systems, and technical support, along with content providers, subject specialists and designers who may or may not come from outside the library. Martin Kurth, Head of Metadata Services at Cornell University, describes the digital project meeting room where these diverse groups are brought together as a space where practitioners use their specialized knowledge of metadata requirements to interpret and negotiate the needs of various project stakeholders. Through this process of "cross-community translation," metadata librarians play key informational, interpersonal, and decisional roles in moving digital library projects forward (Kurth n.d., 9–14). As technical services staff continue to take on these roles, the profession will have to retire the image of the cataloger as a "hermit hiding in the bowels of the library shackled to an OCLC terminal all day" (Murray 2002).

In other words, *catalogers may become known for their interpersonal skills.* If you listen closely, you can almost hear hell freezing over.

Librarians don't catalog. Further unshackling themselves from the stereotype and the bibliographic utility terminal, metadata librarians for digitization projects typically don't produce bibliographic records. After completing tasks such as analyzing project requirements, designing templates, and developing controlled vocabulary lists, the librarian then might hand off production duties to paraprofessionals, student workers, or even volunteers. Since metadata practice was developed for use by non-specialists, its performance requires neither a master's in library science nor several years of training and experience. Those resources are more effectively spent on such activities as consulting with content providers, designing metadata templates, creating data maps and crosswalks, developing project-specific thesauri, and performing quality control.

Emphasis on the collection, not the "item in hand." The cataloging mantra "item in hand" originates from the following principle stated in section 0.24 of AACR2: "The starting point for description is the physical form of the item in hand, not the original or any previous form in which the work has been published." According to these instructions, catalogers should focus exclusively on describing what's in front of them, without allowing cataloging decisions to become muddled by previous iterations of the work. Only after this initial assessment do they proceed to link the item in hand to similar materials — i.e., to build collections — through the application of controlled headings for access points such as author, subject, series, and uniform title.

This process, according to Kurth, becomes inverted in digital library cataloging, with a consideration of the collection as a whole serving as the starting point. Since collection-building and interoperability with other collections are primary goals of digital library practice, metadata analysis for a new project requires an understanding of "the big picture," including such factors as: the current project's goals, requirements and user needs; the scholarly communities served by the collection; other initiatives serving those communities; and interoperability tools such as federated search or metadata harvesting mechanisms. A close examination of the item in hand, or several representative items, is then only a final step in this analysis, with the metadata practitioner creating sample item-level records to serve as exemplars for the rest of the collection (Kurth n.d., 5–9).

Sometimes "good enough" is good enough. Like all cataloging work, metadata practice requires negotiating a balance between quality and quantity. However, key characteristics of digital library work provide a strong argument for prioritizing speed and efficiency over fullness of detail.

- *Collection size.* The types of archival materials frequently targeted for digitization include collections of items such as historic photographs, correspondence, or newspaper clippings, often numbering in the hundreds or thousands of pieces. Each of these collections may be only one of hundreds or thousands held by the repository. At this scale, standard original cataloging treatment (AACR2 rules and LCSH headings applied by experienced MLS holders) at the item level simply isn't feasible.

- *Uniqueness.* Many of the traditional rules were developed in part to assist librarians in deciding whether their item in hand matched an existing bibliographic record or if it required original cataloging. With libraries increasingly digitizing unique holdings only, recording data designed to help distinguish between similar editions has become unnecessary.
- *Online access.* Not least of all, digitized versions of the materials cataloged with metadata records are usually immediately available onscreen. This renders in-depth description much less important, since users can see the items for themselves.

Regardless, catalogers of the "because that's the way we've always done it" school insist on strict adherence to traditional standards when working with digital materials. As a result, they risk exclusion on future projects by perpetuating the view of technical services staff as "overly rigid," making things "too complicated," and focusing on "minutia which [has] of little relevance to the user." Standardization, while important in digital library work, must be secondary to the higher goal of interoperability (DeZelar-Tiedman 2004, 146).

No more monoliths. While it's not unusual for catalogers to learn one set of structural, content, and value standards and use them exclusively until retirement, metadata practitioners must be able to navigate an ever-growing sea of acronyms representing a diverse and fragmented world of tools and guidelines. In addition to MARC, they may need familiarity with other structural schemes and element sets including Dublin Core, MODS, EAD, METS and TEI. Besides AACR2, they might consult other descriptive standards like *Cataloging Cultural Objects, Descriptive Metadata Guidelines for RLG Cultural Materials,* and *CDP's Dublin Core Metadata Best Practices* . Along with LCSH, they may apply terms from additional value standards such as Library of Congress Thesaurus for Graphic Materials (LCTGM), the Art and Architecture Thesaurus (AAT), or the Union List of Artist Names (ULAN).[1]

Although it might be tempting to try sitting out the digital revolution until monolithic metadata standards have materialized, such a strategy is unwise, if not impossible. Prefacing a recent anthology on metadata projects, Hillmann and Westbrooks identified the most consistent and most important of the lessons learned: "Change happens, and it happens constantly. Get used to it, accept it, and plan for it. Waiting for emerging standards to settle down is a futile exercise; it will probably not happen in our lifetimes" (Hillman and Westbrook 2004, xvi). It's true that traditional cataloging standards also evolve, but since such change is more incremental and less, well, radical, it's less likely to be used as an excuse to delay or deny access to materials.

LCSH: off with its head? While application of authority control for names and places remains generally unquestioned, the future of using Library of Congress Subject Headings for topical subject access has become a hot-button issue, with the "How could we possibly abandon it?" and the "How could we possibly continue using it?" camps squaring off. As summarized in recent reports on the future of cataloging, the former group cites LCSH's superiority at clustering related content compared to keyword searching, the economic value of legacy data, and skepticism that current technology is good enough to do without manually assigned headings. The latter group argues that its application isn't cost effective, especially since a relatively small number of users perform subject searching in catalogs, and that the resources invested in it would be better spent developing automatic classification (Calhoun 2006, 33; University of California Libraries 2005, 23–24). While the debate continues, some have started exploring alternatives to LCSH. Among the most frequently cited possibilities are the three F's: full-text searching of enhanced metadata or digitized text; FAST, an OCLC initiative to develop a simplified subject vocabulary based on LCSH strings parsed into facets; and folksonomies, with users applying their own subject tags à la del.icio.us and Flickr.

In digital library work, the LCSH issue manifests itself as a head-on collision between two primary metadata goals: simplicity (records can be created by non-specialists) and interoperability (records can be cross-searched with the libraries' other bibliographic data, which chiefly exists in the form of MARC records cataloged with LCSH). However, as mentioned above, the large scale and limited staff resources available for digital library projects often tips the balance toward a more pragmatic approach. The harsh reality? When describing digitized items that would otherwise have remained uncataloged, some access — with or without LCSH — is better than none.

Perpetual Paradigm Shift

Much debate surrounds the future of cataloging, but no one disagrees that the field is currently undergoing a period of rapid change. Competition from commercial search engines and online merchants, a decline in library purchasing of the print materials around which cataloging departments built their workflow, and an increase in the outsourcing of technical services to vendors are just a few of the factors prompting a reevaluation of established procedures. Although the implementation of updated standards like RDA and the growing awareness of FRBR's entity-relationship model may help streamline operations, the pressure to come up with strategies for developing "more, faster, better, cheaper" cataloging is unlikely to let up any time soon.[2]

For successful evolution to the next stage in cataloging, survival of the fittest won't require specialized training and experience as much as an adaptability to change. At a workshop on educating twenty-first-century cataloging and metadata professionals, Janet Swan Hill explained that those participating in technical services "as the world slips and slides under us" will need such general skills as:

- the capacity to work with people from a variety of backgrounds, skill levels and inclinations
- the ability to read closely, write clearly and precisely, and speak coherently, logically, and persuasively
- the capability to approach work with imagination and a willingness to experiment,

along with the ability "to see when something is not working, let go of it, and move on" (Hill 2005, 18)

In other words, librarians specializing in metadata creation require the same characteristics as their tools: interoperability, extensibility and flexibility. For those working with digital library projects, this means the ability to play well with others, a capability for more than just production work, and an openness to emerging tools and standards.

And, once those standards are established, a healthy willingness to sometimes disregard them.

Notes

1. Although some of these tools were developed for use in cataloging with MARC, the wide and diverse range of digital library projects necessitates custom-designed metadata workflows, so a greater emphasis is placed on selecting the most suitable tools for the job. This is more likely to result in mixing and matching a variety of standards, rather than the one-size-fits-all approach of traditional cataloging.

2. For strategies, see (or, rather, listen to) digitized audio of sessions at the 2006 August RLG Members' Forum: More, Better, Faster, Cheaper (<http://www.rlg.org/en/page.php?Page_ID=20968>).

References

Calhoun, Karen. (2006). The changing nature of the catalog and its integration with other discovery tools. Final report. Prepared for the Library of Congress. Available: <http://www.loc.gov/catdir/calhoun-report-final.pdf> (accessed Nov. 10, 2006).

DeZelar-Tiedman, Christine. (2004). Crashing the party: catalogers as digital librarians. *OCLC Systems and Services: International Digital Library Perspectives* 20 (4): 145–147.

Hillmann, Diane I., and Elaine L. Westbrooks, eds. (2004). *Metadata in Practice.* Chicago: American Library Association.

Kurth, Martin. Found in translation: four characteristics of metadata practice. In *Metadata and the Digitization of Information: A Festschrift in Honor of Thomas P. Turner,* ed. Elaine Westbrooks and Keith Jenkins. Lanham, MD: Scarecrow Press. (In publication.) Available: <http://metadata.library.cornell.edu/kurth-translation-20050408.pdf> (accessed November 10, 2006).

Murray, Richard A. (2002, February). The whimsy of cataloging. *LISCareer.com: The Library & Information Science Professional's Career Development Center.* Available: <http://www.liscareer.com/murray_cataloging.htm> (accessed November 10, 2006).

Hill, Janet Swan. (2005, January). Analog people for digital dreams: staffing and educational considerations for cataloging and metadata professionals. *Library Resources & Technical Services* 49 (1): 14–18.

University of California Libraries Bibliographic Services Task Force. (2005). Rethinking how we provide bibliographic services for the University of California: Final report. Available: <http://libraries.universityofcalifornia.edu/sopag/BSTF/Final.pdf> (accessed November 10, 2006).

This Subfield Kills Fascists: A Highly Selective, Slightly Irreverent Trip Down Radical Cataloging Literature Lane

Brian Hasenstab

Wolf, Steve. "Sex and the Single Cataloger." In *Revolting Librarians*, edited by Celeste West and Elizabeth Katz, 39–44. San Francisco: Booklegger Press, 1972.

Steve Wolf's contribution to the mind-expanding anthology *Revolting Librarians* goes after both LCC and DDC, challenging their classification of gay folks. A year earlier, Sandy Berman's *Prejudices and Antipathies* had found fault with headings in LCSH for HOMOSEXUALITY and LESBIANISM, but this was the first concentrated dissection of how classification systems dealt with such topics. Wolf notes that the term "homosexual," used in both arrangements, was created by straight people to label others, and is thus inherently biased. The majority of those being labeled prefer the term "gay," he argues, and usage should reflect this, though he does not suggest an alternative to the noun form "homosexuality" for the schedules to use. He goes on to show that while LCC no longer classes "homosexuality" as a "sexual deviation," both schemes continue to emphasize a viewpoint from which it is both a crime and a disease, and both link it to prostitution and rape, with LCC additionally linking it with pornography and DDC with adultery. Wolf is particularly outraged by DDC's implication that not just gay sexuality, but any sexuality outside of conventional marriage is a "perversion." The article also expands the discussion to look at the scheme's biases in the larger context of societal prejudices and actual real-world behavior. Wolf throws many sarcastic barbs in LC's direction throughout, and the whole thing crackles with righteous anger.

Marshall, Joan K. *On Equal Terms: A Thesaurus for Nonsexist Indexing and Cataloging.* New York: Neal-Schuman, 1977.

The late, great Joan K. Marshall grew this groundbusting work out of an investigation of the hideously sexist cataloging practices of LC in the 1970s, both in terms of the headings themselves and the way LC assigned them to stuff in their collection. But this thesaurus is more than just a reaction to LCSH (though I'm sure it's been used as a supplement to the "red books" in practice). Even if it's now inevitably dated — in fact, you could argue that Mary Ellen S. Capek's *A Women's Thesaurus* rendered it obsolete — while flipping through its pages, you're likely to hear a rallying cry for people-centered cataloging echoing deep within your mind.

Besides the thesaurus itself, this book also includes the momentous *Principles for Establishing Subject Headings Relating to People and Peoples*, developed by the Committee on Sexism in Subject Headings of ALA's Social Responsibilities Round Table's Task Force on Women (now known as the Feminist Task Force). There's also a brief essay by Marshall, "Sexism and Language," that pithily explains precisely why this work was not only necessary, but vital.

Berman, Sanford. *The Joy of Cataloging: Essays, Letters, Reviews and Other Explosions.* **Phoenix, AZ: Oryx, 1981.**

"Cataloging should be fun. And challenging. And useful." Thus begins this collection of Sandy Berman's critiques of the status quo in cataloging theory and practice, spanning writings from 1969 to 1981. I imagine almost any catalogers, not just radical ones, reading those words will immediately recognize that, yes, cataloging should be all of these things — and that, as Sandy goes on to write, cataloging practice too often fails to be any of these things.

In these pages Sandy of course takes aim not only at LCSH (the target he's most associated with), but also AACR2, ISBD, ALA, Sears Subject Headings, OCLC, DDC, useless library literature, and still others. That he does so with vigor, wit, and an absolute commitment to the needs of users probably goes without saying.

A lot has changed since this salvo was fired. Some of the problems have been fixed; others have been rendered somewhat moot by changes in technology. Most of the specific examples are of items now virtually forgotten. So why should today's forward-thinking, on-the-go librarian stop to read this?

Besides the fact that most of the issues addressed still persist (albeit occasionally in somewhat different circumstances), there are two crucial reasons for you to read this. The first is to help you recognize how many of Sandy's "revolutionary" ideas have become commonplace library procedures. You will be reminded of the extent of his well-documented influence, LC subject headings created long after they were established by Hennepin County Library's Technical Services Division under his leadership. Also, remember changes in technology — not necessarily directly influenced by Sandy, but mirroring suggestions made in his book — such as descriptive elements he considered unnecessary and confusing to users, which today remain in catalogs but do not display in many OPACs.

The other, and probably most important, reason is this: no better introduction to the practical application of the principles of useful, critical cataloging exists. Sandy may not consider his work "radical"—and in a real sense it is not, unless we view helpful, equal access to all types of information for all patrons as a radical goal. Nonetheless, through the breadth of its scope and the depth of its critique, this manifesto comes close to a distilled essence of what our fearless editor calls Radical Cataloging. Read it today.

Greenblatt, Ellen. "Homosexuality: The Evolution of a Concept in the Library of Congress Subject Headings." In *Gay and Lesbian Library Service*, edited by Cal Gough and Ellen Greenblatt, 75–101. Jefferson, NC: McFarland, 1990.

The title is slightly misleading — the historical overview it implies takes up less than half of this piece, while the majority is devoted to areas where LCSH has, as of the piece's writing, failed to evolve. But whatever you call it, this is a great critical examination of the treatment of gay and lesbian topics in LCSH, taking in bias, omission, and reluctance to change.

The evolutionary summary cites etymological research to prove that LC developed headings for terms such as "homosexuality," "lesbianism," "gay," "homophobia," and "sodomy" decades after they became commonly used in mainstream vocabularies. The real heart of the essay, though, is the selection of suggested changes to LCSH, covering new headings and alterations to existing headings. The proposals for changes to current headings argue for the umbrella term GAYS to be replaced with the non-subsuming LESBIANS and GAY MEN, and for AGED LESBIANS to be replaced with SENIOR LESBIANS. (Unfortunately, today GAYS remains and AGED LESBIANS has been supplanted by the slightly less offensive OLDER LESBIANS.) The proposals for new headings embarrass LC with examples of books the institution has itself cataloged which furnish ample literary warrant in each case. Greenblatt's compelling recommendations have apparently had some real influence, for in the intervening years all but two of the advocated new headings have been authorized.

In the decades it takes LC to respond to information seekers' needs, however, literary warrant for more new headings springs up. And so it is with the time passed since the publication of *Gay and Lesbian Library Service*. A new edition of the book is said to be in the works. Here's hoping an updated version of this article appears in it, presenting headings that today's users searching for queer information will need (including more terms relating to bisexual and transgendered people). And that it's as well-researched and convincingly argued as this one.

Weinberg, Bella Hass, ed. *Cataloging Heresy: Challenging the Standard Bibliographic Product; Proceedings of the Congress for Librarians, February 18, 1991, St. John's University, Jamaica, New York, with Additional Contributed Papers.* Medford, NJ: Learned Information, 1992.

This book focuses on critiques of LC bibliographic records as a source for other libraries' copy. Sadly, it is not quite as heretical as some of the more wild-eyed revolutionaries among us catalogers might have hoped. True, there are some exciting moments: Alan R. Thomas's essay on the potential benefits of greater use of Bliss Bibliographical Classification is particularly radical, given the firmly entrenched orthodoxies of DDC and LC in the U.S. And Hope Olson's taking LC to task for its failure to grant sufficient subject access to women's studies materials is especially notable for its fascinating discussion of the major orientations of feminist research and how these differ from the old boys' research model on which LC is based. Further dissident gems are supplied by Sanford

Berman, Sheila Intner, Mary Parr, and Charles Whitlow; however, much of the collection is given over to articles on How Our Library Adapted LC Copy to Our Needs (often involving special collections or special libraries). This is surely of some relevance if your library faces similar problems, but the status quo is rarely questioned, so it's not so relevant to our current quest.

Perhaps the most unusual aspect of the proceedings are the three papers allowed for the defensive position: representatives from OCLC and RLIN turn in predictably dull hype sheets about how their products can help your library be heretical (or, preferably, not); but perhaps the most interesting view in the book comes, somewhat incredibly, from LC. John Byrum lets you know how great a job LC thinks it's doing, and offers some advice for the very few libraries he feels might need to modify LC records: they should make enhancements following standards "in the same way as does LC," of course. This rather amazing document is by turns entertaining — "our cataloging is of sufficient value to most users as is" is pure comedy — and enlightening in its candid explication of LC's view of heresy: "There appears to be little room for it in today's bibliographic setting." A must read for all dedicated catalogers who wish to better know their enemy.

Berman, Sanford. "The 'Fucking' Truth about Library Catalogs." In *Alternative Library Literature, 1992/1993: A Biennial Anthology*, edited by Sanford Berman and James P. Danky, 336–341. Jefferson, N.C.: McFarland, 1994.

Somehow I would have felt this reading list incomplete if it had not somewhere included the word "fucking." Thankfully, Sandy has saved us from this deficiency. Note, however, that the questionable wording of the title is significant, and not only because it presents a prime example of Sandy's well-known defiance of what is acceptable (to some) as "professional language." More crucially, because he uses the very discomfort the word provokes in many to illuminate two important themes: the timidity with which many libraries approach the topic of sex; and the same libraries' preference for specialized jargon over common, "real-word" language. The specific adversary in this essay is, once again, LC. Covered are LCSH subject headings that are "so bizarre and antique that no one would look them up first," lack of cross-references for colloquial sexual terms, examples of LC's failure to apply some of the appropriate headings they *do* have, a list of warranted headings unauthorized by LC, and a call for more contents notes in records for sex-related items. This is just one of the multitudinous useful articles (far too many to scratch the surface of in this highly select bibliography) provided by Sandy that today's progressive cataloger can draw inspiration from (and he continues to provide — check his regular column in *The U*N*A*B*A*S*H*E*D Librarian*). I trust that you've got the skills to find the rest.

Cochrane, Pauline Atherton. *Improving LCSH for Use in Online Catalogs: Exercises for Self-help with a Selection of Background Readings.* Littleton, CO: Libraries Unlimited, 1986.

Cochrane, Pauline Atherton. "Improving LCSH for Use in Online Catalogs Revisited — What Progress Has Been Made? What Issues Still Remain?" in

The LCSH Century: One Hundred Years with the Library of Congress Subject Headings System, edited by Alva T. Stone, 73–89. New York: Haworth Information Press, 2000.

Twenty-two years on, *Improving LCSH* is still a winner for two different reasons. The first and probably more obvious one is the set of recommendations for improving LCSH's subject authority records that Cochrane draws from her exhaustive reading of criticism of LCSH. While many of these suggestions have since been adopted (such as greater consistency in the formation of subdivisions), others have seen little implementation (such as increased linkage between LCSH and LCC). Perusing these bright ideas — even those that are now standard — provokes heavy thought about the way LCSH is structured and formatted, and the way that structure and that format both help and hinder the user at the OPAC. This serious thought-provocation might even set your mind to thinking of some innovations of your own.

The other great thing about this tome is the "selection of background readings." These papers — from as early as 1946 to the year before the collection's original publication, 1985 — comprise what is surely the best historical collection of critiques of LCSH you can find in one place. If you can find a better one, I'll buy you a new barcode scanner.

In the 2000 article, Cochrane reviews three aspects covered in 1986 to see how much LCSH has, in fact, been improved. Her findings are: 1) notes in subject authority records are improved and still getting better yet; 2) the structure of cross-references in LCSH has seen progress but still has some ways to go; and 3) coordination between LCSH and LCC has seen little progress but there is potential for a comprehensive alignment in the near future. She even manages to work in a Phil Ochs quote. Nice.

Olson, Hope A. *The Power to Name: Locating the Limits of Subject Representation in Libraries.* Dordrecht, The Netherlands: Kluwer Academic Publishers, 2002.

I have to admit, I approached this feminist, poststructuralist critique of DDC and LCSH with some trepidation. I'd read several articles by Olson previously, and they had varied quite a bit in their readability, from perfectly accessible ones to those weighted down with impenetrable theoretical jargon. Though the chapters here also vary in degrees of accessibility, the total package falls somewhere in the middle, not exactly reader-friendly, but probably not too forbidding for most college-educated readers.

Olson scrutinizes the foundational writing of Melvil Dewey and Charles Cutter on, respectively, classification and subject headings. First she gives each a close reading, highlighting themes of order, control, and universality vs. chaos, anarchy, and diversity. She is on firm ground here, but the next chapter drifts into fuzzier territory. Olson rereads the same texts, and submits them to a Derrida-style deconstruction. I am by no means an expert on this postmodern critical technique. However, everything I've read which explains it and/or uses it, including Olson, leads me to view it as little more than a glorified justification for twisting an author's words to make them "mean" something other than what was clearly intended. Thus, I have a hard time taking it seriously, and I fail to see why it's worth spending almost 80 pages on, especially when Olson has already presented a valuable critique of this material in the preceding chapter.

The study continues with an analysis of current standards in LCSH and DDC and a look at some examples of books cataloged and classified by LC where numerous feminist topics are not adequately represented. The latter chapter is especially rewarding, since it supplies some practice after all that theory.

Finally, Olson concludes with a Where Do We Go From Here chapter that talks a lot about what qualities she would like to see in future subject access systems, but very little about what such systems would actually look like. While I applaud Olson for her willingness to explore cataloging foundations at such a fundamental level (making this easily the most radical selection on this list), in the end I'm left wishing for more practical solutions to bring such wide-ranging theory a little closer to earth.

Bartel, Julie. "Living Arrangements." Chap. 8 in *From A to Zine: Building a Winning Zine Collection in Your Library.* Chicago: American Library Association, 2004.

It's one thing to rail against the standard library systems for providing subject access, as so many critical catalogers have done. It's quite another to create a new classification scheme and list of subject headings more or less from scratch. That's what Julie Bartel and her coworkers did for the zine collection at the Salt Lake City Public Library.

In this chapter from her book about creating and managing this collection, Bartel begins by describing how a small set of subject headings and a very basic classification system grew out of discussions with colleagues. She admits up front that she is "not, by any stretch of the imagination, a cataloger." I see this as both a strength and a liability. The strength is in the freshness with which she approaches the process. This allows her insights that might not have occurred to those of us who are professional catalogers, with our heads full of preconceived notions about how subject access to a collection should work. It also helps her to focus on the practical needs of the collection and its users, rather than on trying to fit a pre-existing model. The liability is clear to Bartel, and she sees the criticism coming: "If my theories and philosophy are faulty, if I use certain words incorrectly, or if I just don't seem to know what I'm talking about, I hope you'll forgive me." Well, new theories and philosophy should always be welcome in cataloging land, but I have a hard time forgiving misused words, and an even harder time with someone not knowing what they're talking about. Sensitive catalogers will cringe at words like "hierarchical" used in a much different way than we use them — not so much because we cannot forgive the author's ignorance, but because of the potential for creating confusion in the minds of impressionable non-cataloging librarians.

This potentiality builds up considerably when Bartel describes the changes after an offer was made to add the zines to the library's "real" catalog. Bartel launches into a convoluted, self-contradicting discussion of whether zines are better served by MARC records for monographs (which she mistakenly refers to as "book-type records") or those for serials. Most any radical cataloger can tell you that you should be able to use whatever MARC record suits your item's (and your user's) needs. If a zine collection is best served by treating all zines as monographs, go for it. There's no need for a contrived, philosophical argument centered on nonsensical questions ("Is it possible that zines resemble books, rather than serials, in spirit and structure?") to justify this practice. Earlier in the chapter, Bartel wisely reminds us that different techniques are appropriate for different institutions, and that there is no "right" way to do these things. If only she'd kept this in mind when writing the last section.

Gross, Tina, and Arlene G. Taylor. "What Have We Got to Lose? The Effects of Controlled Vocabulary on Keyword Searching Results." *College & Research Libraries* **66, no. 3 (May 2005): 212–230.**

Can arguing for the value of controlled vocabulary be considered radical? Yeah, I know, most catalogers, me included, would consider such an argument quite traditional. At least at first glance. But there's an idea, increasingly trendy among some librarians, that the growing use of keyword searching is making traditional subject searching, and hence controlled vocabulary, obsolete. Now, any person who fully understands how a library catalog works can see that this idea is, to put it mildly, asinine. Unfortunately, some people in the field of librarianship lack such an understanding. Sometimes merely knowing what the hell you are doing can make you "radical."

The "subject searching is dead!" attitude inspired Gross and Taylor to conduct a study of just how important controlled subject terms are, even in keyword searching. In their introduction, they mention that it has been suggested "(in at least one academic library) that subject headings should be stripped from the bibliographic records in the catalog." So they took a sample of search terms from a transaction log of keyword searches in a university library's catalog. Then they conducted searches with those terms in another university library's catalog, and studied the results. Their findings were that more than a third of the records retrieved would not have been found had they not contained subject headings. Furthermore, in several individual searches that each had multiple hits, not a single record would have been found without the subject headings.

I've tried to avoid research articles with your standard "literature review — methodology — results — conclusion" format in this reading list, but this one is well worth your time. And it's good to have ready in case the brain-rot that causes some librarians to devalue controlled subject vocabulary starts to infect people in your library.

Does defending a venerated concept (and practice) in cataloging make you a conservative? Does fighting an increasingly powerful myth about catalogs make you a radical? Does doing both at once make you a radical conservative? Whatever you label it, count me in.

Berman, Sanford. *Prejudices and Antipathies: A Tract on the LC Subject Heads Concerning People.* Metuchen, NJ: Scarecrow Press, 1971.

Marshall, Joan K. "LC Labeling: An Indictment." In *Revolting Librarians*, edited by Celeste West and Elizabeth Katz, 45–59. San Francisco: Booklegger Press, 1972.

Knowlton, Steven A. "Three Decades Since *Prejudices and Antipathies*: A

Study of the Changes in the Library of Congress Subject Headings."
Cataloging & Classification Quarterly **40, no. 2 (2005): 123–145.**

Yes, of course. No selection of readings on radical cataloging would be complete without Sandy Berman's extraordinarily influential examination of bias in LCSH. Arguably the foundational work of modern socially responsible cataloging, this "earthquake of a book" (as Eric Moon described it) set off a firestorm of controversy that continues to smolder today. (Though it seems that many more librarians these days are inclined to agree with Sandy's point of view regarding bias than there were in 1970, the fact that many others still remain unconvinced by his passionate yet clearly reasoned arguments does not bode well for the profession.) In this "tract," Sandy methodically works through 225 headings from LCSH, explaining the problems with each, citing copious sources for his arguments (often with very detailed notes), and suggesting solutions in every case. My description of this methodology might lead you to imagine a rather dry read, but only if you are unfamiliar with the writings of Sanford Berman. (And if anyone reading this does for some strange reason lack such a familiarity, seek this book out immediately!) The book ends with 14 problematic headings provided without suggested reforms, but with an invitation to "do it yourself." This perfect touch reminds us that the work of combating LC's sluggishness is not Sandy's alone, but should be actively contributed to by all.

Joan Marshall's contribution to the aforementioned *Revolting Librarians* was developed from a letter to Sandy Berman which Sandy quoted extensively in *Prejudices and Antipathies*. As it appears in the anthology, the piece is more than a mere footnote to Sandy's book: it's a concise summary of the stance toward bias which both of these heroic librarians shared.

Steven Knowlton studied the 2003 edition of LCSH to determine which of the changes advocated in *Prejudices and Antipathies* had been acted upon. His results show that thirty-nine percent of the headings had been changed in more or less the same way Sandy had suggested, twenty-four percent showed partial adoption of the changes but still remained objectionable in some way, and twenty-six percent were unchanged. This reminds me of the two recurring themes that continually strike me while reading Sandy Berman and a great deal of other radical library literature: so much has been achieved, and so much remains to be done.

Ranganathan's Forgotten Law: Save the Time of the Cataloger

Jennifer Young

As a cataloger, my time is wasted every day doing my job. I have to spend time creating workarounds or dealing with clunky interfaces to library systems. I have to spend time creating macros so I can reduce the number of keystrokes I have to do. I have to spend time configuring external programs that allow me to do some of the things I can't do easily in the integrated library system.

My time is also wasted by following cataloging rules, which were not only created for a 3 × 5 card, books-only world, but are making up for bad OPAC design. Just as the 3 × 5 card confined us, we are allowing ourselves to become too limited by technology instead of using current technology to the fullest, or even creating new technology to serve our needs. Our systems also don't consider all the encoding that we do, so being able to apply search limits can be a frustrating exercise. Linking fields have problems actually linking to the correct records. Too often we're told, "Sorry, it's hard-coded," or "It's working as intended," instead of actually doing something about it. Hey, if too many things are "hard-coded," then maybe you need to change your code. Of course, sometimes problems derive from past library practice coming back to haunt us. Some access isn't necessarily better than no access. It can be quite harmful.

Technological advances have allowed us to become more efficient; unfortunately, we haven't been able to go far enough. Not only does the front end of the OPAC need a revamp, but so does the back end. If we have to have different modules for the catalog, they really need to be integrated better. For example, if I can tell in the catalog module that there is a purchase order attached to a bibliographic record, why should I have to use the acquisitions module to see it? Conversely, why do I have to manually add the 245 field and any 246s to the acquisitions record to be able to search for it in the acquisitions module? Why isn't it pulling the search data from the cataloging module? Of course, this only touches on the problems of why OPACs don't fully utilize the encoding we do in MARC, and even the interoperability between different types of vendors.

With the development of the new cataloging code, many have been discussing the "next generation catalog" and what it should encompass. Most of the discussion of both

RDA and the next-gen catalog has focused on what seem to be fundamentally display issues for users. However, the "one user fits all" concept has to go. One main user community seems to keep being forgotten — catalogers. If I, as the "professional," have problems using a system or a code, how can it be expected that others would find it easier to use? Radical cataloging is the notion that catalogers are users too.

OCLC: A Review

Jeffrey Beall

Introduction

One of the suggested titles I was given for this chapter was "OCLC Sucks." But I rejected that title, for, despite the temptation to use it, I realized it was unfair, untrue, and perhaps even unwarranted. It's easier to write a chapter that trashes an organization than it is to write one that presents an objective analysis of it. I've resisted the temptation to wholeheartedly trash OCLC, easy as that would have been. Instead, I aspire to the high road: objective analysis, keeping in mind that the word *radical* is in this book's title. That's not to say that OCLC is wonderful; it certainly is not. Indeed it is a malevolent organization at times, in the way that all large, rapacious, transnational conglomerates are.

There were two things that led me to reject that title for this chapter. One of them was a series of blog entries by Karen Schneider entitled, "How OPACs Suck."[1] Her title is specious, of course. OPACs do not suck; they have quietly and efficiently been linking researchers and others with desired information for about twenty years. They are a wonderful tool and represent the best implementation of metadata in the history of mankind. Seeing her use the word "suck" in a title in a supposedly reputable publication (the ALA TechSource Blog) looked really stupid to me. The use of that term in that context seemed wholly inappropriate, and I did not want to be guilty of such poor judgment. Who is the spineless editor that allowed such rubbish to be published?

The other thing that influenced me was an interview with LC's Barbara Tillett that appeared in the blog *Library Juice*.[2] The interview dealt partly with gadfly Sandy Berman's harassment of the Library of Congress regarding its choice of terms for the Library of Congress Subject headings. In this interview Tillett said:

> Most of our correspondence contains helpful and constructive suggestions — what criticism we receive is simply not as he characterizes it. There is no onslaught of letters and emails and faxes from outraged librarians or researchers. For the most part, public criticism comes from Mr. Berman or other individuals he has urged to write to us. We're more inclined to react favorably to constructive suggestions than to coercive techniques such as petitions, hostile articles in the library literature, emotional attacks, or letters of complaint to members of

Congress. Methods such as these are almost always counterproductive, whereas more cooperative and positive approaches usually produce good results.[3]

That's the approach I want to take in this article: the cooperative and positive one. If I have trouble sticking to that approach, it's understandable, for OCLC claims to be a "member cooperative" when it is really a profit-hungry leech on libraries.

About OCLC

OCLC was born of cataloging, chiefly cataloging in academic libraries. It's safe to say that the foundation of OCLC rests on the labor of over thirty years of catalogers' work. OCLC's fortunes have been built on the backs of catalogers, librarians who are most often underpaid, overqualified, and under-appreciated.

But OCLC has turned its back on catalogers and on MLS librarians as well. In 2006, I attended the Innovative Users Group meeting held in Denver and heard a talk by Jerry Kline, the president of Innovative Interfaces, Inc. He remarked in his speech that, after the Los Angeles County Public Library, Innovative is the second largest employer of MLS librarians in the state of California. His company values the profession, it values the credential we agree on as the standard for professional librarianship, and it values the people who have earned that credential.

OCLC, Inc. does not share those values. OCLC does not sufficiently value librarianship, the MLS degree, or librarians. This antipathy towards librarians can be measured by observing OCLC employment advertisements. OCLC rarely seeks to hire MLS librarians. One rarely sees a job opening advertised at OCLC that requires an MLS degree. What OCLC values more than anything else is business entrepreneurship. It wants people who are going to come up with the means and strategies for making money for the organization and for destroying the organization's competition. That's what OCLC values.

OCLC fills most of its professional job openings locally. It relies heavily on Ohio State University in nearby Columbus as a source of workers. The organization is filled with employees who have received either advanced business or computer science degrees from the university. Many of the so-called researchers who work in "OCLC Research" (the research department's official name) are computer science students or computer science graduates of the university. Computer science is probably one of the professions that exhibits the most antipathy and condescension towards library science and towards librarians. Computer scientists think they can invent a way to make library catalogs and librarians obsolete (take the so-called Semantic Web, for example), even though despite many years of trying, they have been unable to do so. The Semantic Web, according to Wikipedia, is "a project to create a universal medium for information exchange by putting documents with computer-processable meaning (semantics) on the World Wide Web."[4] The Semantic Web is so far ahead of its time, about one thousand years, that it doesn't work yet. Now computer scientists are working on romantic notions like automatic indexing of images, in which a computer recognizes a house in an image and applies the subject heading "house" to the image automatically. It's as if computer scientists even refuse to consider the value of human-created metadata and think that even crude metadata created by a computer is better than rich metadata created by a human.

Many other professionals at OCLC are hired with bachelor's degrees in various fields and then encouraged to earn an MBA, and many do. Note that the organization does not encourage its employees to study library science; it encourages them to study business. One example of this is Erik Jul. Remember him? He was extremely visible for a while at ALA conferences and on popular email lists. He was ALA's toast of Mayfair. According to the LITA web site,[5] he had a master's degree in classics when he was hired at OCLC as a technical writer. He was one of the OCLC employees who were behind the "Intercat" project, when we all started cataloging websites for the first time in World-Cat. Later Jul became the director of the now essentially defunct OCLC Institute, and then he disappeared from the library landscape. OCLC is very much an Ohio organization — instead of a national organization — when you look at the origins of its workers. It's rumored that Jul now plays a role in OCLC's WebJunction, which is supposed to be a training and knowledge sharing resource for librarians, but in reality it serves mainly as a means of funneling Gates Foundation money into OCLC.

For its non-professional (staff) employees, OCLC has a questionable and perhaps exploitative recruiting method. These staff members are generally non-permanent, low-level technicians. For example, it hires people referred from employment agencies in Columbus to do its contract cataloging work. This is work that in most libraries is done by professionals, but at OCLC, where bibliographic data quality doesn't count for much, they basically take people off the street and teach them to catalog in a day or so, often in languages they can barely understand. This part of OCLC used to be called TechPro, but I can't find any reference to it on the OCLC website any more. Instead they now call the service Contract Cataloging, which I actually think is a better name than TechPro, which sounded like it was made up by a clueless person in OCLC's marketing department. While they have improved the name, they haven't improved the working conditions there. OCLC Contract Cataloging is basically an information sweatshop, where employees are forced to produce such a high quota of metadata that quality suffers greatly. When employees fail to meet the quota, they are let go, and a call is placed to the employment agency, which sends out another employee to replace the one that is let go, much the same way that workers are replaced in the maquiladoras along the U.S.-Mexican border.

OCLC's Mission

The mission of OCLC is to separate libraries from their money. There's no other way to say it. Never mind that OCLC is technically classified as a non-profit, presents itself as a library cooperative, and controls the world's largest bibliographic database. There are dozens of MBAs at OCLC whose job it is to think up new ways to generate revenue from libraries.

One of these ways that they've come up with is monopolization. OCLC buys up small, promising companies that promise to have the potential to generate a lot of revenue, especially from libraries. In the past few years OCLC has acquired the assets of the only two competing bibliographic utilities — WLN and RLIN — and is now positioned as the only bibliographic utility in the country. It has no competition. Long ago, under the leadership of robber baron K. Wayne Smith, OCLC began its practice of gobbling up companies that supply libraries with goods or services. For example, OCLC owns Forest Press, which publishes the Dewey Decimal Classification (DDC). Forest Press comes out with a new edition of DDC every few years so that libraries have to shell out capital in order to buy the latest edition and keep up, in much the same way that Mary Baker Eddy, the founder of Christian Science, would periodically update her *Science & Health: With a Key to the Scriptures* and require her followers to purchase the updated editions just to generate revenue.

One of the types of library suppliers that OCLC currently does not have its hand in is library supplies. Companies like Gaylord and DEMCO supply libraries with things like labels, book trucks, archival materials, etc. I predict that OCLC will fill this product gap and soon acquire one of these companies. The MBA entrepreneurs at OCLC are possibly planning this type of acquisition, for it represents a big gap in library services and supplies that OCLC does not currently cover and, judging from its recent acquisitions, OCLC surely seeks to completely control the all of the library services and supplies market.

Another way that OCLC separates libraries from their money is by means of its being a so-called library cooperative. OCLC uses its status as a library cooperative and as an organization that serves libraries to ennoble itself. It puts forth the attitude: "We serve libraries; we are noble, so everything we do is noble." Librarians are sickened by this attitude because they know how OCLC exploits libraries and librarians. OCLC uses bibliographic data created by librarians and then resells it at inflated rates to other libraries! Also, OCLC loads very poor quality bibliographic records into its WorldCat database and then charges libraries to access and use this data, charging them the same as it charges for higher quality records, such as those that come from the Library of Congress.

A more honest way of looking at OCLC is this: it buys bibliographic data from libraries at exploitatively low rates, and then sells that data back to libraries at exorbitantly high rates. Also, a lot of the bibliographic data it gets is basically free, such as vendor records (brief, low-quality bibliographic records supplied by book vendors) and records from the Library of Congress, which OCLC gets for free or for a very low cost.

Bibliographic Record Quality

One of the reasons that low-quality bibliographic records remain in WorldCat is that OCLC does not provide sufficient incentive for libraries to upgrade the records. Many member libraries have the ability to enhance vendor records or to at least correct them, but few libraries do this because the monetary incentives for enhancing and correcting records that OCLC offers are insufficient. That is to say, the credit a library gets for fixing up a poor-quality record in WorldCat is not enough to motivate libraries to do it. The result is that bad data stays in WorldCat for years and years, and possibly forever. Libraries choose instead to download the records directly into their online catalogs and fix up the records there, where the editing process is easier and generally quicker. If OCLC were to sufficiently increase the incentives it offers for enhancing bibliographic records the data quality in WorldCat would be greatly improved.

Regarding the vendor records — some of which are really, really bad — the question has been asked, "Is it better to have a bad record than to have no record at all?" I think this is a valid question, and the answer you get is going to differ depending on whom you ask. If you were to ask a reference librarian, he would probably say that any record is better than none, because in the course of helping someone at a reference desk, it is more helpful to find at least a minimal record than none at all. Finding even a stub record can help confirm a citation and confirms that a book or other information resource does exist.

On the other hand, I have seen many vendor records that are so bad that they have multiple errors, including typographical and transcription errors, that would render the record virtually unfindable in any database. By this, I mean that if the reference librarian mentioned above were to conduct a search for a book for the patron he's helping, many of the vendor records in OCLC are so bad that he's not going to find them — not because they aren't there, but because the title or other field contains so many errors that it won't be retrieved in a search. In this case there is no difference between inputting bad records and not inputting a record because the result is the same: no record found!

For several years, OCLC has been in the business of loading large sets of bibliographic records into WorldCat that it obtains from, for example, foreign libraries. These records are minimal level, have name and title headings that do not match any authority scheme, and are often missing much of the data required to meet even minimal-level record standards. There are literally millions of these records that OCLC has incorporated into WorldCat that are sub-minimal level, even according to OCLC's standards. OCLC has a webpage entitled "WorldCat Principles of Cooperation." One of the principles enumerated on this page directs libraries to make a commitment to "Create bibliographic records and related data at the fullest possible level, consistent with the standards and guidelines adopted by OCLC."[6] Because OCLC dumps so much dirty data from around the world into WorldCat, this shows that the organization has no desire to follow its own principles of cooperation.

Some libraries have tried to find a way to circumvent the high cost (and low return) of OCLC's exploitative membership by seeking other sources of bibliographic records. MARC data is everywhere on the web, and much of it is of better quality that what's found in WorldCat because you can access the poor-quality records that have been downloaded from OCLC and then enhanced, as described above, locally (that is, in their own OPACs only) by OCLC member libraries. It's also possible to access records that originated in OCLC in the public catalogs of thousands of libraries around the world, a fact that annoys OCLC. Many of the MARC records that OCLC resells to libraries originated from the Library of Congress and are therefore in the public domain, but this doesn't stop OCLC from copyrighting the data and going after people who use this data that once resided in the WorldCat database.

Several years ago, OCLC invented a term for using their records secondhand; they call it "record nabbing."[7] Coining this term was very clever on OCLC's part because it stigmatized a practice that, from a different perspective, is a creative and innovative way of sharing bibliographic data. When you want to demonize something, you give it a negative name. But OCLC now uses the term "resource sharing" to refer to interlibrary loan, and I really don't see how the practice of using OCLC records found in online catalogs isn't really just the same thing: resource sharing. OCLC has pressured many consortia and libraries to "turn off" their Z39.50 ports to stop the practice of this method of resource sharing, thus cutting off a free source of bibliographic data that was being used by small libraries and libraries unable to afford OCLC's predatory pricing policies. In summary, when OCLC makes money on the deal, it's called "resource sharing"; when OCLC doesn't make money on the deal, it's called "record nabbing." A frank and helpful description of the emergence of the concept of record nabbing appeared in the June 23, 2003 issue of *Technical Services Law Librarian*, written by Michael Maben:

> As I was preparing this column in late April, a discussion arose on Autocat concerning usage of OCLC-derived records by nonmember libraries. There was a presentation and discussion about this issue at the February 2003 Members Council meeting. The presentation was done by Gary Houk, OCLC Vice President of Cataloging and Metadata Services. The slides of his presentation are available at: http://www.oclc.org/oclc/uc/feb03/ppt/GaryHouk_NonMem berUseofRecords_files/frame.htm>. OCLC's concern is for "record nabbing," which Houk defined as "the unauthorized downloading of OCLC member cataloging records from library OPACs by all types of libraries from all corners of the world." So the idea is not the unauthorized use of OCLC records from WorldCat, but rather the unauthorized "nabbing" of OCLC-derived records in member libraries' OPACs.
>
> One characteristic of virtually any discussion of OCLC on Autocat is one of extreme hostility towards OCLC by some of the participants. This discussion was no exception. People took issue with OCLC's pricing as forcing libraries to engage in record nabbing. Many people questioned who really owns the records, if the records are under copyright protection, contract issues between OCLC and the library, and the like. Others slammed OCLC's non-profit status and how it evidently took a special act of the Ohio Legislature to maintain that status (having seen OCLC's facilities in Dublin, Ohio, I can attest to the fact that they are bringing in a lot of money). One individual even accused OCLC of being a Ponzi scheme.[8]

OCLC even changed the name of its puppet governing board from "Users' Council" to "Members Council" a few years ago, a public relations move aimed at selling the notion that OCLC is actually a cooperative and not a rapacious conglomerate.

OCLC, as many people know, is headquartered on a "campus" in suburban Columbus, Ohio. It's the same place that is headquarters to the artery-clogging company Wendy's Old Fashioned Hamburgers. On OCLC's campus, there are several buildings named after past OCLC presidents. There's the Frederick G. Kilgour Building, the K. Wayne Smith building, and the Rowland C.W. Brown Building. This last one is named after a now forgotten former president of OCLC. Note that the K. Wayne Smith building was named after K. Wayne Smith *while he was still president of OCLC*. What incredible hubris! I am certain that they will construct a new building soon and it will be named — you guessed it — the Jay Jordan building.

Connexion

In March, 2004, OCLC released version 1.1 of Connexion, its new application for cataloging in WorldCat. The interface is available in a browser version and a client version.

I am most familiar with the client version: i.e., a software program that is loaded (continually) on my computer at work. (I say "continually" because it seems like a new version of the software is released every few months or so.) Connexion replaces Passport, the now-obsolete OCLC cataloging application.

The only way to describe OCLC's implementation of Connexion is this: *complete total laughingstock disaster.* It was probably one of the worst implementations ever of any new software. Everything that could go wrong has gone wrong. I use the perfect tense because the implementation, now two and a half years later, is still going on. The "Known Problems" web page regularly grows after each release of a new version. The OCLC programmers are the Three Stooges of the coding world. They surely must be yet more clueless computer science types from Ohio State University who have never darkened the doors of a library, much less dealt with metadata of any kind.

One of the worst parts of the implementation of Connexion has been the downtime; it often crashes. You'll be cataloging away — or should I say "creating metadata" — and all of a sudden you get a strange, vague error message in a little dialogue box that says something like "Unable to access remote server." This usually means the system has gone down, and it often goes down, especially on Mondays. I think it goes down a lot on Mondays because the beginning coders OCLC hired from the Columbus Coders Discount Employment Agency spend the weekend trying to fix the numerous bugs in the system. They do fix the bugs, but in doing so, they create new ones, bugs that cause the system to crash when heavy usage starts again on Monday.

OCLC is always "very sorry" for the inconveniences these outages cause. These outages mean that literally thousands of library workers cannot do their jobs while the system is down. OCLC has not hired sufficiently skilled programmers to create Connexion. Clearly, they've taken the cheap route and have hired people who are not excellent but only satisfactory. To put it another way, the OCLC programmers are about as good as the data in a vendor record from Europe, loaded into WorldCat, with typos and missing and incorrect data.

OCLC, in its Connexion email list, encourages users to either contact their regional service provider or to contact customer service when the system goes down. There are several problems with this. My experience is that when I contact my regional service provider and tell them (by means of an email) that I cannot connect to OCLC via Connexion, they send me an email the next day saying that the problem has been fixed. In other words, contacting one's regional service provider is a waste of time. If you try to call OCLC, one of their other suggested options when the system goes down, you are put on hold and forced to listen to music that only people in Columbus, Ohio could ever tolerate. After about ten minutes of this insipid music, a customer service representative finally answers. Then you explain the problem and hear silence on the other end. It's clear the person on the other end of the phone has no clue what you are talking about. You get the feeling that you are talking with someone who took her GED instead of finishing high school and took any job she could find. Eventually, however, usually sometime after lunch Mountain Time, the system comes back up and then you are able to begin cataloging again.

The implementation of OCLC Connexion has been an embarrassing disaster from the beginning. It has been a case study of how not to implement a new service. Now that OCLC is a monopoly, the organization will be less mindful of its users' needs. This has already become evident in email postings by OCLC employees to the OCLC Cataloging email list. For example, David Whitehair, the Connexion product manager, now maintains a very dictatorial attitude on the list, refusing, in one instance, to extend the "end-of-service" date of one of the versions of Connexion client, despite the pleas of libraries across the country that were having major troubles implementing the next version.

OCLC Propaganda

Am I the only one who cannot understand a word that Lorcan Dempsey says or writes? Have you ever tried reading one of his articles? They are some of the most incoherent and desultory articles in the history of information. Nevertheless, hiring Dempsey, OCLC Vice President and Chief Strategist, was another clever move on OCLC's part. His flamboyance makes him a popular attraction at ALA conferences. Also at these conferences, there is a tendency among the attendees to believe anything that is said with a British accent (unless it's Michael Gorman who, because he is pro-cataloging, is sometimes stigmatized). Dempsey appeared out of nowhere, purports to "know a lot about emerging technologies," and, of course, has a blog. He lives for new technology. It seems as if he thinks that any new library or information technology is automatically better than the technology that predates it and it must be implemented immediately, especially if OCLC has a hand in it. Dempsey's mission is to make OCLC the center of libraries' technology strategies. The striking thing about Lorcan Dempsey is that he is all form and very little content. You can listen to him ramble for an hour and you leave the conference hall with less understanding of information technology than when you entered.

OCLC also has a large propaganda machine. This machine consists of several very articulate individuals who travel the country attending library conferences large and small and promoting OCLC's mission, which, as you will recall, is to separate libraries from their money. These individuals include people like Alane Wilson, a very eloquent and winsome speaker who travels the country and, like many others at OCLC, attempts to predict the future of the library and information landscape. In their predictions, they always state that there will be certain needs, needs that OCLC just happens to be working on and will be able to fulfill.

OCLC's Research Department always conducts research that supports the organization's goals and views of the information world. Most of their research is carried out in Ohio, as if Ohio were a valid statistical information sample for the whole world. An example of this is a research project carried out by Lynn Silipigni Connaway. You remember her, right? She used to be in charge of netLibrary, another start-up that OCLC gobbled up. She was responsible for distributing netLibrary bibliographic records to thousands of libraries, records that contained many serious errors, such as typos, invalid headings, etc. She proudly distributed this dirty data, and OCLC was only happy to make money from the deal. Anyway, her recent research was entitled "Sense-Making the Information Confluence: The Whys and Hows of College and University User Satisficing of Information Needs." What a pedantic title. Their use of the non-word "satisficing" shows how they always attempt to be on the cutting edge, in this case by using a word that sounds technologically trendy. Guess where the research was carried out: Ohio. How convenient. As Ohio goes, so goes the nation, I guess. The main goal of the research was to show that college freshmen don't use library catalogs anymore. For this the federal grant-making agency Institute of Museum and Library Services awarded thousands of dollars? OCLC wants its research to point to the fact that information seeking behavior is changing, and only OCLC can help you provide the means of supplying information in this new information landscape.

Conclusion

I think it will be fascinating to observe the future of OCLC. I think more and more libraries will begin to conclude that they are not getting their money's worth from the organization, what with the poor data quality and poor computer applications it provides, and with the way it exploits its employees and snubs the library profession. OCLC at some point will be exposed for the profit-seeking multinational corporation it is, rather than the non-profit, cultural heritage organization it presents itself as. When this happens, libraries may be freed from their connections to OCLC and be forced to innovate and will create better, home-grown solutions to library needs than a large, distant, and disconnected organization could ever do. Libraries will foster true resource sharing, sharing that doesn't involve them sending their scarce capital to Ohio. In this way, libraries will be able to spend more of their budgets on buying resources for their users.

References

1. Karen Schneider. (2006). How OPACs Suck. *ALA Tech Source Blog.* Available: <http://www.techsource. ala.org/blog/2006/03/how-opacs-suck-part-1-relevance-rank-or-the-lack-of-it.html>.
2. Rory Litwin, (2006, 6 August). Interview with Barbara Tillett. *Library Juice.* Available: <http://libraryjuice press.com/blog/?p=115>.
3. Ibid.
4. Wikipedia, s.v. "Semantic Web." Available: <http://en.wikipedia.org/wiki/Semantic_Web>.
5. Library & Information Technology Association, "Erik Jul," (2006). Available: <http://www.ala.org/ala/ lita/litaresources/toptechtrends/erikjul.htm>.
6. OCLC, WorldCat Principles of Cooperation," (2006). Available: <http://www.oclc.org/worldcat/contrib ute/principles/>.
7. Gary R. Houk, "OCLC speaks out on record nabbing," *Library Collections, Acquisitions, & Technical Services* 27, 3 (2003):277–79.
8. Michael Maben, "OBS OCLC Committee," *Technical Services Law Librarian* 28(4), 2003. Available: <http://www.aallnet.org/sis/tssis/tsll/28-04/oclc.htm>.

Latina Lesbian Subject Headings: The Power of Naming

tatiana de la tierra

When people walk into the library of their own free will — when it is an act not in response to a mandatory class assignment or work project — what are they looking for? Many times, it is themselves — traces of self, fragments, whole stories. Perhaps it is human nature to search for a reflection of ourselves in literature. It seems as if our very existence, the face in the mirror, is not sufficient. We need artistic, literary, historical, and quantitative proof that we are, and have always been, "here." But we don't always find it.

Libraries are limited by their collections, by the politics of the moment, by biases, and by the administrative and organizational machinery that maintain order in the library. As a result, some of the people who enter in search of themselves walk out of the library empty-handed. Often the inability of a library to meet the patron's needs hits people of color the hardest. As African-American Studies librarian Kathleen E. Bethel writes:

> Many librarians know how disheartening it is for people of color to enter these same institutions and find little reflection of their lived experiences. Of the small amount of material that people of color manage to locate, a major portion speaks of pathological behaviors or may be a misrepresentation of the histories and cultures of non–Western peoples [222].

Latina lesbians and all queers have the well-documented tradition of going to the library as part of critical soul-searching that precedes the "coming out" process — and leaving disappointed. Joan Nestle, co-founder of the Lesbian Herstory Archives of Brooklyn, recounts her expedition to the New York Public Library on Fifth Avenue. It was 1957, she was seventeen years old, and she wanted to write a research paper on homosexuality.

> Too ashamed to ask a librarian about my topic, I toured the endless rows of wooden card catalogue cabinets until I found the letter H. I pulled out the long narrow drawer and flipped through the timeworn cards. Finally, my heart beating, I found the word "Homosexual," followed by a dash and then the words "see Deviancy," and next to this "see Pathology," with suggested subcategories of prisons and mental institutions. I never wrote that paper [67].

Nearly fifty years later, the wooden card catalogs have been replaced by online public access catalogs, and HOMOSEXUALITY is no longer defined in pathological terms. But finding "homosexual" library materials is still problematic, and it becomes even more so when the search is coupled with ethnic identifiers. In the early eighties, after recognizing the dyke within, I did as Nestle and countless others have — I went to the library and looked myself up. At the time, HOMOSEXUAL pointed me to books about dysfunctional identities resulting from overbearing mothers. HISPANIC in association with LESBIAN led nowhere. I wondered if I was the only Latina lesbian in the world.

Latina lesbians who enter the library in search of themselves will look beyond the U.S. border and the English language. Literature in Spanish and materials related to their countries of origin are a priority. This body of literature is not abundant to begin with, and it can be difficult to identify and to obtain. Yet it does exist, and word about authors and titles gets out. U.S. libraries even have some of these books. But can hopeful Latina lesbians find these materials in a library catalog? Generally speaking, no. Not unless they know the title or author in advance. Finding "homosexual" library materials is problematic and it becomes even more so when the search is coupled with ethnic identifiers. Poor cataloging and inappropriate subject headings, or the lack of them, are part of the problem.

To name, to categorize and classify, to label and brand, to make a linguistic determination, to signal, to define, to say, "this is the word, these are the words that will represent you" — this is a powerful thing. Those of us who had to learn another language and culture know about the power of naming, of being named, and of making words our very own.

Language is fluid and political. There was a time when we were all "Mankind." When immigrants were brave, as opposed to "Illegal" and "Alien." When African Americans were "Black" or "Colored." When the "N-word" was the actual word. When Latin@s* were coined as "Hispanic" and Native Americans were "Indians." When the "L-word" meant nothing at all. When terms such as "Homo," "Fag," "Queer" and "Dyke" were hurled like jagged rocks with the intent to cause injury. They still are, but now these same terms have been proudly adopted by some. There was a time when "Male or Female" were the only recognized expressions of gender, "Homosexual or Heterosexual" were the only possible sexual identities, and "Black or White" referred to the entire racial and ethnic spectrum.

The practice of classifying books with defining terms is done with the best of intentions: to increase access to the book, to make it available to library users. But given the subjective human process involved in selecting appropriate subject headings, and considering the political nature of language and the natural evolution of words, cataloging is a perilously imperfect art. Library of Congress Subject Headings can be a reflection of the times. As Joan Nestle discovered in 1957, SEXUAL PERVERSION was the official heading for homosexuality until it was replaced with SEXUAL DEVIATION in 1969. (In 1974, the American Psychiatric Association determined that homosexuality was not a pathology.) But Library of Congress subject headings can also be out of step with the times. Despite established usage, for instance, "Queer," "Transgender," "Latina lesbians," and "Chicana lesbians" aren't official subject headings.

Subject headings carry a lot of weight. The right ones can help a researcher find books on the topic he or she is looking for; the wrong ones, or none at all, can cut off access to them.

Sanford Berman, a politically astute "Rambo cataloger," a horsefly in the Library of Congress's underbelly, has been agitating for changes in subject heading terminology for decades. He, along with like-minded colleagues, uses grassroots techniques — petitions, letter-writing campaigns, and public forum debates — to say, essentially, "White Western male supremacist terminology is wrong; it can, and should, be righted." As the millennial clock was ticking in late October of 1999, Sanford Berman spoke at San Jose State University on the topic announced on a flyer: "Good Luck Finding Information on 'Those People' in Library Catalogs!: Multiculturalism; Poverty; Gay and Lesbian Issues."

In the spirit of Sandy Berman, following is an exploration of words — the ones determined for us and the ones we use to name ourselves — and of books by and about Latina and Chicana lesbians, and of how these books can be found, and lost, in a library catalog.

On Hissspanicsss, Latin@s and Chican@s

Despite the reality that most Latin@s call ourselves Latin@, we are, by Library of Congress standards, "Hispanic"— a term that so many of us have loathed since it entered popular use during the Reagan administration. Chicanos are "Mexican Americans" or may be classified under the broader term of "Hispanic Americans." We hate "Hispanic" because it is "their" word for "us." The one you have to check off on government forms, the one the Census uses to count us, the one that keeps us all under the reign of Spanish and Spain. Elba Rosario Sánchez takes the word on in her poem "Hissspanicsss":

> hiss panicsss
> as in from Hispania?
> where's that?
> non-existent country
> non-existent people
> no history or geography
> no tongue to speak
> of struggle [used by permission of the author]

"Latin@" is not a perfect term either, as there is not a clear-cut geographic, linguistic or historical boundary to Latinidad. A Latin@ can be Puerto Rican or Guatemalan or U.S.-born of Latin American heritage. Latin@s might be fluent in Spanish, English, and/or Spanglish. And depending on the definition of "Latin@," maybe even Portuguese or Creole. The term "Latin@" is also open to discussion. As Juana Maria Rodriguez wrote in an article published in the Latina lesbian magazine *conmoción,*

Is Latinidad in the blood, in a certain geographic space, is it about language and culture, or is it a certain set of experiences? ... Others claim, que lo Latino se conoce, it is an essence that is evident in how we look, talk, dance, eat, play. Is Latinidad really that easy to spot? How many times have we heard, *She doesn't look Latina.*

David Roman writes in *Aztlán* that "the term 'Latino' itself encompasses so many different nationalities, ethnicities, and cultural backgrounds, that to rely on the term as an organizing label of social identity veils that such terms, used to fashion private and public identities, are sites of struggle and historical negotiation" (151). Alicia Gaspar de Alba argues against using "Latina" as a broader term for "Chicana." "It has become politically correct, not to mention expedient, to fit Chicanas under the broader rubric of latinidad, but can Latinas fit under the Chicana umbrella? I know this is a rhetorical question, but I employ it here to suggest that the term Latina, when used as a signifier for Chicana experience, privileges the Latina subject" (107).

Those of us who identify as Latin@ must deal with an added pesky problem — the a/o and o/a of Latina/o and Latino/a. A female is Latina, a male is Latino, yet sometimes, we mean to speak for both male and female, and to avoid sexist linguistics that makes us all pertinent to "he/his," we use Latinos/as or Latinas/os. Likewise, Mexican Americans use Chicano/Chicana or Chicanas/os or Chicano/as. Some of us have found a solution to this complication, visually, at least: Latin@, Latin@s, Chican@, Chican@s. The "@" symbolically embodies both the male and female, an androgynous letter added to a bilingual alphabet. But it has no pronunciation.

Regardless of the imperfections, though, "Latin@" is the term that many of us use to refer to ourselves. David Abalos, in an article published in *The Hispanic Outlook in Higher Education*, writes about the power of naming:

> The language and discourse of liberation and transformation recognizes and honors the right of all people and groups to name themselves. This is not about a fad, being politically correct, or a commercialization of difference; to name oneself and one's community is at one and the same time a personal, political, historical, and sacred act.

Per the twenty-seventh edition of *Library of Congress Subject Headings* (2004), "Latino Americans" and "Latinos (United States)" are referred to "USE" HISPANIC AMERICANS.** The scope note reads, "Here are entered works on United States citizens of Latin American descent. Works on citizens of Latin American countries are entered under Latin Americans. Works on citizens of Latin American countries in the United States are entered under Latin Americans — United States." The subject heading for LATIN AMERICANS is defined in the scope note as, "Here are entered works on citizens of Latin American countries. Works on citizens of Latin American countries in the United States are entered under LATIN AMERICANS — UNITED STATES. Works on United States citizens of Latin American descent are entered under HISPANIC AMERICANS. Meanwhile, there is only one subject heading that uses "Chicano": "CHICANO (THE ENGLISH WORD): BT ENGLISH LANGUAGE — ETYMOLOGY." Otherwise, all listings for Chicano refer one to USE MEXICAN AMERICAN, as in, "Chicano authors: USE MEXICAN AMERICAN AUTHORS."

So, Latin@s and Chican@s must all go to USE hell: we have been de-term-ined to be officially named as HISPANIC AMERICANS and MEXICAN AMERICANS. We can also be classified under MINORITIES or via ETHNICITY. We may also be referred to as [Nationality] Americans, as in COLOMBIAN AMERICANS.

The word "American" is also loaded. When South Americans speak of Americans we mean the Americas — the South as well as the North. When North Americans from the U.S. say "American," they typically mean themselves. By definition, "America" transcends the United States; in practice, popular terminology has made "America" a word pertaining only to the United States. In Colombia, where I come from, "Americans" are referred to as "gringos" or "Yankees" (a term commonly used in Spain). As a U.S. citizen, I am technically an "American," or more specifically, a "Colombian American." I used to think of myself as a Colombian who lived in the U.S. But then, after 25 years of living here as a "resident alien," I became a U.S. citizen. Now, after being a U.S. citizen for 10 years, and as the prospect of returning to live in Colombia dims, I am closer than ever to identifying as an "American." My brother, who grew up in the U.S. and was exiled for 10 years in Colombia, thought of himself as a "Colombian American" when he lived in the U.S. and as an "American Colombian" when he lived in Colombia. Many, but not all, Latin@s identify as "American." Identity is funny that way.

On "Queer"

While there is a diverse terminology for sexual identity, the Library of Congress distills it into variations of lesbian, gay, bisexual, and homosexual. Meanwhile, we are queers, and queens, and transgender, and dykes, and bull daggers, and butches, and lipstick lesbians. We use code words: in the life, familia. Latina lesbians are *mariconas, jotas, patas, tortilleras, areperas, patlache, gallonas,* and *cuaimas,* among other dazzling terms; most are derogatory words that were embraced after the fact, as in "dyke." Library of Congress subject headings do not name the complete gamut of sexual expressions. How do you classify those who have a female body and a masculine identity? Or those who were born with a female body and became, through surgery and hormones and cosmetics, male and relate sexually to women? Or Teena Brandon or Brandon Teena? "Gay" and "Lesbian" are oversimplified terms for a highly complex set of practices and identities.

"Queer" represents a wide range of sexual identities and expressions. It was a term of the working class and used by people of color from early on in the gay liberation movement. For Gloria Anzaldúa, it was a key word. As she said in an interview,

> When I was growing up in south Texas the word "queer" was very much what we called these people. Or "de las otras," which means "of the others," that I wrote about in *Borderlands.* Marimachas and marimachos, jotitas, jotas, tortilleras: these were labels and terms in the Chicano working-class community that I grew up in. When I went and left home and became part of the women of color community and came out as a lesbian, I started not liking to use the word "lesbian." When I would dialogue with myself or with other women of color, I would use "dyke" or "queer."

Anzaldúa's "queer *mestisaje*" and Cherríe Moraga's claiming of "queer Aztlán" placed "queer" within the context of Chicana discourse. "Queer" is a term widely used by Chican@ and Latin@ lesbians and gays. It's in the title of one of Moraga's books, *Waiting in the Wings: Portrait of a Queer Motherhood.* One of Monica Palacios' performance pieces is "Greetings from a Queer Señorita." Terri de la Peña entitled a chapter in her *Latin Satins* novel "Queer of the Year." Leading Latin@ scholars use "queer." Examples include Juana Maria Rodriguez' *Queer Latinidad: Identity Practices, Discursive Spaces*; Licia Fiol-Matta's *A Queer Mother for the Nation: The State and Gabriela Mistral*; Jose Quiroga's *Tropics of Desire: Interventions from Queer Latino America*; and Alicia Arrizon's exploration of queer identity in *Latina Performance: Traversing the Stage.* "Queer" is in the titles of chapters in academic anthologies, such as Horacio N. Roque Ramirez's "Claiming Queer Citizenship: Gay Latino (Im)Migrant Acts in San Francisco" in *Queer Migrations: Sexuality, U.S. Citizenship, and Border Crossings*; Lawrence LaFountain-Stokes' "Tomboy Tantrums and Queer Infatuations: Reading Lesbianism in Magali Garcia Ramis's *Felices dias, tio Sergio*" in *Tortilleras: Hispanic and U.S. Latina Expression*; Oscar Montero's "Julian del Casal and the Queers of Havana" in *¿Entiendes? Queer Readings, Hispanic Writings*; Miguel A. Segovia's "Only Cauldrons Know the Secrets of Their Soups: Queer Romance and *Like Water for Chocolate*" in *Velvet Barrios*; Lázaro Lima's "Locas al Rescate: the Transnational Hauntings of Queer Cubanidad" in *Cuba Transnational*; Yvonne Yarbro-Bejarano's "Laying it Bare: the Queer/Colored Body in Photography by Laura Aguilar" and Gloria Anzaldúa's "To(o) Queer the Writer, Loca, Escritora y Chicana" in *Living Chicana Theory*.

But "Queer" is not an authorized Library of Congress Subject Heading. There are now headings such as QUEER AS FOLK (TELEVISION PROGRAM : UNITED STATES) and QUEER THEORY. But as of the 29th edition of the *Library of Congress Subject Headings* (2006), "Queer" is not even listed with a "USE" referring researchers to "Lesbian," "Gay," or "Homosexuality" categories. This is despite extensive mainstream use of the term that includes queer studies university programs, queer cultural centers, queer theory, queer cruises, and the ubiquitous gay pride chant, "We're here, we're queer, get used to it." I am surprised at the establishment's resistance to this mainstream term. After using "queer" ten times in a 10-page encyclopedia entry on a lesbian topic, I received the following e-mail from one of the editors:

Dear Tatiana,

Thanks very much for your piece.... It's excellent! Would you be willing to do a little tinkering to eliminate, define or explain the contemporary language that can become quickly dated ("queer" for example, has become a term of political advocacy, in our opinion, used mainly within the gay and lesbian intellectual and academic community...) This will help the readers understand the full depth of your piece, I think.

A similar request was made of another entry that I co-authored for this same encyclopedia; we used "queer" twice in that nine-page article. We were not willing to delete "queer" from these encyclopedia entries. We defended "queer" within the context of Latin@ intellectual community, and eventually prevailed, though I did, at the editor's request, define "queer" for readers.

This experience, along with the Library of Congress's hesitation to list "Queer" (at the very least with a USE reference) makes me wonder. Do words that originate in the margins have to work harder to prove themselves to be worthy of use in encyclopedias and subject headings? Are 20,000,000 Google hits not enough to show wide popular usage? Why does "Gay," with over a hundred authorized subject headings, get all the power instead? While LESBIANISM became an official heading in 1950 and GAY MEN became an official heading in 1987, "Gay" is still often used to refer to both male and female homosexuals. While not without its critics, many of whom cite the term's pejorative history, "queer" is a term with the capacity to encompass the LGBTI spectrum. I doubt that all gays and lesbians would be happy with a "Queer" subject heading, but it's just a matter of time before the Library of Congress makes it official.

Mostly, queer Latin@ expressions are categorized in the Library of Congress with the following subject headings: HISPANIC AMERICAN GAYS: UF GAYS, HISPANIC AMERICAN; BT GAYS—UNITED STATES; HISPANIC AMERICAN LESBIANS: UF LESBIANS, HISPANIC AMERI-CAN; BT LESBIANS—UNITED STATES; MEXICAN AMERICAN GAYS: UF GAYS, MEXICAN AMER-ICAN; BT GAYS—UNITED STATES; and MEXICAN AMERICAN LESBIANS: UF CHICANA LESBIANS AND LESBIANS, MEXICAN AMERICAN; BT LESBIANS—UNITED STATES. There are other sub-ject headings that may apply, such as: GAY MEN'S WRITINGS, LATIN AMERICAN: UF LATIN AMERICAN GAY MEN'S WRITINGS; BT LATIN AMERICAN LITERATURE; GAYS' WRITINGS, LATIN AMERICAN: UF HOMOSEXUALS' WRITINGS, LATIN AMERICAN (FORMER HEADING) AND LATIN AMERICAN GAYS' WRITINGS; BT LATIN AMERICAN LITERATURE; AND LESBIANS' WRITINGS, SPANISH AMERICAN: UF SPANISH AMERICAN LESBIANS' WRITINGS; BT SPANISH AMERICAN LIT-ERATURE.

Terminology Is One Thing: Putting It into Practice Is Another

It seems that if researchers were educated about the proper Library of Congress Sub-ject Headings for books by and about Latina lesbians, they could just use these headings and find the materials. In theory, this could be the case, if all books by and about queer Latin@s and Chican@s were given a magical corresponding label such as HISPANIC AMER-ICAN LESBIANS. But searching in real library catalogs such as University at Buffalo's (UB) BISON catalog shows that it's not so simple. Because even worse than inappropriate terms is the lack of subject headings. In these cases, if titles don't contain magical key-words, the books are effectively erased from catalogs. To not name is to eradicate, to make invisible. It is like banning a book that no one ever knew existed to begin with.

Library materials by and about queer people of color are among the most vulnerable, as this body of literature and academic study is at a growing stage. Simply put, since there is relative lack of materials, the ones that do exist may be necessary for survival and for the soul. Yet with the exception of recently published nonfiction titles that are explicitly and centrally about homosexuality and Latin@ culture, most of the body of work by and about Latina lesbians and gays is not accessible via keyword or subject heading searching.

In some cases, there are no subject headings at all. This is particularly true for works of literature; books in Spanish are especially affected. The Library of Congress did not start routinely applying subject headings to literature until the 1990s. Today, some, but not all, works of poetry and prose are assigned subject headings. The following novels, all with queer content by authors known to be lesbian, were in UB's library catalog with-out any assigned subject headings: Rosamaria Roffiel's *Amora* (1989), Sara Levi Calderon's *The Two Mujeres* (1991), Emma Perez' *Gulf Dreams* (1996), and Lola Van Guardia's *Plumas de doble filo* (2002). Likewise, lesbian poetry books such as Sabina Berman's *Lunas* (1988) and Cristina Peri Rossi's *Evohe* (1994) and *Estrategias del deseo* (2004) are without sub-ject headings. Older nonfiction titles may also be in the catalog without any subject head-ings, such as Gloria Anzaldúa's *Borderlands* and Cherríe Moraga's *Loving in the War Years*. This means that someone looking for queer Latina or Spanish writings will not find these books or others unless they know the title or author in advance.

Another significant problem is that Latina lesbian materials are not always assigned both ethnic and sexual identifiers. For instance, Terri de la Peña's *Latin Satins* has five subject headings, including HISPANIC AMERICAN WOMEN, but none of them have the "L-word" or a "Mexican American" subject heading, which is more appropriate than HIS-PANIC AMERICAN since the characters are all Chicana lesbians. Alicia Gaspar de Alba's *Sor Juana's Second Dream* has two subject headings: JUANA INES DE LA CRUZ, SISTER, 1651–1695 — FICTION and MEXICO — CHURCH HISTORY — 17TH CENTURY — FICTION. Considering that the intent of this novel was to lesbianize the iconic Sor Juana, the subject headings could have been better. Likewise, Gaspar de Alba's *The Mystery of Survival and Other Stories* has two subject headings: MEXICAN AMERICAN WOMEN — FICTION and MEX-ICAN AMERICANS — FICTION. Lacking in these headings are references to lesbianism and to the fact that some of the content is in Spanish. My own book, *For the Hard Ones/Para las duras* has four subject headings: LESBIANISM — PHILOSOPHY — POETRY, LESBIANS — IDEN-TITY, LESBIAN EROTICA, and COMING OUT (SEXUAL ORIENTATION). There are no references to the Spanish-language content in the book, or to its "Hispanic" origin.

In some cases, books may get assigned the proper ethnic and sexual identifiers, but not in one subject heading. For instance, Achy Obejas' novel *Memory Mambo* and her short story collection, *We Came All the Way from Cuba so You Could Dress Like This?* the have subject headings CUBAN AMERICAN WOMEN — FICTION and LESBIANS — UNITED STATES — FICTION but not HISPANIC AMERICAN LESBIANS — FICTION.

In general, materials with highly queer titles stand the best chance of getting assigned the proper ethnic and sexual identifiers. Materials with HISPANIC AMERICAN LESBIANS sub-ject headings listed in UB's catalog include *Compañeras: Latina Lesbians: an Anthology; Tortilleras: Hispanic and U.S. Latina Expression; Latina Performance: Traversing the Stage; Waiting in the Wings: Portrait of a Queer Motherhood*; and the magazines *esto no tiene nom-bre: revista de lesbianas Latinas* and *conmoción: revista y red revolucionaria de lesbianas Lati-nas*. Books with MEXICAN AMERICAN LESBIANS subject headings include *Interviews/ Entrevistas; Living Chicana Theory; Chicana Lesbians: The Girls Our Mothers Warned Us About*; and, surprisingly, Ibis Gomez Vegas' novel *Send My Roots Rain*.

But even a direct title doesn't get the exact subject heading. For instance, the anthol-ogy entitled *Latina Lesbian Writers and Artists* has twelve subject headings. Among them are LESBIANS' WRITINGS, SPANISH AMERICAN and HOMOSEXUALITY AND LITERATURE — LATIN AMERICA — but no HISPANIC AMERICAN LESBIANS. Elena M. Martinez's *Lesbian Voices from Latin America: Breaking Ground* has the SPANISH AMERICAN LITERATURE — 20TH CEN-TURY — HISTORY AND CRITICISM subject heading, even though the book focuses on Latin American and Caribbean lesbian writers. Juana Maria Rodriguez's *Queer Latinidad* has HISPANIC AMERICAN GAYS — PSYCHOLOGY, HISPANIC AMERICAN GAYS — ETHNIC IDENTITY and GAYS — UNITED STATES — IDENTITY. There is no "lesbian" label. In this case, the book's content is more gay than lesbian, so these subject headings are technically correct, but the author is a dyke. This means that people searching the catalog for books by Latina lesbians won't find *Queer Latinidad*.

Of course, subject headings aren't the only way to find books in the catalog. Keyword searching can sometimes make up for the lack of proper identifiers. But keyword search-ing is random by nature — the only titles that will come up are those with the keyword search term in the bibliographic record. If the keywords are not in the title, subject headings, notes or contents, which aren't usually entered, the books won't be found. Doing simple keyword searches in UB's catalog, the results were generally paltry. For instance, "Latina lesbian" got four hits, while "Latina and lesbian" got eight. "Chicana lesbian" got five hits while "Chicana and lesbian" got eleven. "Mexican American and lesbians" got ten and "Hispanic and lesbian" got nine. Clearly, keyword searching, powerful as it is, is limited by the information in the bibliographic record.

What is the solution to all this? My Chicana friend from East Los Angeles suggested that perhaps Latina lesbians should infiltrate the Library of Congress and right all the wronged and missing subject headings. Short of this, petitioning catalogers to modify subject headings as appropriate is a good strategy, because the catalogers who have the power to name, to brand, and to label a book are only human. But beyond book-by-book petitioning, writers and publishers need to ensure that titles have a good chance of being catalogued properly, and researchers need to employ bibliographies. Walking into a library with a known title or author beats the whole system. So until the Latina lesbian subject revolution happens, researchers had better be prepared.

Works Cited

Abalos, D. (1999). Perspective: choosing between the languages of oppression and liberation. *The Hispanic Outlook in Higher Education* 9 (17): 18.

American Library Association Student Chapter Speaker Series. (1999, October 25). Sanford Berman. Available: <http://witloof.sjsu.edu/people/alasc/speakers.html>.

Anzaldúa, G. "Words of Gloria Anzaldúa by cult of Anzaldúa [sic]. "Words of Gloria Anzaldúa." Available: http://la.indymedia.org/news/2005/05/127792.php> (accessed March 12, 2006).

Bethel, K. E. (1994). Culture keepers: cataloging the Afrocentric way. *The Reference Librarian* 45–46: 221–31.

Gaspar de Alba, A. (2003). The Chicana/Latina dyad, or identity and perception. *Latino Studies* 1 (1): 106–14.

Nestle, J. (1998). *A Fragile Union: New and Selected Readings.* San Francisco, Cleis Press, 67.

Rodriguez, J. M. (1996). Pensando en identidad. *conmoción* 3: 8–9.

Román, D. (1997). Latino performance and identity. *Aztlán.* 22:2: 151–167.

Sánchez, E. R. (1999). Hissspanicsss [sic]. *When Skin Peels.* Audio recording. San Diego: Calaca Press.

Swine — Juvenile Literature?: Good Cataloging vs. Good Public Service

John Sandstrom

I began my life in libraries as an academic cataloger. Okay, I began as a copy cataloger, who inherited the "problem" shelf when I finished the cataloging classwork for my MLIS. I went on to work in collection development and public services. One of my strengths is that I have worked in most parts of academic, public, and special libraries.

I am also part of that transitional generation of librarians between the manual world and the computer age. I learned how to type catalog card sets, print them on the computer, and finally bypass the cards altogether. When I started working in public services, we had print resources and the card catalog. While getting my MLIS, I learned Dialog I and II. At my first professional job, we started using the Internet.

Being a part of this generation of library science has given me a viewpoint and insight that neither earlier generations of librarians, nor the newer generations, can really understand. I had to learn both ways of doing things as I pursued my degree. Using computers in the library was not something I learned because I had to; computers have been a part of my library training since the beginning of my career. But I also learned the older, pre-computer way of doing things, with typewriters, steel erasers, hard-copy indexes, and card catalogs.

These experiences give me a sense of the history of cataloging and public services that I feel many of my newer colleagues are missing. Right now, I am having the issues between technical services and public services hammered at me as the Manager of Collection Development and Acquisitions, and the Acting Manager of Cataloging and Processing at my library, as well as spending a bit over ten percent of my time each week working the reference desk. I am a generalist who can see the connections between technical services and public services, and how they need to work together.

The purpose of this essay is to ask some questions, based on my knowledge and experience in the "big picture" of the library. So what does all this have to do with cataloging? Good question! Let's answer it with a question.

What is the purpose of cataloging?

Charles Ammi Cutter made the first explicit statement regarding the objectives of a bibliographic system in 1876. According to Cutter, those objectives were:

1. To enable a person to find a book of which any of these is known (finding objective)
   - the author
   - the title
   - the subject
2. To show what the library has (collocating objective)
   - by a given author
   - on a given subject
   - in a given kind of literature
3. to assist in the choice of a book (choice objective)
   - as to its edition (bibliographically)
   - as to its character (literary or topical) (Cutter 1904)

While Cutter's definition of what a catalog is supposed to be and do is fairly old, it still serves its purpose well. When it was developed, catalogs were primarily in book form and index cards were just beginning to be used. In both of these formats, space limitations were a major consideration. Catalogers had to fit all the information about a book into as little space as possible.

In the early days of the computer catalogs, space was still a concern. Memory, in the form of magnetic tape and giant disk packs, was expensive and difficult to access, requiring multiple readers and a mainframe for even the smallest libraries. For over 100 years the rule of thumb was to distill the subject of a book into no more than three subject headings, using whatever set of subject headings had been accepted by your library.

Why are we still working on this limited-space basis? Memory is getting cheaper and cheaper, as are the computers and software needed to access it. There are already hard drives on the market that can contain the entirety of the OCLC database. Why do we continue to limit ourselves to three or four subject headings?

This clinging to old and outdated standards is what provoked the title of this piece. In my library, one of the subject headings for *The Three Little Pigs* is SWINE—JUVENILE LITERATURE, as opposed to PIGS—FOLKLORE. Is this useful? Is it appropriate for the intended audience? My library uses LCSH, and the term "pig" is not a subject heading. Indeed, since we are still following the "three subject headings" rule, our catalogers delete the Sears subject headings that make much more sense for this item.

Would it not provide better public service to allow for all the subject headings of a book to be listed in the catalog? Would it not be easier to provide access to LCSH, Sears, MeSH and any other set of subject headings through the catalog? I'm a librarian and I wouldn't dream of looking up a children's book on pigs under SWINE. Why should we expect our patrons to do so?

A second issue in the interface between cataloging and public services that I'd like to address is call numbers. One of the biggest ways a cataloging department can affect public services is through the call numbers they assign to the materials coming into the library. A book that is misshelved might as well be a lost book, much as a book that has been cataloged to an area away from the rest of the like materials in a collection is also lost. Current examples of this are bilingual picture books and graphic novels.

Think about it. In most libraries, especially public libraries, picture books are all shelved together, usually by the author's last name. Spanish language picture books are shelved in the juvenile Spanish area, again alphabetically by author. However, in several libraries I've worked in, from New Jersey to Texas, bilingual easy readers are treated differently.

First, they are cataloged in the first language that appears on the title page. Okay, we can work with that. The kicker comes when they are assigned their call number. In far too many cases, they get put in the Dewey 400s for that language. So a Spanish-English picture book ends up in the 468s instead of with the rest of the picture books. How many patrons would think to look for them there? How many adult librarians with limited familiarity with picture books and juvenile collections would think to look for them there?

In the case of graphic novels, we have a newer format that is being hammered into the old boxes. Since they're "new," their cataloging is still being worked out. As a result, some libraries put all of them in the 741s with the compilation volumes of various comic strips, even though they aren't comic strips. Other places put them all in fiction, even though some aren't novels. Some libraries catalog nonfiction graphic novels in their respective subject areas. What is the right answer? I don't know. Part of this issue requires us to take a step back and ask an even more basic question: Are graphic novels different enough to be grouped together by format, or should they be treated like any other book?[1] I do know that, due to their popularity, many libraries are pulling them all together in a separate collection regardless of how they are cataloged. In the long run, this may be the best way to serve the public, but it would help all of us if clear guidelines could be developed as soon as possible.

At the beginning of this essay I promised some questions. I don't have definite answers. Answers will vary by the needs of your library and community. But I do have some questions I think we all need to think about and discuss.

What is more important? Pristine, by-the-book cataloging, or cataloging that provides access to the collection in the way best suited to your patron base?

How many access points to an online record are too many? I believe that we need to tailor our cataloging to the needs of our patrons. This increases the number of appropriate subject headings. Increasing the number of access points increases our ability to provide appropriate customer service. Increasing the number of access points improves the usefulness of our catalogs.

Do we really need to choose between one set of subject headings and another? Can't we use all that are relevant?

What is more important? Using the call numbers assigned by the Library of Congress, or consistently keeping multiple editions of a title together where they can be found more easily?

Note

1. From a discussion regarding this paper with editor K.R. Roberto.

References

Cutter, C.A. (1904). *Rules for a Dictionary Catalog*, 4th edition, Washington, D.C.: Government Printing Office.

Cults, New Religious Movements, and Bias in LC Subject Headings

Tracy Nectoux

What's a cult? It just means not enough people to make a minority.
—Robert Altman

As a lowly graduate assistant monographic copy cataloger, I am no stranger to OCLC Connexion, and the sometimes carelessly prepared records that can be exported from it. I spend my days correcting page numbers, adding tables of contents, correcting access points for names, and altering the occasional Dewey number to one more precise and appropriate for my library's catalog. Each day brings new, interesting challenges simply because cataloging feeds my anal-retentive nature so marvelously. As a bibliophile, I get satisfaction from providing information and access for every book that crosses my desk — from the beautiful, half-bound, nineteenth-century collection of Tennyson poems with marbled endpapers, to the simplest of pamphlets listing the winners of cornhusking competitions in depression-era Nebraska. Sometimes I have to remind myself that there are limitations to just how elegant and beautiful MARC records can be. I realize that even if I work at the University of Illinois library until the Angel of Death scratches at my door, I'll never be able to correct every miscataloged book; in the records for our 11 million holdings, there will still be cataloging errors, incomplete records, or (shudder) no record at all. But the cataloging geek in me still enjoys the feeling that when I've completed a record, I at least know that when/if patrons look for it, they will be able to find it.

One rainy afternoon, I happened upon a book that stood out amidst all of the others I'd worked on that day: it was a new encyclopedia edited by Peter B. Clarke.[1] Its classification immediately set me on edge: first, the record was inaccurately classified; secondly, it triggered my sense of unfairness, pushing all of my buttons. This book required much more help than I could give it, because it needed more than just a shiny new MARC record.

As I perused the book's bibliographical record (created by UKM/The British Library), I checked the classification number (standard practice for CCs for all records exported from Connexion), and ... I didn't like it. The record was created by the British Library, and the number it had assigned to the book was (and still is, as of this writing) 200.9034: 19th-Century Religion. Yet, the Subject Added Entry field (650) did not contain a subfield for chronology ($y). I looked through the text and found various religions, scripture, subcultures, and movements, from I Ching, to Baha'i, to Scientology. Clearly, the scope of this book covers much more than popular religions in the nineteenth century. Of course, when classifying records that discuss historical time periods, many catalogers will often default to the earliest period in the work. Yet many of the religious movements and societies in Clarke's text draw upon roots prior to the nineteenth century; thus, I already knew I was going to use a different Dewey number for my library's catalog. Then something struck me, and I looked at the bibliographical record again.

The record contained only one 650 field. Clarke's book, in which he attempts to "convey all the variations and variety of the New Religious Movements that now exist" (vi), was designated only one subject heading: CULTS—ENCYCLOPEDIAS. Admittedly, I was stung by the very word "cults." "New Religious Movements" and "cults" are not — at least in my mind — always analogous. Using only this subject heading seemed inexcusably myopic to me. From just the cursory attention I'd paid to this book, I knew that CULTS would not serve to cover even an eighth of its subject matter. I began looking through the index and scanning the encyclopedia more thoroughly. Clarke's book does indeed contain information on what many, including me, would consider cults: the Unification Church (a.k.a. Moonies); the Branch Davidians; Heaven's Gate; and so on. Clarke also discusses other groups that precariously straddle the fence: Scientology (Church of Scientology), Identity Movement (a.k.a. Christian Identity), Opus Dei, etc. But Clarke also discusses the history of various religious, political, and social movements for which the term "cult" would not even be considered by many in our culture: the Nation of Islam, vegetarianism, the Findhorn Community, Glastonbury, Soka Gakkai (Value Creation), Wicca, Church of Satan, etc. A quick perusal of the text will affirm that including CULTS as a heading is certainly applicable. But to assign *only* this contentious term to a book as complex, comprehensive, and inclusive as Clarke's encyclopedia is doing *all* of the entries a huge disservice.

It is certainly true that anyone reading this essay could present legitimate arguments against my designations for the various groups in the above paragraph, but this further illustrates my point. "Cult" as a descriptive term is powerful and controversial, necessary *and* insufficient. My complaint is not that the Library of Congress offers the heading CULTS for new religious movements; my complaint is that it does not take into account the negative connotations the term "cult" carries, or the limitations it manifests for catalogers.

Admittedly, movements outside of the mainstream (and some within)— whether political, religious, or social — will inevitably be considered somewhere, by somebody, as cults. An Internet search of "Mormonism + cult" results in thousands of entries that expound upon the "evils" of the Latter-day Saints, but I do not think that we would find consensus for this opinion from Mormons themselves. I seriously doubt that members of the Findhorn Community consider themselves cultists. Neither do, for that matter, Taoists, vegetarians, or Wiccans. Yet all of these can be found in Clarke's encyclopedia.

Technically, in the purest definition of the word, "cult" simply means a group of people whose beliefs or adopted customs are outside of the mainstream. The word comes from the Latin *cultus,* meaning "adoration," and it is within this context that the Catholic Church refers to its Cult of the Virgin or Cult of St. John. But most often, modern usage of the word "cult," when applied toward a group of people, carries an unfavorable impression. The word is loaded — whether fairly or not — with negative and destructive connotations. Thus, we're led to the question: why was Clarke's text *solely* classified under the heading "Cults"? It is true that UKM records are often incomplete, perfunctory, and poorly constructed, but I'm not sure that in this case blame can be placed solely on the British Library's shoulders.

I searched for "cults" on ClassWeb, and found that we are instructed to enter "groups or movements whose system of religious beliefs or practices differs significantly from the major world religions" under this heading. According to InfoPlease, there are "twelve classical world religions." Does this mean that everything else should be classified as a cult? It seems that CULTS is to be used for ALTERNATIVE RELIGIOUS MOVEMENTS and NEW RELIGIONS, which are both cross-referenced in the authority record. So, because the term "new religious movements" is part of the book's title, and LC still considers these to be cults, whether or not they have, as Clarke says, "become or are in the process of becoming global religions" (vi), this encyclopedia was classified as a book about "cults," and nothing more, because there isn't any other available alternative.

Classifying all non-mainstream societies and cultures as "cults" unfairly marginalizes and devalues them. In my opinion, this needs to change. We should, at the very least, offer "New Movements" (for new secular movements) as a subject heading related term along with "Sects" (which fits well for new schisms in religious movements), especially for books like Clarke's that include both religious *and* secular movements. In a recent interview with Rory Litwin, LC's Barbara Tillett explained that the "general rule" in assigning subject headings is to "best summarize the overall contents of the work and provide access to its most important topics" (*Library Juice,* 9 Aug. 2006). Clarke's encyclopedia covers the history of new religious movements and societies throughout the world. With just this little bit of information regarding the text, I find it hard to believe that a cataloger would think that CULTS adequately describes the scope of this scholarly work. It is unreasonable to assume that someone looking for information on Baha'i, Buddhism, Taoism, or the Nation of Islam would consider CULTS (or SECTS, for that matter) as a subject heading search. The classification of this book has made it potentially inaccessible to the very people and religions it discusses, and has resigned its discovery to the serendipitous luck of the occasional shelf browser.

So how did I handle this book? A quick perusal of my library's OPAC gave me some ideas. The subject search CULTS produced hundreds of records, with some including RELIGIONS, RELIGION AND SOCIOLOGY, and RELIGION AND LAW along with CULTS AND SECTS. These books ranged from various societies within religious movements, to "global perspectives" regarding them, to "alternative spiritualities" in indigenous and pagan traditions. Unfortunately, as a graduate assistant, changing the subject headings was impossible, since I've not yet been trained in this (not to mention it's against the rules of my job). But I did change the Dewey Decimal number, and I hope that this will help with access for shelf browsers and call number searches.

The monograph in my hand was a second copy, and my concern (outside of my outrage regarding the classification) was that the call number was incorrect in that it limited the book to the 19th century only. Our History Library holds the first copy, so I wrote to Dennis Sears, the library operational assistant there, and explained the incorrect number. I also grumbled a little about the assignment of CULTS. To my gratification, he was also annoyed by the classification, saying that this is a perfect example of the "limits of LC Subject Headings." We decided to reclassify the books under 299.03: "Religions not provided for elsewhere/Encyclopedias." (Which brings me to the "ghetto" of the DDC 290s, which is completely off-topic for this essay, but is a matter that I will address in the future, trust me.) I will pause, however, to mention the LC number in the record: BL31 (encyclopedias of religion). This number is clear and proper, and we took it for our lead when deciding our own DDC classification.

Leaving the responsibility of designating what is and is not a cult to the cataloger's discretion is hazardous, but what other choice do we have? (Even I should acknowledge my biases regarding Scientology, Heaven's Gate, and Identity Movement.) More options in LC subject headings would help ameliorate our inevitable bias and enhance the detachment for which we all strive. I have no argument with including CULTS for Clarke's book, but to have *only* this heading shows a bias against subcultures in our society. Clearly, I wasn't the only one unsatisfied with the original classification, as sometime between my export and the writing of this essay, Duke University added SECTS to the record. This is an improvement; still, many of Clarke's entries do not fall under the definition of "sect": a dissenting or schismatic religious body; *especially*: one regarded as extreme or heretical.[2] The lack of options regarding new movements — both religious and otherwise — is frustrating and gives impressions of closed-mindedness or ignorance toward the nuanced realities of these varied communities.

My thanks to Dennis Sears, whose advice and assistance brought invaluable insight to this essay.

Notes

1. *Encyclopedia of New Religious Movements.* London: Routledge, 2006.
2. From *Merriam-Webster.*

Works Cited

Clarke, Peter B., ed. (2006). Introduction. *Encyclopedia of New Religious Movements.* London: Routledge, vi–xv.
"Major Religions of the World." (2006). *Infoplease.com.* Available: <http://www.infoplease.com/ipa/A0113529.html> (accessed 21 October 2006).
Litwin, Rory. 2006. "Interview with Barbara Tillett." *Library Juice,* 6 August 2006. Available: <http://library juicepress.com/blog/?p=115>.

(The English Word) That Dares
Not Seek Its Name

Carol Reid

With its strikingly muted black cover and provocatively lower-case lettering, Randall Kennedy in 2002 elegantly brought the N-word out of the Ivy-League closet. In *Nigger: The Strange Career of a Troublesome Word*, the Harvard professor argues that reflexive and selective "banning" and double standards may no longer be the way to go with this most infamous of words. He urges a clear-eyed, dispassionate view of its history and, more controversially, suggests that it will (and perhaps even should) continue to gain currency in a non-hateful way, among both blacks and whites. To that point, Christopher Hitchens penned an eloquent rebuttal, albeit as part of a generally good review, in *The Nation* ("Black Mischief," March 4, 2002).

Nigger was widely reviewed and discussed, and the author appeared on a number of television shows, including Bill Maher's *Politically Incorrect*. He also consulted on an episode of the Fox drama *Boston Public* based on the use of his book in a high school classroom. Obviously, it helped that Kennedy is black, but this did not prevent his coming under criticism from other African-Americans. According to Rick Rucker in *Newcity* magazine: "Columbia University prof (and MacArthur 'genius' award recipient) Patricia Williams wrote that 'seeing *nigger* floating abstractly on bookshelves ... makes me cringe.' Kennedy himself cites someone who referred to the title as 'vulgar marketing,' while distinguished Penn professor Houston Baker reportedly commented, 'I see no other reason to do this except to make money.'" (And yet I have to wonder what else one reasonably *could* call a book written on this topic.)

Kennedy had initially given it the subtitle *A Problem in American Culture*. Arguably, a bit of a clunker. Pantheon Books felt, moreover, that this might incline some readers to misinterpret the title as referring to black people themselves being "a problem" and called for a rewrite. Unfortunately, though, press releases and other publicity, plus the Library of Congress's prepublication catalog record, all contained the original wording. Google initially returned a great many hits with the first subtitle, but currently fewer than a dozen remain, compared with the close to 20,000 hits retrieved by the later one. (I chose to include a 246 field in our local record for "Prepublication title: Nigger: a problem in American culture," mainly just to chronicle this minor ironic dustup.)

In any event, the change appears to have been sensible, and the subsequent subtitle an improvement (I like the words *strange*— echoing Lady Day's *Strange Fruit*— and *troublesome*). But in some small way, this nervous editing and second-guessing seems to underscore the often too-careful scrupling the book was written to help dispel. If Pantheon Books wasn't ready for the word *Problem*, was LC ready for the problem of the N-word? Or had the time finally arrived to establish an authority heading for "Nigger (The English Word)"— cross-referenced, perhaps, with "The N Word"?

Literary warrant can comprise a single work, and it seems there might be others that could supply it in this case as well: *Household Words: Bloomers, Sucker, Bombshell, Scab, Nigger, Cyber* (2006); *Why Should I Be Called Nigger?* (2000); *The Use of Nigger in Mark Twain's Adventures of Huckleberry Finn* (1964); and *From Nigger to African American: Education and Critical Consciousness As Crucial Components to Positive Black Racial Label Development* (2003).

Over 500 records in OCLC have the word "nigger" in the title, and these speak to the black experience in a wide variety of ways. Some have argued that the Kennedy book is also largely concerned with racism in general or is just not "linguistic" enough to merit a new heading. But title and text tell us that descriptors like *Racism* and *Invective* are simply too broad; this is a work about a specific word. There are 290 monograph records in OCLC with *Fuck* in the title (again, not about the word per se), but in 1995 LC created the heading FUCK (THE ENGLISH WORD), based on Jesse Sheidlower's book *The F Word*, published by Random House that same year. In fact, there are 99 ... (THE ENGLISH WORD) headings in OCLC, including, notably enough, SPADE (THE ENGLISH WORD), which was warranted by the 2002 book *Call a Spade a Spade: From Classical Phrase to Racial Slur*.

The recent Michael Richards comedy club debacle proved that the N-word remains an explosive one often intricately tied to perceived and actual racism and — in certain cases, at least — still considered taboo. But, despite that fact, or more perhaps because of it, there is good reason to expect that literature addressing the etymology and ethnolinguistic aspects of this word will continue to be produced. LC should do its part to discriminate between the word itself and the racism associated with it by promptly establishing a heading for "Nigger (The English Word)." To delicately decline to do so is to damn with faint phrase.

Folk Art Terminology Revisited: Why It (Still) Matters

Joan M. Benedetti

In 1994, after working for eighteen years as the Museum Librarian at the Craft and Folk Art Museum in Los Angeles, I was asked to assist an editor of the *Art and Architecture Thesaurus* (a database maintained by the Getty Vocabularies Program) in clarifying an important area of art vocabulary. We had each been struggling independently to articulate and resolve practical problems that writers and researchers experience daily in describing art works by a wide range of artists often described as folk artists — and books, catalogs, and audiovisual materials about them and their work. As I indicated in a previous *Art Documentation* article,[1] a passionate debate on this topic had raged openly between scholars and collectors since at least 1977.[2]

As librarians and indexers know, establishing useful vocabulary is not just a matter of accurate naming. The words chosen should retrieve only the most relevant information in library catalogs and on the Internet.

Folk Art and the *AAT*

Making changes in the *Art and Architecture Thesaurus* (*AAT*) is not a simple matter, nor should it be. *AAT* editors work very hard to make sure that all terms accepted for inclusion are terms whose form and meanings have a certain level of scholarly acceptance. They must have what is called literary warrant. This means that they can be found in publications likely to be used by scholars working in the associated disciplines. The *AAT* is a scholar's tool and the *AAT* editor told me in 1994 that widespread popular understanding of terms such as "folk art" does not figure into consideration of literary warrant.

But the *AAT* is also a writer's and a librarian's tool that, when fully implemented and more widely used by book catalogers, will make it easier for anyone to find information about artists like Sanford Darling, Calvin and Ruby Black, Tressa Prisbrey, and Trapper John Ehn, even if one does not know their names and even if one is not sure whether to refer to them as "self-taught artists" or "outsider artists" or "folk artists."

Without the *AAT*, one can search for "folk art" in an index or a library catalog (or on Google) and pull up hundreds, if not thousands, of entries on every type of object that is not, in someone's opinion, "fine art." Or one will find terms that are wrong or objectionable, such as "primitive art" or "naïve art" (the *AAT* states unequivocally that "primitive art" is an outdated designation; they have not yet come to the same conclusion about "naïve art").[3] Sometimes one also fails to locate an item because the cataloger at the Library of Congress or the local library cataloger, overworked and underpaid, simply gave up and put aside the item one is seeking in a problem pile for lack of terminology that is both LC-authorized and appropriate.

Work on terminology is never easy, especially when the terms under consideration are both fluid and controversial. Because the controversy concerning "folk art" has been overheated for many years, it was only in 1995 that the *AAT* added scope notes (the notes in the *AAT* that give the usage parameters of a term) for "folk art," "outsider art," "naïve art," and "self-taught artists." In that year, a consensus about these terms was reached at the *AAT*; this effort was coordinated by Suzanne Warren, with input from me as well as the scholar Alan Jabbour (at that time the Director of the American Folklife Center in Washington, DC), and other writers on the topic whose works had been read, cited, and compared. Five years later, in 2000 (ironically just after the original version of the present article had gone to press), the *AAT* editors further revised "folk art" and "outsider art" to clarify the differences. Following are the *AAT* definitions as of this writing[4]:

Folk art: Refers to art and crafts that are produced in culturally cohesive communities or contexts, and guided by traditional rules or procedures. It includes paintings, ceramics, textiles, sculpture, and other art forms. It is generally distinct from "naïve art," which is created by those without formal training, but not necessarily within a cohesive cultural community. It is also distinct from "outsider art," which usually refers specifically to art created or collected according to a philosophy of avoidance of traditional training.

Naïve art: Refers to art created by non-professional artists or artisans who have not had formal training and are often self-taught. It typically displays the artist's poor grasp of anatomy and lacks mastery of conventional perspective and other hallmarks of trained artists. It includes painting and sculpture, embroidery, quilts, toys, ships' figureheads, decoys, painted targets, and other objects, and often refers to such objects created specifically in nineteenth- and twentieth-century Europe and North America. It is generally distinguished from "outsider art," which includes the more extravagant psychotic drawings and other art created or collected according to a philosophy of avoidance of, rather than simply a lack of, traditional training. It is also usually distinct from "folk art," which is created according to specific cultural traditions.

Outsider art: Refers to art created or collected according to a philosophy of avoidance of the conventional fine art tradition. The concept generally refers to art that fits the ideal described by Jean Dubuffet, who posited that art should be inventive, nonconformist, unprocessed, spontaneous, insulated from all social and cultural influences, "brut," created without thought of financial gain or public recognition, and based upon autonomous inspiration, in direct contrast to the stereotypes of the traditional or official artistic culture. Dubuffet sought such art in the work of psychiatric patients and other insulated individuals. It is generally distinct from "naïve art," which is created by those without formal training, but not necessarily in accordance with the principles described above. It is also typically distinct from "folk art," which is made according to the rules and traditions of a particular culture.

Self-taught artists: Artists with no formal training who create in order to express an often intense and very personal vision or aesthetic, and whose work is usually unmediated by the standards, traditions, and practices of the culture of the art world, as embodied by the international art markets and established art institutions.

One might infer from the above that self-taught artists make outsider art. In fact, in the full *AAT* records for these two terms, "outsider art" is listed as a related concept under "self-taught artists," and "self-taught artists" (along with "folk art" and "naïve art") is listed as a related concept under "outsider art." If "outsider art" is done by "self-taught artists," is "outsider art" the same as "self-taught art"? "Self-taught art" is listed by the *AAT* as an alternative, though not preferred, American English term under "outsider art."

The *AAT* is grammatically correct in preferring "outsider art" to "self-taught art." By sanctioning "self-taught artists," but not "self-taught art," the *AAT* avoids the grammatical error of describing the art, rather than the artist, as self-taught. By sanctioning outsider art, but not "outsider artist," the *AAT* avoids characterizing certain people as outsiders. However, if an individual writer or cataloger would rather use the term "self-taught" instead of "outsider," the *AAT* provides only a preferred name for the artist, not her art — unless "outsider" and "self-taught" are interchangeable. Similarly, we have a name for what is considered outsider art, but how do we describe the artist who makes it? In my opinion, both "outsider art" and "outsider artist," even if value-neutral (which they are not), are not general enough to include all the types of art produced by self-taught artists. The sanctioning of "naïve art" as a sort of benign subset of "outsider art" (while avoiding the characterization of some artists as naïve) seems somewhat jejune.

Technology can be a problem here as well. Even if one's institution allows its catalogers to use *AAT* as well as LC terms, one's OPAC software may not find "self-taught artists" if "self-taught art" is input, and vice versa.

One will still find all the above terms in use by writers. However, in the past decade there has been a noticeable increase in the frequency with which one sees "self-taught" in print and a decrease in the use of "outsider art." In a call for papers for a conference on self-taught artists held at the John Michael Kohler Art Center in May 2000, no other term except "self-taught artists" was used, or even referred to, in the entire four-page announcement. Hardly anyone uses "primitive" anymore, but "folk art" is still in popular usage to describe both self-taught and community-taught or culturally traditional art. Why are these terms controversial? Do they mean the same thing?

The (Folk) Art Game from the Margins

First, let's look at the term "folk art." "Folk art" has been used to describe almost anything handmade, almost anything made by people who have never been to art school, almost anything old-timey or traditional or that looks old-timey or traditional to the individual viewer. It is, therefore, controversial for this very reason: its meaning becomes diluted as it is used equally to describe American quilts made in China and sold through the Sears catalog, twig furniture made by an Otis College of Art and Design graduate in Mendocino, California, and paintings made by elderly artists from childhood memories. What do the above have in common? Virtually nothing other than being promoted as kinds of folk art.

The controversy is even more complicated than that. My years at the Craft and Folk Art Museum (1976–1997) gave me the unusual opportunity of seeing the broadest range of materials on, over, and off the margins of fine art. The Craft and Folk Art Museum exhibited the culturally cohesive as well as the culturally unmediated and collected fine contemporary craft, product design, and both kinds of folk art from all over the world. Yet, for most of that time, our constituency was relatively small vis-à-vis the art world as a whole.

At establishment institutions, there were occasional exhibitions of contemporary craft or folk art, but mostly they were of the small, short-run variety. Textile, ceramic, glass, and furniture collections in encyclopedic museums were primarily accommodated within decorative arts departments, often housed in basement galleries or spaces far removed from the main attractions of painting and sculpture. Painting and sculpture, however they were defined, were undeniably fine art and an art work was much more likely to enter a museum collection if it looked like what one would expect to see in a painting or sculpture gallery.

The fine art exhibition game has had rules, the principal one being the need for a fine art object to have no non-art function. Occasionally chairs and cups displaying parody or other commentary could come in the back door, especially if a bona fide artist — preferably young, white, and male — had made them. If an object met all the above criteria, but had the misfortune to be made of one of the craft media, especially glass, clay, or fiber, it almost always went immediately to "dec arts" or was relegated to "outer Siberia" — the local slide registry. (A notable exception is work by Kenneth Price.) If the artist was a woman, especially a woman of color, the rules of the game were clear: quit the game or go directly to jail; do not pass go, etc.

Of course, there are fine specialized museums that have shown only contemporary craft, or only folk art, or only design. Victims of art apartheid have important ceramic, glass, and currently even "visionary art" museums providing sanctuary. But venues where one could, over a period of time, hope to survey the art of the real whole world are still very rare and are usually too small to actually reflect their entire scope in their galleries at any one time. The only time the Craft and Folk Art Museum collection was all on view at one time was in the auction gallery just before it was all sold off in 1998.[5]

Participants eligible to play the fine art game are, of course, mostly graduates of art schools. What are one's chances if one is a folk artist? However folk artists are defined, they are clearly outside of the fine art game.

For these and other reasons, few people describe themselves as folk artists. Though we may like to think of ourselves as "just folks," the term "folk artist" is generally used by some people (e.g., curators or art dealers) to describe other people. (Howard Finster

James "Jack" Poppitz, *America Don't!* (American, 1997?). Scrap lumber, paint. 20" × 36". Collection of Robert and Joan Benedetti.

was an exception. Finster Folk Art, Inc. even has its own Web site at <http://www. finster.com>.) When artists use the term "folk art" to describe their own work, what do they mean? Usually, they are referring to a style that is self-consciously childlike or crude in some way.[6] In contrast, folk art in the sense of culturally cohesive art is often sophisticated, highly finished, and complex in meaning and form. Just look at Acoma pottery or Japanese textiles.

Folk art in all of its manifestations has continued to grow in popularity and dollar value, so it is not surprising that it is being appropriated by a wider market. I found the term recently in a mail-order catalog describing eccentric hand-painted things that were not very good knock-offs of another art world phenomenon, artist-made furniture or "functional art."

Outside of What?

"Outsider art," as I've already indicated, is problematic at best. Outside of what? Would artists commonly referred to as outsiders describe themselves that way? Works called "outsider" are certainly unconventional, outside the mainstream (another euphemism). As such, they are exciting to art world insiders and they are often emotionally evocative as well. Sometimes they turn out to be the work of people who have been institutionalized, either in prison or mental institutions — about as outside (or maybe we should say as inside) as you can get. The term art brut is sometimes used interchangeably with "outsider art," but the artist/collector Jean Dubuffet (who coined the term art brut and who, over forty years, created the Collection de l'Art Brut in Lausanne), used art brut primarily to apply to the work of institutionalized schizophrenics.[7] "Self-taught" is a more inclusive term than "outsider."

The Problem with Anonymous

For a long time, people who wrote about folk art described one of its characteristics as being anonymous. But what is most often meant when we see "Anon." instead of an artist's name on an object label is simply that the curator or dealer does not know the name of the artist. Somewhere along the line, the fact that many works labeled "folk art" were made by unidentified artists got mixed up with another unrelated fact: in some cultures, makers of things are not encouraged to promote themselves as artists in the Euro-Western sense. This sublimation of the maker's identity can have several causes. In some cases, it is because community values are stronger than individual values. In other cases, it is because the object being called art or folk art by Euro-Western viewers is so bound up in the everyday routine of the maker's culture that it has no specialness for his or her community. Or, the opposite may be true: items may have sacred value and may have been made by religious leaders or healers who serve a communal function.

Euro-Western dealers, curators, or museum viewers may see in sacred objects similarities to what they call art, but their view is an outsider's (!) view in terms of the culture from which the object came. To the object's maker and the community from which it came, these religious objects may have a completely different value that honors the community and

Olga Ponce Furginson, *Folk Treasures of Mexico 1991* (Mexican American, 1991). Papel picado (cut paper). 13½" × 16". Collection of Robert and Joan Benedetti.

not the individual priest or shaman. To take them out of their community context and place them in an art context may honor them in the outsider-viewer's eyes, but in the eyes of the maker's community, the lack of context may have exactly the opposite effect.

Application of any art world terminology to objects produced outside of the art world tends to co-opt the objects thus named, making them part of the Euro-Western art market culture and distorting, rather than aiding, our understanding of them or their makers. The term "anonymous" may carry the implication that the maker wanted to remain unknown, which may or may not be the case. If an artist is actually *unknown*, the object label should say so, and every effort should be made to at least identify his or her community.

Market Exploitation and Other Power Struggles

The potential for market exploitation of outsiders by art world insiders is the greatest source of controversy. Whether or not exploitation is thought to happen more in the world of folk art collecting and exhibiting than in the mostly Euro-Western mainstream art world depends in part on how broadly folk art is defined. Once one realizes that within the art world establishment makers of folk art are all outsiders, taking the next logical step and acknowledging the power relationship that this represents is less difficult. The seriousness and prevalence of exploitative practices is a hotly debated topic, and is beyond the scope of this essay. That larcenous exploitation of both cultural groups and self-taught artists happens in direct relationship to the rise in market value of their art is obvious. That, nevertheless, some folk art makers successfully participate in the market as individuals and as cultural groups is equally without question. As noted above, some genuine self-taught artists, such as Howard Finster in Georgia, were famous self-promoters.[8]

Self-promotion is especially an issue for those who consciously or unconsciously perpetuate the romantic myth of folk art as a product of isolated innocence. Could collectors' well-documented resistance to both accepting a cultural definition for folk art and to accepting that folk artists and their communities (like most people today) are multicultural, operating simultaneously both inside and outside mainstream society, be a power issue? If only people who are outside the art market value system make folk art, and especially if they are seen as naïve or childlike, then it is easier to justify their non-inclusion in the economic rewards of that system.

When the standard of cultural cohesiveness and community value is used to define folk art, it can include many cultural groups. For example, Native Americans practicing traditional art forms are beginning to participate more actively in the market and attempting to control the unauthorized use of their tribal names and cultural symbols. Part of this latter effort is manifested in the rise of community and tribal museums that can control the information and context of objects displayed.

The Power of Museums

After the internal debates of the last decade, Euro-Western museums are beginning to acknowledge the powerful role they play in the art market and are starting to include in the exhibition planning process those communities whose cultural objects are being shown.

This struggle for equity in museums has only begun. Terminology is not more important than behavior. We all know the meaning of the phrase "He can talk the talk, but can he walk the walk?" Who talks and who listens is as important as what is said. But language influences our preconceptions and can be used to either assist understanding or aggravate mistrust. Museums are learning that they can promote understanding through language, not only in exhibition catalogs and label copy, but in publicity releases and in docent talks as well. Why should our library catalogs be exempt?

Eugene W. Metcalf, Jr., who together with collector and sculptor Michael D. Hall edited a collection of essays called *The Artist Outsider,*[9] served on an advisory board at the Craft and Folk Art Museum that helped to establish an adjunct library program we called the Center for the Study of Art and Culture (CSAC). In its short life (1989–1994), CSAC actively promoted diversity and inclusion in museums in several public programs.[10]

Metcalf and Hall's book is a kind of intellectual Trojan horse. It functions both as compilation of the history of interest by the established art world in self-taught artists as well as a critique and record of the highly contradictory ways other constituencies (folklorists, for example) are thinking about this and other art on the margins.

One of the editors and contributors, Roger Cardinal, is credited with having invented the term "outsider art."[11] According to contributor historian Kenneth L. Ames, however, "We probably need to get rid of the whole idea of outsider art. It does more harm than good."[12] Folklorist Michael Owen Jones feels that "a different picture would emerge in exhibits and publications if more collectors and curators really got inside the art of outsiders. An *emic* or insider approach would reveal that much of [all] people's behavior is traditional.... Instead of a collection of oddities by those who are abnormal, the art of outsiders is really a window onto what makes us human, including the need for tradition and the urge to create aesthetic forms in our everyday lives."[13]

Museums have a special responsibility for clarity in these matters. According to Gene Metcalf, "Museums ... cannot avoid the struggle, the political struggle that emerges when you talk about the nature of art in culture ... Who determines the display? Curators, consultants,

Artist unknown, *Tree of Life*. Candelabra (Mexico, State of Puebla, 20th C.). Ceramic, black glaze. 14" × 7". Collection of Robert and Joan Benedetti.

the makers of the objects, the public, or who? Where is the display? Who is it made for? We have to accept that when we interpret objects, we're also interpreting people."[14]

How we make and view art is significantly affected by how we are taught and by the communities in which we learn. The word "community" in this context means the different kinds of groups that teach us, not just the community where we grew up, but also other groups that influence us, that share some common interest. In this culturally diverse and free society, we often enrich our cultural habits by participating in different cultures where we work, play, pray, or go to school.

The Power of Art School

One of the most significant cultural immersions we can have is to go to school beyond high school, especially if we do it full time, and especially if it is related to a potential vocation. After we have been to law, business, medical, library, or art school, it is hard to see the world the way we did before we had that experience. Even if we have gone to an art school with a reputation for being open or progressive, we inevitably have picked up the dominant culture of that art school, which is invariably proactively or reactively influenced by the prevailing art world culture. Professional schools, after all, are expected to prepare their students to operate successfully within the predominant professional culture. This function is coded more in art schools than in business schools, but students will probably consider it a very useful part of their training.

Mainstream contemporary art is now very diverse, but certain cultural values have not changed in Euro-Western art schools in a very long time. A value of very long standing is of the artist as "maverick," as "poet," as "outsider." My sense is that people who are wed to the outsider idea are often also wed to the concept of artists as being necessarily social mavericks. This latter concept may work within the international art market and established art institutions, but increasingly, the Euro-Western art world has to rethink these categories, including that of the "great artist."[15]

Although art schools are today attempting to expose their students to the values of people who may have a more integrated relationship to their expressive culture,[16] the Euro-Western idea of the artist as primarily an inventor, as a contributor of new ideas, as someone who is special for this reason, is still predominant in art schools and in the larger society. This value, which happens to be compatible with the historic, political, and economic values of this country, contributed a great deal to the development of interest in collecting American folk art earlier in this century and, not by chance, coincided with the establishment of the first museums of modern art by some of the same collectors.[17]

Lynda Hartigan, a former curator at the National Museum of American Art, described the history of folk art collecting, including the work of self-taught artists, in her important essay in the catalog of the Herbert Hemphill collection at the NMAA.[18] She notes that the first folk art objects collected in the late 1920s tended to be the work of itinerant portrait painters, ladies' handiwork such as hair wreaths and mourning pictures, or weathervanes and antique tools. These objects were culturally traditional or functional items. Collecting simple tools, advertising signs, architectural elements, or furniture and displaying them as sculpture seemed in the same spirit as the modernists' "found objects." In fact, some of the first folk art collectors were modernist painters.

Later, in the 1950s and 1960s, during the height of interest in American abstract expressionism, a more idiosyncratic kind of folk art became fashionable. Although the makers of this art were called folk artists because they had not been to art school, their art had more in common with Dubuffet's *art brut*. These artists had not been taught by cultural tradition. They were self-taught. The irony for those who believe the most important value art schools teach is independence of thought[19] is that the works of self-taught artists seem to express an even more radical break with convention.[20]

Often described as visionary,[21] these artists seem to come from a wholly different perspective that gives rise to the concept of outsiderness. I believe that this is partially because self-taught artists are not immersed in art school values. Art schools may articulate independence as an essential value, but invariably turn out graduates who have values in common that are recognizable at some level in their artwork. This is not necessarily good or bad. It is the inevitable expressive outcome of any group's learning/working experience.

My point is that communal learning experiences, whether as part of a family, an ethnic group, or an art school, all leave a distinctive cultural imprint. If one does not attend art school, one's work will express other (personal and cultural) experiences unfiltered by the art school experience. If one has been taught by, and identifies very strongly with, a particular cultural community, one's work will show evidence of that tradition. Art school will overlay another filter over any other cultural experience, not canceling out what came before, but modifying it and adding other, usually identifiable aspects.

The Power of Words and Their Importance in Our Profession

In popular usage, the term "folk art" continues to be used for almost any expressive work done outside the sphere of influence of art or design schools. This is what Holger

Howard Finster. *At the Sound of His Trumpet* (American, 1997). Painted plywood. 12" × 50". Collection of Robert and Joan Benedetti.

Cahill meant when he called the exhibition of folk art he mounted at the Museum of Modern Art in 1932 *American Folk Art: The Art of the Common Man in America, 1750–1900*.[22] For the most part, objects collected by Cahill and the other first-generation folk art collectors were culturally traditional objects; their makers were culturally taught, not self-taught.[23] With some notable exceptions,[24] folklorists have also used the term "folk art" in a way that excludes what is self-taught. Focusing on the cultural context of the objects, they use "folk art" to describe the visual (or material culture) equivalent of folklore, which describes the oral traditions of a particular cultural group. "Folklife" is now commonly used to describe all of the expressive behavior of a particular culture, including folk music, folk dance, folklore, and folk art.[25] At the Craft and Folk Art Museum, the term "folk art" was used in this latter sense in order to distinguish between culturally taught and self-taught expressions. That is how the *Art and Architecture Thesaurus* defines it as well. But the popular sense of "folk art" as an umbrella term to describe the art of the common [wo]man will undoubtedly continue. After thinking about the issue for at least three decades, I now believe it would be useful for this related, popular meaning of the term to be acknowledged in the scope note by the *AAT*. I don't believe it would detract from the current preferred definition, which is useful to scholars, collectors, and librarians.

I believe that librarians and curators, who use words so much, should take this widespread confusion into account when cataloging, writing, and talking about this material. There are relatively few folk art specialists within the art history or folklore disciplines. Folk art is a subject about which many non-specialists, both lay people and scholars outside of folk art studies, wrongly assume a level of common understanding, not realizing the extent of the subject's complexity.

One thing is certain: both the popular and scholarly meanings of these words are still evolving. The controversy is still heated because our ideas about people and society are changing more rapidly than our ability to find words to express our new ways of seeing the world. Words are powerful because they reflect people's relative positions of power, their points of view, their ideas, and their feelings. "Sticks and stones will break my bones, but words can never hurt me," is not true. Carelessly used words can hurt people's feelings and prevent them from participating constructively in society, or they can lead to self-destructive behavior. The inaccurate use of words is not only counterproductive, it can damage cultural communities, which hurts us all indirectly. As an art librarian and as a person living in the world today, I have been concerned about these issues in my work and in my life.

Notes

1. See "Who are the folk in folk art?: inside and outside the cultural context," *Art Documentation* 6, no. 1 (Spring 1987), 3–8. The original version of the present essay was written as a lecture given for the Contemporary Arts Forum in Santa Barbara in conjunction with its 1995 exhibition *Visions from the Left Coast: California Self-Taught Artists*. It was published as "Words, Words, Words: Folk Art Terminology — Why It (Still) Matters," *Art Documentation* 19, no. 1 (Spring 2000).

2. Kenneth Ames' book *Beyond Necessity: Art in the Folk Tradition* (Winterthur, DE: Winterthur Museum, 1977) was published in conjunction with an exhibition of the same name, which occasioned a conference on

folk art at the Winterthur Museum. Curators, scholars, and collectors were invited, and the last-named group especially took exception to Ames' critique of the application of fine art principles to folk art.

3. According to Patricia Harpring, Managing Editor, Getty Vocabulary Program, "We will not categorize 'naïve art' as outdated, because major museums still use it in the sense defined in the AAT. See for example the NGA site, where one of the styles ('school' on their Web page) for which one can search is 'naïve art' at <http://www.nga.gov/collection/srchexpd.shtm>. It was in fact repeated requests from museum curators and other users who brought to our attention the problem with the AAT's original conflation of 'naïve art' and 'outsider art.' They needed separate terms to disambiguate the style of— for example — the anonymous itinerant early American portraitist Beardsley Limner from Dubuffet." (E-mail to author, December 11, 2006.)

4. *The Art and Architecture Thesaurus Online,* one of the Getty Vocabularies, a project of the J. Paul Getty Trust. Available: <http://www.getty.edu/research/conducting_research/vocabularies/aat> (accessed January 6, 2007).

5. The Craft and Folk Art Museum closed for sixteen months at the end of 1997, reopening in April 1999 in partnership with the City of Los Angeles Department of Cultural Affairs.

6. The folk art collector and ex-painter Herbert Hemphill coined the phrase "faux naïve" to describe his own forays into this painting style. See Lynda Roscoe Hartigan, *Made with Passion* (Washington, D.C.: Smithsonian Institution Press, 1990), 6.

7. The art collection that originally inspired Dubuffet is described in *The Prinzhorn Collection: Selected Work from the Prinzhorn Collection of the Art of the Mentally Ill* (Champaign: University of Illinois Press, 1984). See also "Art Brut and Psychiatry," by Dr. Leo Navratil, founder of the House of Artists at the Gugging Psychiatric Hospital, Lausanne, Switzerland, in *Raw Vision* 15 (Summer 1996), 40–47. A photograph of the artist-residents in front of the House of Artists is featured on the cover. According to Navratil, "Dubuffet stressed that the typical Art Brut artist creates his art for himself, not for others." He relates the story by Michel Thevoz of a seventy-five-year-old woman who knit beautiful pictures, but refused an exhibition of her work because she always unraveled everything she knitted so the wool could be reused.

8. The artist Howard Finster is possibly the best-known self-described folk artist to date. He appeared on the Johnny Carson show and a drawing of his was used on the cover of a Talking Heads album. He died in 2001, and his family continues to sell his work and the work of his children at his former Georgia home, "The Garden of Earthly Paradise," and on his web site, <www.finster.com>.

9. Michael D. Hall and Eugene W. Metcalf, Jr., with Roger Cardinal, eds., *The Artist Outsider: Creativity and the Boundaries of Culture* (Washington, D.C.: Smithsonian Institution Press, 1994).

10. I owe a great deal of my present thinking to Gene Metcalf, John Vlach, and others who served on the center's Advisory Board.

11. Roger Cardinal, *Outsider Art* (London: Studio Vista, 1972).

12. *The Artist Outsider,* 270–271.

13. *The Artist Outsider,* 327–328. Both Ames and Jones were on the CSAC Advisory Board, as was Toni Peterson, a cofounder of the *AAT.*

14. "Proceedings of the First Meeting of the National Advisory Board," December 6, 1990 (Los Angeles, CA: Craft and Folk Art Museum, Center for the Study of Art and Culture, 1990). Photocopy.

15. Joanne Cubbs' essay "The Romantic Artist Outsider," in *The Artist Outsider,* 76–93, reveals the romantic fallacy of these ideas. She makes the interesting point that "the outsider myth is primarily a heroic male text" (see page 91, note 2).

16. Cross-cultural exposure was part of the California Institute of the Arts idea from its beginning in 1970, with ethnomusicologist Nicholas England, former dean of the Music School, and Ghanian musicians Alfred and Kobla Ladzekpo on the original faculty. Steven Lavine, CalArts president since 1988, has further institutionalized the concept by creating several intercultural programs that place CalArts students in community organizations. These programs provide arts training for high school students throughout Los Angeles. Lavine co-edited with anthropologist Ivan Karp *Exhibiting Cultures: The Poetics and Politics of Museum Display* (Washington, D.C.: Smithsonian Institution Press, 1991) and *Museums and Communities: The Politics of Public Culture* (Washington, D.C.: Smithsonian Institution Press, 1992).

17. For example, both Abby Aldrich Rockefeller, who founded the Museum of Modern Art, and Gertrude Vanderbilt Whitney, the founder of the Whitney Museum of American Art, had large folk art collections.

18. Lynda Hartigan, *Made with Passion.* For a historical overview (and a virtual who's who and who was who) of twentieth-century American folk art and self-taught art collecting, see the curator's lively seventy-page biographical essay on Herbert Hemphill, her equally lively notes, and the catalog's excellent bibliography (which serves as a checklist for the basic documents on the subject). The essay itself, with the addition of material on the western United States, could serve as the primary text for a course in the history of collecting self-taught art.

19. Another irony is that this work, along with other kinds of folk art and crafts, began to be taken seriously by the art world only when it was presented in a typical art gallery environment: "neutral ... white walls, pedestals, and spotlights" [*Made with Passion*, 28]. According to Lynda Hartigan, "Artists spearheaded the first folk art rush ... [and] artists were generators of the second wave ... during the late 1960s.... Based in New York, the first group had championed modernism.... Spread throughout the country, the second group ... embraced contemporary folk art ["contemporary folk art" is a euphemism for the work of self-taught artists] because it reinforced the latter's search for individuality" [*Made with Passion*, 39–40].

20. Along with M.O. Jones (quoted above), Lynda Hartigan points out that this is not always the case (*Made with Passion*, 80, note 159); just because something seems different or eccentric within the viewer's frame of reference does not make it so within the artist's community. When we place a high value on what we perceive as eccentric, we must understand that this is a relative value.

21. The American Visionary Museum in Baltimore is an example of the popularity of this particular synonym for "self-taught." Others include the publications *Visions from the Left Coast: California Self-Taught Artists* (Santa Barbara, CA: Santa Barbara Contemporary Arts Forum, 1995); *Naives and Visionaries* (New York: E.P. Dutton, 1974); *Howard Finster: Man of Visions* (New York: Alfred A. Knopf, 1989); and, especially, *Raw Vision: The New International Journal of Outsider Art* (subscription information: <http://www.rawvision.com>). Two other, more modest, publications for collectors of self-taught art deserve mention: *Folk Art Finder* (quarterly, now defunct; published from 1980 to 2000) and *Folk Art Messenger* (<http://www.folkart.org>). These two titles, as well as the American Folk Art Museum's journal, *Folk Art* (<http://www.folkartmuseum.org>), are prominent examples of the popular use of "folk art" as an umbrella term, although in practice they are all more focused on self-taught than traditional folk art.

22. "The work ... is folk art because it is the expression of the common people, made by them and intended for their use and enjoyment. It is not the expression of *professional* artists made for a small cultured class, and it has little to do with the fashionable art of its period. It does not come out of an academic tradition passed on by schools, but out of craft tradition plus the personal quality of the rare craftsman who is an artist" [Cahill, *American Folk Art*, 6]. This was the third in a series of folk art exhibitions mounted by Cahill and was drawn almost entirely from the collection of Abby Aldrich Rockefeller, who had just founded the Museum of Modern Art three years before. The two earlier shows, *American Primitives* (1930) and *American Folk Sculpture* (1931), were organized by Cahill at the Newark Museum under the influence of the progressive museum director John Cotton Dana. According to Cahill's biographer, John Vlach, "Dana believed that there was an art of everyday life that was as important as the art of high style civilization.... Cahill learned [from Dana] that the broader base of the social pyramid deserved more attention than it was getting" ["Holger Cahill As Folklorist," *Journal of American Folklore* 98 (April–June 1985): 153].

Cahill's three folk art exhibitions, together with the published version of his *Index of American Design*, edited by Erwin O. Christensen [New York: Macmillan, 1950], largely served — until the start of interest in self-taught art in the late 1960s — to embody in the popular imagination what is meant by "American folk art." The documented objects are principally Anglo-Saxon American, mostly from those states that were among the original colonies, and were made primarily from Revolutionary War times to the end of the nineteenth century. These were, of course, the items still available to Holger Cahill, his colleagues and friends, when they went "picking" in eastern seaboard antique stores and attics of the early twentieth century. See also Wendy Jeffers, "Holger Cahill and American Folk Art," *Antiques* 148, no. 3 (September 1995), 326–35.

Though Cahill has rightly been credited for making a place for the folk art of the earliest (primarily Anglo-Saxon) immigrant populations in American art museums, a less well known individual, Allen H. Eaton, working with the Russell Sage Foundation, was doing comparable work concerning more recent American immigrant folk art at exactly the same time. Eaton's book *Immigrant Gifts to American Life: Some Experiments in Appreciation of the Contributions of Our Foreign-Born Citizens to American Culture* [New York: Russell Sage Foundation, 1932], was published the same year that Cahill's *American Folk Art: The Art of the Common Man* was exhibited at the Museum of Modern Art. *Immigrant Gifts* describes Eaton's efforts (mostly in fairground settings and ethnic club exhibition halls) at organizing exhibitions of "arts and crafts of the homelands" during a period when the flood of immigration was drawing reactionary voices at least as shrill as those heard in the United States today. It is clear that the relative popularity and social acceptance of Cahill's work was largely a matter of the political context in which the two men worked.

23. There is continued confusion about "the possibility of genuine contemporary [folk] expression" [*Made with Passion*, 29]. In fact, as mentioned above in note 19, the term "contemporary folk art" has come to mean something completely different — it is a code phrase for self-taught folk art. Those who are interested in early American items in particular have difficulty accepting that culturally traditional folk art's parameters can include contemporary material, especially items whose cultural origins are mixed or aimed at the tourist market. Holger Cahill and his first-generation collecting peers thought that "the great period of American folk art covers about two hundred years, from the second quarter of the seventeenth century up to the

third quarter of the nineteenth" [*American Folk Art: The Art of the Common Man in America, 1750–1900* (New York: Museum of Modern Art, 1932), 8]. But a third generation of collectors and curators has a different point of view. The clearest manifestation of this viewpoint yet is in an exhibition that originated at the Museum of International Folk Art. See Charlene Cerny and Suzanne Seriff (eds.), *Recycled, Reseen: Folk Art from the Global Scrap Heap* (New York: Harry N. Abrams, 1996).

24. Michael Owen Jones, Professor of Folklore at UCLA, and Alan Jabbour, ex-director of the American Folklife Center in Washington, D.C., have taken centrist positions on this controversy, while others, such as John Vlach, Professor of Folklore at George Washington University in Washington, D.C., have sought to exclude self-taught artists completely from folk art studies. This exclusion is based on the grounds that, from the perspective of folkoric studies, the term "folk art" can by definition be applied only to objects that are the products of cultural communities. This is, of course a much more strict definition than what is in general use, especially in the popular consciousness, but for a museum or library that has to deal with both types of art, it is a very useful distinction.

25. A good definition of "folklife" is in the language of the 1976 American Folklife Preservation Act [P.L. 94–201]: "the traditional expressive culture shared within the various groups in the United States: familial, ethnic, occupational, religious, regional" [quoted in Mary Hufford's *American Folklife: A Commonwealth of Cultures* (Washington, D.C.: Library of Congress, American Folklife Center, 1992), 5].

Rearranging the Deck Chairs on the *Titanic*: A Drowning Cataloger's Call to Stop Churning the Subject Headings

Christopher H. Walker

The Library of Congress Subject Headings thesaurus (LCSH) is the largest and most nearly comprehensive subject thesaurus in the world, beyond the wildest ambition of the Medical Subject Headings (MeSH) thesaurus, the Sears thesaurus used in many school and some public libraries, the ERIC thesaurus of education terms, or the *Répertoire de vedettes-matière* maintained by Library and Archives Canada for French-language headings. It is promulgated by the Library of Congress, which maintains strict editorial control over the terms hallowed for inclusion, though institutions that are members of the Subject Authority Cooperative Program (SACO) can and do suggest additions and alterations. The Library of Congress Cataloging Policy and Support Office issues frequent bulletins (the *Cataloging Service Bulletin*) detailing:

(1) **New headings**, that have been forged so that adequate subject access can be assigned to materials being published about new topics; and
(2) **Changed headings**, where the established form is being altered.

Some of the heading changes are in pursuit of the ever-elusive goal of standardizing a tool that has grown in tiny increments over the best part of a century. Others reveal shifts of emphasis, worldview, and culture. Some are quite irritatingly arbitrary; others are concessions to fashion or to the dwindling size of the database of shared Western culture that used to underpin so many of our institutions.

New Headings

Study of the New Headings list can provide some insights into what society, or at least libraries and publishers, are interested in. The New Headings list is also one measure for tracking the transformation of slang and jargon into common or official use.

The addition of a new heading to the lexicon depends on two things. First, a publisher has to produce an item (generally a book) that would require a new subject heading before the bibliographic description could be considered adequate. Second, a conscientious cataloger has to recognize that the new heading is needed, and take the trouble to submit the new idea for consideration, rather than just trying to catch the new concept between the cross-hairs of two or more related ideas already represented by existing terms in the thesaurus. The book (or other material) that demonstrates the need for a new term is called the heading's "literary warrant."

Below are sample new headings from LCSH lists of the last two years. The list is far from complete; I excise the obvious, the boring, and the trivial.

New Headings That Point to Social and Cultural Change ... Or Not

In some instances surprise derives from the fact that the phenomenon newly assigned its own subject heading is as old as the hills, yet has seemingly only now attracted the attention of a book publisher and provided the literary warrant for a "new" heading. The following are all from New Headings lists within the last three years:

ALCOHOLIC FATHERS

BELLY DANCERS

CROSS-BORDER SHOPPING

ENDANGERED LANGUAGES

FAIRY GODMOTHERS

FAMILY SECRETS

FEAR OF DENTISTS (hmmm... perhaps what we felt before Spring 2006 was mere trepidation, not outright "fear"...)

FLIRTING

INSECT PHOBIA (They're supposedly harmonizing all the old headings, to impose greater consistency, right? Here's an example of why this laudable goal can never, ever be achieved: because new headings that are not in step follow on the heels of the old ones that have been changed. Why is it FEAR OF DENTISTS (note plural), but INSECT PHOBIA (note singular)? And do we prefer the common term "fear," or its ten-cent equivalent, "phobia"?)

MARSH ARABS (I think there have been marsh Arabs since the seventh century CE, but no one cared about them until now, I guess.)

MASCULINE BEAUTY (AESTHETICS) (I think masculine beauty was discovered by the Roman emperor Hadrian, if not before.)

MEXICAN AMERICAN MOTHERS

MUEZZINS

NEIGHBORS

REASONABLE DOUBT

SHEET MUSIC

STAFF MEETINGS (Wouldn't it be lovely if these were indeed only now being invented? Think of all the productive hours we could have spent doing actual work if there had been no staff meetings until 2006.)

WORKING CLASS MEN joined the lexicon in 2005, 20 years after the heading WORKING CLASS WOMEN. (Perhaps there's hope for Mexican American fathers, if they wait long enough.)

Before the Flowers of Friendship Faded, Friendship Faded

Another group of brand-new headings represent phenomena that have arrived, flourished, dwindled, and passed in real life, but that suddenly acquire an official subject heading, mysteriously added to the lexicon now that nearly all need for it is probably gone.

The classic case for this category was the new heading EX-NAZIS, which entered the thesaurus in 1995, after nearly all ex–Nazis were dead. From recent lists:

CAMP (STYLE) (This heading came along in Summer 2006, almost a decade after Charles Pierce died of old age.)

CONFEDERATE CEMETERIES

MAD SCIENTIST FILMS

NAVAJO CODE TALKERS

RECORD STORES

A heading was promulgated in Summer 2004 for UGLY CONTESTS, but let us hope that the phenomenon has already passed from the cultural scene.

The above group has a complementary parallel in the short list of headings that are actually withdrawn from the lexicon and not just left, rusting and disused, on the shelf. The heading YELLOW PERIL continued to be available (though, one hopes, no longer assigned) until 1989, connected to EASTERN QUESTION (which is still valid, though it lacks any scope note to guide catalogers or patrons as to its correct use) as a broader term.

Say Wha' ?????

Some new headings are annoying because they are *wrong or incomplete.* LC frequently gets slang wrong, and sometimes other things.

In Spring 2004 LC coined the heading DISCOURAGED WORKERS. Nearly all workers get discouraged by Friday afternoon at the latest, but that isn't what the heading is supposed to mean. The scope note confirms that what they were after is a term for unemployed people who stop job-hunting and drop off government statistical reports. "Job Seekers" or "Job Hunters" would have been better than "workers."

The Fall 2006 list gives MOORE'S LAW as a new heading, which is great; but wouldn't the heading have been improved by a cross-reference to the Moore, Gordon, for whom Moore's Law (a formula explaining the pace at which computing power divided by unit cost increases with technological advance) is named, and a 550 see-also reference to MOO-ERS'S LAW, with which it is frequently confused? It would have taken only a few minutes to write at the same time a new heading for MOOERS'S LAW (the principle that learners will not master new knowledge until the inconvenience of not knowing exceeds the cost of the effort and time to learn), with a cross-reference to Mooers, Calvin N. (already an established heading available in the file), preventing future trouble and confusion.

POSTNATAL EXERCISE appeared in Fall 2006; but surely, if we set aside those kooks who hold a radio up to Mommy's tummy to see if they can get a fetus to kick in the womb, *all* exercise is post-natal?

New Headings That Really Do Point to Social and Cultural Change

Other new headings describe and document genuinely new trends or features of life in the twenty-first century. Some are encouraging signs of progress. Others are signposts showing us headed over the nearest cliff. (We might not all agree as to which are which.)

ANTI-SWEATSHOP MOVEMENT

CHILD SUICIDE BOMBERS (MAY SUBD GEOG) (especially after they are blown to smithereens)

CIVIL UNIONS

COMPETITIVE EATING (I think they mean contests, as at fairs and festivals, rather than the effort to tear open care packages in Darfur before the aid organization runs out of bundles.)

COMPULSIVE WASHING

COMPUTER ANXIETY (it's listed as **May Subd Geog**, but I generally find that it fades if I go into the other room)

DEBT-FOR-NATURE SWAPS

ENERGY DRINKS

EX-GAY MOVEMENT

FATHERHOOD RESPONSIBILITY MOVEMENT

FLAVORED ALCOHOLIC BEVERAGES

FOR-PROFIT UNIVERSITIES AND COLLEGES

GAY CONSERVATIVES

GENERATION Y

HUMAN TRAFFICKING (MAY SUBD GEOG) (Wasn't this covered by SLAVE TRADE? The new heading has Use-from cross references from WHITE SLAVE TRAFFIC and WHITE SLAV-ERY. What gives? Is there no human trafficking, then, in persons of color? Wishful thinking, or outright racism?)

INTERNALIZED HOMOPHOBIA IN LESBIANS

ISLAMOPHOBIA

MAKEOVER TELEVISION PROGRAMS

ONLINE DATING

PERSONAL CONCIERGES

POST-RETIREMENT EMPLOYMENT

ROADSIDE MEMORIALS

SEXUAL REORIENTATION PROGRAMS (A sanitized form of heading. It would have been more straightforward to simply call the phenomenon GAY PEOPLE, PSYCHOLOGICAL TORTURE OF, because the established form seems to imply that there might be reciprocal "programs" to reorient heterosexuals into gay people — as if society would ever tolerate such a thing.)

STRAIGHT-EDGE CULTURE

SLACKERS (It took them awhile to get around to establishing this one.)

SLASHER FILMS

SPECIAL NEEDS OFFENDERS

SUDOKU

SUICIDE BY COP (What a lovely decade we're headed into.)

THOUGHT SUPPRESSION (DITTO.)

VIRAL MARKETING

WHEELCHAIR RUGBY (Well, a note of hope, or at least wholesome fun.)

There are, of course, innumerable new headings that have to do with computers and technology. These are seldom surprising or interesting, and are generally perfectly à propos.

PHISHING

SPAM FILTERING (ELECTRONIC MAIL)

A few headings are so specialized and specific that only someone who has already read or skimmed the book that provided the literary warrant for creating the subject heading could possibly guess what it means.

BUILDERING

EXCITED DELIRIUM SYNDROME (What the devil is that?)

HUMAN ZOOS (I remember a *Twilight Zone* episode about this, but surely most of you readers are too young to respond to the association there.)

KRUMPING

MUSIC AND PROBABILITY

NANODIAMONDS (Gnomes and gremlins give them to their itty-bitty fiancées, perhaps.)

POLKABILLY MUSIC (I live in the part of the world where entire radio stations are devoted to polkabilly music, but I bet the concept is new to many of you.)

SOIL NAILING

SLOW FOOD MOVEMENT

WRONG-WAY DRIVING (Of course I know what that is, but do we really need a heading for it?)

So much for new headings. Some are startling and some mundane, but we can all agree that at least some of them are needed, and welcome. What about changes to the headings we already have?

Heading Changes

Advocates for the current habit of churning over the established headings in order to make trivial changes that then have to be implemented in a search-and-replace snipe hunt through every English-language library catalog in the world will tell you without a wince of shame or apology that there is method to their madness. Barbara Tillett's interview with Rory Calhoun for *Library Juice* <http://libraryjuicepress.com/blog/?p=115> is one of the best places to collect the official program about this. Supposedly they are rewriting old headings in an effort to impose consistency on the forms of the headings and the structure of the thesaurus itself. Moving place or time period subdivisions into a more consistent pattern, for instance. Another mania: rewriting headings that were formerly inverted so that the word with news value came first on the card. They're hunting down and ironing those out, mostly, into natural word order. Example: LABOR, PREMATURE, changed to PREMATURE LABOR in December 2006. But God forbid they do anything, even that, in a consistent manner. This dominant change pattern hasn't stopped them from changing

> CAPE HORN and
> CAPE OF GOOD HOPE

to

> HORN, CAPE and
> GOOD HOPE, CAPE OF

(both in Summer 2006).

Compound Complex Running-in-Place, See: White Queen, Antics of

Other massive shifts occur when global edits are attempted to systematize orthography. They cannot leave hyphenated words alone, for example. They love to take the hyphen out of compound noun clusters. Paradoxically, however, they sometimes put a hyphen *into* clusters that never needed one before.

They put hyphens into all the headings for "middle-aged" this, that and the other (MIDDLE AGED WOMEN—LIFE SKILLS GUIDES became MIDDLE-AGED WOMEN—LIFE SKILLS GUIDES, etc.) and they added a hyphen to SHAPE(-)NOTE SINGING; but they took the hyphens out of ROLLER-SKATING and CLOVER-LEAF WEEVIL. Incidentally, there is no heading for MIDDLE-AGED MEN—LIFE SKILLS GUIDES, with or without hyphen. If men won't even ask for highway directions, they're certainly not going to consult a LIFE SKILLS GUIDE.

WET-NURSES became WET NURSES in Summer 2005, so it now covers both RNs who participate in t-shirt contests as well as surrogate breastfeeders. Breastfeeding lost the former space between the two words of the compound, in that same list, which was probably a good change.

In Fall 2006 they changed ALDER FLEA-BEETLE to ALDER FLEA BEETLE (three words);

but in the *very same headings change list* they made PARSNIP LEAF-MINER into PARSNIP LEAFMINER, closing up the gap between the words. Delightfully consistent. Not.

Early in 2006 they changed FLOWER POTS IN ART to FLOWERPOTS IN ART. (I had worried myself nearly into a frazzle over that little space, and I bet you had, too, hadn't you?)

The Spring 2006 list responded to overwhelming patron requests and changed

ABYSSINIAN EXPEDITION, 1867–1868 to
ABYSSINIAN EXPEDITION (1867–1868).

Then there's the maddening effort to re-systematize class nouns so that certain groups will always be plural, in the established heading, while others that were established in the plural form now (for reasons best known to the Cataloging Policy & Support Department) must be rewritten in the singular. They've been at this a long time. You'd think they'd be done. My valued colleague Lori Leatherman notes that when (in 1995) they changed BANANA to BANANAS, it drove her ... banana.

- PARSNIPS devolved into a single
  PARSNIP, in Fall 2006, while just three or four lines below *it in the very same list,*
- PHILODENDRON put out a fresh tendril and pluralized into
  PHILODENDRONS and, on the next page (I know the suspense is killing you, readers)
- SYCAMORE metastasized into SYCAMORES.
- BLOOD PHEASANTS was changed to
  BLOOD PHEASANT in Fall 2005 (There were two left, but Vice President Cheney shot one of them in the face on a hunting trip in Montana. There was no inquest.)
- The Summer 2006 list changed MASTODON to MASTODONS. (I thought they were extinct; how can they be multiplying?)
- SWASTIKA IN ART became SWASTIKAS IN ART
- CONGA (DRUM) became
  CONGAS. It's delightful that we have two of them now, but in the process of making this trivial change to the plural form, we've obscured the differentiation between the percussion instrument and the dance.
- LESBIAN COMMUNITIES became
  LESBIAN COMMUNITY toward the end of the George W. Bush administration. Maybe they are trying to herd all the lesbians into a single community so they'll be easier to round up and put in a
- HALLIBURTON-BUILT NO-BID-CONTRACT FEDERAL INTERNMENT CAMP (MAY SUBD GEOG). (Or is that Camps, plural?)

One wonders if they ran up and down the halls of the Library of Congress, shouting and exulting, when they found the harmless old heading TREASURE-TROVE, which "needed" to be made into TREASURE TROVES, changing both from singular to plural *and* having its hyphen surgically removed. The discovery must have produced EXCITED DELIRIUM SYNDROME.

Sometimes, though, discovery or possession is no longer nine points of the law. VON WILLIBRAND'S DISEASE became VON WILLIBRAND DISEASE in Fall 2006, while WILSON'S SNIPE went completely incognito as the COMMON SNIPE in the same list. (Wilson's patent ran out, maybe.) But this pattern, never fear, is as Tweedle-dum inconsistent as all the others. ALBERT SQUIRREL was recast as ALBERT'S SQUIRREL in Spring 2005.

How Much Is That Canis Lupus Familiaris in the Window?

The other broad category of heading changes (besides tinkering with the form) is supposedly to make the thesaurus more useful to patrons. Doesn't that sound like a good idea? Sure it does. The problem is that they can't seem to make up their minds which patrons to serve better. Some changes are in the direction of relying less on supposedly old-fashioned or erudite terms, replacing them with words from common parlance. Certainly examples come to mind pretty easily where such a change was appropriate and welcome. We all reached a point — generally long before LC recognized it — where a heading like NEGRO ATHLETES needed to be changed. These only raise a ruckus when the thesaurus squirms briefly on a new term and then changes again. Let's never revisit the difference between AFRO-AMERICAN and AFRICAN-AMERICAN, and if somebody on the committee starts worrying about that hyphen, hit him for all of us, ok? It would be courteous to acknowledge that numerous similar heading changes of this kind continue to be apposite, replacing cumbersome headings with headings that much better reflect common usage. Some of these doubtless actually assist patrons to find what they're looking for. Changing DRUGS—OVERDOSAGE to DRUGS—OVERDOSE was a good idea. Changing the subdivision—WEBLOGS to —BLOGS (Summer 2006) caught up with a universal shift in usage a little faster than LC's typical glacier-slow recognition of verbal obsolescence.

The movement toward common language terms, generally speaking, is the effort that Sanford Berman and his friends and associates urged on from outside LC, using the systematically reformed headings that were the hallmark of the Hennepin County Library catalog for years. Many of those headings were eventually adopted by the Library of Congress and promulgated as part of LCSH. You can identify a lot of those, in the national thesaurus, nowadays, by a 670 note in the heading that alludes to "Hennepin." Those headings are the work of Sandy Berman and his team. The story of how that reformist lexicon clashed, interacted, and was subsumed by LCSH is a well-worn tale that needn't be rehashed here. The movement to make the subject headings more user-friendly was a shared goal, to some extent, despite the frequent fireworks over specific proposals.

The trouble is that there is an equal and opposite trend at work, trying to make the English-language subject lexicon more ready to become the skeleton of an international system. This is also a rational goal. An international subject-term system, coded in such a way as to be machine-convertible to other languages, is a wonderful idea. Such a baseline thesaurus would enable efficient sharing of bibliographic records internationally. It would form a useful companion to the international effort to agree on the principles of bibliographic description currently embodied in the successive rollouts of discussion papers about functional requirements for bibliographic records (FRBR, which, incidentally, has yet to have an LCSH term established for it, despite the gallons of literary warrant ink poured out over it already). Scholars in ivory tower committee rooms are working on how to implement the concept.

But in the meantime one may question whether, for instance, all the changes from Linnaean taxonomic terms for flora and fauna to common English field names aren't moving the prospect of an internationally useful thesaurus further away? There may have been only one field of activity among all the fields of knowledge where almost every country used the same terms: biological nomenclature — and the gnomes at LC are well advanced on their program of stamping it out.

What a shame it was, during the 1990s, to watch glumly as the committee hunted down and exterminated all the—FAUNA and—FLORA from the thesaurus (they changed into plants and animals).

Further examples from the Summer and Fall 2006 lists:

* AILURUS FULGENS was changed to RED PANDA
* CONGRIDAE to CONGER EELS
* SCROFULARIA became FIGWORTS
* DERMACENTOR OCCIDENTALIS to PACIFIC COAST TICK
* AOTES TRIVIRGATUS became THREE-STRIPED NIGHT MONKEY (Note the hyphen, which perhaps someday they will come back and take out.)
* OREOSOMATIDAE became
  OREOS (FISH); note the plural form and the parenthetical qualifier meant to restore differentiation from the flagship cookie of the Nabisco product line. However, in the very same list,
* SMOOTH OREO DORY dropped the "dory" (whatever a dory is) and became simply SMOOTH OREO (Note singular form and lack of qualifier.)
* ZAPODIDAE became
  JUMPING MICE, which may be considered charming, but it required that
  ZAPODIDAE, FOSSIL become
  JUMPING MICE, FOSSIL, which seems just wrong. (Jumping fossils?)

Well, you can't make an omelet without breaking a few dinosaur eggs, maybe. All for the greater good. But, okay, in the *same week* in which they changed POSSODES SITCHENSIS to WHITE PINE WEEVIL, they changed SNOWBERRY to SYMPHORICARPOS, but they simultaneously changed SYMPHORICARPOS ROTUNDIFOLIUS to ROUNDLEAF SNOWBERRY. I am not making this up. The underlying rationale is evidently that plants with fat leaves should retain — or in this case, gain — Latin designations.

Excuse me. I need to go lie down for a moment in a darkened room, with a cold cloth over my eyes.

The Moving Finger Writes, and, Having Writ, Moves on

Some changes take official note of the fact that time marches on and history happens. In Fall 2006, MALAWI—POLITICS AND GOVERNMENT—1964- got split into

* MALAWI—POLITICS AND GOVERNMENT—1964–1994, and
* MALAWI—POLITICS AND GOVERNMENT—1994-.

Washington pundits take very little note, generally speaking, of Africa (look at Darfur); but, eventually they did notice that, Lion or no Lion, President Hastings Banda had fallen from power and was dead. It took them only twelve years.

Other changes, or lack of changes, reflect official U.S. government policy. The heading CYPRUS—POLITICS AND GOVERNMENT—1960– was split in Summer 2006 between:

- CYPRUS—POLITICS AND GOVERNMENT—1960–2004 and
- CYPRUS—POLITICS AND GOVERNMENT— 2004– because there were, of course, no fundamental changes or milestones in Cypriot politics and government between those years. No, there weren't. I said no, there weren't. I'm stuffing my fingers in my ears, I can't hear you!

Vernacularization vs. Gentrification

The most perplexingly schizoid category of subject heading changes is the push-me, pull-you efforts to, on the one hand, change supposedly stuffy old headings into more contemporary terms derived from natural speech, while simultaneously changing other headings from words used in common speech to gentrified terms or foreign words.

Examples of the former type abound. For instance, they decided in Summer 2004 that the word "aged" was getting, well, elderly. So they changed most instances of it to either "elderly" or "older." As they worked through the list they came to

- POOR AGED, and changed it to
- ELDERLY POOR. Fine, I guess. But seeing it in the list reminded me that in 1995 they changed the heading
- POOR AS CONSUMERS to
- LOW-INCOME CONSUMERS. I wondered at the time if that change signaled doom for the plain, unvarnished heading POOR, which has a see-from cross reference from LOW-INCOME PEOPLE. Jesus said, "The poor ye shall always have with you" (Mat. 26:11), but I knew that wouldn't necessarily protect them from LC. However, poor remains a valid heading as long as they're not buying anything. Or purchasing. Whichever. (See below.)

All that's just fine, and would be one sensible way (supposing one agreed with the general prospect of churning the headings at all) to make the official lexicon more user-friendly. However, changes like those above seem totally incompatible with an equally large category of headings that have been changed from natural common English terms to foreign words. SISTINE CHAPEL was changed in 1996 to CAPELLA SISTINA (VATICAN PALACE, VATICAN CITY). Note that the palace in the qualifier is still a palace (English), and not a *palazzo* (Italian). Boy, that makes sense. They've gone on with these. In more recent lists, COOKERY, SEYCHELLES was changed to COOKERY, SEYCHELLOIS (how pinky-up), but ZITTAUER GEBIRGE (GERMANY) was changed to ZITTAU MOUNTAINS (GERMANY).

And Again, Say Wha' ?????

Some changes seem simultaneously arbitrary and trivial. It is hard to see justification for them in any likelihood that the old heading was becoming irretrievable due to a shift in English usage.

- CABLES, SUBMARINE—ATLANTIC and
- CABLES, SUBMARINE—PACIFIC were changed to
- TRANSATLANTIC CABLES and

  TRANSPACIFIC CABLES. Were they moving them apart in the catalog so they'd be less exposed to simultaneous terrorist attack?
- PAVIA, BATTLE OF, 1525 was changed in 2003 (after an irritating two-step process) to PAVIA, BATTLE OF, PAVIA, ITALY, 1525 (to distinguish it from all those other Battles of Pavia that were fought in 1525 in some other country.)
- BRUNEI NEWSPAPERS became

  BRUNEIAN NEWSPAPERS. No doubt this makes the heading match some pattern better. But are there really any native speakers of English who are sure what the adjectival form of the place name Brunei is? Aren't they all likely to search, if they search for this material at all, for the combination of "newspaper" and "Brunei"?
- GUERRE DES BOUFFONS became, in Fall 2006, QUERELLE DES BOUFFONS. The clowns didn't make up, exactly, but the conflict was ratcheted down a notch.
- They changed the heading HARLEQUIN to

  HARLEQUIN (FICTITIOUS CHARACTER). I was heartbroken; I was so hoping he was real.
- BOARD GAME PLAYERS became

  BOARD GAMERS, but if the intent was to make them sound less like hopeless geeks, I don't think this will work, and I'll bet you a nickel this will have to be changed back someday.
- FIRE ISLAND (N.Y.) was changed, to make it conform to some pattern or other, to the ugly heading

  FIRE ISLAND (N.Y: ISLAND)
- Ranganathan's Fourth Law must have been in mind when LC split the heading UMBRELLAS AND PARASOLS into two files, one for UMBRELLAS, and one for PARASOLS. (Saves the time of the reader. All that material about parasols in the national database did clutter up searches for umbrellas. It was terrible.)

Changes to Accommodate Trends, Fashion, and Shifts of Usage That Seem Arbitrary or Ephemeral

For instance, in Fall 2006 they hunted down all the headings that included the expression "biological diversity" (surely straightforward enough to find easily by keyword searching) and replaced them with "biodiversity"; a snappy word in vogue, to be sure, but one surely doomed to need to be changed back, someday soon, when the fashion for it fades. Someone wiser than I will have to explain to you why this change is compatible with the shift away from ECODISTRICTS (established 2003) to ECOLOGICAL DISTRICTS (replaced it in 2004).

- KINGS AND RULERS—MISTRESSES was changed to
  KINGS AND RULERS—PARAMOURS. Okay, now Piers Gaveston is covered by it, strike one blow for gender parity; but "paramours"? Isn't that just a bit Belle Époque? Does anyone say "paramours" anymore? And shouldn't the main heading be just "Rulers," or "Sovereigns," if we're systematically tinkering with old headings to achieve gender neutrality? "Paramours"? If we're after natural language, what happened to "lovers" or "romantic partners"? "Paramours"?
- The free-floating subdivision—BUYING changed to—PURCHASING in Fall 2006. They were standardizing, because BUYING had been authorized under some specific headings, and PURCHASING under others; but surely they flipped the wrong ones, if the intention is to enable natural-word searching by patrons. Which word is more common in regular speech? The Airlie House Conference was in 1991. The gremlins are still finding subdivisions that they want to flip around or tinker with under the guidelines promulgated at that meeting. Job security? Or OBSESSIVE-COMPULSIVE DISORDER (May Subd Geog)?

The Unwilling, Picked from the Unfit, in Pursuit of the Inedible

Suppose we could, in fact, persuade the subject thesaurus gurus to slow or stop the constant churning of the established headings in search of the illusion of perfect consistency, or, at the very least, declare some sort of moratorium. What might make more sense than churning the headings? How about expanding the syndetic structure? How about providing more scope notes? How about providing more correlative call number matches?

They Made a Desert and Called It a Folksonomy

Okay, we've vented an omer of spleen, but let's clarify. It's the constant tinkering, and not the LCSH system itself, that's being teased, harassed, and critiqued here. Large and unwieldy as it sometimes may seem, LCSH is more baby than bath water. There's no useful alternative of comparable scope. Elsewhere between covers with this essay (or rant) there are doubtless going to be discussions of "folksonomies," as people call them, but I'm not going to enlist under that banner. Louise Spiteri, in an article that's friendly to the general concept of this feral young member of the taxonomic genus, puts her professorial finger pretty squarely on the strengths and weaknesses of folk tagging (Spiteri 2006). While calling for further study, she concludes correctly that with respect to library catalogs, at least, folksonomic metadata has the potential to supplement, but never to supplant, controlled subject vocabulary. Folksonomic tagging may have its uses for individual patrons or small user communities. Personally I've witnessed the effects of uncontrolled end-user subject tagging on a large data archive by too numerous a community, and it was not pretty. It threatened the usability of the information, and it certainly degraded retrieval. Grist for another paper and venue, perhaps. Jeffrey Beall, in one of his typically provocative and cogent papers, recently pointed out that while new cataloging and metadata schemes often point in useful directions and open our minds to places where our systems must expand and grow, the robustness of our best old systems is probably too valuable to jettison (Beall 2006).

If Seven Maids with Seven Mops Swept It for Fifty Years...?

The effort to impose complete consistency on a reef of lexical coral that has grown with typically organic lack of tidiness seems quixotic to me, and invokes that trite quotation from Ralph Waldo Emerson that you're probably all braced for here. It's also pragmatically impossible, as examples above illustrate. The tinkerers can work their fingers to the bone, but they will never impose total consistency on LCSH — particularly without first achieving consensus on whether the goal is an English vernacular thesaurus or the scaffolding for an international one.

The intellectual energy behind LCSH as a developing conceptual system attempting to map the fields of human knowledge began to dissipate, perhaps, as its sister system — the Library of Congress Classification schedules — neared completion. LCSH was tied to a linear system for ordering books on a shelf, a tangible task. Like the Dewey system, LC classification eventually reached a point where it had achieved workable functional success. They had solved their problem with the LCCS, and as Pauline Atherton Cochrane says in a recent interview (Cochrane 2001), librarians dropped out of the classification research think tanks in droves, satisfied. They abandoned the conceptual struggle, pretty much, to information science and commercial developers. Ideas for improving the essential structure of LCSH continued to be voiced — see the three bibliographies of critical reviews cited in the bibliography below — but have had limited impact on the growth of the system.

In the meantime, is there any conceivable improvement to the existing system that might be more valuable than the proliferation of these little tinkers' dams that come out in the weekly lists?

Well, at the risk of being a nag, we might remind them that *the system's syndetic architecture is profoundly deficient.* The terms selected for headings only sporadically offer connections to broader, narrower, or related terms. Phyllis Richmond pointed this out in 1959. That will soon be fifty-year-old advice. It had no Calhoun–esque budget-saving implications, so it was never implemented, but it's still an accurate assessment of one of the system's major weaknesses.

The requirement to cite literary warrant before any new heading is forged doubtless seems efficient to tech services managers, but it hobbles the system, leaving conceptual holes. The situation could be made less dire and doily-like if, on occasion, the cataloger were encouraged to write scope notes (which does seem to be happening), to ponder the new heading's syndetic connections and articulate them before moving on to the next heading, and if they were also encouraged to write new headings for the related concepts that constitute gaps made obvious by the new one. An example is mentioned above: MOORE'S LAW, which could have been distinguished from a new heading for Mooers's Law, even if the piece providing literary warrant for the one did not contain discussion of the other. In many cases, the same reference sources checked to confirm usage of the term being established would provide the information needed to write related headings that are going to be needed sooner or later; this would enrich the system and provide guidance to catalogers, who would not have to start from scratch when they discover the need for the missing related term. Not doing this exposes ridiculous situations, such as the articulation of RECOVERED MEMORY two years after the heading for FALSE MEMORY SYNDROME was written.

Another weakness of the older headings is the lack of scope notes. We applaud the observation that new headings added nowadays frequently do have scope notes, sometimes exemplary ones. But working catalogers are still all too often floundering in the dark when we stumble across an old one that may or may not be appropriate for the item in hand. Karen Plummer points out a group of important LCSH terms that make no use of the expertise embedded in a specialized field's available subject taxonomies, resulting in terms for key mathematical concepts that do not map well against accepted usage and lack scope notes to guide catalogers in their proper use (Plummer 2006).

The only point at which LCSH continues to grow conceptually toward the potential richness of a faceted system is in the occasional articulation of multiple classification number correlations (e.g., "use BF for the psychological aspects of this topic, but Q300 for its technical aspects"). More of these, when appropriate, would be far more helpful than worrying about the hyphen in STRAIGHT-EDGE CULTURE.

In short, the energy used to make micro-changes to individual headings in the LCSH lexicon would go a lot farther if it were applied toward reinforcing its structure, resulting in a sturdier system. In the meantime, while we're waiting for the next weekly list of micro-changes, the last Alder flea beetle has invited me to go phishing. Call us if those fossil Zapodidae start to jump around. I don't want to miss that.

Acknowledgments

The author would like to thank innocent colleagues, including K. R. Roberto, Lori Leatherman, Rory Calhoun, Annie Copeland, and Jeff Edmunds for encouragement, examples, and collaboration of various kinds. Special thanks for the gracious indulgence of Kathryn La Barre, who made an edited transcript of her interviews with Pauline Cochrane available to me for this project. None of these should be blamed for the accuracy, tone, or peevishness of any of the above. I should also apologize to Richard Harkness, Edward FitzGerald, Gertrude Stein, Tacitus, Oscar Wilde, the Walrus, and Bob Merrill for tampering with brief snippets from their writing. I don't know what came over me.

Disclaimer: The author has crept into this anthology on false pretenses, and abused the indulgence of the distinguished editor. When at his desk on a normal workday, he is not really a "radical" cataloger, at all. Indeed, he would have to plead guilty to being a prominent advocate for the practical utility of adhering closely to national cataloging standards, for a variety of reasons that could occupy another article as long as this one. However, he sees no incompatibility between adhering to national conventions and agitating for national conventions that make a little more sense.

Bibliography

Beall, Jeffrey. (2006). The death of metadata. *Serials Librarian* 51 (2).

Cataloging Support Bulletin. Washington, D.C.: CPSO. Available: <http://www.loc.gov/aba/#subjects>.

Cochrane, Pauline Atherton. Interview by Kathryn La Barre, Urbana, Ill., Oct. 27, 2001. Tapes and original transcripts on deposit among the Cochrane papers at Syracuse University, Syracuse, N.Y.

Cochrane, Pauline Atherton, and Monika Kirtland. (1981). Critical Views of LCSH — the Library of Congress Subject Headings: A Bibliographic and Bibliometric Essay; an Analysis of Vocabulary Control in the Library of Congress List of Subject Headings (LCSH). Syracuse, N.Y.: ERIC Clearinghouse on Information Resources, Syracuse University.

Conway, Martha O'Hara. (1992). The future of subdivisions in the Library of Congress subject headings system: report from the Subject Subdivisions Conference, sponsored by the Library of Congress, May 9–12, 1991. Washington, D.C.: Library of Congress, Cataloging Distribution Service.

Fischer, Karen S. (2005). Critical views of LCSH, 1990–2001: the third bibliographic essay. *Cataloging & Classification Quarterly* 41 (1).

Plummer, Karen A. (2006). Mathematics subject headings for the pre–K–12 community: a comparison of key terms from the National Council of Teachers of Mathematics (NCTM) Mathematics Standards to ERIC Thesaurus Descriptors and the Library of Congress Subject Headings. *Cataloging and Classification Quarterly,* 52 (2).

Richmond, Phyllis A. (1959). Cats: an example of concealed classification in subject headings. *Library Resources and Technical Services* 3.

Shubert, Steven Blake. (1992). Critical views of LCSH ten years later: a third bibliographic essay. *Cataloging and Classification Quarterly,* 15 (2).

Spiteri, Louise F. (2006). The use of folksonomies in public library catalogues. *Serials Librarian* 51 (2).

Litwin, Rory. (2006, 6 August). Interview with Barbara Tillett. *Library Juice.* Available: <http://libraryjuicepress.com/blog/?p=115>.

Who Moved My Pinakes?
Cataloging and Change

Tina Gross

"Two of the great libraries of antiquity were in Pergamum and Alexandria....
Later writings have referred to Pinakes from both libraries. Pinakes is plural
of pinax, a word that means tray or dish. It is thought that such trays had
slightly raised edges and that wax could be poured in the middle; when hard-
ened, the wax could be written in with a stylus. If this was indeed the medium,
it is no wonder that no remnants have survived. Writers have quoted from the
Pinakes of Alexandria, which was created by Callimachus. The work may have
been a catalog, or it may have been a bibliography of Greek literature. Callimachus has been given credit as being the first cataloger of whom we have
knowledge."
>   — Arlene G. Taylor, *The Organization of Information*
>   (Libraries Unlimited, 2004), 50

"If You Do Not Change, You Can Become Extinct."
>   — Spencer Johnson, *Who Moved My Cheese?*
>   (Putnam, 1998), 46

Rhetoric about "fear of change" has long been present in discussions of the future of cataloging, but lately it's been more widespread than ever. If you think that dismantling LCSH would be a bad idea, or if you don't embrace the term "legacy metadata," it must be because you're threatened by change and worship the status quo. As Thomas Mann puts it, "professional librarians who raise objections to the abandonment of cataloging and classification" are "dismissed as dinosaurs whose 'resistance to change' springs not from their concern for the maintenance of high professional standards, but from a selfish fear of losing job security."[1]

If some catalogers fear losing their jobs, that would hardly be surprising, given the constant talk in some circles of how irrelevant and obsolete their work is. (You would think that we're clinging to truly ancient bibliographic technology — Deanna Marcum will have to pry the pinakes from my cold dead hands!) It may even be true that such fear factors into their views on what cataloging should be like in the future, but that doesn't mean they fear change itself, nor that they would resist any and all changes to cataloging. People don't fear all change in general, and we should emphatically rebuff attempts to characterize resistance to particular changes as motivated only by an inclination to cling to the status quo.

I have two goals in writing this. The first is to call out the disingenuousness and stupidity of "fear of change" rhetoric. It should be the object of ridicule and contempt, not something that cows us. The second is to argue that change rhetoric is actually a threat to a genuine agenda for the improvement and modernization (and not just cheapening) of cataloging and library catalogs.

"Fear of change" is frequently invoked in the corporate world in order to dismiss opposition to something that is about to happen (usually something involving loss of job security), or to characterize that opposition as irrational or hidebound. According to the rhetoric, when layoffs are coming, what the potential victims are afraid of is "change," not of losing their health insurance or not being able to pay their rent. That a change might be dreadful, and that to resist it might be the most rational and ethical response, is not conceivable within this framework.

Change rhetoric ignores the obvious fact that people do not generally fear or resist changes that they perceive to be positive. Having your salary doubled would be as significant a change as losing your job to downsizing, but no one would react to a big raise with fear. Imagine if, instead of simplification and reduction, the major reform of cataloging being proposed was to get rid of backlogs by hiring additional professional staff and providing the necessary institutional support. Imagine if new timesaving technologies and vendor services were used not to facilitate the downsizing of technical services departments, but to free up catalogers to provide richer subject access and spend more time on authority control. Obviously, either of these scenarios would be wildly out of step with the current direction of the field and its priorities. They would be a total departure from the status quo, and yet they would not drive catalogers to "rambling gripe sessions about the end of the world."[2]

Much of the time, a change is good or bad depending on one's position. Change rhetoric frequently serves to veil the interests of those promoting the change — a reorganization that results in layoffs and hardship for some results in large bonuses and increased profits for others. Change rhetoric presents such occurrences as inevitable and necessary; they are never actions that those in positions of power undertake to further their own interests. Their perspective is presented as objective — change itself is desirable, and thus to react with skepticism or resistance is inherently bad, while openness and flexibility (terms which, in the context of change rhetoric, are usually used to extol compliance and passivity) are inherently good.

This is essentially the view advanced by *Who Moved My Cheese?*[3], the sickening motivational book on which the title of this piece is based. It's frequently ordered in bulk by management to be distributed to employees, especially those about to experience a "change." Using a parable about mice (and "littlepeople") in a maze, it conveys that one should view change (the absence of cheese where cheese used to appear, and the search for New Cheese somewhere else in the maze) as a potential blessing and something to be accepted without questioning or complaining. In *One Market Under God*, Thomas Frank describes it as an "asinine and chronic best-seller" and a "work of breathtaking obscenity" which manages to "both call for childlike innocence before the gods of the market and openly advance a scheme for gulling, silencing, and firing workers who are critical of management."[4]

Change rhetoric often plays a crucial role in pushing through reorganizations and downsizing that result in fewer people having to do more work for less pay and benefits. Unfortunately for many of its ill-fated readers, the lesson *Who Moved My Cheese?* expounds, that "you can believe that a change will harm you and resist it. Or you can believe that finding New Cheese will help you, and embrace the change. It all depends on what you choose to believe,"[5] is patently untrue in the real world.

Even if they choose to believe that they would benefit from the search for New Cheese, it remains a fact that "two years after a layoff, two-thirds of the victims say they are working again, according to the Bureau of Labor Statistics. Of those two-thirds, only 40 percent, on average, make as much as they had in their old jobs....The rest are making less, often much less. Out of 100 laid-off workers, then, 27 make their old salary again, or more — and 73 make less, or are not working at all."[6] Cajoling workers to become "change-masters" when they are about to be laid off does not change the fact that their lives are likely get objectively harder.

The drive to implement "lean and mean" business practices has transformed the economy, to the benefit of a tiny few — while productivity has increased, income inequality has grown massively.[6] For nearly thirty years, "incomes on the middle rungs of the economic ladder have stagnated, despite strong economic growth and strong productivity growth, while most of the rewards of the strong economy have gone to the wealthiest Americans. Their incomes have exploded."[8]

"Fear of change" rhetoric is one of the ideological tools that have been used to bring about this situation. But as Frank explains, "There is no social theory on earth short of the divine right of kings that can justify a five-hundred-fold gap between management and labor; that can explain away the concentration of a decade of gain in the bank accounts of a tiny minority. 'Change,' like the American corporation itself, is the product of argument and social conflict."[9]

In discussions about cataloging, change rhetoric is less about class warfare and more about cost-cutting to accommodate the budgets that prevailing trends prescribe. In the largely nonprofit world of libraries, the ultimate aim of cuts is obviously not to benefit stockholders and executives (except possibly in that the lack of resources available for things such as libraries is connected to the rich paying little or no tax on the wealth that has been shifted to them). Library administrators don't seek to line their own pockets, but to adjust to the budgets and priorities handed down to them, whether they agree with them or not (agreeing with them, of course, makes one more likely to be an administrator). Nevertheless, the outlook that drastically scaling back to "lean and mean" operations is the only possible way forward comes straight from the business world. It's not surprising that change rhetoric would come along with it.

Frank argues, "'Change' is not a benevolent doctrine. On the contrary: Management theorists wield 'change' like a weapon. 'Change' cleans out resistance. 'Change' blasts through the defenses. 'Change' levels city blocks. 'Change' means 'do it or die.'"[10] As in the business world, "change" is wielded like a weapon in the ongoing debates about the future of cataloging. It serves there, as it does everywhere, to advance an agenda of pared-down efficiency and to characterize rational and reasonable defense of some "old practices" as irrational clinging to the way things used to be.

Karen Calhoun's "The Changing Nature of the Catalog and Its Integration with
Other Discovery Tools," a report commissioned by the Library of Congress, is perhaps
the most controversial document in the current stage of the "cataloging wars." She asserts
that "taking advantage of research libraries' opportunities for leveraging their investments
in their catalogs and collections requires overcoming some daunting obstacles. Many
research library leaders, most staff members, and some university faculty are not ready
for change of this magnitude."[11] One of the challenges to the feasibility of her plans is
"resistance to change from faculty members, deans or administrators."[12]

In typical fashion, change is casually presented as something that people resist in
and of itself, but perhaps a much more revealing appearance of "change" is in the report's
"Blueprint for phased implementation."[13] The eighth step of the blueprint is to "manage
change," which includes the substeps "Train managers and staff to understand and cope
with the dynamics of personal and organizational transition" and "Recruit and train
change agents."[14] What this means may not be apparent to someone who doesn't read corporate management theory, but Calhoun includes a footnote referring the reader to *Managing Transitions: Making the Most of Change* by William Bridges.[15]

Bridges's book is not as hideous and devoid of humanity as *Who Moved My Cheese?*;
there are no "littlepeople" gathering up their courage by telling themselves "It's MAZE
time."[16] Bridges is candid, indicating that his advice is for managers facing a situation in
which "Industries are consolidating, and the last one in is a loser. Technology is transforming how business is done, and holding on to the familiar old ways will leave an
organization out in the cold. The other firms in the field have restructured and slimmed
down and outsourced and abbreviated their products' time-to-market drastically. Their
competitors can't *not* change."[17]

Bridges addresses managers and advises them that if they are not forthright and
humane in "managing transition," they risk creating an "exhausted and demoralized workforce"[18] and dooming their change to failure, while *Who Moved My Cheese?* addresses
employees and attempts to dupe them into self-policing their doubts. What the two
approaches have in common is that they both aim to provide the vital service of helping
management restructure, slim down, outsource, and abbreviate without being hindered
by employee resistance. Calhoun's adoption of a business model, thoroughly critiqued by
Thomas Mann,[19] wouldn't be complete without invoking it.

By far the most emphatic use of "fear of change" rhetoric in cataloging debates was
a message with the subject "'Culture wars' in cataloging" which was posted by David
Banush on the Program for Cooperative Cataloging (PCC) email list.[20]

Banush asserts that there are two unequivocal camps in the cataloging world. On
one side are those who want to do away with old practices, "primarily managers and
administrators," and on the other "more conservative forces, which seem to include many
front-line staff, are vigorously (sometimes stridently) defending the status quo, or even
the status quo ante."[21]

Banush goes much further than most, elaborating a jaw-dropping analogy between
cataloging and "the welfare states of Europe." What they have in common are bureaucracy,

over-regulation, high costs, and a need to forgo tradition and being "comfortable and secure" in order to become more efficient and competitive. And of course, they both face the obstacle of workers who "do not want to change."[22]

Evidently trade unionists in Europe resist the elimination of social services and work benefits because they're "threatened by change," and not because they believe that their quality of life is more important than the competitiveness that business would gain if it were substantially lowered. In one way, it is difficult to believe that Banush really wants to compare library leaders who claim they want to modernize cataloging with corporations determined to wipe out social spending, and laws protecting workers for the sake of higher profits, and package the entire project as dynamism. But an uncritical adoption of the priorities and values of business and profit are utterly in keeping with the corporate mindset from which change rhetoric originates.

According to Banush, those who expressed opposition to Calhoun's report or to LC's series decision "feel too threatened by change to consider reforms anything but heresy or betrayal." He gives no hint that the concerns expressed about the Calhoun report were in reaction to specific proposals. He seems to think that an uncontroversial proposal such as "Enable much better browsing and organization of large retrieval sets"[23] is just as troubling to catalogers as "Urge LC to dismantle LCSH."[24]

If you believed Banush, you would never think that many catalogers would be ecstatic to see most of the changes proposed by the University of California report. It would seem that there was a hysterical reaction to the entire report, every bit as much to something expected like "Add enriched content such as Tables of Contents, cover art, publisher promotional blurbs, content excerpts (print, audio or video), and bibliographies"[25] as to "Consider using controlled vocabularies only for name, uniform title, date, and place, and abandoning the use of controlled vocabularies..."[26] This would make perfect sense if "change" is what catalogers are opposed to, and not the impoverishment of access.

Perhaps because change rhetoric fits so well with the traditional stereotype of catalogers as rule-obsessed hermits, it has largely become part of the stereotype. Echoes and adoptions of it are widespread. Just as I was writing this, a posting on the AUTOCAT email list, discussing recent events at LC, said "This is the 21st century and things have changed. And since things have changed so do WE have to change. I realize that change is scary, but it has to be done."[27] The same contributor went on, later in the same day, to say, "I don't understand why LC's series decision, which to me was a delegation of work, caused such an uproar ... other than the fact that it was a CHANGE."[28]

Uncanny! There could hardly be a more perfect specimen: the only explanation is that CHANGE is scary. Tellingly, one of the actual reasons for the uproar (the "delegation of work" meaning an increased workload for libraries) is mentioned but passed over.

In reality, the uproar being made by defenders of cataloging is in response to the notion that the conceptual categorization and collocation of works made possible by catalogers are unnecessary and expendable. We object to giving users only search results that are "incomplete, haphazard, indiscriminate, biased toward recent works, and largely confined to English language sources."[29] We resist the forestalling of future search and retrieval improvements that depend on controlled vocabulary and classification.

We reject the idea that no one will care if library users can no longer retrieve a list of works by an author, or about a particular topic, without being inundated by irrelevant junk. We are not resigned to the revival of information organization problems that were solved by the end of the nineteenth century. That would be change, but it wouldn't be progress.

If it's just "change" that catalogers and their defenders are opposed to, their view would have to be that everything should just stay the same. It would be impossible to explain why dissatisfaction with online catalog design and functionality is nearly universal among them, or why many who objected to the LC series decision are also frustrated with the ongoing RDA development process and fear that it might end up a disappointing cop-out that sidelines FRBR and is merely AACR3 by another name.

How has the cataloging community reacted to FRBR and the changes it will bring? The responses have been varied — some catalogers are ecstatic about the possibilities, some doubt that it's all it's cracked up to be. Some are following its development closely, some aren't. Some feel that they don't yet grasp it, some even feel intimidated by it. But it could not be credibly argued that the reaction has been one of resistance. No one has said, "It's time to circle the wagons against this abomination — FRBR (not MARC) must die!"

When Deanna Marcum says "Big changes are on the way,"[30] we know even before she continues with "The series authority records are but the first step ..." that the "big changes" she's talking about aren't FRBR or FRSAR or the Virtual International Authority File. She isn't talking about RDA, or even the replacement of MARC with another encoding standard. She doesn't mean expanding upon current cataloging practices, or replacing them with more advanced ones, but simply eliminating them.

There are numerous initiatives and projects that could contribute to revolutionizing library catalogs, some of which are mentioned in the preceding paragraph. They will require time and resources if they are to meet their potential, and their realization may add time to the cataloging process.

The vast majority of the "fear of change" axe-wielding crowd aims to drain resources from cataloging. They have little or no role in the genuine innovations taking shape, although they present their agenda as embodying progress.

It goes without saying that big changes are coming in cataloging, and in librarianship in general. What has yet to be resolved is whether these changes will actually mean progress and improvement or the gutting of our mission. Against the latter, recalcitrance, opposition, and resistance are desperately needed.

Notes

1. Thomas Mann. (2006, 19 June) What is going on at the Library of Congress? Available: <http://guild2910.org/AFSCMEWhatIsGoingOn.pdf>.

2. David Banush, e-mail to PCCLIST (Program for Cooperative Cataloging mailing list), May 24, 2006. Available: <http://listserv.loc.gov/cgi-bin/wa?A2=ind0605&L=pcclist&T=0&P=4815>.

3. Spencer Johnson. (1998). *Who Moved My Cheese?: An A-Mazing Way to Deal with Change in Your Work and in Your Life*. New York: Putnam.

4. Thomas Frank. (2000). *One Market Under God: Extreme Capitalism, Market Populism, and the End of Economic Democracy*, New York: Doubleday, 248–249.

5. Johnson, 65.

6. Louis Uchitelle, "Retraining Laid-Off Workers, but for What?" *New York Times*, 26 March 2006.

7. Editorial, *Newsday*, September 4, 2006.

8. John Ydstie, "Does Wealth Imbalance Threaten Society's Fabric?" *All Things Considered*. National Public Radio. February 5, 2007. Available: <http://www.npr.org/templates/story/story.php?storyId=7190876>.

9. Frank, 250.

10. Ibid., 240.

11. Karen Calhoun. (2006, March 17). The Changing Nature of the Catalog and Its Integration with Other Discovery Tools. Final Report. Prepared for the Library of Congress. Available: <http://www.loc.gov/catdir/calhoun-report-final.pdf>.

12. Ibid., 13.

13. Ibid., 16.

14. Ibid., 20.

15. William Bridges. (2003). *Managing Transitions: Making the Most of Change*. Cambridge, MA: Perseus.

16. Johnson, 45.

17. Bridges, x.

18. Ibid., 140.

19. Thomas Mann. (2006, March 17). The Changing Nature of the Catalog and Its Integration with Other Discovery Tools. Final Report. Prepared for the Library of Congress by Karen Calhoun. A Critical Review. Library of Congress Professional Guild AFSCME Local 2910. Available: <http://www.guild2910.org/AFSCMECalhounReviewREV.pdf>.

20. Banush.

21. Ibid.

22. Ibid.

23. Calhoun, 19.

24. Ibid., 18.

25. University of California Libraries Bibliographic Services Task Force (2005). "Rethinking How We Provide Bibliographic Services for the University of California." Available: <http://libraries.universityofcalifornia.edu/sopag/BSTF/Final.pdf>.

26. Ibid., 5.

27. Jerri Swinehart, e-mail to AUTOCAT mailing list, February 6, 2007.

28. Ibid.

29. Mann, "What is going on," 21.

30. Deanna Marcum to ARL directors, May 5, 2006. Available: <http://www.ala.org/ala/alctscontent/alctspubsbucket/bibcontrol/Marcum050506.htm>.

The End of Prohibition

Carol Reid

As former newsletter editor of NYLA's Intellectual Freedom Round Table, and organizer of several Banned Books Week programs at the New York State Library, I am very familiar with the phrase "banned books." It has a pithy, alliterative appeal, and I'm sure it rings a bell for many people, especially regular library visitors. However, a rash of conservative editorials arguing that no books were in fact banned in public libraries during 1995 and '96 — never mind in other years or in school libraries — gave rise to a resolution of appeasement at the 1996 ALA conference to the effect that we change the name of Banned Books Week to "Challenged Books Week" or something equally awkward and literal-minded. However, no one, to my knowledge, recommended the moniker "Prohibited Books Week," which would have actually been in accordance with Library of Congress subject headings.

We can debate the political connotations of a term like "banned books" till the catalogers come home, but as for Banned Books Week, I see it basically as an expression, a catchphrase, a sort of synecdoche — the idea being that these are books that *would* have been banned had the protestors gotten their way. And the only reason they typically don't is that librarians are continually being educated and encouraged to defend the First Amendment, largely through the publicity and support that events like Banned Books Week provide. Ironically, it is in part *because* of Banned Books Week that few or sometimes no books at all are banned from public libraries in any given year. "Book banning" does not necessarily mean the same thing to every person in every time and place. But to most people it implies censorious intent, generally with a narrower focus than "censorship."

A keyword title search in OCLC on "banned + books" or "book + banning" produced 159 records, a dozen or so titles dating back more than fifty years, proving that these expressions have been around for a while, but also indicating a lot more relevance and resonance of late, primarily due to the annual commemoration of Banned Books Week. However, instead of assigning the heading BANNED BOOKS to these materials, LC instructs us to use PROHIBITED BOOKS, which seems to be a locution having largely to do with Catholicism and other orthodox religious and governmental bodies. As the authority record lacks a citation, I can only guess at the origin of PROHIBITED BOOKS, which I suspect to be the Catholic

Church's onetime list of off-limits reading material, the *Index Librorum Prohibitorum.* Although "prohibited books" is not a phrase in common parlance, and the *Index* itself is now defunct, it does have a certain authoritative and historical import.

OCLC yields eighteen monographic records with the words "prohibited + books" in the title and PROHIBITED BOOKSin a subject field. With the exception of *Books Prohibited in Eire under the Censorship of Publications Act, as on 19th February, 1948; Index of Prohibited Books, Revised and Published by Order of His Holiness Pope Pius XI* (1930); and a few other related titles, virtually all of this material was published well in advance of the twentieth century. Although a subject search on PROHIBITED BOOKS will lead one, for example, to *Banned Books Week: Celebrating the Freedom to Read*, it is safe to assume that the average patron would choose to look under BANNED BOOKS instead. And it's a waste of time to reroute users of the "red books" from a likely heading to an unlikely one, despite the fact that all roads will eventually lead to Rome.

LC subsumes BOOK CENSORSHIP under CENSORSHIP— which seems an increasingly outmoded concept if it ever really made sense — and makes BANNED BOOKS a "see" reference from PROHIBITED BOOKS. CENSORSHIP as a subheading (FILM—CENSORSHIP, MUSIC—CENSORSHIP, etc.) wasn't introduced until 1999 and was not established as a main heading until 2002. Bibliographic records for the Banned Books Week resource guides all contain the headings CENSORSHIP, PROHIBITED BOOKS, and BOOKS AND READING. Some have FREEDOM OF INFORMATION added to the mix. Only a few of the thirty-four records for the resource guides, though, chose to include the subject CHALLENGED BOOKS, which is technically the most accurate descriptor for much of this content, although not the wording that probably leaps to mind for most seekers of knowledge about Banned Books Week.

CHALLENGED BOOKS was added to the LC National Authority File in 1996, and the following year LC decided to authorize a heading for BANNED BOOKS WEEK as well, appearing at that juncture to be pointedly gainsaying BANNED BOOKS itself. Such a comparison almost seems to suggest a political compromise — which is to say, until and unless ALA can be persuaded to soften the name of Banned Books Week to placate those factions who *would* censor books but don't like to be publicly accused of such proclivities, the week will reluctantly require being called by its actual name. But by failing to authorize a heading for the activity itself, LC can appear to cooperate with those who wish to downplay its significance. (Although, frankly, this sort of thing is usually more often a case of not wanting to spend money on a new frock when an old smock can still cover the area.)

Homely metaphors and conspiracy theories aside, how many catalogers does it take to change a light bulb? The answer is just one when it's Sanford Berman, who for years petitioned the Library of Congress to change INCANDESCENT LAMPS, ELECTRIC to the more searcher-friendly LIGHT BULBS, or at any rate to establish the latter, which it finally did in 1990. (Before that time, LC had had a "strict policy" against revising subject authorities.) Berman used to hold one up, to the amusement of his listeners, in order to illuminate that story; it's a great metaphor for seeing the light on a subject. Perhaps we can turn on the powers that be to creating a heading for BANNED BOOKS (or switching it with PROHIBITED BOOKS) and adding a cross-reference for BOOK BANNING. ALA and the Library of Congress should be the last places on earth where material on "banned books" is banned, or made needlessly (if not to say "prohibitively") hard to find.

North American Indian Personal Names in National Bibliographies

Frank Exner, Little Bear

Introduction

North American Indian personal names require special attention in authority control and cataloging because they do not necessarily follow rules developed for European names. Everyone who lives in the United States, except full-blooded American Indians, either is an immigrant or is descended from one or more immigrants (Hook 1982). Therefore every name form in the world can be found somewhere in the United States, and these name forms need to be managed with understanding and sensitivity.

North American Indian Naming

Black Pipe's Story

Black Pipe's story demonstrates the principles of North American Indian naming. *The Indian Sign Language* (Clark 1982) is a reprint of a nineteenth century U. S. Army training manual for officers working with the Plains tribes in the 1870s and 1880s. He told the story of an old Cheyenne warrior about personal names and naming:

> When a child is first born, whether a boy or girl, it is called a baby,—a girl baby or boy baby,—afterwards by any childish name until, if a boy, he goes to war; then, if he "counts a coup," he is named for something that has happened on that journey, from some accident, some animal killed, or some bird that helped them to success. Or, after returning, some one of the older men may give the young man his name.
>
> When I was small, I was called "Little Bird." When I first went to war and returned to camp, the name of "Long Horn" was given me by an old man of the camp. Then the traders gave me the name Tall-White-Man, and now, since I have become old, they (the Indians) call me Black Pipe. This name was given me from a pipe I used to carry when I went to war. I used to blacken the stem and bowl just as I did my face after these trips, and was especially careful to do so when I had been successful.

North American Indian Name Forms

North American Indian cultures in the United States and Canada today have three name forms: those derived from a European model, traditional forms, and names that mix the two (IFLA 1996, Ingraham 1997).

Sherman Alexie (2000), a Spokane/Coeur d'Alene poet and novelist born in October 1966, has a European-style name (IFLA 1996, Ingraham 1997). The name "Sherman Alexie" identifies a specific individual within his genealogical line but contains no additional descriptive information. North American Indians often use hyphens to connect the separate words in a naming concept (e.g., Tall-White-Man [Clark 1982]) or concatenate the words into an unbroken string (e.g., the author Martin Brokenleg [Mitten 1999]) to force the proper treatment of their names in English listings. Names like these can be treated as a European name form; equivalent mixed-form names would appear as *Tall White Man* and *Martin Broken Leg.*

Sitting Bull (Utley 1993), who received his name before the first census of the Lakota people, is a traditional name form (actually the translation from Lakota of a traditional name form). Tamaque (Ingraham 1997, 347), the Lenni Lenape man's name that means *Beaver*, is both traditional in form and is expressed in the tribe's own language.

Mixed-form names combine a traditional name and a European-form name. Dr. Janine Pease-Pretty on Top, the founding president of Little Big Horn College in Montana, has a mixed-form name. Pease was her father's name and passed on to her and all of her siblings, thus the first half of her hyphenated second name follows the European model. (Hyphenated family names are becoming more common in the United States.) Pretty on Top is descriptive, thus the second half of her second name is a traditional one. Janine, her first name, clearly follows the European model.

Another mixed name form is John "Blackfeather" Jeffries. John Jeffries is Tribal Chair of the Occaneechi Band of the Saponi Nation, and his name, when written this way, is of the European form. Blackfeather is his tribal name; his name, when written this way, is of traditional form. As a result, with his tribal name within his European name, John "Blackfeather" Jeffries is a mixed form.

North American Names Through Life

North American Indians do not necessarily have one name only. Clark (1982, 266) noted Black Pipe's names as:

1. Little Bird
2. Long Horn
3. Black Pipe

During the period that his tribe used the names "Long Horn" and Black Pipe, traders called him "Tall-White-Man." Name changes where the "new" name replaces the "old" name constitute a name sequence. Name changes where two or more names are used at the same time constitute a name set.

The story of Sitting Bull's early life is an example of a name sequence (changing traditional names that tell an autobiographical story). When he was a child the future chief's name was changed to Slow when his deliberate manner asserted itself so that his name reflected the most important aspect of his character. But his heroism in battle showed that he could think and act quickly when speed was needed. As a result, the young man was honored with his father's name, Sitting Bull, which contains both fierce and deliberate aspects.

And North American Indians may have more than one name at the same time (a name set). Young Bear (Young Bear and Thiesz 1994) says that these different names often carry different social expectations. When making an ordinary social request, his common name (Severt Young Bear) is used. When making an extraordinary social request his tribal name (Hehaka Luzahan or Swift Elk) is used because its use both honors him and carries important duties. For example, if Severt Young Bear (his common name) is asked to sing at a pow-wow, there is no social pressure on him and he can do as he wishes. On the other hand, if Hehaka Luzahan or Swift Elk (his tribal name) is asked to sing at a pow-wow, he feels obliged to comply.

Effects of Colonization

Prior to contact with Europeans, North American Indians lived in oral cultures. Colonization brought both spoken and written European languages along with the institutions (e.g., schools and governments) of the colonizers. Over time, then, the oral cultures adopted new languages (partially or fully) and writing (some individuals more fluently than others).

The personal names of North American Indians may represent a pre-contact culture, a mixed state (some fully traditional oral people, some people fully integrated into the European-based culture, and many people between these extremes).

North American Indians do not necessarily have one name only. Clark (1982, 266) described the name sequence of one of his scouts:

Little Bird
Long Horn
Black Pipe

During the period that his tribe used the names *Long Horn* and Black Pipe, traders called him *Tall-White-Man*.

Certainly the name *Little Bird*, when it was first bestowed, was not spoken in English. Since the scout's tribe is unknown, his language and the pronunciation of his first name are also unknown. Little Bird, Long Horn, and Black Pipe could reasonably appear in an army biography or history that named scouts in English or in a tribal history written by anthropologists writing in several languages (Waldman, 1985).

Since *Tall-White-Man* was a name given to the scout by traders, it probably would only appear in English. Thus, this single scout might well be known by three names in two languages. This does not include names that might have been given by other tribes with whom Black Pipe interacted. A complete authority analysis of the personal names of Clark's scout, then, would require working knowledge of several languages describing two cultures within multiple contexts.

North American Indians often use hyphens to connect the separate words in a naming concept (e.g., Tall-White-Man [Clark, 1982, 266]) or concatenate the words into an unbroken string (e.g., the author Martin Brokenleg [Mitten, 1999]) to force the proper treatment of their names in English listings. Names like these can be treated as a European name form; equivalent mixed form names would appear as *Tall White Man* and *Martin Broken Leg.*

Some individuals indicate the possibility of a name set by their recorded name. For example, Robert (Gray-Wolf) Hofsinde, the author of *Indian Costumes*, has two names, "Robert Hofsinde" and Gray-Wolf, that could be used interchangeably since neither is more right than the other.

Another example is the name "Eastman, Charles Alexander (Ohiyesa)." Dr. Alexander, a Wahpeton Dakota Indian who lived from 1858 to 1939, became the first American Indian to receive an M.D. degree. He received the name Ohiyesa as a youth when he was raised traditionally and the name Charles Alexander Eastman when he went to school in Wisconsin. He served in both the American Indian and White American worlds; thus, "Ohiyesa" and "Charles Alexander Eastman" were a name set (Giese, 1996).

North American Indian Names in National Bibliographies

The following paragraphs describe how the test sets of names and national authority files were developed.

The Set of Names

The name test set provides the personal names with which to survey the selected national library authority files. Requirements for the set of names included:

- Reasonable expectation of presence in national library authority files
- Reasonable size
- Representatives of the three name forms
- Presence of apparent name sets

The first requirement is met by basing the test set on the 2,021 names found in four major bibliographic lists composed of book material available through the book trade. They can be expected in the catalogs of the Library of Congress and the National Library of Canada and may or may not be in the catalogs of other national libraries.

Working with a list containing 2,021 names would be very unwieldy. One option to ease the situation would be to take a random sample of 322 names. Powell (1997, 80) suggests 322 as a proper sample size for a population of 2,000 to 2,200 individuals. However, such a random sample would provide no assurance that the requisite name forms and name sets would be present; any selection process that guaranteed the presence of all name forms and name sets, in fact, would require a bias negating randomness. Another way to structure the names test set would be to select names from the list according to a detailed standard. Following this option, names were selected from the original list of 2,021 names by including:

- All names that appear on two or more lists
- All traditional names
- All mixed-form names
- The names of authors known from their biographies to be North American Indians

Applying these rules, the original list of 2,021 names was reduced to a test set of 185 names.

The Set of Libraries

There are many lists of national libraries. Entering "National Libraries" in the Google search engine produced 24,400 hits, many of which are lists of national libraries from sources all over the world. To select the set of libraries for this research, the following rules were applied:

- The list must be sponsored by an international agency.
- The list must include national libraries from around the world.
- The list must include national libraries that have shown an interest in the authority control of personal names.
- The list must include access to the national libraries that will facilitate this research.

The most significant international agency in the field of library and information science is the International Federation of Library and Information Agencies (IFLA). It publishes a list, *Web Accessible National and Major Libraries*, which includes 54 national libraries with the URL for each.

To assure an institutional interest in personal name authority control, only national libraries represented in *Names of Persons: National Usages for Entry in Catalogues* (IFLA, 1996) were accepted for this chapter. This produced a set of 50 libraries including national libraries of large and small countries on virtually all continents that have demonstrated a concern with personal name authority control and that provide access for research. Unfortunately, most of the 50 libraries do not make authority files available through their online OPACs. Since this study depends on access to online name authority files through national library OPACs, only ten libraries were queried. The libraries were:

- U.S. Library of Congress
- National Library of Canada
- Bibliothéque nationale de France
- Danish National Library
- Koninklijke Bibliotheek (The Netherlands)
- Oesterreichische National Bibliothek (Austria)
- Narodni knihovna Ceske republiky (Czech Republic)
- Biblioteca Nacional de Chile (Chile)
- Latvijas Nacionalas bibliotekas (Latvia)
- National Library of Australia

For each of these libraries, a search on an author's name produces both the national OPAC's authorized name choice and all of their recognized variant names.

Analysis

The data was gathered on instruments that resemble content analysis forms. Every name in the name test set is checked against each selected national library's authority file.

As the name test set is made up of individuals who are members of nations indigenous to the U.S. and Canada, and whose publications are sold in both countries, their names should reasonably be in both authority files. The Library of Congress name authority file (LCNAF) and the name authority file of the National Library of Canada (NLC/BNC) were analyzed using the following method:

- Determine the number of authors who appear and subtract it from 185 (the number of names in the name test list).
- Determine the number of author names whose authorized forms differ from the name test set.
- Divide the number of differing names by the number of present names.

Next, the state of North American Indian personal names in the eight national library test authority files throughout the world was measured. The authorized forms of the test author names that appeared in four or more national authority files were compared with each other, indicating the level of uniformity within international authority control.

Table 1: The SAS FREQ procedure applied to all authorized forms

National Library	Traditional Names	European Names	Mixed Names	Unusual Names	Not Found	Total Names
AUSTRALIA	No.=5 %=2.70	No.=28 %=15.14	No.=7 %=3.78	No.=1 %=0.54	No.=144 %=77.84	No.=185 %=100.00
AUSTRIA	No.=3 %=1.62	No.=3 %=1.62	No.=4 %=2.16	No.=0 %=0.00	No.=175 %=94.59	No.=185 %=100.00
CANADA	No.=34 %=18.38	No.=90 %=48.65	No.=28 %=15.14	No.=2 %=1.08	No.=31 %=16.76	No.=185 %=100.00
CHILE	No.=0 %=0.00	No.=5 %=2.70	No.=1 %=0.54	No.=0 %=0.00	No.=179 %=96.76	No.=185 %=100.00
DENMARK	No.=9 %=4.86	No.=21 %=11.35	No.=6 %=3.24	No.=1 %=0.54	No.=148 %=80.00	No.=185 %=100.00
FRANCE	No.=4 %=2.16	No.=22 %=11.89	No.=6 %=3.24	No.=3 %=1.62	No.=150 %=81.08	No.=185 %=100.00
USA	No.=32 %=17.30	No.=99 %=53.51	No.=23 %=12.43	No.=2 %=1.08	No.=29 %=15.68	No.=185 %=100.00
TOTAL	No.=92 %=4.97	No.=287 %=15.51	No.=79 %=4.27	No.=11 %=0.59	No.=1381 %=74.65	No.=1850 %=100.00

Most authorized forms in the tested national authority files take the European form, with the remaining names divided between traditional and mixed forms. But 92 authorized forms (from nine national authority files) took traditional form and 79 (also from nine national authority files) took mixed forms. So a total of 171 (9.24 percent) of authorized forms examined were not a European form and need rules that allow the control of traditional and mixed-form names.

Regarding cross-reference formation, one approach to a multi-word concept name (whether traditional or mixed-form) was the rotation of name elements. For example, LC lists the authorized form for Adam Fortunate Eagle as Eagle, Adam Fortunate. The chosen cross-references are:

- Nordwall, Adam
- Fortunate Eagle, Adam
- Adam Fortunate Eagle

This last unsupported form is a particularly interesting and instructive example of North American Indian naming. Adam Nordwall was a leader in the 1969 takeover of Alcatraz Island by a coalition of North American Indian activists including members of the American Indian Movement. During the standoff that followed, Adam Nordwall was given the name Fortunate Eagle (Fortunate Eagle 1992). Virtually all references, at least in North American Indian literature, refer to either *Adam Fortunate Eagle* or *Fortunate Eagle*. LCNAF, however, appears to have applied the English name paradigm, so that *Eagle* was taken as a family name and *Adam Fortunate* as given names.

The first reference is a reasonable selection according to *AACR2R* (1998) Rule 22.2C1, since Adam Nordwall was the author's birth name. The second reference appears to follow rule 26.2A.3 because a patron might reasonably be expected to look for the author under this name (especially since it is the author's current mixed-form name). The third reference is peculiar; a patron is unlikely to look for the author Adam Fortunate Eagle under *A*. (This approach is like including "Nelson Mandela" as a cross-reference to "Mandela, Nelson.") The pattern seems to take care of all possibilities by rotating every entry element until the possibilities are exhausted. Though this pattern is amenable to automation, it does not appear to meet any intellectual standard.

Another example of odd references is the set chosen for the author Archie Fire Lame Deer. "Lame Deer, Archie Fire, 1935–") was the authorized form chosen by LC. They were:

- Fire, Archie, 1935–
- Deer, Archie Fire Lame, 1935–
- Archie Fire Lame Deer, 1935–

The following commentary on the above authority record is based on *Lame Deer* (no date), a World Wide Web site that includes the story "Lame Deer, Or How My Family Got Its Name."

The chosen authorized form, "Lame Deer, Archie Fire," is correct. The family name is Lame Deer, Archie Fire are given names; "Fire" has been a middle name for three generations: Archie Fire Lame Deer, John Fire Lame Deer (Archie's father), and Josephine Fire Lame Deer (Archie's daughter).

The first cross-reference, "Fire, Archie, 1935–," makes no sense, since "Lame Deer" was part of the author's name from birth. The third cross-reference, "Archie Fire Lame

Deer, 1935–," follows the same pattern as "Adam Fortunate Eagle," and seems equally unlikely to be used as a search point.

The second reference, "Deer, Archie Fire Lame, 1935–," is interesting because it appears to both follow a standard authority control practice and break a principle of naming among North American Indians. Clack (1990, 107–108) said, "References are made if ... [t]he name is a compound or multipart name and the parts are likely access points." If "Deer" is a likely access point, "Deer, Archie Fire Lame" is a reasonable reference; if, however, "Deer" is not a likely access point, "Deer, Archie Fire Lame" is not a reasonable reference. It seems to this researcher that, since both mixed and traditional names can comprise one concept expressed as two (or more) related words, searching on the second (or later) word is a way of changing the name. A changed name is not a likely access point, so this kind of reference does not seem acceptable.

North American Indian Names in North American National Libraries

The authority files of the Library of Congress (one of the four U.S. national libraries) had records for 156 of the 185 test names, and the authority files of the National Library of Canada had records for 154 of the 185 test names. However, the authorized form, not the author's presence, was being tested. Some names had dates added to an author's name when an authority record was created to separate people with the same name (current NACO policy is to add birth and death dates automatically). These dates could be expected in the authority files tested but not on the list of test names, so their presence should not be considered a deviation from the test set.

The LCNAF authorized forms for 39 of the 156 names differed from the form on the test list, a rate of 25 percent. Since bibliographers prepared the four bibliographies selected for this research, main sources of information (usually the title pages) were probably used to create the test names. In most cases LCNAF authorized forms were also derived from the main sources of information, so a 25 percent rate of difference is higher than might be expected.

The authorized forms for 31 of the 154 names in the National Library of Canada authority file differed from the forms on the test list, a rate of twenty percent. As with the Library of Congress, bibliographers prepared the four test bibliographies, so the main sources of information (usually title pages) were probably those used to create the test names. Since Canada's authorized forms were also selected from the main sources of information, a 20 percent difference rate was surprising.

Reasons for the differences between the Library of Congress' and the National Library of Canada's authority files may include:

- The author's name on a title page may be a cross-reference in LCNAF (for authors of more than one book). An example is the choice of "Brave Bird, Mary" or "Crow Dog, Mary."
- The author's name may be a multi-word traditional form or a mixed form and

LCNAF may have created the authorized form incorrectly. An example is the choice of "Fortunate Eagle, Adam" or "Eagle, Adam Fortunate."

The differences exhibited by the 39 different names included:

- Fullness of name: e.g., "Big Crow, Moses" in the test list versus "Big Crow, Moses Nelson" in the authority record.
- Added title: e.g., "Blacksnake" in the test list versus "Blacksnake, Governor" in the authority record.
- Added label: e.g., "Black Hawk" in the test list versus "Black Hawk, Sauk Chief" in the authority record.
- Name in the named person's original language: for example, "Buffalo Bird Woman" in the test list versus "Wahenee" in the authority record.
- Both European-form name and name in author's language: e.g., "Eastman, Charles Alexander (Ohiyesa)" in the test list versus "Eastman, Charles Alexander" in the authority record. This record hid a name set.
- Unsupported form: e.g., "Fortunate Eagle, Adam" in the test list versus "Eagle, Adam Fortunate" in the authority record.

North American Indian Names Outside North America

Only 75 of the 185 test names appeared in one or more of the eight national authority files of countries outside North America. Of those test names:

- Thirty-eight names appeared in one list only
- Fourteen names appeared in two lists
- Nine names appeared in three lists
- Six names appeared in four lists
- Six names appeared in five lists
- Two names appeared in six lists
- No names appeared in seven or eight lists

This section will discuss those names that appear in at least half of the eight lists. Fourteen names appeared in four or more test national authority files; six names appeared in four lists, six more names appeared in five lists, and two names appeared in six lists.

The names appearing in four or more lists were:

- Black Elk (five lists)
- Brave Bird, Mary (six lists)
- Craven, Margaret (four lists)
- Eastman, Charles Alexander (Ohiyesa) (four lists)
- Iwabuchi, Akifumi (four lists)
- La Flesche, Francis (four lists)
- Least Heat-Moon, William (five lists)
- Littlefield, Daniel F. (four lists)

- Rostworowski de Diez Canseco, Maria (four lists)
- Schoolcraft, Henry Rowe (five lists)
- Seattle, Chief (five lists)
- Snow, Dean R. (five lists)
- Tanaka, Beatrice (five lists)
- Tum, Rigoberta Menchu (six lists)

Traditional names were reported in different ways by different national authority files. For example, the Oglala Lakota author Black Elk was called:

- Elan Noir (his tribal name in French): French cross-reference
- Zwarte Eland (his tribal name in Dutch): Netherlands cross-reference
- Schwartzer Hirsch (his tribal name in German): Netherlands cross-reference

Clearly, entries for a traditional name can include translations of the name in any language. This is a result of names that both identify and describe the individual, since conceptual names lend themselves to translation. As discussed earlier, the presence of birth or death dates to separate identically named individuals is not considered a deviation from the names on the test set.

The authorized forms for the fourteen authors were:

Black Elk
    Australia: Black Elk, 1863–1950
    Austria: Black Elk
    Denmark: Black Elk
    France: Hehaka Sapa
    Netherlands: Black Elk (1863–1950)

Brave Bird, Mary
    Australia: Brave Bird, Mary
    Austria: Crow Dog, Mary
    Chile: Crow Dog, Mary
    Denmark: Crow Dog, Mary
    France: Crow Dog, Mary (1954–....)
    Netherlands: Crow Dog, Mary

Craven, Margaret
    Australia: Craven, Margaret
    Czech Republic: Craven, Margaret
    Denmark: Craven, Margaret
    Netherlands: Craven, Margaret

Eastman, Charles Alexander (Ohiyesa)
    Australia: Eastman, Charles Alexander, 1858–1939
    Czech Republic: Eastman, Charles Alexander 1858–1939
    Denmark: Eastman, Charles Alexander
    France: Eastman, Charles Alexander (1858–1939)

Iwabuchi, Akifumi
> Australia: Iwabuchi, Akifumi
> Denmark: Iwabuchi, Akifumi
> france: Iwabuchi, Akifumi
> Netherlands: Iwabuchi, Akifumi

La Flesche, Francis
> Chile: La Flesche, Francis, –1932.
> Denmark: La Flesche, Francis
> France: La Flesche, Francis
> Netherlands: La Flesche, Francis (Francis; –1932)

Least Heat-Moon, William
> Australia: Heat Moon, William Least
> Czech Republic: Least Heat Moon, William
> Denmark: Heat Moon, William Least
> France: Heat-Moon, William Least (1934–....)
> Netherlands: Heat Moon, William Least (pseud. Van: William Trogdon)

Littlefield, Daniel F.
> Australia: Littlefield, Daniel F.
> Denmark: Littlefield, Daniel F.
> France: Littlefield, Daniel F.
> Netherlands: Littlefield, Daniel F. (jr.)

Rostworowski de Diez Canseco, Maria
> Australia: Rostworowski de Diez Canseco, Maria
> Austria: Rostworowski de Diez Canseco, Maria
> Chile: Rostworowski de Diez Canseco, Maria
> France: Rostworowski de Diez Canseco, Maria

Schoolcraft, Henry Rowe
> Australia: Schoolcraft, Henry R. (Henry Rowe), 1793–1864
> Chile: Schoolcraft, Henry Rowe 1793–1864
> Denmark: Schoolcraft, Henry Rowe
> France: Schoolcraft, Henry Rowe
> Netherlands: Schoolcraft, Henry Rowe (Henry Rowe; 1793–1864)

Seattle, Chief
> Australia: Seattle, Chief, 1790–1866
> Austria: Seattle
> Denmark: Seattle, Hovding
> France: Seattle, Chief (1790–1866)
> Netherlands: Seattle (ca 1786–1866)

Snow, Dean R.
> Australia: Snow, Dean R., 1940–
> Czech Republic: Snow, Dean
> Denmark: Snow, Dean R., 1940–

France: Snow, Dean R. (1940–....)
Netherlands: Snow, Dean R. (Dean R.; 1940–)

Tanaka, Beatrice
Chile: Tanaka, Beatrice
Denmark: Tanaka, Beatrice
France: Tanaka, Beatrice (1932–....)
Latvia: Tanaka, Beatrice
Netherlands: Tanaka, Beatrice

Tum, Rigoberta Menchu
Australia: Menchu, Rigoberta
Austria: Menchu, Rigoberta
Chile: Menchu, Rigoberta, 1959–
Denmark: Menchu, Rigoberta
France: Menchu, Rigoberta (1959–....)
Netherlands: Menchu, Rigoberta (Rigoberta; 1960–)

At least one of the 14 authors was included in each of the eight test bibliographies. The authorized forms for five names were the same in all of the national authority files containing them. The authorized forms for nine of the names were different in different national authority files. One of the foundations of the international authority control movement is standardization, so a different name presentation rate of 64 percent indicates that standardization is far from being accomplished.

Three of the authors ("Craven, Margaret"; "Iwabuchi, Akifumi"; and "Rostworowski de Diez Canseco, Maria") had identical authorized forms in all of the national bibliographies including them. All of the authorized forms except one, for Daniel F. Littlefield, were identical; the national authority file of the Netherlands adds ("jr.") to "Littlefield, Daniel F."

Two additional authors ("Eastman, Charles Alexander" and "Tanaka, Beatrice") appeared in several national authority files with identical authorized forms with birth and death date extensions.

Four of the 12 test names found in the national authority file of the Netherlands followed the authorized form with a repetition of the author's given name as well as a date extension in parentheses. For example, the Danish authorized form for Francis La Flesche was "La Flesche, Francis" but the authorized form in the national authority file of the Netherlands was "La Flesche, Francis (Francis;–1932)." The Danish authorized form for William Least Heat-Moon was "Heat Moon, William Least" but the authorized form in the national bibliography of the Netherlands was "Heat Moon, William Least (pseud. Van: William Trogdon)."

The authorized forms in the national authority files of Australia, Austria, Denmark, and the Netherlands for the Lakota author Black Elk were "Black Elk" with or without date extensions. But the main entry in the national authority file of France was "Hehaka Sapa," the author's name in Lakota.

The Australian authorized form for Mary Brave Bird is "Brave Bird, Mary." The authorized forms in the six test national authority files are all "Crow Dog, Mary" with or without a date extension. Crow Dog is the family name of the author's first husband; Brave Bird is the family name of the author's second husband.

The national authority file of Chile stated that its records are taken from LCNAF. The LCNAF authorized form for Mary Brave Bird, however, is "Brave Bird, Mary," and the Chilean authorized form is "Crow Dog, Mary." Apparently, Chile's national authority file, while it might originate in LCNAF, does not maintain its authorized forms scrupulously.

The authorized forms for Rigoberta Menchu Tum in all seven of the national bibliographies examined were "Menchu, Rigoberta," with or without a date extension. At the time that she won the 1992 Nobel Peace Prize and wrote her best-known book, "Rigoberta Menchu Tum" was already her name.

Overall, the analysis of the 14 names contained in multiple national authority files (nine of which had more than one authorized form) indicated a lack of standardization among authorized forms.

Cultural Distance

This section will discuss new bibliographic evidence for cultural distance. Table 2 lists the number of test names found in the ten tested national authority files.

Table 2: Authorized forms of test names found

National Library	Found	Not Found	Total Names
USA	No.=156 %=84.32	No.=29 %=15.68	No.=185 %=100.00
CANADA	No.=154 %=83.24	No.=31 %=16.76	No.=185 %=100.00
AUSTRALIA	No.=41 %=22.16	No.=144 %=77.84	No.=185 %=100.00
DENMARK	No.=37 %=20.00	No.=148 %=80.00	No.=185 %=100.00
FRANCE	No.=35 %=18.92	No.=150 %=81.08	No.=185 %=100.00
NETHERLANDS	No.=19 %=10.27	No.=166 %=89.73	No.=185 %=100.00
AUSTRIA	No.=10 %=5.41	No.=175 %=94.59	No.=185 %=100.00
CZECH REPUBLIC	No.=9 %=4.87	No.=176 %=95.13	No.=185 %=100.00
CHILE	No.=6 %=3.24	No.=179 %=96.76	No.=185 %=100.00
LATVIA	No.=2 %=1.08	No.=183 %=98.92	No.=185 %=100.00

Obviously, more test names can be found among the national collections of the United States and Canada. These, after all, are the nations where North American Indians live.

There also appears to be a direct correlation between the national bibliographic collections of the countries that colonized North America (and the nations which were colonized by North America's colonizers) and the number of books by North American Indian authors. So the Australian National Library (Australia, like most of North America, was colonized by Great Britain) has more books than the National Library of France (France colonized only a small part of North America).

The next category to examine is the national authority files of western European nations that did not colonize North America: Denmark, the Netherlands, and Austria. These national bibliographies have 37, 19, and 10 test names respectively. These countries have close cultural ties to the colonizing countries, but were not themselves colonizers. True, Denmark's national bibliography has two more test names than France's. This could simply be an artifact of the study, or it could be a result of the breadth of vision of Scandinavian cultures.

The national bibliography of the Czech Republic includes nine of the test names. Moreover, the cultural ties between eastern Europe and the colonization of North America are significantly weaker than those of non-colonizing western European nations.

In a very interesting example, the national bibliography of Chile includes six of the test names. Chile was colonized by Spain, a country that colonized very little of what is now North America. During the era of colonization Spain, Britain, and France were antagonistic. In addition, Chile has indigenous cultures that, in terms of its national history, parallel the indigenous cultures of North America. Maybe Chile's national bibliography is as rich in the names of South American indigenous authors as the Library of Congress is in the names of indigenous North Americans.

Finally, the national bibliography of Latvia includes two of the test names. Its cultural ties to western Europe (not to mention North America) may be even more remote than the connections of the colonizers and the Czech Republic.

Currently there is a trend to integrate eastern Europe and western Europe (economically and politically if not culturally). It is an interesting question whether such an effort at integration might be reflected in national bibliographies.

Conclusion

This article interweaves two disparate threads. First is the structure of North American Indian personal names and naming. Two name forms and two name patterns were identified in addition to the standard European form.

Then a set of test names was applied to ten national bibliographies. Two conclusions appeared: a lack of consistency and bibliographic cultural distance. The lack of consistency may present a problem (or at least an issue to be resolved) for the international authority control movement.

So is bibliographic cultural distance a reality? Based on the evidence in this study, it appears to be. And it does make sense that there would be a relation between a nation's culture and the works included in its national bibliography. Continued research is needed, for the concept could be important.

Bibliography

Alexie, S. (2000). Biography. Available: <http://fallsapart.com/biography.html> (accessed 21 February 2004).

Anglo-American Cataloguing Rules: Second Edition, 1998 Revision. (1998). Chicago: American Library Association Editions.

Clark, W. P. (1982). *The Indian Sign Language.* Lincoln: University of Nebraska Press.

Fortunate Eagle, A. (1992). *Alcatraz! Alcatraz!: The Indian Occupation of 1969–1971.* Berkeley, CA: Heyday Books.

Giese, P. (1996). All native books. Available: <http://www.kstrom.net/isk/books/all_idx.html> (accessed 21 February 2004).

Hook, J. N. (1982). *Family Names.* New York: Macmillan.

IFLA (International Federation of Library Associations and Institutions). (1996). *Names of Persons: National Usages for Entry in Catalogues* (fourth revised and enlarged edition). Munich: K.G. Saur Verlag GmbH & Co.

Ingraham, H. (1997). *People's Names: A Cross-Cultural Reference Guide to the Proper Use of Over 40,000 Personal and Familial Names in Over 100 Cultures.* Jefferson, NC: McFarland & Company, Inc.

Lame Deer, Josephine Fire. Lame Deer, or how my family received its name. Available: <http://www.geocities.com/Wellesley/Garden/3922/jo-lamedr.html> (accessed 21 February 2004).

Mitten, L. (1999). New Indian books. Available: <http://www.nativeculture.com/lisamitten/indbks.html> (accessed 21 February 2004).

Powell, R. R. (1997). *Basic Research Methods for Librarians* (third edition). Greenwich, CT: Ablex Publishing Corporation.

Utley, R. M. (1993). *The Lance and the Shield.* New York: Henry Holt and Company.

Waldman, C. (1985). *Atlas of the North American Indian.* New York: Facts On File, Inc.

Young Bear, S., and Theisz, R. D. (1994). *Standing in the Light: A Lakota Way of Seeing.* Lincoln: University of Nebraska Press.

Useful Cataloging

Chris Dodge

Radical surgery aims to remove the roots of disease. Radical politics depart extremely from business as usual. What defines radical cataloging? *Webster's Third* says "radical" can relate to roots or origins, meaning "original, fundamental, inherent," and that's the sort of radical toward which the words that follow will incline.

Assertions and Opinions:

• Catalog users are best served by catalogers less concerned with correctness than *usefulness*, Sanford Berman has long asserted. I agree.
• Primary sources are too frequently neglected.
• Things written long ago oft remain germane.

Herewith are documents from my files, the first reprinted from two issues of *MSRRT Newsletter* in 1998 and 1999.

Politics of Cataloging

Librarians, according to stereotype, are stodgy, shushing women with their hair in buns. While this image is decried within the profession, many librarians direct their own prejudices toward catalogers. This class of person, popular wisdom goes, has marginal social skills and obsesses neurotically upon matters of "bibliographic *petit point*." Unfortunately, there is an element of truth in this generalization. The professed concern is largely for cataloging *correctly* rather than usefully, and for following proscribed rules (or interpreting them "accurately") rather than considering catalog searchers. Two principles that steer subject catalogers are specificity and standard terminology. At times, however, these principles are applied dysfunctionally. As a case in point, look at the Library of Congress record for George B. Schaller's *Wildlife of the Tibetan Steppe*. If you'd expect a user to be able to find this work by searching for WILDLIFE—TIBET, you are sadly mistaken. LC's subject headings assigned are: UNGULATA—CHINA—CHANG TANG PLATEAU and MAMMALS—CHINA—CHANG TANG PLATEAU.

More insidious access problems exist at a higher level. Dozens of books and government documents have appeared in recent years on the topics of GATT, NAFTA, MAI, and other treaties and international agreements. Systematically these have not been assigned specific access points by name of treaty. One veteran cataloger at LC reports that about twenty years ago treaties were moved from the subject file to the names file "on the grounds that they were in fact uniform titles of named documents." From that point, descriptive catalogers were supposed to establish names of treaties that would then be used as subject headings by the subject catalogers. The latter were supposed to return books to the descriptive catalogers when this hadn't been done, and remind them to do it. "Unfortunately nobody is appointed to remind the subject catalogers to remind the descriptive catalogers," another LC cataloger notes. "It has probably been overlooked more times than it has been done ... [and] has become a rather large can of worms." The head of LC's Cataloging Policy and Support Office has not responded to queries about this issue. [From *MSRRT Newsletter*, September/October 1998.]

Politics of Cataloging, II

Last year we criticized the Library of Congress for failing to assign treaty-specific subject headings to records for materials on GATT, NAFTA, and MAI. ("Politics of Cataloging," *MSRRT Newsletter*, Sept./Oct. 1998). After no response last fall, a belated dialogue ensued this past April after the commentary piece was sent to LC's Cataloging Policy and Support Office. Here are selections from the email correspondence:

LC: Dear Ms. Dodge ... Headings for treaties are established in the Library of Congress name authority file according to AACR2 rules. These headings are then assigned as subject headings to works about the treaties. For example, the AACR2 heading for NAFTA is "Canada. Treaties, etc. 1992 Oct. 7," The heading for GATT is "General Agreement on Tariffs and Trade (Organization)." Subject catalogers typically assign the heading for a treaty only to a general work on the treaty as a whole, not to a work that is only tangentially about it ...." [This was followed by 180 words, literally citing chapter and verse — "Subject Cataloging Manual: Subject Headings, H 2227, sec. 2.b"— describing what subject catalogers do, namely, use our best judgment to decide if headings are warranted.]

CD: Thank you for your response. Happily, it seems as though some retrospective work has been done at LC in assigning specific headings to works about NAFTA. Dozens of such titles remain, however, that have not been assigned "Canada. Treaties, etc. 1992 Oct. 7." Among the most obvious: *NAFTA: What You Need to Know Now*; *The NAFTA Puzzle: Political Parties and Trade in North America*; *North American Free Trade Agreement: Summary and Analysis*; *NAFTA: An Assessment*; and *Corporte* [sic] *Counsel's Guide to the North American Free Trade Agreement*. Certainly these and other titles warrant specific assignment. (As an aside, would you care to explain to public library catalog users why "Canada. Treaties, etc. 1992 Oct. 7" is used instead of "North American Free Trade Agreement"?) On a smaller scale, regarding works about MAI, why no specific subject heading assignment to *MAI: The Multilateral Agreement on Investment and the Threat to American Freedom* or *MAI: The Multilateral Agreement on Investment and the Threat to Canadian Sovereignty*?

LC: As time permits, I will check the titles you report and add the heading for NAFTA where appropriate. It appears that some may have been cataloged prior to the time the treaty was signed and ratified and the heading established. Many were cataloged by the Government Printing Office, not by the Library of Congress. Thanks for letting us know about these. [This is followed by an "explanation" for the form of the heading for NAFTA: "Library of Congress follows the Anglo-American Cataloguing Rules, 2nd edition, in establishing headings."] The heading "OECD Multilateral Agreement on Investment" was established only a few months ago. We are in the process of updating the appropriate bibliographic records to add the heading. I notice that the name authority record for this treaty does not currently have references from the forms "MAI" or "OECD MAI." I will arrange to have those references added.

CD: Many thanks for your attention to this matter.

LC: I have some additional information to provide to you regarding MAI. This treaty is still a draft which has not yet been adopted and ratified. That is the reason why the Library of Congress had not established a heading for it and has not assigned it as a subject heading. It is not our practice to establish headings for proposed treaties, laws, etc. The LC office in Nairobi, Kenya erroneously established the heading "OECD Multilateral Agreement on Investment" in our name authority file recently, contrary to our standard practice. We have removed that heading from the file. Until such time as the treaty is actually approved and adopted, we will continue to assign only topical headings to works about this proposed treaty. If and when the treaty is adopted we will then establish a heading for it.

CD: Since there are whole works about MAI [cited previously], why not gloss a subject heading thusly?: Multilateral Agreement on Investment (Proposed). I am suggesting that if this is not currently policy, that it be made so.

LC: Thanks for the suggestion. I'm sorry that we are not in a position to consider changing our policy at the present time. We catalog so much material on proposals or drafts for legislation, treaties, etc., that it is not practical for us to establish headings for entities of this type that do not yet exist in reality. It would be too time-consuming to have to monitor these proposals and update headings if and when the proposals are actually adopted.

CD: Would you say 'We catalog so many materials on World War II history that it is not practical for us to establish [related] headings'? If there are whole works about a subject, why not make it policy to establish and assign a heading? If that subject is a proposed treaty, why not gloss it with the word 'proposed' in parentheses? Claiming that the MAI doesn't exist because it hasn't been signed is a disservice to catalog users. Try explaining to a public library patron that there is no subject heading for this reason. It's widely recognized. Here's one web search directory result: *Yahoo! Category Matches: Business and Economy > Trade > Law > International > Multilateral Agreement on Investment (MAI)*.

LC: The Library of Congress operates with very limited resources and is under a mandate by the U.S. Congress to give the highest priority to reducing our arrearage of many millions of uncataloged items to which no access at all currently exists. Given these constraints on our time and resources, it is not practical for us to provide the level of detailed access to material on proposed treaties that you advocate. We appreciate hear-

ing your opinion on this matter. Should circumstances permit, at some time in the future
we might consider a change in our practice to provide this enhanced level of access. However, at this time it is impossible for us to do so. [From *MSRRT Newsletter*, Summer
1999.]

Bibliocide I

In January 2005, when I was working as librarian at *Utne Magazine* (now *Utne Reader*
again), I wrote to the head of Collection and Bibliographic Services at Minnesota's Hennepin County Library, identifying myself as a colleague, catalog user, and former HCL
cataloger, trying to answer questions for myself and for a library intern cataloger at Utne:

> Once, I told my intern, users of the HCL catalog could search for "mystery stories" and
> immediately be presented with links to many "see also" headings — showing that the library
> collection included, for example, gay mystery stories and lesbian mystery stories, among oth-
> ers ("culinary mystery stories" also comes to mind). These links provided not only more
> specific access, but hit lists that weren't unmanageably large. Now — as I showed my intern —
> a search for "mystery stories" results in "See 'Detective and mystery stories,'" from which one
> goes, dysfunctionally, to a hit list of nearly 11,000 titles. [As of September 2006, the heading
> has been changed to "Mystery fiction," probably mystifying those used to searching "Detec-
> tive and mystery stories," and the list has grown to well over 12,000 titles.] Not only is it a
> problem that a step is bypassed showing "see also" references, but there's now only one "see
> also" heading left, to "Noir fiction."
> Ah, I said. Let's look up author Michael Nava, a gay author whose first books were pub-
> lished by a gay press, whose characters are typically gay detectives. A look at the MARC
> record for the oldest of his books held by HCL (*The Little Death*) shows seven headings
> tagged 695:
>
> | | | |
> |---|---|---|
> | 695 | $a Lawyer-detectives $z California $v Fiction. | |
> | 695 | $a Gay mystery stories. | |
> | 695 | $a Chicano lawyers $z California $z Los Angeles $v Fiction. | |
> | 695 | $a Chicano detectives $z California $z Los Angeles $v Fiction. | |
> | 695 | $a Mystery stories, Chicano. | |
> | 695 | $a Gay detectives $z California $z Los Angeles $v Fiction. | |
> | 695 | $a Gay Chicanos $z California $z Los Angeles $v Fiction. | |
>
> My question is: Why aren't these indexed? Why were these access points removed? And do
> you have a count of how many such headings exist in the HCL bibliographic database?
> I'll never forget the day I tried to find a citation for a book I'd cataloged, and couldn't find
> it because access to a subject heading had been removed. Frankly, I was horrified.
> Gone now are access to materials on such topics as "new baby in family" and "moving to a
> new neighborhood." Gone is access to books assigned such generic headings as "Minnesota
> poetry"— for poetic works by Minnesota authors — and "Minnesota fiction." Gone is access
> to works representing countless genres from "Restaurant cookbooks" to "Eco-fiction." My
> mind boggles.

I closed the letter "Hoping for answers."

Some weeks later I received a discouraging reply offering not answers but excuses,
it seemed to me, noting that as of October 2002, HCL subject headings "that did not
conform to standard forms" were no longer authorized. The reply also referred me to a

product called NoveList on the library's website, a product itself based on the library's now inadequate catalog.

Bibliocide II

As Sandy Berman has often pointed out — and strived in various ways to change (including petition campaigns and direct correspondence) — the Library of Congress has a history of failing to promptly establish warranted subject headings, ones that are clear and useful. An issue of *The U*N*A*B*A*S*H*E*D Librarian* from 1985 contained some of Berman's letters requesting the addition of subject headings for which literary warrant existed (for example, FAMILY PLANNING, HUMAN SERVICES, MARXISM, VIOLENCE AGAINST WOMEN, WOMEN'S SHELTERS); the addition of new terms for new topics (i.e., PAY EQUITY, MEN'S MOVEMENT, FEMINIST THEOLOGY, TEENAGE ABORTION); and the replacement of biased terms (i.e., "Eskimos/Inuit," "gypsies/Romanies," "man/humans," "city council-men/city council members," "women as jurors/women jurors," "aged/seniors," "underground press/alternative press").

I can report that the Library of Congress has made progress since then. But LC still has no headings for Marxism, Leninism, Trotskyism, or Maoism — all are subsumed under the broad heading COMMUNISM, which means that anyone looking for material specifically on any of these variants must wade through 4,966 bibliographic records, when last I checked.

Oddly, LC *does* have a heading for MARXIAN ECONOMICS now, with a cross-reference from MARXIST ECONOMICS. An authority record note indicates that the source of the literary warrant is a book titled *Marxist Economics for Socialists*. So why isn't the heading MARXIST ECONOMICS? And why no MARXISM?

Further, LC retains countless out-of-date terms with the result that reasonable catalog searches prove fruitless. As a case in point, try searching for "French films" or "French movies" in the LC catalog. It's as if the concept didn't exist. Not only does LC eschew the term "films" and retain the archaic MOTION PICTURES, its catalogers fail to make appropriate cross references here. (The same goes for Chinese films, German films, etc.)

If a non-expert catalog user somehow learns to search for MOTION PICTURES, that user may discover that LC makes a distinction between films based on where they are shown. The scope note under MOTION PICTURES—FRANCE reads: "Here are entered general works on motion pictures shown in France or produced by French film companies. Works on motion pictures produced by French film companies and shown outside of France are entered under MOTION PICTURES, FRENCH." As a result of this, and concomitant confusion, countless library catalogs have some of their Truffaut and Renoir films (and works about them) listed under MOTION PICTURES—FRANCE, some under MOTION PICTURES, FRENCH.

Those who wonder if LC cataloging policy makers enjoy causing aggravation would do well to take matters into their own hands. Change MOTION PICTURES to FILMS, add appropriate cross references (to FRENCH FILMS from MOVIES, FRENCH, for example), and use headings such as FILMS—FRANCE only for works about how film as a medium is viewed, thought about, and written about in individual countries.

What Is Going On at the
Library of Congress?*

Thomas Mann

The judgments made in this paper do not represent official views of the Library of Congress.

What is going on at the Library of Congress? Several recent decisions by the current LC administration have produced firestorms of protest, both inside and outside the Library, that LC is abdicating its professional responsibilities to the national system of shared cataloging, as well as undermining its core mission to acquire, catalog, make accessible, and preserve its own unparalleled holdings — especially its book collections. Among these recent decisions are:

1. The commissioning of "The Calhoun Report" to provide an ostensibly objective cover to justify abandoning the system of Library of Congress Subject Headings (among other recommendations to downgrade LC's cataloging and classification operations). [See <http://www.guild2910.org/AFSCMECalhounReview.pdf>.]
2. The unilateral decision to stop creating Series Authority Records, in violation of the standards the Library previously agreed to in the national Program for Cooperative Cataloging. [For an overview of the damage this will do to researchers, see the national petition, with 3,495 signatures, to protest this move at <http://www.peti tiononline.com/MARC830/petition.html>.]
3. The decision to accept digital formats for preservation purposes in place of paper copies or microfiche for traditional materials that are not "born digital." (In May of 2006 Beacher Wiggins, the Director for Acquisitions & Bibliographic Access, and Deanna Marcum, Associate Librarian for Library Services, agreed to cancel print titles from the Emerald group of publications in exchange for access to digital versions; in the previous month they agreed to stop collecting American doctoral dissertations on microfiche from University Microfilms in exchange for electronic access to digital versions. (LC, according to its national library responsibilities, had up to then

*Prepared for AFSCME 2910, The Library of Congress Professional Guild

maintained the only full set of dissertations in preservable form in any American library.) It was decided that "access" to electronic copies was less expensive. Recent papers on the astronomical economic costs of maintaining digital formats, as contrasted to microfilm-even apart from the still unsolved technical problems of emulation and migration-were simply disregarded; they may be found at <http://jodi. tamu.edu/Articles/v04/i02/Chapman/> and <http://hurstassociates.blogspot.com/ 2006/04/article-digital-black-hole.html>.)

4. The decision by the Library's Copyright Office to dumb down the cataloging of copyright receipts by recording only the information on the registrant's application form, without any inspection of the actual deposited items. (An essay on the problems this will create for future researchers is at <http://www.guild2910.org/CopyrightCatalog. pdf >.)

5. Perhaps most disturbing of all, the continual starvation and dilution of the Library's book-cataloging operations over a period of several years, with the claim that "inelastic funds" necessitate a massive retrenchment in this area, when in fact it is the administration's change in "vision" that now ranks the digitization of copyright-free special collections as a higher priority for the Library's funding than maintenance of traditional book cataloging operations.

The cumulation of these decisions marks a tipping point in imposing an agenda that has long been the goal of the current administration — a goal that will have profound negative implications for research libraries, as well as for individual scholars, throughout the nation. This goal can be characterized as "moving the Library into the digital age"— the "digital age," however, as it is envisioned from a decidedly blinkered perspective.

Characteristics of the blinkered "vision"

Several characteristics of LC management's vision for the future of LC, and of research libraries dependent on LC systems, are matters of great concern:

• It puts much greater emphasis on digitizing LC's "special collections" (manuscripts, maps, photos, etc.— in general, our non-book formats) at the expense of cataloging and classifying our "general collections" (i.e., the books).
• It effectively subordinates LC's book collections as being less important to scholarship than its non-book formats.
• Its new concentration on special formats entails a de-valuing of cataloging and classification operations for book formats — effectively a turning away from maintenance of the cataloging systems that research libraries everywhere depend on.
• It puts inordinate faith in Internet search mechanisms (Google-type relevance ranked keyword searching, Amazon-type user preference ["folksonomy"] tracking) for providing access to books, at the expense of entry through vocabulary-controlled headings and authority-controlled names, titles, and series, the loss of which will be profound for systematic (rather than haphazard) searches.
• Its advocates' confidence in the adequate operation of Internet-type search mecha-

nisms that "relevance rank" keywords from digitized full texts is itself predicated on the wishful-thinking assumption that copyright restrictions on book digitization will be greatly relaxed in Google's favor.

• Its proponents are acting as though those copyright restrictions are *already* legally relaxed, by attempting to dismantle the access systems (cataloging and classification) that remain necessary for efficient access to printed and non-digitized books — as well as to any digital counterparts they may have.

• It asserts that substantial onsite collections of printed books are themselves no longer necessary in research libraries, and that books ought to be housed in remote storage warehouses to avoid "costly duplication" among research library collections; consequently neither LC nor any library following our lead needs to concern itself any more with the shelving of large collections of physical books in subject-categorized groupings for onsite subject browsing.

• Its belief that merging book records (either catalog records or digitized full texts) into a single huge database of "everything" searchable simultaneously ("seamlessly") through a single Google-type search box would effectively bury books amid mountains of irrelevancies that would make substantive scholarship much more difficult to accomplish.

• Its understanding of what "the user" wants is severely skewed by misrepresentations of what user studies actually report.

• Its proponents are relying on "feedback" from only a small coterie of like-minded "digital library" advocates, to the neglect of most users of LC cataloging and classification systems.

• It is essentially writing off efficient access to all books that are not in the English language — sources that would be systematically retrieved in the conceptual categories created by cataloging and classification but which will not be retrieved by Google-type keyword searches or Amazon-type reader referrals.

• It is effectively changing the very mission not only of LC itself, but of all research libraries, from that of promoting systematic scholarship, especially (though not exclusively) within book literature, to that of simply providing "something" (usually not books) delivered quickly and remotely, and discoverable only through haphazard and non-systematic keyword or user-referral mechanisms.

It is perhaps hard for the outside world to believe that such massive changes in the national library system — and such prospective losses of access to *books*— have already progressed as far as they have. Any further debate on these issues, by either AFSCME 2910 members or the outside scholarly community, needs to be informed by a look at the pattern of LC management's own statements and actions.

In LC management's own words

In a May 5th, 2006 letter to the directors of the Association of Research Libraries, Deanna Marcum, the Associate Librarian for Library Services, says the following:

When I spoke to the Association of Research Libraries shortly after I was appointed Associate Librarian for Library Services, I spoke of the necessity of rethinking our bibliographic infrastructure. I charged all of the directors with redesigning our services and products *with the needs of the end-user—the individual researcher—in mind.* I also charged the Acquisitions and Bibliographic Access Directorate ... with streamlining their processes *to make information held by the Library of Congress more conveniently and more quickly accessible to our users....*

Despite the call from petitioners for restoration of funds to replace retiring staff, our decision to stop creating series authority records was not a cost consideration. We, like all of you, are looking for ways to invest more of our inelastic funds in *services that add value for researchers, students and the general public.* We are using the opportunity the comes with retirements to *reconsider areas in which to invest our staff resources.* We have millions of items in our **special collections** that are not available to the public because they do not have even cursory bibliographic description. *We know that increasingly our users go first to Google and other Internet search engines to find information they are seeking.* We have made it a priority to **increase access to content rather than to continue bibliographic practices** that, though helpful to other libraries, do not add **immediate** value **for the user....**"

Big changes are on the way. The series authority records are but the first step in refocusing the Library of Congress to take advantage of the promises of technology, *to focus on the actual needs of information seekers,* and to build a 21st century library that is as effective *in the digital age* as the traditional library *has been* in the *world of print.* [Emphasis added, here as below]

Dr. Marcum's vision for the "digital age," as expressed here, consistently reiterates her comments elsewhere, as reported (for one example) in the distributed minutes of LC's March 24, 2004, Cataloging Management Team (CMT) Meeting:

Deanna reminded the CMT of the "Out-Sell study" commissioned by the Council on Library and Information Resources and issued in October 2002, *Dimensions and Use of the Scholarly Information Environment: Introduction to a Data Set Assembled by the Digital Library Federation and Outsell, Inc.,* (available at <http://www.clir.org/pubs/abstract/pub110abst. html>). This study asked more than 3,000 faculty and students at nearly 400 academic institutions, ranging from community colleges to the Ivy League, where they went to fill their information needs. **Deanna said the study showed that faculty and students have enormous respect and trust for libraries, but they don't use them.** *Instead, they turn first to Google.* Most members of the CMT nodded in agreement. Deanna said this finding raised the question of how much to invest in the ways libraries have been providing information... . She asked the CMT to think about cataloging **from the perspective of users, not necessarily of other libraries.** She also predicted that the future of libraries would be closely tied to relationships with Google and other similar organizations.

[Arts and Sciences Division Cataloging Chief] Judy [Mansfield] mentioned research by Prof. Karen Markey Drabenstott (University of Michigan School of Information) showing that **end users "always" construct keyword searches as one or two words....**

Deanna said that the Library of Congress needed to undertake a massive effort to digitize its collections, notwithstanding obstacles posed by copyright law. The Library would need to negotiate settlements with intellectual property rightsholders...

Dennis [McGovern, of the Social Sciences Cataloging Division] pointed out that *Library of Congress Subject Headings (LCSH)* inform the *Dewey Decimal Classification* and the Faceted Application of Subject Terminology (FAST), and therefore have a life of their own even if students don't search directly using LCSH. LCSH is also important to researchers outside their own fields since the headings and reference structure present a view of the organization of knowledge in all fields. Numerous other databases use LCSH. In reply to a question from Dennis, *Deanna said that there is a good deal of research showing that subject analysis is less important now than in the past.* She repeated that *helping people get to information* is the work we have to do....

Deanna said that Google was seeking agreements with libraries to digitize the content they owned. If Google succeeds in digitizing a library of eight to ten million volumes and making the content available on the Web, what happens to every other library? *She said Library of Congress cataloging would not be needed in these circumstances. The LC role might be to augment the digital core with its special collections.*

... Jeff [Heynen, Chief of the History and Literature Cataloging Division] said that "our biggest problem" was that the Library of Congress is committed to applying consensual standards which take years to establish and change.

Deanna closed her remarks by saying she was thrilled that CMT members were thinking as broadly and creatively as they could. [emphasis added]

Of the many points touched on here, let us concern ourselves first with Dr. Marcum's expressed concern for "the user."

A Skewed Vision of the Library's Users

The passages just quoted places emphasis, commendably, on serving "the needs of the end user." What is problematic is Dr. Marcum's vision of who that end user is. In the letter to ARL directors she says "We know that increasingly our users go first to Google and other Internet search engines to find information they are seeking." And in the CMT minutes she claims that the *Dimensions* study "showed that faculty and students have enormous respect and trust for libraries, but they don't use them." This assertion, however, is directly contradicted by the study itself, which found, from over 3,200 interviews, that 55.4 percent of all respondents (and 59.7 percent of undergraduates) still regard browsing as "an important way" to get information. Two thirds of faculty and grad students use print resources for research all or most of the time. 52 percent of undergrads use print for coursework all or most of the time. (For additional evidence of students' continued library use, from multiple other surveys, see "Survey of User Studies" at <http://www.guild2910.org/google.htm>.)

Second, she says — accurately — that students do turn "first" to Google. But her implication is that the typical student today uses *only* Google — i.e., the user does *not* use the library *in addition to* Google. This is clear from the way she has repeatedly represented that user in several of her speeches. Indeed, AFSCME 2910 members need to be clearly aware that Dr. Marcum has portrayed "the user" that research libraries need to be concerned with not as a serious scholar but rather as undergraduate with a certain mind set:

And let's suppose that I am one of your students with a term paper coming due. And let's suppose further that I've been assigned to write about the foreign policy of President Fillmore.

Now, in the old days, I might have walked to the library ... . But today, let's say it's cold outside on campus, and I don't want to go to the library. *I want to stay in my cozy dorm room*, where I have a computer ... .

I ... have the option, *sitting there in my cozy computer-equipped dorm room*, of *ignoring the library*, and going online to, say, the Google commercial search service. *With Google, all I have to do is type my subject*—"President Fillmore Foreign Policy"—into a search box and click on "Go." If I have used "Advanced Search" to get only references containing all four words, up will come what Google calls the first ten references out of "about 14,200." I don't have to go through multiple organizational layers, guessing and clicking, to get *something* on my subject. [Speech on "The Challenges of Managing Information" to the 2005 Presidents Institute of the Council of Independent Colleges, 6 January 2005 [emphasis added]; same example used in "The Future of Cataloging" January 16, 2004 <http://www.guild2910.org/marcum.htm>]

In another speech, to the Great Lakes Colleges Association, 13 April 2006, Dr. Marcum uses the example of a now college-aged "Calvin" from the comic strip *Calvin and Hobbes*, who also wishes to avoid the burden of "making the physical trek from his dorm all the way to the campus library." In past times he "still had to go to the library building to get [information]. *He didn't like that,*" she says. She continues:

Eventually, you [college administrators and head librarians] *made it easier* for him by setting up an e-mail address, through which he could consult with a reference librarian *without going to the library*. And you installed a computer program that enabled him to do key-word searching of the online catalog. But before long, Calvin looked at Hobbes, and Hobbes looked at Calvin, and they both nodded — yes, *there's an easier way. Go to the Web, get the Google search box, type in a keyword*, and get back **not catalog information**, *and* **not advice**, *but* **information itself** — the stuff you really need *to write a term paper*. On the Web he could do that *without having to go to the library or anywhere else outside his dorm room, except that candy-bar machine*. Calvin *really* liked that. [emphasis added]

The "user" who is portrayed repeatedly in Dr. Marcum's speeches as someone who avoids the library entirely is not the user who is described in a wide variety of user studies (*supra*). Nevertheless, it is just *this* dorm-bound undergraduate whom Marcum consistently portrays as "the user" that research libraries should be striving to accommodate.

It is noteworthy that there are a variety of ways, not one, to deal with the student who does not "like" to have to go "all the way" from a "cozy dorm" room into a physical library. One is to *educate* that person to an awareness of the range of resources and search techniques that he or she is missing by avoiding the library and confining search inquiries to the Google alone — as opposed to endorsing the rank superficiality of scholarship on "Millard Fillmore Foreign Policy" that Google, at its best, enables. (See "Research at Risk," *Library Journal* [July, 2005] regarding the results that Google actually turns up on Fillmore.) This is not Marcum's recommendation, however; she sees the Google Book Search project as essentially *eliminating the need for education*. In the same Great Lakes speech she says:

The project, Google said, would greatly advance its stated mission, which is nothing less than, quote, "to organize the world's information and make it universally accessible and useful." Additionally, Google is working toward providing, quote, "*the perfect search engine,*" which, quote, "*would understand exactly what you mean*" (in your requests as a searcher) and "*give back exactly what you want.*"
  That set of intentions is breathtaking.
  Google, it would appear, will greatly *accelerate* digitization of huge libraries ... Also, Google keeps working on ways to enable users of masses of digitized material to find what they want **with ease and precision**.
  Hearing this, Calvin suddenly **lost interest in literacy training**. A new time-machine-like technology was in sight to simplify his homework again. [emphasis added]

Marcum's solution to the problem of how to serve "the user," then, essentially recommends that libraries (a) put more digitized full-text content into Google, to increase the quality of what is available, and (b) to rely entirely on Google's search software to provide efficient access to it because (c) Google makes educational "advice" from librarians and "literacy training" on how to do research unnecessary.

Digitizing Special Collections as a Priority Higher Than Cataloging and Classifying Books

Further, Marcum recommends specifically that the Library of Congress concentrate on digitizing its special collections (mostly copyright-free non-book material) rather than expend labor on its general collections — its books. Note, again, the consistency of her 2004 and 2006 views:

> [2004] If Google succeeds in digitizing a library of eight to ten million volumes and making the content available on the Web, what happens to every other library? **She said Library of Congress cataloging would not be needed in these circumstances. The LC role might be to augment the digital core with its special collections.** [emphasis added]
>
> [2006] We have millions of items in our **special collections** that are not available to the public ... . *We know that increasingly our users go first to Google and other Internet search engines to find information they are seeking.* **We have made it a priority to increase access to content rather than to continue bibliographic practices** *that, though helpful to other libraries, do not add **immediate** value for the user.* [emphasis added]

Service to "the user" in this world does not value libraries' creation of mere catalog records ("bibliographic practices") for *books*. Nor does it value the intellectual labor of creating *authority controlled* names or titles, or *standardized* subject headings — why should it when Google's keyword search software is envisioned as providing access "with ease and precision"? Apparently "the perfect search engine" would "understand exactly what you mean" and "give back exactly what you want" simply on the basis of relevance-ranked keywords and user referral folksonomies ("people who ordered this also ordered these"). Is it any wonder, then, that LC is already moving to curtail authority work, or that it has commissioned an "outside" study — the Calhoun Report — to recommend that LC Subject Headings be entirely abandoned?

Endorsing Ignorance

Further, "the user" in this vision does not just use Google *first*— he or she does not use the "content" of any physical library *at all*. "The user" wants *only* "something" that can be found online, and won't bother to trudge "all the way" to the library to get any other "content." The highest levels of LC administration now believe that such behavior is to be simply accepted and endorsed as inevitable. In the digital-library mind set, it is an unshakeable article of dogma that "advice" from librarians and "literacy training" will always be ignored by the Calvins of the world, so why even bother to provide such education? This is tantamount to an abandonment of the ideal of education for an endorsement of ignorance — we shouldn't even bother to provide instruction or advice on information literacy, because "Calvin" wouldn't *like* that. The willfully ignorant undergraduate *is* "the user" whose immediate wants we need to dumb down our operations to serve.

In Marcum's vision, providing whatever "content" we can digitize, as long as it is *immediately* and *remotely* available *through Google's search software*, trumps all other considerations of what LC in particular, and research libraries in general, ought to be doing.

Shared Remote Warehouses in Place of Substantive Onsite Book Collections

In the new vision being promoted by LC's administration, it is not even necessary for research libraries to maintain substantial onsite book collections! Such collections, of course, can be browsed for subject access because they are shelved according to the subject classification system created by the Library of Congress; and browsing enables researchers to recognize relevant books whose keywords, in a variety of languages, cannot be specified in advance.

LC tried a decade ago to abandon the practice of shelving books in subject categorizations; the idea then was to shelve them by height, and within height groupings by acquisition order. Of course, abandoning the shelving of books by subject would also entail saving a lot of money in classifying them to begin with — the goal then (as now) was to abandon the maintenance of as much of the LC Classification system as possible (particularly Cuttering). That attempt, however, was stymied by a strong report from the Task Group on Shelving Arrangement that rejected the idea:

> Based on surveys, comments, and discussion with Library of Congress reference librarians and subject specialists, both in CRS and public reading rooms, learned opinion favors retaining a classified collection on Capitol Hill not only to enhance in-depth research for the most complex questions, but to enable continuous and efficient evaluation of collections for collections development and management purposes, and also to facilitate risk management assessment....
>
> The consensus of all survey participants, as expressed in their written comments, is that the use of the stacks in browsable classified arrangement, allowing additional subject access to information in related books, is essential to meeting the mission of the Library of Congress,..."to make its resources available and useful to the Congress and the American people..." [*Working Group on Reference and Research Report to the Task Group on Shelving Arrangement*. October 30, 1997]

Even the Congressional Research Service weighed in with its own report, pointing out the adverse effects that height shelving would have on its ability to serve Congress:

> According to a recent CRS survey, 52 percent of CRS staff responding to the questionnaire indicated they regularly go to the stacks to browse or select appropriate books for 5 percent or more of requests. A majority favors continuing to shelve books needed for congressional research in classified order in the stacks. The survey identified several reasons for this opinion. In particular, the current system allows additional subject access that browsing like works in a single location provides, to meet the needs of Congress, and especially to meet

RUSH deadlines. Short deadline requests handled by CRS comprised 79.8 percent of FY96 requests (388,500 requests out of 487,000).

Of particularly serious concern to the Congressional Research Service is that under the proposed fixed location shelving scheme, materials most immediately affected would be current incoming books, those most frequently used for congressional research.

Despite the gain of perhaps 33 percent shelf space for books that are arranged by size and fixed location (reportedly the experience of the New York Public Library), 87 percent of CRS staff who responded to the survey still preferred retaining subject arrangement of books on the Hill, even though this might mean more library materials stored off-site to continue classified arrangement of books needed for congressional research in the stacks. [*CRS Response to Shelving Alternatives in Library of Congress Stacks.* June 4, 1997]

Scholars throughout the country continue to regard browsing library book collections arranged in subject classified order as essential to their research; this fact is confirmed repeatedly in a variety of user studies (see, again, the Survey of User studies appended to the Calhoun Report review at <http://www.guild2910.org/>). One survey elicited the finding that "The importance of serendipitous browsing in library collections *cannot be overemphasized* by the majority of faculty space holders."

That LC is once again primed to stop shelving books by subject was hinted at in a memo circulated to staff by Dr. Marcum on 11/7/03, in which she recommends the reading of an article by Richard Atkinson, "A New World of Scholarly Communication," that appeared in *The Chronicle of Higher Education* (November 7, 2003). Atkinson regards the duplication of printed books in multiple research libraries — the maintenance, in his words, of "many parallel, redundant research collections" — as a practice that is "outmoded and no longer affordable." He specifically labels as "self defeating" the maintenance of "the Association of Research Libraries' membership index — which ranks the association's more than 120 member libraries largely according to the number of volumes they hold on their shelves"; in his view, this traditional measure of library quality "provides no incentive for consortium members to forgo acquiring holdings that are otherwise available to the system as a whole. Even though the membership index rewards inefficiency and waste, we continue to treat it as a meaningful measure ... in a networked digital age, *excessive attention to the local management and ownership of physical materials impedes the responsible stewardship of the scholarly and cultural record*" [emphasis added]. His recommendation is that research libraries rely on shared remote warehouses for the storage of their book collections.

Remote storage warehouses, of course, do not shelve books in classified subject groupings; they are housed randomly in tubs (but retrievable through bar code correlations). Advocacy of such a scheme effectively eliminates the very possibility of browsing books on the same subject shelved contiguously — the books would neither be onsite to begin with, nor arranged by subject in the remote warehouses.

The Calhoun Report, commissioned by LC, strongly endorses Atkinson's proposal. Both Calhoun and Atkinson take Association of Research Libraries (ARL) libraries to task for maintaining onsite collections whose books duplicate each other (and which could be locally browsed).

That is cause enough for concern, but other statements made by Dr. Marcum point in the same direction. In her "Challenges of Managing Information" speech" (*ibid.*, 2005), she says:

How libraries did it last night — indeed, in the last few decades — just isn't going to work anymore. It isn't going to work because what we were doing was loading physical libraries with such an increasing quantity of books and journals that we were pushing out the students and learning activities that libraries should serve. My guess is that the need for more shelves is what your campus librarians have complained about most.

What you should do depends on your situation, but here's what some others are doing about this nearly universal problem. Some are freeing library space by acquiring or building relatively inexpensive repositories off-campus for print resources that are the least used.

No one has any problem with a recommendation to send the "least used" material to offsite storage. But Marcum continues:

Some are containing costs further by collaborating with nearby colleges to build such off-campus repositories for their combined usage. Some colleges are collaborating further by making their collections accessible to students at all schools in a consortium, whose librarians then work together on *non-duplicative book and journal purchasing.* [emphasis added]

Warehouses, here, are to be used not merely for the "least used" books, but also to house copies of *current* books to avoid duplication among many local libraries. The concealed proposition, again, is that scholars no longer have any need to browse in substantial onsite book collections.

In a more recent speech, "The Future of Libraries in a Digital Age" (an "Address to Faculty and Librarians of Kenyon College, Gambier, Ohio, 17–18 April 2006"), Dr. Marcum cites with approval a number of ideas advanced by a colleague from California:

I hold in high esteem a friend of mine in the library community named Jerry D. Campbell, who is chief information officer and dean of University Libraries at the University of Southern California, in Los Angeles. In a recent issue of *EDUCAUSE Review*, a journal that deals with information technology in higher education, he has published an article entitled, "Changing a Cultural Icon: the Academic Library as a Virtual Destination." There he argues that, quote, "the library is relinquishing its place as the top source of inquiry." [<http://www.educause.edu/apps/er/erm06/erm0610asp>] Let's think about what he has to say.

The Web, he says, has become the world's largest, easiest-to-use store of information. Libraries might once have argued for their survival on grounds that much Web-accessible information is unreliable, and many publishers have resisted digitizing monographs. However, we're discovering that works not digitally available are getting ignored. And so libraries, themselves, are digitizing books. In addition, major efforts to digitize more books — millions, in fact — have recently been announced by search-engine companies such as Google, which plans to digitize large parts if not all of five major research libraries. *Now, almost everybody believes that eventually the Web "will have it all," says Campbell, who adds: "For most people, including academicians, the library — in its most basic function as a source of information — has become overwhelmingly a virtual destination."*

Dr. Campbell does not believe that the Library of Congress, his libraries at USC, or your own Kenyon should *immediately* close their doors. Academic libraries must continue current operations through a *transition* period *until everything is on the Web....* what I take Campbell to mean is that *eventually all of us will go to the open Web for scholarly material,* **not to the campus library or even to its particular Web site.** We will go "Googling" or "Yahooing" via the Internet to find what we need from wherever. [emphasis added]

Do libraries then disappear? Not exactly, Campbell says. Instead, some services, though "derivative" and not collectively "a fundamental purpose for the library," in his view, may "hold the key to its future." What are these services?

The "services" in question are, according to Campbell and Marcum, providing "quality learning spaces," "creating metadata," offering "virtual reference services" (although "Campbell thinks the future of library reference service is uncertain"), "teaching information literacy" (although, in line with her comments above, Marcum adds, "Will making everything Web-accessible reduce the need for literacy training...? Perhaps..." It is noteworthy that no reason occurs to Dr. Marcum to justify the continuance of instruction). The other "services" are choosing digital resources and "maintaining resource licenses," "collecting and digitizing archival materials," and "maintaining digital repositories."

It is noteworthy that the maintenance of substantial onsite book collections, arranged in subject-classified arrangements to facilitate browsing and direct access, does not even appear on the radar screen. It isn't even mentioned as *one* of the multiple "services" that future research libraries need to provide. It is simply not a concern of the digital age vision shared by Marcum, Campbell, Calhoun, and Atkinson. As Marcum mentions at the end of this speech, "Perhaps Campbell is right that the book-based library may eventually disappear and the Web may become the library of the future." That, in any event, is the clear goal: to get research libraries out of the business of having to deal with onsite printed book collections.

What then happens to libraries as places if they don't have substantial book collections on the premises? Dr. Marcum sees future library buildings as "providing spaces in which learners can use ... resources, individually and collaboratively, in multiple ways, including ways of their own invention. Computer banks, electronic classrooms, distance learning labs, special program facilities, collaborative study lounges, copy centers, even cafes and canteens and corners for contemplation — these are increasingly valued features of libraries. *Physical* libraries." (This is from her speech "Libraries: Physical Places or Virtual Spaces in the Digital World?" at the National Library of Medicine, November 5–6, 2003). As she said to the college presidents audience of her "Challenges of Managing Information" talk (*supra*), "If you aren't figuring out how to get a little café in your library like the big book stores have, well, just keep right on using it as a place that supports books, not students." Libraries, of course, should not be devoting their resources to maintaining onsite book collections; Marcum, Campbell, and Calhoun believe that, instead — not *in addition to*, but *instead*— they should be digitizing "everything" to provide "direct access," which is envisioned *only* as *remote* access to *digitized* texts, not as onsite-browsing access to printed books shelved in subject categories. The printed books, again, should be shelved in remote warehouses, to prevent "costly duplication."

Recapitulation

In sum, because the Google Book Search project is envisioned as providing access "with ease and precision" to "the digital core" of millions of *books*, it is no longer necessary for the Library of Congress to expend its efforts and resources in this area — LC should, *instead*, concentrate on digitizing its special collections. This radical change in priorities ("Big changes are on the way") has been a consistent feature of Marcum's vision for years. The reason is obvious: since "the user" can rely on Google digitizing and keyword searching to provide adequate access ("with ease and precision") to *books*, what's left for LC to do, then, is simply to digitize the unique, *non-book* collections in its custody that Google will not find at Michigan, Stanford, Harvard, Oxford, and NYPL.

Providing leadership in the cataloging and classification of book collections is no longer regarded as necessary at the top levels of LC administration. Cataloging and classification are themselves regarded as replaceable by keyword searching, relevance ranking, and user-referral mechanisms.

Objections

Are objections to this "vision" merely instances of "resistance to change"? Are they really just attempts to preserve "the status quo" when a wholesale "transition" to digital libraries is offered as the sole alternative to the maintenance of traditional libraries? Do objections from professional librarians reflect only short-sighted and selfish concerns to maintain the "comfort" of old-fashioned but outdated practices? Are so many professionals' objections, both from AFSCME 2910 and the larger research library community, simply crass attempts to keep unnecessary library jobs from being eliminated?

Or is it possible that the digital age proponents and consultants have only a very partial grasp of the truth, and that their attempt to force the whole of our responsibilities onto the Procrustean bed of a Google search box may actually be counter-productive, indeed *destructive*, to scholarship?

Is it possible that they in fact have no actual contacts with "the user" whose needs they profess to understand and represent?

Is it possible that their high administrative positions have isolated and insulated them from the needs of real researchers (not made-up cartoon characters), and from feedback on how badly Google actually works when the goal is scholarship rather than mere quick information seeking?

Is it possible that they do not grasp the importance of maintaining traditional book resources and access mechanisms within real libraries as *alternatives* to Google, when users' first-choice Google searches do not provide what they ultimately need?

Is it possible that they also lack feedback from any substantive first-hand experience in using their own libraries' book collections — the ones they are in charge of — for scholarly research?

Is it possible that they are misrepresenting the user studies to which they appeal as the ground for their beliefs?

Is it possible that they lack first-hand experience in struggling to read the e-book formats they would impose on everyone else?

Is it possible, when they confidently assert that *almost everybody* believes that eventually the "Web will have it all," that their circle of acquaintances is much too limited to be representative of either the library profession or the much larger scholarly world it must serve?

Is it possible that they do not perceive any real differences between quick information seeking, on the one hand, and substantive scholarship, on the other?

Is it possible that they do not understand that "hit and miss" retrieval mechanisms which provide "something" quickly, while appropriate (and necessary) in some situations, are no substitute for alternative mechanisms that provide systematic and comprehensive retrieval when much more than "something" is required?

Is it possible that, on the basis of misread statistics, highly selective feedback from a too-limited "choir," and lack of personal experience in using cataloging and classification systems, that they cannot discern if a real baby is being thrown out with the bath water?

One would hope that none of these possibilities is in fact a reality. If even a few of them were, then ALA President Michael Gorman's call for renewed emphasis on library education would be fully justified.

The Continuing Need for Library of Congress Subject Headings in Online Catalogs

Since I have quoted so extensively from opposing viewpoints, I will give my own critics the opportunity to challenge some passages from my own book *The Oxford Guide to Library Research* (3rd edition; Oxford U. Press, 2005). It is a text that I wrote in the hope that it might play an important part in just the kind of educational effort Gorman has called for. In the current debates within the library profession, I hope the book as a whole will demonstrate that there is much more substantive value to traditional library practices than has been recognized by many proponents of the digital "vision." The first passage, from Chapter 2, provides an example of the continuing need for Library of Congress Subject Headings, and for online catalogs with mechanisms (unlike Google's) that can *display* such headings:

> One researcher interested in the history of Yugoslavia asked for help at the reference desk because, on his own, he'd simply done a Boolean combination of the keywords "Yugoslavia" and "history," and had been overwhelmed with too many irrelevant records. The solution to this problem was the use of the online catalog's *browse displays*. When doing a subject (not keyword) search under **Yugoslavia**, a browse display of many screens' length was automatically generated; it included headings such as these:
>   **Yugoslavia–Antiquities**
>   **Yugoslavia–Antiquities–Bibliography**
>   **Yugoslavia–Antiquities–Maps**
>   **Yugoslavia–Armed Forces–History**
>   **Yugoslavia–Bibliography**
>   **Yugoslavia–Biography**
>   **Yugoslavia–Biography–Dictionaries**
>   **Yugoslavia–Boundaries**
>   **Yugoslavia–Civilization**
>   **Yugoslavia–Civilization–Bibliography**
>   **Yugoslavia–Commerce–History**
>   **Yugoslavia–Commerce–Pakistan**
>   **Yugoslavia–Commercial treaties**
>   **Yugoslavia–Constitutional history**
>   **Yugoslavia–Description and travel**

Yugoslavia–Economic conditions
Yugoslavia–Encyclopedias
Yugoslavia–Ethnic relations
Yugoslavia–Foreign economic relations
Yugoslavia–Foreign relations–Great Britain
Yugoslavia–Foreign relations–Soviet Union
Yugoslavia–Foreign relations–United States
Yugoslavia–Geography–Bibliography
Yugoslavia–History–1992–2003
    [NT cross-reference to **Yugoslav War, 1991–1995**]
Yugoslavia–History–Bibliography
Yugoslavia–History–Chronology
Yugoslavia–History–Dictionaries
Yugoslavia–History, Military
Yugoslavia–History–Soviet occupation, 1979–1989
Yugoslavia–Kings and rulers–Biography
Yugoslavia–Maps
Yugoslavia–Pictorial works
Yugoslavia–Politic and government [with period subdivisions]
Yugoslavia–Relations–India–Bibliography
Yugoslavia–Relations–Pakistan–Chronology
Yugoslavia–Road maps
Yugoslavia–Social conditions
Yugoslavia–Social life and customs
Yugoslavia–Statistics
Yugoslavia–Strategic aspects
Yugoslavia–Yearbooks

These are only a sample of the full list. The researcher, in this case, was delighted: he could immediately see that he had many more options for his topic than he had realized. He was particularly excited by the —ANTIQUITIES subdivisions, which his keyword search under "history" had missed entirely.

Note also that all of this material would have been missed if the searcher had simply typed "Yugoslavia" and "history" into a blank search box in a massive full text database such as the newly-proposed Google Print project [now Google Book Search], which plans to digitize millions of books. The Google software cannot display browse menus of subjects-with-subdivisions and cross-references, allowing researchers to simply recognize options that they cannot specify in advance. Library catalogs provide much more efficient and systematic overviews of the *range* of books relevant to any topic. Searching for all relevant book texts via a simple Internet-type search box would be like trying to get an overview of a whole country while looking at it only through a bombsight. While the Google project may enhance *information seeking*, it will greatly curtail *scholarship*—which requires connections, linkages, and overviews — if it is regarded as a replacement for real libraries and traditional cataloging. (See Chapter 3 for more on Google Print [Book Search].)

I cannot recommend this too strongly: use your library catalog's browse displays. When there are multiple screens of subdivisions, *take the time to look through all of them.* You will *usually* be able to spot important aspects of your topic that you would never have otherwise noticed. This technique is almost tailor-made to solve the frequent problem of getting too much junk via keyword searches.

The larger a library's catalog, the more researchers must rely on *menu listings* that enable them to simply *recognize* relevant options that they could not specify in advance. There are three such menus you need to look for: the cross-reference lists of NT and RT terms, the alphabetically adjacent narrower terms in the red books, and — especially — the rosters of subdivisions that automatically appear in online-catalog subject searches. A great deal of intellectual time and effort by catalogers goes into the creation of these menus; without them, you simply have to guess which terms to use; and, as in this **Yugoslavia** example, no one will be able to think up beforehand all of the relevant topics that could readily be of use in researching the country's history. Online browse displays of subject subdivisions are the kinds of things real users would kill to have in Internet searches — but Net search engines simply cannot produce them. This radical advantage is available to researchers only in library catalogs.

The Continuing Need for Substantial Onsite Book Collections Shelved in Subject Classified Order

The second passage from *The Oxford Guide to Library Research*, from Chapter 3, is an example the continuing need for onsite book collections arranged in subject classified arrangements for in-depth browsing:

Let me offer one more example of the need for focused browsing of contiguous full texts. A scholar from France, working on a study of the writer Paul Valery and his times, needed to pin down an important bit of information regarding Valery's connection to the famous Dreyfus case, in which a French military officer of Jewish descent was convicted of treason, and, only years later, acquitted. The woman had hearsay information from Valery's children and daughter-in-law that he had signed his name to a "petition" or "liste" on the issue at the time, but had no specifics of place or date. The large online *Tresor de la langue francaise* database of full text sources did not solve the problem, nor did biographies of Valery, nor did the *Historical Abstracts* or *Francis* databases (the latter having an emphasis on French studies), nor did two massive published bibliographies on Valery (each over 600 pages). I finally had to go back into the bookstacks, where, at the Library of Congress, we have 186 volumes on 6 shelves in the classes DC354–354.9 ("Dreyfus case"). As a shortcut, I was particularly looking for a volume that a browse display in the computer catalog had alerted me to, with the subject heading **Dreyfus, Alfred, 1859–1935 — Trials, litigation, etc. — Sources**. (The — **Sources** subdivision indicates a published compilation of primary sources concerning the actual event.) This volume, shelved at DC354.8.Z65 1994, however, did not reprint or identify the particular newspaper petition with Valery's signature. On the shelf above it, however, I noticed another book which, it turned out, did indeed have the necessary information. As an extra serendipitous bonus, the same volume turned out to contain additional information about one of Valery's close friends — information that solved another problem for the researcher that she hadn't specifically asked about.

Once again, a search of the computer catalog — even by call number — could not identify *which one* of the 186 volumes had the exact information that was needed. If all of these volumes had been scattered by acquisition number, or shelved according to their many different heights, it would not have been possible to find the right book without making separate requests and waiting for 186 individual deliveries. (The volumes could not even be delivered *en masse* if they were not shelved next to each other in the first place.) In the real world, the prospect of that degree of "hassle" effectively precludes the necessary scholarship from being accomplished. Libraries that do not take into account the Principle of Least Effort in information-seeking behavior are simply not functional, no matter how much money they may save; the purpose of a research library is to facilitate scholarship, not to save funds.

I emphasize the point because many library administrators these days do indeed think that "remote storage" techniques can be used within central library buildings themselves. This is something academics need to watch out for: if your library committees do not take active steps to prevent this erosion of shelving by subject, you will wind up with book collections that cannot be browsed *or* focus-examined down to the level of individual pages or paragraphs. In that case, you will no longer have systematic access to the "depth" parts of the books not contained on their catalog records: not just tables of contents and indexes, but maps, charts, tables, illustrations, diagrams, running heads, highlighted sidebars, binding information, typographical variations for emphasis, bulleted or numbered lists, footnotes, and bibliographies. All such material is readily searchable by focused browsing of subject-classified book collections. Further, the browsing search mechanism that presently allows you to recognize relevant books, or individual pages and paragraphs within them, will be replaced by blank search boxes on computer screens that require you to specify in advance, in detail, every word or phrase that may possibly be related to your topic.

The recently announced Google Print [Book Search] project, aims to digitize the full texts of fifteen million books, from a variety of research libraries, and make them freely available for keyword searching on the Internet. It is not yet clear exactly how the project will segregate works still under copyright protection (life of author plus 70 years) from those in the public domain; but in any event the announcement of the operation has caused some observers to assert that local, onsite book collections will no longer be necessary if every text is keyword searchable on the Internet.

There are, however, real problems with such a naive assumption. Those who hold it are apparently innocent of experience in the ways real scholars must actually work. Let me return to the above examples... .

Similarly, with the Paul Valery example, the researcher told me it is highly unlikely that she could have found the necessary information even in a huge full-text database like Google Print [Book Search]. One problem is that Google may not be able to mount copyrighted texts, which would include the French book that provided the information in this case. The other, more serious problem is that the researcher did not know in advance the right keywords to type in. Again, the Valery family members simply said the writer had, at some point, signed a "petition" or a "liste." It turns out that it was actually a subscription fund to provide money for the widow of one of the individuals involved in the scandal; and the text in question, *L'Affaire Dreyfus et la Presse* (Armond Colin, 1960), reports that the names were published in the journal *La Libre Parole* in 1898. The researcher, however, did not know the name of this journal in advance; nor does the French text use the words "petition" or "liste" to describe the roster — it uses the words "souscription" and "souscripteurs" instead. In other words, the scholar would not have been able to type in the right keywords to find the information even if the copyrighted text were fully searchable online.

It is noteworthy that a search in the Google Web engine on "Valery" and "Dreyfus" already produces over 3,500 hits, and one on "Paul Valery" and "Dreyfus" produces 344. Keyword searching in a Google Print [Book Search] file is likely to produce similar mounds of chaff— especially since the single instance of Valery's name in the entirety of the *L'Affaire Dreyfus et la presse* (272 pages) would not have ranked this text at the top of any retrieval set derived from all of the words on 4.5 billion pages, or from the frequency of "hits" on this one very obscure book. Focused browsing in classified bookstacks, enabling scholars to simply recognize what they cannot specify in advance, remains crucial to advanced scholarship.

It is especially noteworthy that any proposed use of Google Print to replace classified bookstacks would entirely segregate foreign language materials into multiple electronic "zones" that could not be searched simultaneously by the specification of English keywords. With classified bookstacks, on the other hand, books in all languages are grouped together by subject in the same locales; and oftentimes researchers can simply notice relevant foreign books on a topic simply by their illustrations or other visual cues. Google Print enthusiasts would unwittingly re-create in reality the disastrous consequences mythologized in the Tower of Babel story.

Google Print [Book Search] will be a wonderful supplement to classified bookstacks in real research libraries, but a terrible substitute. The overriding reason is that mere relevance-ranking algorithms cannot solve the massive problem of out-of-context keyword retrievals in full text databases. Any large digitization project without the filtering, structuring, segregating, and channeling elements provided by traditional library categorizations would do much more actual harm than good — assuming, as the digital paradigm does, that digitized book collections would replace rather than supplement onsite print collections — because the efficient *categorizing of books by subject* is not a problem that technology can solve through any *ranking* algorithms of keywords. *Information seeking* at the level of finding discrete data would improve, but *scholarship* (being dependent on contexts, connections, and webs of relationships) would be made much more difficult under the "replacement" scenario. Any attempt at a structured overview of resources would be precluded right from the start by inadequate filtering, segregating, linking, and display mechanisms.

Faculty Library Committees need to be aware that most library administrators fail to note the distinction between (a) general browsing to see what's available, versus (b) focused searching for definite, and very specific, information likely to be found within a limited range of full texts, *recognizable* within that range even when its keywords cannot be specified in advance. If this difference is blurred, then all of the (valid) objections against general browsing as the primary way to do systematic research come into play, and none of the arguments for recognition-access to the depth contents of contiguous full texts are noticed. Although all historians, anthropologists, linguists, and others have experienced the advantages of direct access to classified bookshelves, almost no one bothers to write down the numbers of contiguous volumes examined, as in the above examples. It just takes too much time, and most academics have never perceived a need to do so. Nor do they articulate clearly the crucial need, in many research situations, for recognition access rather than prior-specification search techniques. (It is the dismissal by library administrators of any concern for recognition mechanisms that is especially galling to working academics, as it is usually done with the patronizing air that advocacy of anything other than computerized keyword retrieval is merely "sentimental" rather than rational.) Until recently, scholars could simply assume that no research library administrator would even think of undermining the practice of shelving books by subject. Unfortunately, that assumption is no longer a safe one — the abandonment is being actively promoted by bean counters who overlook the operation of the overall system in which the beans are situated.

The book provides numerous other concrete examples of the practical utility of LC cataloging and classification in solving the growing problem of too much junk being retrieved through Internet search mechanisms. The point is that Internet search mechanisms do not eliminate all difficulties — they in fact create as many problems as they solve. And those problems require *other* mechanisms for their solutions than Google and Amazon type access.

What Is Going on at the Library of Congress?

So what is the bottom line here? The question with which this paper began is, What is going on at the Library of Congress?

There is substantive evidence, provided by *patterns* of statements both from LC management and from the sources it relies on, that the Library of Congress is striving mightily to get out of the business of providing systematic access to large collections of printed books through the provision of LC Subject Headings (in an online catalog that is not merged with Google) and through the provision of subject-categorized shelving of actual volumes arranged according to the LC Classification system. It sees the digitization of book collections being essentially accomplished completely by Google's Book Search project (and some others), in spite of copyright restrictions. It also envisions keyword searching of these digitized book texts, with computer-algorithm "relevance ranking" of the results (and Amazon-type reader-preference tracking) as being adequate to meet the new goal of research libraries, which is simply to provide *something* delivered *quickly* and *remotely* to "the user." Questions regarding the *quality* of resources made available on the Internet are all to be answered simply by digitizing *everything*— in spite of copyright restrictions and in spite of the fact that Internet search mechanisms cannot *find* the quality material, or adequately segregate it from the mountains of chaff, through keyword and user-tracking softwares.

As with research libraries in general, the goal to which LC in particular should now devote itself no longer includes the component of providing complete and systematic subject access to printed books (i.e., to show "what the library has" in its book collections); rather, in furtherance of the goal to provide merely "something" remotely, the new emphasis is on revealing the content of non-book special collections over the contents of books. (Google will be trusted to provide the latter.) "The user" whom the Library is striving to satisfy is not the scholar who requires complete and systematic access to relevant books, nor does that user any longer require mechanisms enabling him or her to recognize important works (in a wide variety of languages) whose keywords cannot be specified in advance in a blank Google search box. Rather, "the user" whose satisfaction is paramount is the uninstructed undergraduate who has a term paper due quickly, who does not want to leave her cozy dorm room and trudge all the way to the library, who does not have time to read entire books in any event, who wants only English language material, and who cannot be bothered with anything that does not come up immediately in a Google search. Moreover, LC management's goal of focusing on the wants of *this* user includes the assumption that such students will not simply use Google *first*, and then go to the library, but that they will avoid going inside any library *at all*; this "user" wants *only* full texts that can be tapped into remotely. Digitizing those texts for remote access is now seen as *constituting* all that is needed to provide adequate "access" to them; no matter how bad, or how overwhelming, keyword retrievals may be, the proven alternative filtering mechanisms of conceptual cataloging and classification are now regarded as outmoded. And professional librarians who raise objections to the abandonment of cataloging and classification be dismissed as dinosaurs whose "resistance to change" springs not from their concern for the maintenance of high professional standards, but from a selfish fear of losing job security.

And so the Library's management in recent years has consistently disparaged the work of its own professional catalogers, has invited a string of outside speakers to tell them how irrelevant and outmoded their work is "in a digital age," has changed Library priorities to avoid hiring new professional catalogers as old ones retire, has restricted catalogers' ability to extend the subject headings system, and has generally sought to promote the belief that authority control, standardization of headings, and the shelving of actual books in subject categories — that all such practices are now no longer necessary because keyword searching in Google Book Search is, or soon will be, an adequate substitute. For some time now, LC management has been looking for every excuse it can find to dismantle as much as it can of its own cataloging and classification operations.

The imminent loss of the LC systems will have profound implications for research libraries throughout the world, and for all of the scholars in all academic disciplines who depend on them. The dismantling of these access systems, already taking place, will make scholarly research in large *book* collections much more difficult to do at all, and impossible to do in any systematic manner. Retrieval of books through Google and Amazon type search mechanisms, in place of systematic cataloging and classification, will produce results that are superficial, incomplete, haphazard, indiscriminate, biased toward recent works, and largely confined to English language sources. LC's abdication of leadership in cataloging and classification is on the brink of dragging down the capacities of research libraries all over the nation to promote substantive scholarship over "quick information seeking." In the new "vision," the Internet, and not large, onsite book collections, is now regarded as central to substantive research; and research libraries themselves are viewed mainly as feeder-streams to provide "content" to Google, rather than as providing *alternatives* to Google in both content and search method capabilities. This re-centering of focus constitutes an abandonment of the mechanisms that provide systematic subject access to printed books. The national library of the United States is giving away the birthright of American scholars in exchange for a mess of Internet pottage.

That is what is going on at the Library of Congress. If scholars in this country, in all subject areas, want to maintain efficient, deep, extensive, and systematic access to book collections in research libraries, they had better speak up now.

Don't Class Me in Antiquities!
Giving Voice to Native American Materials

Kelly Webster and *Ann Doyle*

Introduction

Kelly Webster, Monographs Cataloger at the O'Neill Library at Boston College, and Ann Doyle, Branch Librarian for Xwi7xwa Library at the University of British Columbia's First Nations House of Learning, share a conversation about some of the issues related to the cataloging and classification of American Indian materials, and give an overview of some alternative practices.

KW: Have you ever noticed how American Indians are treated in Library of Congress cataloging? In both obvious and subtle ways, American Indians are treated as a remnant of the past. Although there have been some positive changes recently, such as the efforts being made to work with tribes to establish the preferred form of tribal names, there is still bias and problematic treatment of Native topics in the Library of Congress classification schedules and subject headings. The E schedules in LC classification are a dumping ground for all things Indian. Medicine, education, psychology? You won't find material on those topics in the R, L or BF schedules if it involves Native Americans, because historic practice segregated us into a historic people. We are still here, though, and people working in library services to Native peoples are finding established practice a barrier to information access and promoting use of the library.

AD: We face similar issues here in Canada. Cataloging practices not only fail to provide access for Aboriginal students and others using the academic libraries, they obscure an increasingly rich interdisciplinary literature and constitute a significant barrier to use of the public libraries. Years ago, as a library school student in 1980, I did a collection analysis of three special collections of Aboriginal materials. It turned out that although the local public library was comparatively well-stocked, the Aboriginal staff at the neighborhood Native Resource Center still felt that it was a poor collection. At the time, the bricks and mortar of this barrier to the public library collection were not clear to me. In retrospect, I see that the lack of appropriate description and classification were significant blocks to access for Aboriginal people. The student paper concluded with the *Guidelines* *for the Evaluation and Selection of Indian Materials for Adults* from the ALA Adult Services Division Subcommittee on Indian Materials.[1] Those criteria written in 1971 still hold true today!

The guidelines included questions such as, "Are the contributions of American Indian culture to Western civilization given rightful and accurate representation? Is American Indian culture evaluated in terms of its own values and attitudes rather than in terms of those of another culture?" Another consideration mentioned was the effect of the material on a Native person's self-image. Along with selection guidelines we can use a cataloging perspective to ask ourselves, "How does the language of cataloging contribute (or not) to the meeting these evaluation requirements?"

KW: In library school we didn't touch on any issues related to this, but right before I graduated, I came upon the work of Sandy Berman and got my eyes opened. His writing about racism and ethnocentrism in Library of Congress subject headings got me thinking about how Native topics are reflected in LCSH. Then I started my first professional job and cataloged my first book about American Indians. I turned to the E schedule and saw, "Pre–Columbian America. The Indians." I thought at first that was where all books on Indians went: in the historical section. I remember my cheeks actually burned as I thought about having to follow that practice. I was used to that kind of ignorance out in the world, but the thought of having to perpetuate it in my job as a cataloger felt terrible. Eventually I found that my book would go in the next section of the classification table, Indians of North America, but that drew my attention to the subtle implications in LC classification and its treatment of Indians. What is signified by the placement of Indians of North America after Pre–Columbian American and before Discovery of America? The use of that problematic last phrase implies the Indians were either gone by the start of American history, or just didn't matter enough to be counted as part of it. Shortly afterward, I attended my first American Indian Library Association meeting. One of the agenda topics was a discussion of a memo Sandy Berman had sent to AILA, regarding several possible changes to LCSH.[2] The suggestions included changes to the umbrella heading Indians of North America, correcting specific tribal names, and the proposal of a subject heading then used at Hennepin County Library: NATIVE AMERICAN HOLOCAUST (1492–1900). The ideas were well received, but unfortunately never acted on until now. Since then, I've tried to learn all I can about the issues and what can be done to remedy some of the problems.

Some Examples of How Standard Practice Is Problematic

AD: There is a growing international body of work by LIS scholars and practitioners that talks about that feeling you had of your cheeks burning. Library and Archives Canada completed an Aboriginal community consultation process in 2003. Its report recommended that deficiencies in subject headings and cataloging practices be given priority citing the following rationale: "There is a need to re-teach the 'experts,' such as cataloguers, about the terms used to describe Aboriginal peoples. Issues of racism and ignorance are raised by present cataloguing standards and terminology."[3]

Classification systems carry systemic biases; they reflect the values and perspectives of their makers. In the case of Native American/Aboriginal topics, the LIS literature cites the following issues as problematic in mainstream library cataloging practices: marginalization; historicization; omission; lack of specificity; failure to organize materials in effective ways; lack of relevance; and lack of recognition of the sovereignty of American Indian nations. Inaccurate and inappropriate subject representation also affects reference services because it limits both the efficiency and accuracy of information retrieval, and thereby erodes the quality of services to patrons.[4]

The treatment of Aboriginal people in LC classification is a great barrier to effective access. Hope Olson's *The Power to Name* cites Gillian Rose's spatial metaphors of the ghetto and the diaspora to describe a fundamental dynamic of marginalized groups and topics. The ghetto isolates by concentrating in a single area and the diaspora scatters within a homogeneous mass so there is no identifiable existence. Library catalogs replicate this dynamic by ghettoizing Indigenous peoples in North America in a single area of the classification schedule, regardless of discipline. Subject headings that are either too general or nonexistent diasporize Indigenous topics throughout a Western knowledge taxonomy.

Over thirty-five years ago, Thomas Yen-Ran Yeh's careful analysis of the LC classification identified many of these problems. For example, he cites the segregation of the American Indian from the class for the History of America, and the complete exclusion of the American Indian from the local history schedule [F1-975]. He notes that the last date in the schedule for American Indian history is E83.895, "Chippewa War, 1898," which suggests that American Indians do not live in the twentieth century, but as Kelly says, in Antiquities. Yeh's suggested corrections elicited a dismissive response from the Library of Congress: "It is quite clear from the tables themselves that the intention of the creators of the classification was to treat the modern Indians as remnants of a vast group of peoples who once populated the entire New World long before the arrival of the Europeans. This conceptualization of the Indians is still valid today, it seems to us."[5] This example of those in power defining how knowledge of different groups is made accessible might be dismissed as a product of that time, but the problematic classification Yeh highlighted has yet to be changed.

KW: The practice of classifying all things Native American in the E schedule is problematic no matter what kind of collecting is being organized, for the reasons Ann describes. Its limitations are especially obvious when working with a collection that is heavy on materials about Native Americans, whether it is a tribal library or a special collection in another type of library. Once I did some cataloging at Little Big Horn College on the Crow reservation, and of course there was a lot of material shelved at E99.C92. If the book were about Crow medicine, you'd find it there squeezed in with Crow history and Crow art and Crow philosophy, instead of in the R schedule. Those shelves were so crowded that it was difficult to locate anything. After I'd completed my work there, I found that someone had drawn up an alternate scheme specifically for that library that would allow for the dispersal of Crow materials throughout the range of LC class numbers; for example, Crow education would be classed with other works about education and Crow art with works about art, and so forth. I wish I had seen that when I started, but it did make it clear to me that libraries need more than just an alternate scheme to improve access through classification — they also need staff trained to use it and keep it updated, and the staff time to adapt almost all the records received through copy cataloging. Both of things are luxuries that even large libraries don't often have.

AD: The failure of mainstream subject headings to describe even such basics as Aboriginal Nations comes up regularly at the X̱wi7x̱wa Library. The university where I work is located on the traditional, unceded lands of the Musqueam Nation. Musqueam elders are an integral part of the university; they provide support for student and staff services, consult on protocol, serve as language instructors, and frequently open campus events and ceremonies. Musqueam leaders serve on administrative bodies, such as the university senate. When the Musqueam people come to the library and ask, "Where are the library materials on Musqueam? Where are all the materials written by the anthropologists, and the linguists, and the historians on our people?" I have to reply, "There is no word for Musqueam in the library world, there is no section on the university library shelves for Musqueam." Musqueam is subsumed and erased under COAST SALISH INDIANS, a generic heading that also swallows other First Nations in the area. These examples are representative of the mainstream cataloging treatment of First Nations people and topics in the lower mainland of British Columbia where I live, and for many other parts of the country. The X̱wi7x̱wa Library cataloging practice, however, is an exception in that it aims to accurately represent names of First Nations, Aboriginal people, places, and concepts. At X̱wi7x̱wa, Musqueam is named and does have a place on the shelves. The library uses the standard MARC record fields to carry variant personal names: for example, using both Degonwadonti and Beth Brant for the Tyendinaga Mohawk writer. The University of British Columbia has provided core funding for the library's continued work in this area, and supports an Aboriginal classification scheme.

There is a burgeoning interdisciplinary literature produced by First Nations/Aboriginal scholars who are designing and conducting research, as well as publishing. At the same time, governments at all levels are funding research that seeks to address socioeconomic conditions of Aboriginal people, which produces another body of interdisciplinary literature ranging from health to education to resource development and commerce. The ongoing treaty negotiations and claims processes also produce a body of associated literatures. Of course, many sectors are also interested in how Aboriginal knowledges of local environments and Aboriginal views of the world can enrich their endeavors. There is a knowledge sector dedicated to mining Aboriginal knowledges, such as traditional use and environmental knowledge. From Aboriginal perspectives, there is a strong repatriation impetus that seeks to reclaim Aboriginal property in all forms, including intellectual property and cultural property, and to access knowledge produced by Aboriginal people and relevant to Aboriginal interests that is held in public institutions and repositories. There is a pressing need for design and development of classification tools, including accurate, relevant subject description, that give voice to this rapidly expanding universe of Aboriginal materials.

KW: Another example of how inappropriate terminology affects access that comes immediately to mind is the LC subject heading INDIANS OF NORTH AMERICA—RELOCATION, which was changed from the earlier heading, INDIANS OF NORTH AMERICA—

REMOVAL. I suppose the change was made to bring the heading into line with patterns for other groups, but it feels like a slap in the face, frankly. All the pain and betrayal and death that went along with the forced removal of tribes is just not reflected in the term "relocation." This impedes access because a patron doing research in this area, especially a Native patron, might not think to associate this term with the actual events. It's one of the many ways that the library can come across as a white institution, adding another barrier to promoting its use in Native communities. Then there are glaring omissions from LCSH of terms and concepts such as First Nations, Urban Indians, and Federal Indian Law.

A Change Is Going to Come ... Some Examples of Alternative Practice

Fortunately, there are many organizations and people around the world working to develop and put into practice alternative ways of organizing and providing access to Indigenous works in their collections, some of which we will describe below. There are also efforts to help improve standard practice. For instance, the American Indian Library Association recently established a Subject Access and Classification Committee which plans to submit proposals for new LCSH terms through the Subject Authority Cooperative Program (SACO), which allows libraries to submit subject headings and classification numbers to the Library of Congress. We are grateful for the many thesaurus projects underway that can guide us in this work.[6]

Australia

Aboriginal Thesaurus: The National Library of Australia is developing this tool to improve access to Aboriginal and Torres Strait Islander works. As Heather Moorcroft, one of the compilers, states on the project web site, "It is important that the Indigenous voices of Australia are heard and felt through proper representation in catalogues. It is very important that we as thesaurus makers are imaginative and creative and do not rely wholly on the literature itself because so much has been written ABOUT Aboriginal people, and not so much BY Aboriginal people, but this is changing. This means that we need to find the 'right' words in other ways."[7]

New Zealand

Māori Subject Headings: The Māori Subject Headings grew out a research project on the information needs of Māori people which found that subject representation of Māori topics was inappropriate and library classification and arrangement were not understood. The Māori subject headings aim to provide improved access to the Māori body of knowledge held in public institutions for Māori people.

Canada

Brian Deer Classification Scheme: <http://www.library.ubc.ca/xwi7xwa/deer.pdf> The Brian Deer system of classification was developed by a Kahnawake Librarian for the

National Indian Brotherhood/Assembly of First Nations. Gene Joseph, Gitxsan Dakelh, the founding librarian (1993) of the X̱wi7xwa Library at the University of British Columbia, selected this Indigenous scheme for the collection, recognizing that the future of a new library, including the development of its collections and the quality of its services, depends on the organization of the knowledge and the ways in which it is named. At the X̱wi7xwa Library, the knowledge organization aims to be congruent with and to reinforce Indigenous worldviews and experience in support of a mandate to make the university's vast resources more accessible to Aboriginal peoples. Brian Deer classification has been used by several Aboriginal libraries in B.C., including the Union of BC Indian Chiefs and the En'owkin Center.

British Columbia First Nations Names: <http://www.library.ubc.ca/xwi7xwa/bcfn. pdf> The X̱wi7xwa Library maintains and continues to develop an authority list of First Nations in the province of B.C. The authority list is used in cataloging materials held by the library, as well as in providing training in Indigenous information literacy skills for students and library staff. The library strives to reflect current First Nations' use of names and spelling.

Library and Archives Canada (LAC): Following a consultation with the Aboriginal community, LAC noted concerns raised about cataloging practices and proposed a phased review of its Canadian Subject Headings identifying Aboriginal peoples and their cultures. As a first step, they are currently considering revising headings containing the term "Indians" to prefer the more specific names of Aboriginal groups or nations.

First Nations House of Learning Thesaurus: The Library of Congress has authorized the development of the First Nations House of Learning Thesaurus. The thesaurus of First Nations/Aboriginal subject vocabulary will expand on the existing 5,500 First Nations/Aboriginal subject headings in use at X̱wi7xwa Library using cultural warrant in addition to literary warrant and consultation as sources for vocabulary.

United States

Dewey Classification at the American Indian Resource Center (AIRC), City of Huntington Park in Los Angeles County, California: This collection makes use of Dewey classification that has been adapted to more adequately organize materials about American Indians. Many materials have been reclassified to favor the subject area over the American Indian aspect, so that materials could be spread throughout the collection and not crowded into the 970 range.

Luiseno Culture Bank: This database, which collects Luiseno artifacts and information gathered from museums, libraries, and private collections, uses a hybrid scheme that applies categories derived from the elders to augment LCSH.

Mashantucket Pequot Thesaurus Project: Cheryl Metoyer, currently a professor at the University of Washington Information School and Chief Academic Affairs Officer for the Mashantucket Pequot Tribal Nation, has worked with many tribes to help develop their libraries and archives. She is leading a research project to develop this thesaurus for improved access to collections at the tribe's research library and archives.

National Indian Law Library (NILL) Thesaurus: NILL uses a locally developed thesaurus in addition to Library of Congress Subject Headings for its collection of federal Indian law and tribal law materials. It is a particularly well-developed tool, with scope notes, detailed guidelines, and subdivisions.

National Native American Thesaurus: University of California, Berkeley: John D. Berry, the Native American Studies Librarian, has been developing this thesaurus for use with the National Native American Bibliographic Database. The thesaurus project follows in the footsteps of the well-developed Chicano Thesaurus, the first edition of which was produced at the University of California in 1979.

Native American Educational Services (NAES) Public Policy and Tribal Research Center and Archives Subject Index: NAES, located in Chicago, has a non-circulating collection of over 10,000 materials in a variety of formats focusing on the development of Native American communities in the 20th century. Its collection is being recataloged using this homegrown, tribally centered classification system developed by its faculty and driven by the awareness that a system reflecting a Native perspective was required to meet patron needs.

Conclusion

Accurate and culturally appropriate cataloging of Native American/Indigenous materials is not just a Native American issue, but a national and international issue. It is critical for the self-determination efforts of Indigenous people to have intellectual access to collections of materials documenting their/our histories, cultures, and languages held in libraries. This documentary heritage may be seen as the cultural and intellectual property of Native Americans barricaded behind current cataloging practice. It is also critical in terms of access to new knowledge, emergent scholarship, and contemporary works. The lack of accurate representation and access affects not only the education of Native American children but the education of all children and citizens. The spread of problematic cataloging records perpetuates stereotypes and inaccuracies. Moreover, the ubiquitous bibliographic utilities and international use of LC and DDC transmit these records worldwide. These are significant concerns for catalogers, librarians, and educators, and they warrant our vigilant attention.

Notes

1. *ASD Newsletter*, vol. 8, no.3, Spring 1971. The Adult Services Division (ASD) subsequently developed into the ALA Reference and User Services Association.
2. Sanford Berman, "When the subject is Indian." *American Indian Libraries Newsletter* 18, no. 2 (Winter 1995). Available: <http://www.nativeculturelinks.com/ailanewsW95_LCindians.html>.
3. Library and Archives Canada. *Report and Recommendations of the Consultation on Aboriginal Resources and Services*. Ottawa: Minister of Public Works and Government Services Canada, 2004, 23.
4. See: Berman, Calliou, Carter, Lawson, Lee, Lincoln, Martens, Moorcroft, Tomren, Szekely, Yeh, and Young.

5. Thomas Yen-Ran Yeh, "The Treatment of the American Indian in the Library of Congress E-F Schedule." *Library Resources & Technical Services* 15, no. 2 (Spring 1971): 129.

6. The American Indian Library Association's Subject Access and Classification Committee is compiling a more complete list of these projects. Please contact Kelly Webster through AILA if you know of examples to add.

7. National Library of Australia. *The Aboriginal Thesaurus.* First Roundtable on Library and Archives Collections and Services of Relevance to Aboriginal and Torres Strait Islander People. State Library of South Australia, Adelaide, 4 May 1995. Available: <http://www.nla.gov.au/niac/libs/thesaurus.html> (accessed 08 December 2006).

Selected Further Reading

Listed below are resources that include discussion of cataloging Indigenous materials, and the works cited in this article. For more general resources see the bibliography *Library Services to Indigenous Populations: Viewpoints & Resources* (Chicago: Office for Literacy and Outreach Services, American Library Association, 2005).

Byrne, Alex, Alana Garwood, Heather Moorcroft and Alan Barnes, comps. (1995). *Aboriginal and Torres Strait Islander Protocols for Libraries, Archives and Information Services.* Deakin, A.C.T. Australian Library and Information Association. Available: <http://www.ntu.edu.au/library/protocol.html> (accessed 08 December 2006).

Calliou, Sharilyn. (1992). "Sunrise: activism and self-determination in first nations education 1972–1998." In *Aboriginal Self-Government in Canada: Current Trends and Issues.* 2nd ed. Saskatoon: Purich.

Carter, Nancy Carol. (Winter 2002). "American Indians and law libraries: acknowledging the third sovereign." *Law Library Journal* 7: 7–26.

Doyle, Ann. (2006). *Naming and Reclaiming Indigenous Knowledge: Intersections of Landscape and Experience.* Proceedings of the Ninth International Society of Knowledge Organization, Vienna. Wurzburg: Ergon Verlag.

Frosio, Eugene T. (Spring 1971). Comments on the Thomas Yen-Ran Yeh proposals. *Library Resources and Technical Services* 15, 2: 128–131.

Herlihy, Catherine S., and Fraser Cocks. (1995). "The Luiseno Culture Bank: expanding the canon." *Cataloging and Classification Quarterly* 20, 1: 61–81.

Lawson, Kimberley L. (2004). *Precious Fragments: First Nations Materials in Archives, Libraries and Museums.* Unpublished MLIS Thesis. Vancouver: University of British Columbia.

Lee, Deborah E. (2001). "Aboriginal students in Canada: a case study of their academic information needs and library use." *Journal of Library Administration* 33(3/4): 259–92.

Library and Archives Canada. (2004). *Report and Recommendations of the Consultation on Aboriginal Resources and Services.* Ottawa: Minister of Public Works and Government Services Canada.

Lincoln, Tamara. (2003). "Cultural reassertion of Alaska Native languages and cultures: libraries' responses." *Cataloging & Classification Quarterly* 35(3–4): 265–90.

Lincoln, Tamara. (Spring 1987). "Ethno-linguistic misrepresentations of the Alaskan Native languages as mirrored in the Library of Congress system of cataloging and classification." *Cataloging & Classification Quarterly* 7(3): 69–89.

MacDonell, Paul, Reiko Tagami, and Paul Washington. *Brian Deer Classification System.* Student paper. Available: <http://www.slais.ubc.ca/people/students/student-rojects/R_Tagami/517/index.htm> (accessed 08 December 2006).

Māori Subject Headings Nga Ūpoko Tukutuku. Available: <http://www.natlib.govt.nz/en/whatsnew/4mshupoko.html> (accessed 06 December 2006).

Martens, Monica. (Spring 2006). "Creating a supplemental thesaurus to the LCSH for a specialized collection: the experience of the National Indian Law Library." *Law Library Journal* 98 (2).

Moorcroft, Heather. (February 1993). "The construction of silence." *Australian Library Journal* 42 (1): 27–32.

Moorcroft, Heather. (February 1992). "Ethnocentrism in subject headings." *Australian Library Journal,* 40–45.

National Library of Australia. The Aboriginal Thesaurus. First Roundtable on Library and Archives Collections and Services of Relevance to Aboriginal and Torres Strait Islander People. State Library of South Australia, Adelaide, 4 May 1995. Available: <http://www.nla.gov.au/niac/libs/thesaurus.html> (accessed 08 December 2006).

National Library of Australia. Library of Congress Subject Headings (LCSH) for Aboriginal and Torres Strait Islander People. First Roundtable on Library and Archives Collections and Services of Relevance to Aboriginal and Torres Strait Islander People. Available: <http://www.nla.gov.au/niac/libs/martin.html> (accessed 08 December 2006).

Nuckolls, Karen A. (1994). Subject access to diversity materials: the Library of Congress Subject Heading shortfall. In *Racial and Ethnic Diversity in Academic Libraries: Multicultural Issues,* eds. Deborah A. Curry, Susan Griswold Blandy, and Lynne M. Martin, 241–51. New York: Haworth Press.

Olson, Hope A. (Fall 1998). Mapping beyond Dewey's boundaries: constructing classificatory space for marginalized knowledge domains. *Library Trends* 47 (2): 233–55.

Olson, Hope. (2002). *The Power to Name: Locating the Limits of Subject Representation in Libraries.* Dordrecht, Netherlands: Kluwer Academic.

Tomren, Holly. (2003). *Classification, Bias and American Indian Materials.* Unpublished paper. San Jose: San Jose State University.

Szekely, Chris. (1997). *Te Ara Tika=Guiding Voices: M_ori Opinion on Libraries and Information Needs.* Wellington: New Zealand Library and Information Association and Te Ropu Whakahau.

Yeh, Thomas Yen-Ran. (Spring 1971). "The treatment of the American Indian in the Library of Congress E-F Schedule." *Library Resources & Technical Services* 15 (2): 122–29.

Young, Mary L., and Dara L. Doolittle. (1994). "The halt of stereotyping: when does the American Indian enter the mainstream?" *Reference Librarian* 47: 109–19.

Teaching the Radical Catalog

Emily Drabinski

During a recent information literacy session for a group of first-year students enrolled in an African-American women's history course at Sarah Lawrence College, I discussed the changing Library of Congress (LC) subject headings for this field: NEGRO WOMEN; BLACK WOMEN; AFRICAN-AMERICAN WOMEN; etc. A student raised her hand and asked whether students specifically interested in the history of White women needed to search the catalog using the term WHITE. My colleague, a reference and instruction librarian with five years of experience, answered yes. While we might wish that LC acknowledged White as a racial category and marker for domination, it does not. LC is rooted in historical structures of White supremacy; as such, the catalog presumes White to be the normative term. The librarian got it wrong.

We must get it right. Currently at stake is, first off, the problem of giving students wrong information. A class busily searching for works about WHITE WOMEN will come up empty, when a search for WOMEN would serve them quite well. A second stake, less obvious but more insidious, is the risk that by teaching a catalog uncritically, we hide and extend the universalizing, hegemonic tendencies of our classifications into our teaching.

This chapter takes up the moment where critical classification theory intersects with critical pedagogy. Considering critical interruptions of classification as a social and polit- ical project, I argue that classification schemes are socially produced and embedded struc- tures; they are products of human labor that carry traces of all the intentional and unintentional racism, sexism, and classism of the workers who create them. Political efforts to change terminology or localize classification schemes are inevitably limited by the nature of classification itself. We cannot do a classification scheme objectively; it is the nature of subject analysis to be subjective. Teaching, done critically and done well, offers a potential way out of this dilemma. This will require a challenge to our standards-based information literacy discourse, and a turn toward radical pedagogical theory.

Classification in the Library

Classification is at the heart of the work of a library. A library is arguably nothing more — or less — than a set of materials classified according to some set of standard principles. All classifications, including those in libraries, function according to a set of three ideals described by Geoffrey C. Bowker and Susan Leigh Star in their critical study of classification: they apply a system of classificatory principles to a given set of objects; an object can reside in one and only one category; and all objects are accounted for in the classification.[1] In libraries, the classification can include National Library of Medicine, Dewey Decimal, Library of Congress, SuDocs, and others, or some local scheme; the objects classified are varied concretizations of knowledge, including books, films, journals and journal articles, and audiovisual materials.

Classifications consist of two separate parts. First, the classification includes a system of categories that allow for the arrangement of knowledge objects by subject to allow for browsing. The Dewey Decimal Classification (DDC) consists of ten decimal divisions (100s, 200s, etc.), each containing ten narrower divisions (110s, 120s, etc.). The Library of Congress classification (LC) has 21 general subject divisions, further divided by narrower intellectual divisions.

A second aspect of cataloging is a controlled vocabulary. A controlled vocabulary is a thesaurus of terms applied to knowledge objects by cataloging librarians and used by library patrons to access materials in Online Public Access Catalogs (OPACs). The hierarchical classification and the controlled vocabulary together contain all knowledge objects in a given system. Every object in a library will be placed in a subject division and assigned controlled terms; nothing lies outside of the system. Library classifications in the ideal are ambitious, totalizing projects: they seek to contain not only the present sum of human knowledge, but also to encompass any new knowledge generated in the future.

Thesaurus Problems

Scholars and activists have pointed out two central problems with library classifications. A brief discussion of the work of Sanford Berman and Hope Olson lays bare the central issues with library classifications as we know and use them.

In 1969, Sanford Berman published a letter in *Library Journal* calling attention to the chauvinistic headings in the Library of Congress subject heading list.[2] He went on to publish a broad attack on LC headings in 1971's *Prejudices and Antipathies*.[3] His work took issue with what he called "the realm of headings that deal with people and cultures," arguing that "the LC list can only 'satisfy' parochial, jingoistic Europeans and North Americans, white-hued, at least nominally Christian (and preferably Protestant) in faith, comfortably situated in the middle- and higher-income brackets, largely domiciled in suburbia, fundamentally loyal to the Established Order, and heavily imbued with the transcendent, incomparable glory of Western civilization."[4] Berman's writings, as well as his activist work as a cataloger with the Hennepin County Library, has inspired a generation of radical librarians to work for change in cataloging systems.

The language used in the classifications is also a reflection of broader social structures. The thesaurus acts as a meta-text, a symbolic representation of values, power relations, and cultural identities in a given place and time. For example, LC lacks a controlled term for conflicts related to the Israeli occupation of Palestinian territories. Users seeking information about Israeli incursions into Palestinian territories will find works classed under a general heading for ARAB-ISRAELI CONFLICTS. This denies the specificity of Israeli attacks on Palestinians. Further, ISRAELI-ARAB CONFLICT is listed as a cross-reference for ARAB-ISRAELI CONFLICTS, suggesting that in LC, Arabs are the originators of regional disputes.

Berman did not take issue with the fundamentals of library classifications. The goal of library classifications — to bring human knowledge together under a single unifying, universalizing structure and language — was central to Berman's point. Berman wrote in his 1971 Introduction, "Knowledge and scholarship are, after all, universal. And a subject-scheme *should*, ideally, manage to encompass all the facets of what has been printed and subsequently collected in libraries to the satisfaction of the worldwide reading community."[5] Thus, Berman's political claim was in some ways a limited one: The primary problem with Library of Congress classification is a lack of correct language. Structural critiques of classifications, however, suggest that Berman's pragmatist, yet reformist, stance is fundamentally limited.

Structural Problems

A second aspect of critical intervention has to do with the structural limitations of library classifications. Hope Olson outlines two central challenges to the structure of classifications. First, the classifications are hierarchical, and prescribe a universalizing structure of "first terms" that masquerade as neutral when they are, in fact, culturally informed and reflective of social power. For example, Olson discusses the status of WOMEN as a narrower term in relation to FEMALE. "In the case of 'Women,' the broader term 'Females' puts this heading into a biological context that divides all species by sex. Narrower terms are lower in the hierarchy. In the case of 'Women,' 'Abused women,' 'Abusive women,' 'Aged women,' and so on are lower in the hierarchy..."[6] In order to provide a context for the knowledge objects in a library, classifications seek to define hierarchies, not only in broader and narrower terms, but also through the use of related and "see also" references that create a web enfolding everything in the knowledge universe into a single, hierarchical net.

Hierarchies centralize power in the "first term," be it in a dictator in a fascist government, the father in a patriarchal family, or the quarterback in a football team. Less visible is the way that hierarchies privilege only a single aspect of a given object. For example, a man who is a football quarterback may also be a father, a brother, and stamp collector, but for the purpose of the hierarchy that embeds him on the football field, he is only a quarterback. The other relevant parts of his person — his ability to stay in the pocket, scramble, throw the long ball, and so on — are derivative of his "first term," his quarterback-ness. The other parts of his person — his presidency of a local philatelist society, perhaps — become irrelevant. Hope Olson calls this the hierarchy of samenesses. "[W]e divide first by one facet, then by another and another and so on in a prescribed citation order. The result is a hierarchical arrangement that gathers effectively by the first facet following the idea that we gather what is the same and separate what is different."[7]

Imagine a book about our quarterback that also discussed his struggles with racism in the NFL. A cataloger might assign QUARTERBACKING (FOOTBALL), because it is about football, rather than RACISM—UNITED STATES about racism in America. The book would then be visible to sports researchers, and less so to researchers studying racism in America. The range of options is enormous; a cataloger might also choose RACISM IN SPORTS, AFRICAN-AMERICAN ATHLETES—SOCIAL CONDITIONS, DISCRIMINATION IN SPORTS, and so on. In library classifications, the work of choosing the "first cut" for a given book is by catalogers. This is a very human and very subjective process: What is this book in my hand primarily about? Is it about football, or is it about racism? And which among this set of relevant headings should be assigned? This decision has material effects for browsers, who may or may not find or a book depending the classification. The hierarchy in classifications is not simply that of privileging a single term over others, but also the privileging of certain kinds of sameness and difference.

A final structural problem with classifications is their permanency. Even the most flexible classification requires that a knowledge object be placed into a given category "for good." Once a book is placed in a category, even a new category, it usually stays there. Catalogers do revise headings, but the vagaries of cataloging under capitalism generally reward the production of new records. What happens, then, to emerging knowledges that are necessarily in motion? I am thinking here, for example, of materials that address the lives and experiences of transgender and gender-variant people. This identity group is in a state of acute formation — new language is used daily by transgender and gender-variant people to describe their experience, and new identities are constantly coming into being and passing into some other identity. LC figuratively arrests this becoming by placing a book into a classification category based on a vocabulary that may be supplanted by the text itself. For example, books about gender variance fall under the headings TRANSSEXUALS or TRANS-SEXUALITY, though many in those communities identify "transgendered" as the appropriate umbrella term. Surely people can continue to change regardless of LC subject headings; however, the headings do fix certain identities and not others in place and time.

The State of Interventions

Library classifications are necessary. Indeed, we can hardly begin to make sense of knowledge without them. Classifications order objects in material space — they place books in an order on shelves — and grant intellectual access to collections by collating books according to some logic. And yet they are problematic. Library classifications use the hegemonic language of the powerful: they reflect, produce, and reproduce hierarchies; they order sameness and difference and prevent the full representation of minority literatures; they arrest the linguistic transformation in emerging fields of knowledge and identity production. These are large problems, and solutions have tended toward two approaches: attacking the language problem, and attacking the structural problem.

Sandy Berman is perhaps our most famous cataloging activist. Since 1971, his work on transforming subject headings both at the local level (in Hennepin County) and at the Library of Congress has yielded positive linguistic change (LC's elimination of the obviously racist heading YELLOW PERIL in 1989, for example), and has called attention to the hegemonic nature of classification. Yet his work sustains and upholds the value of LC. As Berman struggles to change the thesaurus, he leaves the structural problems untouched. This failure is important. Berman's approach suggests there is some "right" language that could be universally understood and applied. The politics of language are rarely so tidy, and language is virtually always contested. For example, in her interview with Library Juice's Rory Litwin, Barbara Tillett, LC's chief of the Library of Congress Cataloging Policy and Support Office, recalls: "Before we made the change from 'Gypsies' to 'Romanies,' staff members from CPSO attended a seminar on the topic at the Holocaust Museum and consulted closely with a renowned expert and advocate in this field. After we changed the heading to 'Romanies' [in 2004], we received complaints from several individuals and a few organizations that opposed our discontinuing usage of the term Gypsies."[8]

Imagine other instances where the politics of a particular identity term are so contentious that it's difficult to imagine settling on a "right" word. Think of the reclamations of identity terms like "n*****," "queer," "fat," and "crip" for use by some members of those identity groups. Should LC reflect these self-identifications? Berman's struggle for "right language" does not account for the ways in which language is inherently political and contextual.

What about these structural problems? If classifications are necessary, how can we resist the structural aspects that we don't like: the hierarchical ordering of samenesses, their lack of flexibility? Some librarians, including Olson, have focused on the generation of local classifications. Rather than pouring energy into improving a single, universalized classification like LC, Olson and other librarians focused on creating user-centered classifications for particular collections. Examples include the *Art and Architecture Thesaurus*, which uses a faceted classification scheme to classify art objects for art researchers, and the use of folksonomies in digital environments, both discussed elsewhere in this volume.

A second approach to these structural limitations might be to apply technologies to reduce our reliance on structured classifications. A combination of free-text searching and strong relevance algorithms might allow users to retrieve relevant search results without the need for an underlying classification. Anyone who has waded through thousands of JSTOR results in search of a relevant document can tell you we're not there yet. Olson discusses her project of mapping a local thesaurus onto DDC as a second technological solution, combining a localized feminist thesaurus with a standard organizational structure to highlight sexism in DDC and make feminist research easier.[9]

Challenging and changing thesauri, developing local solutions, and utilizing new technologies all have potential use in our radical toolbox. However, none of these solutions will work everywhere all of the time, and none account for the persistent and growing reliance on standardized schemes like DDC and LC. Those of us who practice with LC need a fourth strategy for undoing the perils of the classification.

Teaching the Radical Catalog

Neither changing the language nor changing the structure can eliminate the fundamental limitations of classification systems. Classifications are inherently static — at least at any given moment in time — and inherently universalizing — at least in relation to a given field of knowledge objects. If these characteristics are indeed fundamental, we might incorporate radical pedagogies into our work as teachers to transform users' relationships to these systems.

Public services librarians increasingly think of ourselves as teachers. This turn in our professional identity is noted by James Elmborg, who cites the shift away from individual reference transactions and toward group instruction as empirical evidence of an increased professional focus on "information literacy" as an object of professional elaboration.[10] Further evidence of our profession's emphasis on teaching can be seen in the emphasis of the Association of College and Research Libraries (ACRL) on the development and implementation of standards of information literacy. The ACRL Information Literacy Competency Standards for Higher Education ("the Standards") map a closed universe of library skills and abilities that constitute the information-literate student. They create a hierarchy of information literacy skills, naming them with scientific precision. The Standards constitute the text from which librarians draw the content of our lessons. They form our primary pedagogical text; as such, they both demonstrate the limitations of our current pedagogical thinking, and indicate potential points of radical intervention.

Radical Alternatives

In 1970, Paulo Freire published his seminal work, *Pedagogy of the Oppressed*. Among his many arguments for "education as a practice of freedom,"[11] Freire offered a definition of the pedagogy of the ruling classes. He called this "banking education," which he described as follows: "The banking concept (with its tendency to dichotomize everything) distinguishes two stages in the action of the educator. During the first, he cognizes a cognizable object while he prepares his lessons in his study or his laboratory; during the second, he expounds to his students about that object. The students are not called upon to know, but to memorize the contents narrated by the teacher. Nor do the students practice any act of cognition, since the object towards which that act should be directed is the property of the teacher rather than a medium evoking the critical reflection of both teacher and students."[12] In banking education, then, the student serves as a passive receptacle for the knowledge of the teacher. Critical thought is not encouraged; memorization and regurgitation is rewarded.

If we turn again to the Standards, we see that current information literacy approaches hew quite closely to the "banking education" that Freire describes. ACRL has developed a cognizable object — "information literacy" — and advocates for a pedagogy that conveys these skills to students, and then assesses their ability to reproduce the outcomes favored under the Standards.

Alternative Strategies

Freire offers an alternative pedagogy, one that focuses, not on the one-way exchange of knowledge from a knowing subject to an ignorant object, but instead on the posing of problems that are then grappled with by individuals, all of whom are subjects, all of whom both teach and learn. He calls this "problem-posing education."[13] Instead of passively teaching classifications, a critical library instruction program might instead teach students to engage critically with the classifications as text, encouraging critical thought in relation to the tools.

When we teach the catalog — or any other classified retrieval tool — as a reality that must be accommodated by the student, we perpetuate the dominance of story "told" by the classification. Problem-posing education allows us to "unveil" the hegemonic production and reproduction of the problematic language cited by Berman and the troubling staticity of hierarchies of sameness articulated by Olson. In the words of Freire, "whereas banking education anesthetizes and inhibits creative power, problem-posing education involves a constant unveiling of reality. The former attempts to maintain the *submersion* of consciousness; the latter strives for the *emergence* of consciousness and *critical intervention* in reality."[14] When we come to understand the limits of and power enacted by classifications, we are able to use them for their concrete purposes — finding books on library shelves — and to transform our relationships to them via critical engagement.

Elmborg, working from a background in critical literacy studies, makes precisely this claim. Citing the work of Olson, he says, "For information literacy to have a critical dimension, it must involve both an understanding of how various classification systems work, and also an exploration of how they create and perpetuate such powerful categories for representing 'knowable reality and universal truth.'"[15] By embedding the problems of classification in our content and in our method, we empower students and ourselves to work critically with systems that can never be "fixed" by our cataloging divisions.

Intervening in the Library Classroom

What might a critical engagement with classification-as-text look like in a bibliographic instruction classroom? Surely we must continue teaching students how to use the library catalog, database indexes, and other classified information retrieval systems. Students cannot succeed unless they know how to navigate our many and varied classifications, with all their limitations and political difficulties. How might we teach these tools while simultaneously including critical reflections on the tools themselves?

A first step is certainly to learn from the work of critical education theorists. As Elmborg notes, drawing on the critical work of Allan Luke and Cushla Kaptizke, librarianship has tended away from critical approaches to the work of teaching.[16] In addition to Freire, librarians could benefit from relevant thinkers such as Lisa Delpit, whose writing engages cultural and racial conflict in classrooms; Henry Giroux, whose work on public pedagogy lies at the root of radical pedagogy in the United States; and Peter McLaren, whose work focuses on teaching against capitalist and imperialist narratives. This pedagogical shift will require stepping back from the standards-and-assessments approach that so dominates the teaching literature of librarians and a step towards the extensive theoretical work already undertaken by teachers in other fields.

As teachers, we will need to relinquish some control in the classroom. While our focus has long been on our expertise, we will need to be willing to be learners, along with our students. My colleague, a white woman, was blind to the structures of racism built into the library catalog; she didn't understand the difference, because she didn't conceive it as such. A group of ready learners grappling with the problems of classification might come to understand such a critique together. We will need to remove ourselves from positions of dominance and engage in critical learning with the students who come to our classrooms struggling, like us, to make sense of the library.

Notes

1. Geoffrey C. Bowker and Susan Leigh Star, *Sorting Things Out: Classification and Its Consequences* (Cambridge, MA: MIT Press, 1999), 10.

2. Sanford Berman, "Chauvinistic Headings," *Library Journal* 94 (February 15 1969): 695.

3. Sanford Berman, *Prejudices and Antipathies: A Tract on the LC Subject Heads Concerning People* (Jefferson, NC: McFarland & Company, 1993.)

4. Berman, *Prejudices and Antipathies*, 15.

5. Berman, *Prejudices and Antipathies*, 15.

6. Hope Olson, "The Power to Name: Representations in Library Catalog," *Signs* 26 (Spring 2001): 645.

7. Hope Olson, "Sameness and Difference: A Cultural Foundation of Classification," *Library Resources and Technical Services* 45 (July 2001): 119.

8. Litwin, Rory. (2006, 6 August). Interview with Barbara Tillett. *Library Juice*. Available: <http://libraryjuicepress.com/blog/?p=115> (accessed December 15, 2006).

9. Olson, Power to Name, 661.

10. James Elmborg, "Critical Information literacy: Implications for Instructional Practice," *Journal of Academic Librarianship* 32 (2006): 192.

11. Paulo Freire, *Pedagogy of the Oppressed* (New York: Continuum, 1990): 62.

12. Freire, 61.

13. Freire, 62.

14. Freire, 62.

15. Elmborg, 192.

16. Elmborg, 193.

Browsing Bergman, Finding Fellini, Cataloging Kurosawa: Alternative Approaches to Cataloging Foreign Language Films in Academic Libraries

Michelle Emanuel and *Susannah Benedetti*

Introduction

Many academic libraries collect foreign language films to meet patron needs, both curricular and recreational. Cataloging video recordings is time-consuming and complex, and foreign language titles involve additional challenges. Over time, cataloging resources such as *Anglo-American Cataloguing Rules* (AACR2), *International Standard Bibliographic Description*, and *Bibliographic Formats and Standards* have come to address audiovisual materials in their rules and guidelines correlating to the MARC format. Most academic libraries utilize these resources for cataloging video recordings, whereas archival institutions generally use *Archival Moving Image Materials: A Cataloging Manual* (AMIM), originally published by the Library of Congress's Motion Picture, Broadcasting, and Recorded Sound Division in 1984. The Library of Congress's decision to use AMIM for its moving image cataloging has created a leadership void for libraries using AACR2 to catalog video recordings. Apart from a smattering of Library of Congress Rule Interpretations for AACR2 Chapter 7 on Motion Pictures and Video Recordings, the vanguard has provided little guidance in this area. As a result, standards for bibliographic description of motion pictures and video recordings have not been collectively accepted or codified. Libraries face ambiguity in cataloging these formats, with the result that catalog records and access points (especially of complex materials such as foreign language films) vary widely among institutions. Librarians make local decisions on description, access, and classification, resulting in duplicated efforts, stand-alone procedures, and inconsistent results. Copy catalogers have grown accustomed to "fleshing out" minimal-level video records in shared utilities such as OCLC to meet their local standards. They might add access points for alternate titles, the names of actors, directors, and cinematographers, genre headings, or summary notes to enrich the catalog for keyword searching. Depending on the distributor, however, there are often discrepancies between descriptive information found on the container and in the film credits, and catalogers who must rely solely on the container risk the omission of vital information required by patrons in search of foreign language films, such as country of production, original language, and the presence or absence of subtitles. Enriching the catalog with elements not necessarily found in the chief source of information makes the library collection more accessible at the expense of traditional cataloging rules. This article describes efforts at the University of Mississippi and the University of North Carolina–Wilmington to meet the specialized needs of foreign film enthusiasts, including faculty and students of film studies and foreign languages.

Literature Review

Library catalogers generally provide subject access to film and moving image materials within the confines of the Library of Congress Subject Headings (LCSH). The flagship thesaurus was created largely to describe print materials and is less than perfect for providing access to feature films, not to mention foreign films with essential elements of language and nationality. Similar to its use of AMIM for descriptive cataloging, the Library of Congress utilizes a specialized archival vocabulary for its own moving image materials. Issues facing catalogers using LCSH for moving image materials have been addressed in the literature. Miller notes that the Library of Congress's public documentation for treatment of moving image materials is noticeably meager compared to that for books and even music.[1] The extent of the guidance is found in the *Subject Cataloging Manual: Subject Headings* instruction sheet for Visual Materials and Non–Music Sound Recordings; fiction films are assigned the form heading "Feature films" as well as "[f]orm headings that express either genre (for example, "Comedy films," "Western films") or technique (for example, "Silent films," "Experimental films")."[2] Beyond this directive, the film cataloger is left to struggle with the ambiguous correlation between subject headings (what an item is about) and form/genre headings (what an item is, or the genre of which it is an example). Although this issue also challenges catalogers of literary and musical works, it is especially vexing for feature film videos due to the lack of consensus and broad range of practices in evidence in existing records. Miller concludes, "The cataloger who must work with LCSH or a compatible vocabulary is still left without a useable, comprehensive source of form/genre headings for moving-image materials."[3] In separate studies, Taves and Yee concur that LCSH is fundamentally unsuited to moving image materials due to its lack of appropriate genre terms, and they compare it to the specialized taxonomy *Moving Image Genre — Form Guide* (MIGFG), created at the Library of Congress's Motion Picture, Broadcasting, and Recorded Sound Division in 1998. As one of the creators of MIGFG, Taves voices the hope that its ongoing list of over 150 genre terms could transcend its archival constituency and assume relevance in the academic community where film studies are increasingly prominent.[4] MIGFG offers definitions, scope notes, and examples for each of its terms, and its specificity allows the cataloger to assign precise genre terms, such as MELODRAMA for the film *Terms of Endearment*. Utilizing LCSH for this film results in less than adequate topical headings such as MOTHERS AND DAUGHTERS—

DRAMA. Yee acknowledges the richness of the terms found in MIGFG, but laments that widespread usage is unlikely since the taxonomy is not based on national or international standards for subject heading or thesaurus construction.[5] She recommends that libraries using LCSH for moving images assign topical headings in the 650 field, but also in the 655 field as genre/form headings where relevant. Yee briefly addresses this issue in terms of foreign films, comparing the headings "Motion pictures — [country]" and "Motion pictures, [nationality]" and identifying them as notable examples of LCSH headings that could be useful for genre/form access.[6] Ho examines ten years of messages (1993–2003) on the electronic cataloging lists AUTOCAT and OLAC-LIST and analyzes catalogers' questions and responses about applying form/genre headings to foreign films in order to improve access. List messages indicate that the majority of patrons want to search for foreign films by language and country of origin, and catalogers are eager to provide this level of access. Due to a lack of standards authorizing the use of most topical headings as form/genre headings (especially when qualified by nationality or subdivided geographically), many libraries are adapting LCSH headings and subdivisions for this purpose. Many libraries assign the subject heading FOREIGN FILMS as a form/genre heading so that a search can retrieve all foreign films in the catalog. Others use some variation of the headings "Feature films — [country]," "Motion pictures — [country]" or "Motion pictures, [nationality]." Libraries that choose to provide subject access by language operate even further outside cataloging standards, creating local headings such as GERMAN LANGUAGE VIDEOS.[7] Ho recognizes that widespread use of these techniques and a lack of standards has created great inconsistency between individual library catalogs and within the shared database WorldCat. She concludes that it could be beneficial to incorporate nationality and/or language access elements into authorized form/genre headings for foreign film use. While the larger issue of subject and genre/form access to feature films has been addressed over the years, at the current time there is no viable alternative to LCSH and no additional guidance available. Many libraries continue to adapt LCSH headings locally and in a variety of ways in order to improve access; this paper will explore and compare experiences at two academic libraries.

Birth of a Project

At the University of Mississippi (UM), the video cataloger serves double duty as the Modern Languages subject selector. Therefore, the foreign language video collection has been tailored to meet the needs of those primary users. Upper-level foreign language courses frequently use films in lieu of literary texts; the faculty want more than just film adaptations of the novels they are reading. As the field becomes increasingly interdisciplinary, foreign language departments develop film studies courses, or courses on cultural studies through film. At UM, approximately twenty percent of the firm order budget for Modern Languages materials is spent on feature films and documentaries, with an additional five to ten percent spent on pedagogical titles, such as those from the Films for the Humanities catalog. But it is not enough to purchase these titles; they must be cataloged in a way that they can be found from many access points. While searching for a method to rework the foreign film collection, the UM cataloger crossed paths with the UNCW cataloger, and became intrigued with the method they had implemented.

In 2000, the William M. Randall Library at University of North Carolina Wilmington (UNCW) held roughly two thousand feature films on videotape and DVD. The interdisciplinary film studies program launched a popular major in 2001 and gained departmental status in 2003. These developments spurred significant expansion of the library's video collection, and the Film Studies Department's library budget expanded by thirty-three percent as new faculty were hired, new courses were offered, and new research areas were undertaken. In the last two fiscal years, the department spent over sixty percent of its library budget on videos. By 2006, the library held approximately nine thousand feature films. Of those, twenty percent are foreign language films, reflecting the significance of this field of study. UNCW offers a robust curriculum in foreign film, including upper level courses in French, German, Spanish, and Japanese cinema, new Asian cinemas, new wave cinemas, Brazilian literature and film, and history and perspectives in world cinema. The department benefits from ongoing interdisciplinary involvement of faculty from the Foreign Languages & Literatures Department.

Cutting Edge Cutters?

At UM, Modern Languages professors are known to send their students in search of films for individual projects with instructions as specific as "Find a film by François Truffaut that we did not view in class," and as vague as "Find a feature film from a Latin American country other than Mexico." While the first example is fairly obvious — use an author search for "Truffaut, François"— the second example can be rather challenging for the average undergraduate, and even more so for the reference librarian on duty. To serve the needs of these patrons, the foreign language film collection at the University of Mississippi was reclassified to include the country of production as a geographic Cutter based on *Subject Cataloging Manual: Shelflisting* G 300 Regions and Countries Table. All Argentine films are classed together, as are all Chilean films, all Colombian films, all Chinese films, all Taiwanese films, etc., rather than being classed by the language "Spanish" or "Mandarin," because the faculty are making these distinctions as well. The rest of the call number is derived from the original language title, since foreign language films are generally cited in critical works by their original title rather than by their translated title, which can vary according to the distributor. Therefore, Federico Fellini's *Juliet of the Spirits* (*Giulietta degli Spiriti*) is filed as PN1997.I8 G585 2002, rather than Cuttered by "J." Documentary films, however, are filed by the LC classification of their subject matter, and not by a derivative of PN1997.

Cataloging guidelines at UNCW define foreign films as those produced outside the United States in a non–English language. Foreign films are classified in PN1997 and Cuttered by language. The result is that films in a particular language file together, regardless of the country of origin (i.e., Portuguese language films file together whether they are Portuguese or Brazilian productions). This decision benefits language-based study, such as a project to find French language films produced outside of France, in Francophone countries such as Canada, Belgium, or former African colonies such as Gabon or Senegal. In addition, classifying by language avoids the cataloger's predicament of determining a primary country of origin for a multinational co-production. The co–production is an increasingly common European funding model, resulting in films like *Caché* (credited as "une coproduction France-Autriche-Allemagne-Italie") and *Il Cerchio*, a co-production between Iran, Switzerland, and Italy. In this climate, a film scholar observes, "given the intense movements of film finance and people beyond national borders and former political division lines, classifying films as belonging to a national cinematic tradition is becoming increasingly problematic."[8] The second Cutter of the foreign film call number is based on the prominent container title. UNCW implemented this policy in 2005 in large part to simplify shelving for staff who continually reported discrepancies between call number title Cutters and container titles, interpreting them as errors in need of correction. UNCW follows cataloging standards by transcribing the title proper from a film's title frames in the 245 field of the MARC record.[9] For example, the title proper of Vittorio De Sica's 1949 neorealist Italian film is *Ladri di biciclette*. Some foreign video containers display titles in their original languages, but many substitute translated titles for the American market. For example, the video container for *Ladri di biciclette* features the translated English title *The Bicycle Thief*, and UNCW uses this title for Cuttering purposes (PN1997.I8 B529 1998). Richter notes that the marketing and packaging of foreign films can be fraught with inconsistencies since different video distributors may market the same film under different English titles, especially in the case of Chinese films.[10] Despite potential discrepancies, the reclassification has proved successful for staff shelving and patron browsing.

The Subject Was "Roses $v Drama"

At UM, the subject headings "Feature films" and "Foreign films" have been subdivided geographically to reflect the original country of production, even if the copy in hand has been distributed by an American studio such as MGM/UA, Sony, Columbia-TriStar, etc. The heading "Motion pictures, [language]" was not applied during the latest update, but may be added in the future.

At UNCW, all foreign films are assigned the headings "Feature films" and "Foreign films." As noted, "Feature films" is an accepted form heading according to the *Subject Cataloging Manual: Subject Headings*, but there is no such guidance for clarifying whether the topical heading "Foreign films" is allowable as a genre/form heading. In order to allow patrons to search for all foreign films, UNCW made the local decision to adapt this heading for form/genre access. In terms of providing geographic access, foreign films are also given the heading "Motion pictures, [nationality]," i.e. "Motion pictures, Spanish." This is another topical heading that has been locally adapted for form/genre access, allowing users to perform a subject search to find all films produced in a certain country.

Based on the Book

At UM, literary adaptations are filed with the call number of the literary author, so that multinational adaptations of the same novels can be filed together. For example,

Roger Vadim's 1959 adaptation of Choderlos de Laclos's *Les liaisons dangereuses* (PQ1993.L22) would be filed next to Stephen Frears's 1988 *Dangerous Liaisons* and Milos Forman's 1989 *Valmont*. Likewise, René Clément's 1960 *Plein Soleil* (*Purple Noon*) would be filed next to Anthony Minghella's 1999 adaptation of Patricia Highsmith's *The Talented Mr. Ripley* (PS3558.I366).

UNCW classifies literary adaptations with all other feature films, Cuttering them by title using one of ten predetermined genre class numbers.[11] Adaptations in foreign languages are classed in PN1997 as noted above. Adaptations with the same container title file together, such as Orson Welles' 1948 *Macbeth* and Roman Polanski's 1971 *Macbeth*. This practice separates adaptations of the same work released under different titles, however, such as *Throne of Blood*, Akira Kurosawa's 1957 adaptation of *Macbeth* set in feudal Japan. Although this practice scatters an author's different works throughout the feature film collection, a film's cinematic identity was judged to take precedence over its literary provenance. In addition, this practice avoids the necessity of determining when a film is a formal adaptation as opposed to homage, spoof, or loose interpretation. Local guidelines would need to be established on making this thorny determination, perhaps based on whether or not the original literary work is formally credited in the film titles. There is no reference to Shakespeare or *Macbeth* in the credits of *Throne of Blood*, for example, so under these guidelines would it not be considered a true adaptation? Meanwhile Billy Morrissette's 2001 *Scotland, Pa.* credits Shakespeare's play up front as the basis for its noir tale of a cook and his wife who usurp management of Duncan's hamburger stand in 1970s Pennsylvania. Taves observes, "While useful for scholars tracing such questions as fidelity to the original text, such a term [adaptation] needs to be applied either in its broadest sense or not at all, since quick archival cataloging does not allow for judging as to whether the adaptation is significantly related to the source or not."[12] UNCW has chosen not to classify literary adaptations by their authors' call numbers, but takes care to trace authors as added entries in 700 fields with titles of works noted in $t. In this way, reference librarians can instruct patrons to search by author and/or title in the online catalog and determine what adaptations are available and where they are shelved.

Location, Location, Location

At UM, foreign language films are filed together, and literary adaptations (American, British, and foreign language) are filed together, but the other genres remain lumped together. Additionally, for issues related to shelving, DVDs are shelved separately from VHS, and among the VHS, oversized videos are placed in a third location, though all videos (regardless of format) are Cuttered alphabetically in the catalog module. Therefore, the entire collection is not as browsable as the foreign language section. In general, circulation of the collection has increased exponentially since the reclassification project, and users have been vocal as to the improved browsability and ease of searching.

At UNCW, the video collection is separated into four physical locations: foreign films, English language feature films, non-feature films such as documentary, pedagogical, and instructional videos, and oversized videos. DVDs and VHS are filed separately within each location, and all videos are browsable in open shelves. The video collection is extremely popular with faculty, staff, students, and community guests. Circulation has increased every year since 2001, with DVDs accounting for over twenty-five percent of total circulation in 2006. The collection's continued growth resulted in the creation of a new cataloging staff position in 2005 to focus primarily on DVDs and other audiovisual materials.

Conclusion

Cataloging to accommodate local needs is not a new concept, or one limited to video recordings. In the majority of academic music libraries, for example, books and scores are classified according to Library of Congress Classification, while sound recordings are filed by accession number.[13] Some libraries use accession numbers because their sound recordings are housed in closed stacks and do not require classification for browsing purposes. Others with a high volume of records, cassettes, or compact discs use accession numbers to economize staff time as well as avoid Library of Congress Cutters that could expand to unwieldy lengths. Accession number systems vary by local needs or precedents and may be straightforward or idiosyncratic. Documentation is critical for any decision to deviate from standards in order to explain the rationale and ensure internal consistency.

The local procedures in place at UM and UNCW illustrate issues facing catalogers of foreign films, specifically how to balance access for patrons with adherence to cataloging standards. Both libraries have adapted topical LCSH headings for form/genre access, but have taken different approaches to accommodate language and nationality. UM classifies its foreign films by country of production, while UNCW classifies by original language. UM geographically subdivides the headings FOREIGN FILMS and MOTION PICTURES while UNCW assigns FOREIGN FILMS without a geographic subdivision, and qualifies MOTION PICTURES by country of production (i.e., MOTION PICTURES, BELGIAN). While these methods are effective for the libraries' local constituencies, their differences are noteworthy. A UM patron's successful search strategy for French language films or films produced in Belgium would not retrieve the same results in the UNCW online catalog, and vice versa. The same search in WorldCat might retrieve different results altogether, based on the local practices of the institution that created the record, specifically with regard to access points, subject headings, form headings, and genres variously subdivided and qualified. The result is that searching for foreign films by language or nationality is a hit-or-miss prospect requiring tenacity and creativity to be certain that all results are being retrieved. Unlike its substantial contribution of MARC records for books that it catalogs, the Library of Congress does not typically contribute video records to OCLC. Copy catalogers thus download video records created by various libraries and institutions according to countless standards; the records often require significant access point enhancement, subject heading editing, and call number reassignment in order to conform to local practices. Making local record changes is a basic element of copy cataloging, but the level of individualized and duplicated effort involved with foreign and feature film records is striking. As long as there is a lack of codified national standards and guidance for cataloging motion pictures and videos, libraries like those at the University of Mississippi and the University of North Carolina–Wilmington will continue to catalog in a vacuum according to "home-grown" practices. This scenario shapes workflow, processing time, and cataloging productivity, and the ripple effects will continue to affect OCLC and WorldCat, diluting the integrity of the shared database for catalogers and patrons alike.

Notes

1. David Miller. (2000). Out from under: form/genre access in LCSH, *Cataloging & Classification Quarterly* 29, no. 1/2 (2000), 178.

2. Cataloging Policy and Support Office, Library of Congress, *Subject Cataloging Manual: Subject Headings*, 5th ed. (Washington, D.C.: Cataloging Distribution Service, Library of Congress, 2000), H2230.

3. Miller, 180.

4. Brian Taves, Toward a Comprehensive Genre Taxonomy, *The Moving Image: the Journal of the Association of Moving Image Archivists* 1, no. 1 (2001), 135–36.

5. M. M. Yee, Two Genre and Form Lists for Moving Image and Broadcast Materials: A Comparison, *Cataloging & Classification Quarterly* 31, no. 3/4 (2001), 253.

6. Ibid., 259.

7. Jeannette Ho, Applying Form/Genre Headings to Foreign Films: A Summary of AUTOCAT and OLAC-LIST Discussions, *Cataloging & Classification Quarterly* 40, no. 2 (2005), 81.

8. Dina Iordanova, Feature Filmmaking Within the New Europe, *Media, Culture & Society* 24, no. 4 (2002), 533.

9. Joint Steering Committee for Revision of AACR, *Anglo-American Cataloguing Rules*, 2nd ed., 2002 rev. (Chicago: American Library Association, 2002), 7.0B1.

10. Wayne Richter, email to AUTOCAT mailing list, November 13, 2006 Available: <http://listserv.acsu.buffalo.edu/cgi-bin/wa?A1=ind0611b&L=autocat#7>.

11. William Madison Randall Library, University of North Carolina–Wilmington, Feature Film & Television Cataloging Guidelines. Available: <http://library.uncw.edu/web/technical/Cataloging/featurefilm.html> (accessed October 23, 2006).

12. Taves, 143.

13. Linda Crow, Shelf Arrangement Systems for Sound Recordings: Survey of American Academic Music Libraries, *Technical Services Quarterly* 8, no. 4 (1991), 19.

User-Centered Serials Cataloging

Wendy Baia

The fulfillment of local library users' needs in obtaining desired information and resources provides the guiding motivation for daily decision-making and establishing local library cataloging policies, practices and procedures for catalogers with a user-centered philosophy. Adding the words "user-centered" to "cataloging" should be unnecessary, since this is ostensibly the foundation for all cataloging. The reality is often, however, far different from the professed goal. The history of many arcane and user-unfriendly cataloging rules and practices is testament to the actual implementation of much unexamined, inflexible rule-centered or "We must do exactly what LC does" cataloging practice. If catalog records accessed by our local library OPACs were actually satisfying user needs to the highest degree possible, would there be so many recent complaints about the increasing irrelevance of our libraries and OPACs to today's library patrons?

The comfort level with the online environment — including online ordering, banking, Googling, surfing, blogging, e-mailing, instant messaging, match-making, etc.— continues to increase. In contrast, the comfort level with our library catalogs has decreased per the 2003 *OCLC Environmental Scan*.[1] A 2005 report prepared by OCLC confirmed this trend and concluded that libraries are "increasingly less visible" based on "a database of over 270,000 information consumer views, habits and recommendations from over 3,300 people in six countries."[2] Although libraries are facing competition as never before and in-person reference interviews have severely declined, our cataloging practices are now visible worldwide to more general scrutiny through our OPACs than in earlier eras, when patrons had to come into the library to consult the mysteriously constructed card catalog.

Numerous recent reports echo the criticisms of the 2005 report, *Rethinking How We Provide Bibliographic Services for the University of California*: "The current Library catalog is poorly designed for the tasks of finding, discovering, and selecting the growing set of resources available in our libraries."[3] Karen Calhoun's controversial 2006 report, prepared for the Library of Congress, declared: "The cost-effectiveness of cataloging tradition and practice is under fire."[4] Saving the time of the user has clearly not always been the most urgent goal in the design of our OPACs, or in the implementation of many local cataloging practices. Users want, and have come to expect, self-sufficiency, and our OPACs have fallen short.

The philosophy and principles of user-centered cataloging can be applied to all formats. This chapter will focus on its applicability to the cataloging of serial publications. With user-centered serials cataloging, the cataloger tries to evaluate serial catalog records from a user's point of view. Unfortunately, some catalogers who do original cataloging in OCLC concentrate most of their efforts on producing "perfect" (i.e., rule-following) original bibliographic records with little thought to how easily these records will be retrieved and how they will display in the local catalog. Serials catalogers who look only at the MARC record and don't make it a regular practice to retrieve and view serial records in the local OPAC might think their rule-perfect records are impeccable, when, in reality, most users who want certain serials may not be able to easily find them. When they are lucky enough to find the right records, users may be confused by unfamiliar jargon or cataloging conventions that don't make common sense.

This paper will focus on serials cataloged according to AACR2 rules and MARC format, although it is likely that other metadata schemes will become increasingly more significant in the near future.

The Legalist and the Pragmatist: Bridging the Divide

On my first day on the job at the University of Colorado at Boulder (CU), I was introduced to another cataloger, who said in the course of a brief conversation, "We don't catalog for PAC." (PAC was the name of the CU OPAC at that time.) This was over 17 years ago, but I still clearly remember her exact words, since I was appalled by this statement. I uncharacteristically said nothing at the time to avoid getting into a heated philosophical debate and possibly making an enemy on my first day. This person was not a monster, but as I discovered later was a dedicated, caring cataloger. Her philosophy — that we catalog for OCLC rather than our local users — was diametrically opposite to mine.

Each cataloger brings to her work a unique set of individual characteristics and personal history that influence the work she finds satisfying and the decisions she makes in the workplace. Each cataloger has an implicit or explicit cataloging philosophy that may be in conflict with disparate cataloging philosophies of other catalogers, supervisors, or library administrators. A cataloger with a "save the time of the user" orientation may become frustrated when her colleagues take a rigid stance against violating cataloging rules that cause confusion and non-retrieval of catalog records. She may also become exasperated when colleagues demand rigid consistency in certain cataloging practices when this consistency is mindless and serves no genuine purpose.

Most catalogers probably assume that their cataloging is user-centered since they may interpret "user-centered" to apply to any record that adheres to all applicable cataloging rules and standards. In fact, catalogers who Andrew Osborn termed "legalistic" might not even consider challenging any rules, since rules are to be obeyed. To Osborn's legalist cataloger, "There must be rules and definitions to govern every point that arises; there must be an authority to settle questions at issue."[5] Osborn lists three problems resulting from a legalist cataloging philosophy:

- Cataloging becomes an end in itself.
- Once it is decided to formulate rules and decisions for all points, the process must go on indefinitely.
- Codification tends to obscure reasons and principles. People learn arbitrary rules without understanding the principles. [6]

Osborn saw the legalist as the main danger to cataloging and a major cause of "The Crisis in Cataloging," the name of his perceptive 1941 article. He depicted legalistic catalogers debating the correctness of minute description details that are of significance only to catalogers while huge cataloging backlogs built up in their libraries. Osborn's favorite type of cataloger was the pragmatist, for whom "rules hold and decisions are made only to the extent that seems desirable from a practical point of view.... The pragmatist emphasizes the differing needs of varying types of libraries."[7]

An understanding that strict adherence to rules is not an arbitrary refusal to listen to common sense but a deeply felt need to do what legalist catalogers think is right, can help a pragmatic cataloger maintain reasonable working relationships with legalists. With this understanding and positive strategies, the user-centered cataloger has a better chance of presenting her viewpoint amicably and possibly influencing the adoption of more user-centered practices. Sometimes supervisors or library administrators are the ones who insist on rigid adherence to standards that don't always make common sense. Depending on how severely attempts to adopt alternative innovative solutions are crushed, the user-centered cataloger may decide that she needs to find a workplace more in line with her own philosophy.

Chameleon Serials

Those who are drawn to serials cataloging enjoy the challenges of bringing order and understanding to resources that defy order and do not obey cataloging rules. Serials catalogers who last in this specialty generally take pleasure in the Sherlock Holmes–like challenges of solving complex serials cataloging problems. There is a wonderful sense of triumph when finding an innovative solution to a difficult problem that first seemed to defy any good solution. The variety of problems confronting the serials cataloger never ceases to amaze, no matter how many years a cataloger has spent unraveling serial aberrations.

When cataloged as a serial, the physical volumes of a publication are shelved together in chronological order, saving the user time in locating them. Cataloging as a serial saves cataloging time since new monograph records don't need to be produced for each edition. Having one OPAC serial record rather than many monograph records generally also saves the users' time since they don't have to negotiate among many separate monograph records, and it is immediately clear from the serial holdings which is the most recent available edition. Cataloging a publication as a monograph is often a better option when each edition or volume has varying subject content and information, such as a table of contents, important editors or issuing bodies that merit inclusion in the record. Unfortunately, however, the ability to make user-friendly consistent local decisions about what to cata-log as serials may be curtailed by the presence of programs, such as OCLC's PromptCat, where monograph records may be batch-loaded without review.

Serials catalogers make decisions on how supplements and special issues should be treated. They figure out the relationships among serials that may be companion publica-tions, issued in different editions, or different languages. A serial may suddenly be issued with monographic or serial supplements, or start out as a periodical and then turn into a monographic series, or vice versa.

Besides officially changing title and being published with varying alternative, and sometimes distinctive, titles, serials commonly change place of publication, publisher, frequency, regularity of publication and numbering. A serial may begin by being part of one or more series and then switch the series in which it's issued. Sometimes numbers are mistakenly repeated and issues are misnumbered. Publishers exhibit a never-ending variety of creative numbering. In aptly expressing the sentiment of long-time serials cat-alogers who are never able to say we've seen it all, Reynolds provides us with the follow-ing examples: "I remember a fishery publication that stated its frequency in terms of when the salmon were spawning and a local softball newsletter that expressed its frequency in terms of the season's schedule."[8]

The first law of serials cataloging (just invented by the author) states that, "Any serial that changes once is more likely to change again, with a good chance of it changing back to a previous title." In many larger libraries, serial bibliographic records are often a con-glomeration of the original bibliographic record combined with updates completed by different catalogers. Documenting who did what is helpful when questions arise later — as they often do. Our serials catalogers add a 947 field with codes that document significant updates to serial bibliographic records. We also use these codes to generate cataloging sta-tistics.

An additional serials cataloging aid is a serials sampler, a local annotated compila-tion of sample serial records, which illustrate the library's major local serials cataloging practices and contains practical solutions to tricky problems. A serials sampler can be help-ful in training new serials catalogers and can jog the collective memory when challeng-ing situations arise. It helps avoid the frustration of, "We know we had a problem like that a few years ago, but we can't remember the title of the serial, or exactly how we han-dled it."

Online Serials

The world of the serials cataloger changed dramatically when online serials began to proliferate. In 2005, in its second major study of the online publishing policies and prac-tices of 400 international journal publishers, the Association of Learned and Professional Society Publishers found that:

- 90 percent of journals are now online, compared with 75 percent in 2003.
- Back issues were available online from 91 percent of the publishers, with many hav-ing digitized back to the first issues.[9]

In the past decade, many libraries began canceling print journals in favor of online versions. The e-journal that was once the exception is now not only mainstream for many academic libraries but also has generated many new cataloging practices and workflows. When a publication is issued online, there is no longer an efficient way, using the usual channels, for the cataloger to become aware of changes that need documentation in the catalog record. Without physical issues referred to them — usually by check-in or public services staff or monographic catalogers — serials catalogers suffer the uneasiness of knowing that their catalog records for online serials won't be as current or accurate as they should be when changes to these serials occur. In addition to up-to-date OPAC bibliographic information, the maintenance of accurate serials holdings statements of online availability becomes difficult, if not impossible, and many libraries initially did not even try to provide these.

The emergence of providers of outsourced e-journal records with up-to-date online holdings, such as Serials Solutions, created another revolution in serials cataloging. The cataloging of e-serials is well suited to outsourcing, since no physical issues are involved. The provision of a continual supply of new and updated outsourced e-journal records, however, doesn't mean there's nothing for the library to do locally. With tens of thousands of outsourced records, it is unrealistic to expect 100 percent perfection or 100 percent satisfaction of local needs. Significant changes in e-journals may not be described in existing outsourced records. Important access points may be missing. When mistakes are discovered or updates are needed, local updating of the record may be only temporary since an updated provider record will usually overlay your local record.

With Serials Solutions, libraries have a variety of customization options, such as a 130 uniform title with "(Online)" and the addition of a 655 genre field heading for ELECTRONIC JOURNALS. At CU, we also have been able to exert some degree of local control by protecting certain fields through our ILS, so they will not be overlaid when updates are loaded. We currently protect the 246 (variant title), 590 (local note), 730 (added title), and 947 (local cataloger update) fields. We will probably also protect the 776 linking fields we add or update locally for other formats, so that hotlinks will display in the catalog when we have the same serial in another format. When libraries have the same serial in different formats on separate records, it is important for the existence of all formats to be easily recognizable. This is especially important when different formats have different titles and may not be retrieved in the same search.

The receipt of vendor-supplied e-journal records has caused numerous libraries to move from a one-record approach for all formats — favored by many public services staff as well as many user-centered catalogers — to a separate-record policy for the same serial issued in print and online. This can be expeditious for the loading of e-journal records, but a disadvantage for identification and retrieval of the same serial in different formats. With a separate record policy when e-serials are cataloged locally, catalogers at least have the ability to assure consistency of relevant access points in records — e.g., an OPAC search of a 246 added title will retrieve records for all formats. When many thousands of records are batch-loaded, it is not practical to scrutinize each new or changed outsourced record to assure consistency of relevant access points.

Unfortunately, systematic scrutiny of all outsourced records in order to catch errors or provide locally customized information generally isn't feasible when thousands of records are batch-loaded, much to the frustration of user-centered serials catalogers, who generally only become aware of obvious errors or needed updates when they are reported by public services staff. This loss of local control is a price many libraries are willing to pay for the receipt of many more e-journal records — especially for serial aggregator titles — than the libraries could catalog in-house.

Creativity in Serials Cataloging: Heresy or Necessity?

The word "creativity" generally has positive connotations when used in most contexts. In our profession, when someone says, "Look at that creative cataloging," it generally isn't a compliment. Just the notion of creative cataloging often raises a red flag with an image of a novice, an incompetent, a defiant renegade, or a radical kook. Sometimes these interpretations might be correct, but sometimes creativity is a necessity. It is essential that serials cataloging creativity serve the specific purpose of improving retrievability and understanding of serial records and faster access to the serials themselves. This creativity is not the spur of the moment variety in which a cataloger decides to add her own personal flair to an original OCLC or other shared database catalog record for the primary purpose of expressing individuality or artistry. It is also not creativity that results from ignorance of the rules and national standards. These latter two kinds of "creativity" are more apt to lead to confusion or misunderstanding.

Before making a decision to implement an innovative practice or go counter to established rules, the cataloger must first not only know the rules and standards that govern daily work, but also fully understand the principles behind the rules. Then, common sense and his own ingenuity can guide the cataloger when confronted with new and tricky situations. Shared bibliographic databases require catalogers to uphold agreed-upon standards when entering original records. There should be a lot more flexibility in one's own local catalog, as long as the catalogers have carefully developed guidelines for any necessary local adaptations. It is now commonplace for thoughtful catalogers to input original records according to all required OCLC or any other shared database standards, and then adjust the records as needed in their local catalogs. It is important to distinguish between the positive benefits of creative solutions to problems in one's local catalog rather than problem-causing creativity in a cooperative national or consortial database in violation of agreed-upon standards.

Conflicts between satisfying local needs and adhering to existing accepted cataloging rules and standards has long been a troubling dilemma for many thoughtful common-sense-oriented catalogers. When conflicts occur, the cataloger must determine if not complying with certain rules or normal practices might cause immediate problems (by causing inconsistency in consortial catalogs, for example) or future problems, such as those faced when moving to a new ILS. For example, don't leave out indicators or code them incorrectly because it doesn't make any difference in your current local system. Your next system may be far more sophisticated, and information left out or miscoded is often more difficult to correct or add than if it were done right the first time.

Dire predictions of disaster have been forecasted by my more legalistic colleagues if locally customized practices are adopted rather than following all national standards for the local OPAC. The consistency argument — that users come to expect things a certain way and will be confused if you suddenly do it another way — is valid in some circumstances, but not in others. Our catalogs are made up of records that reflect a variety of cataloging rules, from pre–AACR to AACR2 (2002). In a few years, there will be records cataloged according to RDA standards. As long as essential, accurate, and current information is included in the record, and the record is easily retrieved and understood, few users know or care which rules or standards are represented in our OPACs.

Serials Cataloging Questionable Rules and Practices: Damage Control

Edmund Burke's maxim "Those who don't know history are destined to repeat it" can serve as a warning to those who think national cataloging codes and standards couldn't possibly contain user-unfriendly rules. Knowledge of the history of many user-unfriendly cataloging rules and practices helps remind us that cataloging rules are made by human beings who are not prescient or perfect. Some rules have unintended consequences that only become apparent later, as catalogers struggle to apply these rules to complex situations that could not be foreseen by the rule-makers. Many of the most egregious rules have been changed, but it often takes a long time for this to happen. User-centered serials catalogers try to find alternative treatments when rules and practices inhibit access and understanding.

Successive Entry Cataloging

Successive entry cataloging is the epitome of a current, and often user-unfriendly, serials cataloging practice. It requires the creation of a new serials bibliographic record for each rule-defined main entry author or title change. A method developed forty years ago to handle title changes more efficiently in a card catalog environment is today colossally inefficient for staff acquiring, checking in, and cataloging serials. It is confusing and frustrating to users who have to select the right record, often amidst a list of similar titles. With the continuing proliferation of e-serials, wherein many publishers and platforms list all volumes on one web page, the presence of separate bibliographic records for these serials serves no purpose.

Successive entry cataloging was first introduced with AACR1 in 1967, and adopted by LC in 1971. Successive entry cataloging requires that when the title of a serial changes, the old record is ceased, and a new record is created for the new title, linked by a "Continues" note on the new record and a "Continued by" note on the old record. If a serial is entered under corporate body and the corporate body changes, successive entry cataloging requires the creation of a new record under the new corporate body.

When successive entry cataloging was first adopted, some catalogers overenthusiastically created successive records in OCLC for what now would be considered minor changes not requiring new successive records, e.g., a change in a title from "and" to "&." Successive records were also created for serials that had titles that flip-flopped back and forth, sometimes with a record covering only a few issues of a journal. After rationality eventually reasserted itself, LCRIs for fluctuating titles and minor title variations were developed to avoid the creation of new records for these situations. Serials catalogers who didn't succumb to these overzealous successive records were ahead of the game when these excessive successive records were consolidated in OCLC. A particularly loathsome example of excessive successive that I remember well from around 30 years ago was a daily German newspaper that had a variant title the first day it was published. All the daily issues were reprinted and bound together in one volume, but a cataloger dutifully created two OCLC successive records for this.

A cure for the often confusing and time-consuming proliferation of successive records is the re-adoption of latest entry cataloging, allowing serials to be recataloged under the latest title or author main entry. In an online environment, an existing OPAC record often can be easily and quickly updated to incorporate the latest title change, whether major or minor. Users have an easier time finding the right record since fewer records are needed to represent one serial. Unfortunately, local implementation of nonstandard latest entry cataloging is generally no longer practical due to the importance of consistency in consortial catalogs and the need to comply with OCLC guidelines.

As long as successive entry cataloging is still the national standard, serials catalogers can halt the damage by:

• Never rushing to create a new successive record if a questionable title change may turn out to be a "fluctuating" title or a minor title variation that fits into the minor title change guidelines adopted with AACR2 2002 (21.2C2). Instead, use a 246 field for the new variant title. If it is unclear whether a non-online title change is a stable change, you can add a 246 field for the title in question and put a note in the check-in record to show the next issue to you.
• Displaying the 780 (Continues) and 785 (Continued by) linking fields near the top of the OPAC record, preferably right below the 245 title. These linking fields are likely to be overlooked if they display at the bottom of the OPAC record.
• Hotlinking the 780 and 785 linking fields in the OPAC.

The Ruth Lilly Special Collections and Archives at University Library at Indiana University–Purdue University Indianapolis developed an innovative solution to avoid producing many successive records for a large collection of foundation annual reports. They decided to catalog the annual reports of each foundation as an archival collection. Cataloging the reports as serials would have required them to create numerous successive records for the varying titles and foundation names, which would cause both maintenance and access problems. Instead, each foundation's reports were cataloged on one record under the foundation's most recent name with a 245 title of [Annual reports]. They then put the inclusive dates of the collection in 245 $f. Alternative titles were included in 246 fields and foundation name changes in 710 fields.[10]

Description Based on the Earliest Available Issue in the 260 Field

AACR2 requires the 260 "publication, distribution, etc." field to contain the publishing information of the first or earliest available issue. Requiring earliest information in the 260 field, rather than current information, flies in the face of common sense; users are more often looking for recent, rather than older, issues, and staff ordering and checking in serials need to select the correct record. According to existing rules, current significant publishing information is placed in a note, which may appear near the bottom of the OPAC record, where it is more likely to be unnoticed. The implementation of a proposed rule to allow multiple 260 fields would have helped solve the identification problem, but so far this hasn't happened.

For 260 damage control, the following options might be considered:

- Change the place of publication and publisher in the 260 field to the latest place and publisher when first cataloging a serial and update this information when significant changes occur. Put earlier significant publishing information in a 550 (non-commercial publisher) or 500 (commercial publisher) note.
- Consider the former practice of adding [etc.] after place and publisher. This at least alerts users to the fact that changes have occurred, and they might look in the record for further information. For example:

    San Francisco [etc]: Beckham [etc.] 1910–

362 Field: Dates of Publication and/or Sequential Designation

There are two major problems with the 362 "Dates of Publication and/or Sequential Designation" field:

- The presence of the 362 dates of publication in a record can cause confusion for patrons, who often think this information reflects the library's holdings.
- The 362 information is placed in separate fields depending on whether the first or last issue is in hand. This creates a confusing display when a 362 0_ formatted ending date (last issue not in hand) displays before a 362 1_ unformatted beginning date (first issue is in hand). This distinction reflects cataloging rule fussiness that is of no benefit to users. An example:

    -[v. 149] (June 1932)
    Began with: Vol. 1 in Nov. 1857

For 362 damage control:

- Display the 362 field below the library's holdings.
- Provide a display label for the 362 that might be called "Publication history" rather than "Publication dates."
- Use only one 362 unformatted note, such as:

    Began with Vol. 1 in Nov. 1857 and ceased with v. 149 in June 1932.

Use and Placement of Notes

Serials catalogers sometimes add notes to the bibliographic record without considering how the whole record will read to users. Notes are sometimes added out of logical order; a note that needs to come first to explain another note may display after the other note, or both notes may be widely separated. Catalogers sometimes use library jargon that probably wouldn't be understood by the uninitiated because this jargon has become second nature to catalogers. Some libraries leave notes in records describing LC holdings, supplements, or related publications the library doesn't own. A "Description based on:" note for an issue the library doesn't own can also mislead local users.

For 5XX damage control:

- Consider the serial bibliographic record as an integral whole rather than a collection of separate fields.
- View the OPAC record as if you were an inexperienced OPAC user or library staff member trying to assist users.
- Use commonly understood language rather than library jargon.
- Don't clutter up the OPAC record with unnecessary detail that will obscure important information.
- Combine related information into one 500 note rather than splitting it out into separate fields (e.g., 500 and 515) when this makes common sense.
- Delete information from OCLC records not relevant for your OPAC users, e.g., "Description based on" notes for issues you don't own.

130 (Uniform Titles)

LCRI 25.5B requires that a uniform title be assigned to a serial when you catalog a serial with a title proper that conflicts with another serial's title. User identification of the right record can be time-consuming when many successive records with the same title, but different qualifiers, exist for the same serial. Places of publication and date qualifiers in uniform titles can be misleading, since the earliest place of publication and/or only beginning date (or earliest available date) of publication is included. After viewing a browse display that contains a uniform title with a different place or year than that of desired volumes, users may think they haven't found the right record.

For 130 damage control:

- Be conservative in creating or using successive records that require similar uniform titles distinguished only by dates.
- Delete misleading uniform titles, especially when your library doesn't own other serials with the same title
- Consider adding a dash to the 130 date qualifier for open serials and adding full publication dates to the qualifier for ceased serials. For example:
    American photography (New York, N.Y.: 1985–)
    Advances in applied psychology (1993–2001) [fabricated example]
- Add 730 fields with uniform titles with later places of publication.

Serials That Split into Parts, Have Cumulations, Cumulative Indexes or Supplements

Separate records can often be found in OCLC for serials that split into parts, have cumulations, cumulative indexes, or supplements. Separate records don't always make sense for libraries that want to bind or shelve the volumes together. Finding the right OPAC record can become unnecessarily complicated when separate records exist for these situations, especially when all related volumes have the same main title.

For damage control to avoid a plethora of unnecessary records for split serials, cumulations and cumulative indexes, consider just updating the existing serial record. For a serial that splits into separate sections, add a note and 246 fields for the parts and continue to check in the parts on the record for the original serial. An example:

245 00 European journal of pharmacology
246 30 European journal of pharmacology. $p Environmental toxicology and pharmacology
246 30 European journal of pharmacology. $p Molecular pharmacology section
500   Beginning in 1989, some vols. are devoted to a specialized subject area. Vol. 172
           (1989)—includes Molecular pharmacology section; vol. 228 (1992)—includes Environmental toxicology and pharmacology section.

CONSER Standard Record

The newly adopted CONSER standard record for serials is a promising user-focused development. It will be implemented by CONSER participants once approved by the Joint Steering Committee for Revision of *Anglo-American Cataloguing Rules*. Finally, after decades of standards requiring time-consuming transcription of details in conformity to some rules that make no common sense, this new standard contains elements "that were identified as having the highest value in supporting users' efforts to find, identify, select and obtain the resources they need, as well as navigate the relationships among titles."[11] Although this standard is mandatory only for CONSER participants, many libraries follow CONSER standards, so that we may expect that many OCLC records contributed beginning in mid– to late–2007 will reflect these guidelines.

Some of the time-saving user- and cataloger-friendly recommendations are:

130   No longer needed for translations and language editions or to resolve conflicts except for monographic series and generic titles entered under title.
245 $b Other title information will generally not require transcription unless it is needed for clarification. Parallel titles and acronyms will be recorded only in the 246 field.
245 $c A statement of responsibility is not required if an authority record exists in the national authority file.
260 $a Only the first named place of publication is required. For online resources, the place of publication is required only when readily available.
260 $c Not required.
321   Former frequencies are not required. A "Frequency varies" note can be used to replace existing field 321 information when the 310 current frequency field needs to be updated. This new rule frees the cataloger from having to search through issues to record changing frequencies—a tedious task for large retrospective sets.
362   1. Only first indicator 1 for unformatted serials will be used. This will correct some past illogical displays where a 362 0 for the closing date precedes a 362 1 for the beginning date. 2. Abbreviations aren't required; what appears on the issue can be transcribed.
538   World Wide Web note isn't required for remote access electronic resources.
776   Use 776 $i rather than a 530 note.

The User-Centered Serials Cataloger

A user-centered serials cataloger possesses a philosophy, knowledge, and characteristics that are oriented towards satisfying local user needs in identifying and obtaining desired serial resources. Possession or development of the following characteristics assists in the achievement of this goal:

- Knowledgeable about applicable cataloging rules, standards, policies, practices and procedures.
- Knowledgeable about the MARC format and other metadata schemes as they become more prevalent.
- Knowledgeable about the local system, including: which fields and subfields are indexed; the rules for public display of different fields; which fields are hotlinked; what changes the library can make locally; and what must be done by the ILS vendor.
- Knowledgeable about how your catalog record integrates into your consortial catalog. Is there a master record? How are other libraries' holdings attached? If you make changes in your record, what impact does it have on the consortial catalog?
- Knowledgeable about the unpredictable nature of serials.
- Knowledgeable about how users search and what information is important and helpful to them. The needs of the inexperienced are just as important as the needs of the most sophisticated. This knowledge can be gained by:
  — Searching for serial records in the OPAC as a patron might search and trying to read serial records as a patron might.
  — Working at reference and information desks.
  — Soliciting feedback from public services colleagues.
  — Reading literature on users' needs.
  — Studying user transaction logs.[12]
  — Library needs assessments.
- Maintaining good communication with public services colleagues. This can be accomplished by:
  — Being responsive to public services requests and concerns. Saying "No, we can't do that. It's against the rules" should not be an automatic response. When a specific request has to be denied due to undesirable consequences unknown to the requester, it is often possible to find an alternative solution. You may not be able to do what the requester asks, but you can usually do something to alleviate a problem.
  — Conducting local library presentations on accessing and understanding serial records in the OPAC.
  — Actively soliciting feedback from public services colleagues.
  — Working together on committees where both public services and technical services viewpoints are represented.
- Being flexible. When circumstances change, you can quickly adapt to different responsibilities and changing rules.
- Thinking creatively to find innovative solutions to difficult problems.

- When encountering a problem, determining if this is an isolated incident or indicative of a larger problem that needs investigation.
- Adopting practical workflows and procedures that are cost-effective; they have value proportional to the time and money involved.
- Developing "defensive cataloging" strategies — comparable to defensive driving strategies. Anticipating potential problems and implementing solutions to prevent them. The more experience one has working with serials, the easier it is to be proactive.
- Being a holistic cataloger. Seeing the purpose of your work as furthering your library's mission. Staying current on the evolving roles of libraries.
- Understanding the library workflow from acquisitions to access.
- Being curious. Wanting to learn about new library and technology developments.
- Being a questioner. Wanting to know why things are done the way they are, and evaluating if there is still a valid reason to continue to do them this way.
- Being analytical. Carefully considering all factors to determine the best approach or solution.
- Using intuition as a viable guide in decision-making.
- Expressing your unorthodox views in a non-combative way.

Conclusion

Imagine the audience reaction at a major cataloging presentation if a well respected head of a cataloging department stated that there are "too many rule followers, not enough problem solvers" — as Rick Anderson said in a 2006 videoconference.[13] The gasps of horror and disbelief that would erupt would most likely vastly outnumber the cheers of "Right on!" Anderson was referring to the library profession in general, but this criticism is certainly applicable to catalogers — as heretical as it is for a rule-driven profession. The user-centered serials cataloger's dream is to work in a library where risk-taking and innovation in the cataloging department are not just lip service, where responsiveness to patrons' needs is the guiding force initiating significant changes from traditional ways of operating. In the ideal world, the user-centered serials cataloger would be the norm rather than being considered a radical. The term "user-centered" should be redundant when prefacing "cataloging."

Serials cataloging standards appear finally to be moving in the right direction to make catalog records fit real-world developments and needs. RDA and the CONSER standard record, although both are still in draft form at the time of this writing, look promising in overcoming some of the user-unfriendly problems with past cataloging rules. As we have learned from the past, however, bad cataloging rules take a long time to change. We don't always have appropriate rules when they are needed. No set of rules can anticipate every possible situation. The more time we spend agonizing over the perfect application of arbitrary and nonsensical conventions, the less time we have to make resources available to users who want them.

Cataloging is a cooperative profession where input on changing standards is often solicited, but the best ideas don't always win. User-centered serials catalogers need to remain vigilant and exercise their judgment when they encounter situations that require alternative solutions. It's important for serials catalogers to become involved in local OPAC development, since all their beautifully crafted and meticulously updated MARC serial records will be unviewed if people don't want to bother with library catalogs, or if it is too difficult to find desired resources through the OPAC. FRBRized catalogs with Amazon-like content, such as reviews and scanned images and text, will become the OPACs of tomorrow. Colorful library homepages with RSS feeds and library blogs are already becoming more common. The future of catalogers will not be questioned by library administrations when catalogers are providing an innovative service that reflects their knowledge, experience and user-oriented motivation.

References

1. Cathy De Rosa, Lorcan Dempsey, and Alane Wilson. *The 2003 OCLC Environmental Scan: Pattern Recognition: A Report to the OCLC Membership.* Dublin, OH: OCLC, 2004. Available: <http://www.oclc.org/reports/escan/introduction/default.htm>.
2. *Perceptions of Libraries and Information Resources: A Report to the OCLC Membership.* Dublin, OH: OCLC, 2005. Available: <http://www.oclc.org/reports/2005perceptions.htm>.
3. The University of California Libraries, Bibliographic Services Task Force. *Rethinking How We Provide Bibliographic Services for the University of California: Final Report, December 2005.* Available: <http://libraries.universityofcalifornia.edu/sopag/BSTF/Final.pdf>.
4. Karen Calhoun, *The Changing Nature of the Catalog and Its Integration with Other Discovery Tools.* Ithaca, N.Y.: K. Calhoun, 2006. Available at: <http://www.loc.gov/catdir/calhoun-report-final.pdf>.
5. Andrew D. Osborn, "The Crisis in Cataloging." *The Library Quarterly* 11, no. 4 (October 1941): 395.
6. Osborn, "The Crisis in Cataloging" 397–98.
7. Osborn, "The Crisis in Cataloging" 401.
8. Regina Romano Reynolds, "Serial Conversations: An Interview with Regina Romano Reynolds." *Serials Review* 32, no.2 (2006): 123.
9. John Cox, and Laura Cox. Scholarly Publishing Practice: Academic Journal Publishers' Policies and Practices in Online Publishing. Second Survey, 2005. Available: <http://www.alpsp.org/publications/pub13.htm>.
10. Joseph C. Harmon and Brenda L. Burk. "Better Service through Flexible Rules: Cataloging a Collection of Annual Reports in a Most Un-CONSER-Like Manner." *Cataloging & Classification Quarterly* 31, no. 1 (2000): 43–50.
11. CONSER Standard Record, 12/22/06. Available: <http://www.loc.gov/catdir/cpso/conser.html>. ("The final version of the CONSER documentation and the LCRIs will be available at this location until the 2007 Update 2 of Cataloger's Desktop.")
12. For a discussion of this topic, see: Patricia M. Wallace, "Periodical Title Searching in Online Catalogs." *Serials Review* 23, no. 3 (Fall 1997).
13. Rick Anderson, "Always a River, Sometimes a Library." *Soaring to Excellence.* Teleconference broadcast February 3, 2006. Program overview available at: <http://www.dupagepress.com/COD/index.php?id=986>.

"Why Isn't My Book on the Shelf?" and Other Mysteries of the Library

Robin Fay

While this may not be the most radical of cataloging ideas, it is a good example of how easy it is to take current technologies and implement small changes to provide more interaction with users.

As a result of the University of Georgia Libraries' MARC record data having been through four conversions (including most recently to Unicode), discrepancies have occurred through both the actual data migrations, as well as potential for human error. Although the libraries have a Database Maintenance Section dedicated to investigating potential problems in the catalog, some discrepancies cannot be easily identified through access reports, and are most likely found through human intervention.

The University of Georgia Cataloging Department's Database Maintenance Section had a "report an error" HTML form on its website for several years to try to capture user submitted errors and discrepancies in the libraries' Voyager catalog (GIL). In order to report an error or discrepancy, the user needed to open a separate browser window, open the Database Maintenance website, find the "report an error" link, and then fill out the information. While it was a good idea, unsurprisingly it was not highly used, even by library staff. In 2004, after seeing a similar reporting structure embedded into the Library of Congress catalog, a light bulb went on. Why couldn't that existing HTML form be hooked into the libraries' catalog?

Utilizing JavaScript to grab bibliographic information, the HTML form was revamped slightly and linked into the libraries' OPAC. When users find a record with discrepancies, lacking data, or any number of issues, they click on a link at the bottom of the screen to report the error. The link opens a new popup window, with bibliographic information already in place. The user fills in her name, email address, a brief statement about the suspected problem, and chooses whether she would like to be contacted for follow-up. Behind the scenes, the bibliographic record ID is sent along with this information to the Database Maintenance staff.

Giving users of the libraries' catalog an opportunity to report discrepancies as they stumble across them not only facilitates a more streamlined reporting mechanism but gives the user a direct line of contact to the "behind the scenes" cataloging staff, thus providing an unique opportunity for customer service. This new path to communicate directly with staff has provided both patrons and library staff a means to quickly identify and route potential problems or issues. Public services staff frequently use the link when they are at the reference desk, as well as in their own offices. Collection development staff use it to alert cataloging staff to erroneous information or discrepancies in the catalog (such as older material for which there is a newer record with a more appropriate call number). Library patrons use the form for a variety of reasons — in some cases, as a desperate measure to find anyone to help them!

Staff members always respond quickly to these emails and follow up as appropriate. This service is often used as opportunity for library education, informing users of various related policies and services.

Reported errors and cataloging questions average 25 emails per month through this venue. On the surface this seems like a very small number, but considering the minimal amount of initial and follow-up work, the rewards greatly outweigh that effort. Over the course of a year, approximately 250 questions are sent directly to the Cataloging Department for investigation through this medium.

Selected real reported errors:

- No error. I just want to know what "discharged" means. Is the book on the shelf or not? — library user (student)
- There is a typo in one of the subject heading dates — should not be 1957. — library user (student)
- Book not on shelf where it ought to be — library user (student)
- Do we really have 2 copies of this and is one still in the In Process collection [a temporary, and publicly accessible, location for monographs that haven't yet been fully cataloged]? Or do we really only have 1 copy and the In Process one should be merged? Or do we have 2 copies and the In Process once should be made copy 2? — library staff
- This record shows that it is part of a series of records from the "Mineralized Society of America." That's Mineralogical Society of America! — library user (faculty)
- Both 600 tags in the MARC bib are not displaying as proper subjects in Full Display, and I had trouble searching for them as proper authorities. Perhaps they could be updated? Thanks. — library user (student)
- My date of birth is NOT 1940... — library user (author)

This mechanism provides a way for library users to provide input into the library catalog and to help fix or resolve issues and questions when they arise. Additionally, users are given a choice of receiving a response from a member of the Database Maintenance Section. Database maintenance staff are given the opportunity to interact directly with library users, albeit virtually. This service extends beyond database maintenance staff to other cataloging, collection development, and access services staff members, when reported errors outside of the scope of the section are routed elsewhere.

While the "report an error" form is an obvious example of a service which can be easily incorporated into most ILS, it does help facilitate a stronger and more public relationship between the Cataloging Department and the library users. In some ways, that concept is the beauty of this very simple form. That's what makes it a little part of the concept of radical cataloging: taking what we are already doing, examining it to see how we can improve it and create a more interactive experience for our users, given the limited resources that we all have.

Report Type			Affiliation		
GIL errors	*Student*	*Faculty/Staff*	*Library*	*Other/Visitor*	
Copy/volume/location	1		23		
Item Status (missing, etc.)			17		
Title (incorrect, filing indicator/indexing etc.)	3	2	40		
Holdings (incomplete, etc)	3	1	17		
Call number (recataloged/ classification, duplicate, etc.)	2	1	23	1	
Authority/headings	3	1	25	3	
Other (bib: content notes, questions about cataloging, etc.)	2	3	41	1	
Total GIL errors	**14**	**8**	**186**	**5**	**213**
Routed to other depts.	*Student*	*Faculty/Staff*	*Library*	*Other/Visitor*	
E-reserves	5				
Patron record questions	1	2			
Request assistance	2	3		1	
System problems	17	1		1	
Other		1			
Total routed reports	**25**	**7**	**0**	**2**	**34**
Total errors reported via form					**247**

Table 1: GIL Report and Error Form Statistics 2006

AACR 2 — Bendable but Not Flexible: Cataloging Zines at Barnard College

Jenna Freedman

Disclaimer

First, I feel that I need to acknowledge that I am not a cataloger. I am a radical, though, if that helps, and I also care a lot about the catalog. (Don't all reference librarians say that?) I will attempt in this article to illuminate the zine cataloging practice at Barnard College, with technical detail when necessary, and I will stand by everything I have written. However, you must know that my *perspective* is that of a reference librarian, and so I may come at things from a different angle than catalogers may expect or want. Sorry about that!

Definition

The other thing I that need to do, before I really get started on how we catalog zines at Barnard, is to explain what a zine is. You will want to know that "zine," which rhymes with "spleen," not "spine," is short for "magazine" or "fanzine." Zines are self-publications that generally have small, self-distributed print runs, are free of paid advertisements, are motivated by a desire to contribute their knowledge or experience to their community (anarchists, art girls, isolated teenagers, mamas, punks, wrestling fans, etc.), and do not have a masthead.

Not every zine fits every criterion I have listed above, because that is how zines are. They defy even the rules that define them. For example, *Beer Frame*[1] had paid ads and *Bamboo Girl*[2] a shiny cover. Both were printed by someone other than the publisher, but what both retained — unlike *Bust*,[3] which made the transition from zine to magazine — was the control of the original writer. Paul Lukas may have printed ads in *Beer Frame* and Sabrina Margarita Sandata may have had a lot of contributors to *Bamboo Girl*, but both zines remained completely controlled by their creators. This is not to say that *Bust*, a third wave feminism magazine that began as a zine, sold out or anything — not at all — but having a staff, national ads, an ISSN, a glossy cover, and over 90,000 readers[4] has got to impact a publication's ability to stay true to the vision of its tiny circulation/pseudony-mously edited beginning.

If you still do not quite get it, here is a rundown of one zine I pulled off the shelf at random: *Rainbow Flavoured Angst*, #1. It is a 20-page 4.25" × 5.5" zine by Hanh Nguyen. It includes a Magic Markered cover cartoon about racism, a two-page introduction, an essay on identity, a poem and essays about the war in Vietnam, a poem about a death penalty victim, an article about a husband getting advice from the author's aunt, a how-to article on writing a "letter to authority," a piece about a classmate's ignorance, guest pieces on citizenship and a poem, a cartoon about American hypocrisy, a tribute to Matthew Shepard, some political quotes, and what is known in the trade as an "outro"(the opposite of an intro...duction). You also get the author's first name (her last name is included in an essay, so your discovery of her first name is incidental), email and postal addresses, the cost of the zine ($1 or two stamps or a zine trade). There is neither a date nor subscription information. The content is variably handwritten and word-processed. There are drawings, photos, and clip art throughout. The back has a picture of the Simpsons, a quote from the Boondocks, and what look like two photocopied stickers.

Introduction

Perhaps because of their name connection with magazines, many librarians' first impulse is to deal with zines as serials. That designation is one of the two biggest decisions librarians dealing with zines must make — whether zines are to be regarded strictly as serials or not. The other tough call is library catalog vs. stand-alone database. At Barnard, in both instances we use a combination of the two. I'll explain our thinking and processes on these issues, and also attempt a summary of our cataloging practices.

Serial or Monograph

The truth is that some zines are serials and some are monographs, or "one-offs," as they are called in zine publishing. Based on their presentation, we identify as monographs zines that are not numbered and zines that although they may be numbered have a distinct title (e.g., *I Dreamed I Was Assertive*, "The I.V.F. Issue"). Issues of serials that have distinctive titles can be analyzed separately — that is, each issue can be cataloged as a monograph, with the serial title entered as a series statement. We prefer to catalog zines as monographs when we can, so that they can be fully described and so that original records are uploaded into OCLC's holdings, which Barnard serials records currently do not, due to a quirk caused by our shared catalog but affiliate status with Columbia University. Numbered zines without discrete titles are serials. The title fields are coded:

```
245 14 $a The I.V.F. issue
440 _0 $a I dreamed I was assertive ; $v no. 8
```

Some of the challenges with the serials are that they are generally not published very regularly, their authors move around a lot, and zines are not always consistently named and numbered. We just deal with those issues as best we can. Zine catalogers attempting to adhere to the AACR must be open minded and a little creative.

ILS or Stand-Alone

Although it required sacrificing some control over what we can describe and how, we chose to catalog the zines in our Voyager/Endeavor catalog, CLIO. We wanted the zines to be represented not only in our catalog but also in WorldCat. For us the priority was achieving visibility for the materials, and the legitimacy their presence in WorldCat would bestow upon them. The primary access points we provide are author, title, subject headings when possible (more about that later), and a keyword-rich abstract about the zine if it is a monograph, and about the author and series if it is a serial.

What we lost by choosing standardization was the ability to create and utilize our own genre terms and keywords, upload scanned zine covers, provide summaries for each issue of a serial zine, etc. Furthermore, with a stand-alone catalog, staff members in addition to our one MLS cataloger could have contributed more, relieving him of some of the burden. It is likely that some of the above sacrifices are not totally AACR's fault; rather, we cannot catalog as fully as is truly possible, due to the limited time of our cataloging department and the limited cataloging knowledge and skills of our zine librarian.

The Record

Table 1. A sample catalog record of a zine monograph

100	Author	Lee, Charisma.
245	Title	Dear Franka Potente I had/have a crush on you because you're a good actress.
300	Physical Description	50 p. : ill. ; 14 cm.
440	Series	Brewster ; no. 7
260	Publisher/ Date	Denver, CO : C. Lee, [2004?]
655	Other Subject Terms	Zines.
500	Notes	A personal zine. Title from cover.
520	Summary	Charisma is a high school dropout, LiveJournal user, and Filipina-American punk. Her type- and handwritten personal zine discusses racism in society and in punk rock, as well as Filipino history and identity, zines, and crushes. She also discusses the use of antidepressants.
	Material Type	Book
852 $b	Location	Barnard Rare Books (Non-Circulating)
852 $h	Call Number	Zines L347b no. 7
	Status	No information available

The summary is provided by a work-study student. We have decided to emphasize the presence of important keywords over the quality of the writing. The current student,

Barnard junior Marissa Edelman, writes wonderful abstracts, and then I mess them up by shoehorning in phrases like "LiveJournal user," and awkward references to other zinesters' sexual preferences or religions in anticipation that future researchers will want to compare personal zines to entries in blogs like LiveJournal or have a specific research interest in bisexual zines. The abstracts are neutral, not zine reviews. They also provide information about the zine's physical characteristics (e.g. "typewritten with a screen printed cover"). When describing a serial, rather than a monograph, the student is directed to focus on the writer, rather than the zine itself, as the former is theoretically less likely to change than the latter. That is, it is more likely that Celia Perez, author of *I Dreamed I Was Assertive*, will remain Latina, married, and a librarian than it is that she'll write about riding the bus in Tampa (she lives in Chicago now) or compare biscuit and egg breakfasts in every issue. While only "Latina" is permanent, as opposed to "married" and "librarian," given how long zine careers typically last, it is not so dangerous to include these descriptors. Things that are regular features, like book recommendations, do get mentioned in the abstract.

We assign one or more genre types in the notes field (500). Genres include among a few others:

- Compilation zine: zines edited by one or more people, with multiple contributors, typically on a common theme, (e.g. Issue 6 of Emily Pohl-Weary's *Kiss Machine*, "Girls & Guns," where female writers were encouraged to contribute stories about their experiences with weapons).
- DIY zine: DIY stands for Do It Yourself. These are how-to guides. One of the best known of these is *Stolen Sharpie Revolution*, by Alex Wrekk, which teaches the reader how to make and distribute a zine — and also which libraries have them.
- Fanzine: a zine devoted to one topic. When the term was first coined, the writers were science fiction fans, and later the term was adopted for punk rock aficionados who wrote about their favorite bands. Now a fanzine can be about anything, including *Buffy the Vampire Slayer*, the television series (*All Slay*).
- Literary zine: related to chapbooks, these zines can contain stories or poems. They generally differ from chapbooks because of the motivation of the author. Zine authors are not necessarily trying to get published "for real." Some of them take their writing very seriously, but they are less likely than chapbook authors to be in MFA programs or doing a lot of poetry readings.
- Mamazine: zines about parenting, by parents of any gender. Popular topics include home schooling, retaining one's punk identity, activism, and details about the lives of the contributing mamas.
- Personal zine: these can contain journal entries, poems, lists (top ten, to do, peeves), essays, soundtracks, book reviews, drawings, cartoons, and more, all to do with the author's life. An example of a personal zine (also known as a perzine) is the poignantly titled *Proof I Exist* by Billy.
- Political zine: zines often made by activists on themes of importance to them, including feminism, media, prisoners' rights, sexual assault, sizeism, and war.
- Split zine: this is not a thematic genre. Instead it indicates that two (occasionally

three) people published a zine together. Typically, though, the zine was not exactly created simultaneously in one location, and it is usually presented as two separate zines that share center pages, with one zine seeming to be upside down and backwards compared to the other, and vice versa, similar in format to some bilingual newspapers or magazines.

There are two zine locations: Barnard and Barnard Rare Books. Neither circulates at the moment (while we work out the logistics), but the former is open stacks. We attempt to collect two copies of each zine, the first for the archive ("rare books") and the second for the stacks. Zines in both locations are shelved in call number order.

Michael Elmore, Head of Technical Services at Barnard and the designer of our zine cataloging system, devised the method of using the word "zines" at the beginning of the call number (in the 852 $h) and following that with a Cutter number — author if appropriate and available, title if not. The idea behind this was making "zines" searchable.[5] (This was before LC allowed zines as a subject heading in July of 2005, thus allowing us to enter the term in the 655.)

The "No information available" status is one of those Columbia things over which we at Barnard have little control. It has to do with the functionality of Columbia's Voyager catalog. It is an unfortunate fact that our current standard cataloging does not serve zines as well as it could, because of the issues of AACR flexibility and cataloger time mentioned earlier. Therefore, I created a secondary catalog, an Access database that resides on my personal drive and on a shared server. I am not really supposed to be spending much time on this database, as my boss does not particularly want to pay both Elmore and me to catalog the same materials. I do it anyway, on my lunch hour, because I want the information to be available after the revolution comes. This file is local to the library's shared network only and serves as a pre-cataloging database, since all of the pre-processed zines are in there. In my database, in addition to the basic access points listed above, I include a record for each issue, with information on topics mentioned in the zine, even if they are less than 20 percent of the contents. I log how it is presented visually (styles like cut-and-paste or collage, whether it is typewritten or font heavy, etc.), provenance, e-mail addresses and URLs, whether or not there is a copyright statement, what color the cover is, and more. (See Table 2.)

Table 2

ID	596
Title	Brewster
Subtitle	Dear Franke Potente I Had/Have a Crush on You...
Issue #	7
Author 1	Lee, Charisma
Author 2	
Editor 1	
Editor 2	
Zine Subject	beer coupon
	typewritten
	anti-depressant use
	assimilating, relating to whites

Table 2 (cont.)

Zine Subject	punk shows
	US Filipino history, chronology
	riding the bus
	crushes
Description	Filipina-American
	punk
	high school dropout
	LiveJournal user
ISSN/ISBN	
Publisher	
Date of Publication	after 2001
Place of Publication	Denver, CO
Copyright	
e-mail address	geekcore@ureach.com
Where acquired	gift of Celia C. Perez
Material type	monograph
Genre	personal zine
URL	
Holdings	two copies
Notes	second copy gift of Yumi Lee (different title: Dear Yumi Hwang-Williams I Had/Have a Crush on You Because You Are the Colorado Symphony Orchestra Concert Mistress)
	handwritten
	clip art
Cover	red cover on Yumi's copy
Record created	7/27/2005
Record modified	2/7/2007

Blank fields generally indicate that there was no data provided in the zine. Brackets indicate that the information was not explicit in the zine, but that the information was gleaned by a postmark, or a mention of an event that dated it, and so on.

MARC

Here is the MARC record for the same zine from our Voyager catalog, cataloged using encoding level 3.

Table 3

008		051110s2004 coua 000 0 eng d
035	__	$a (NNC)5464848
040	__	$a NNC $c NNC
100	1_	$a Lee, Charisma.
245	10	$a Dear Franka Potente I had/have a crush on you because you're a good actress.
260	__	$a Denver, CO : $b C. Lee, $c [2004?]
300	__	$a 50 p. : $b ill. ; $c 14 cm.
440	_0	$a Brewster ; $v no. 7
500	__	$a A personal zine.
500	__	$a Title from cover.

Table 3 (cont.)

520   __ $a Charisma is a high school dropout, Live Journal user, and Filipina-American punk.
             Her type- and handwritten personal zine discusses racism in society and in punk rock, as
             well as Filipino history and identity, zines, and crushes. She also discusses the use of
             anti-depressants.
655   _0 $a Zines.

You will see that we have interpreted *Brewster* as an analyzed monographic series, meaning that we have created individual monographic records for each issue we have, with Brewster as a series statement. It is issue #7 (in the 440 field), and the title of this issue, "Dear Franka Potente..." is the 245. This is the only issue of *Brewster* that we have in the collection. This system allows us to shelve the zines together under an author Cutter if there is one, and also makes it possible for us to abstract each named issue individually. When a zine is a straight-up serial, the abstract describes the author and the regular features or general qualities of the zine rather than running through the contents of the individual issue. We do not go to much effort to collect all the issues of a zine. Individual zines are more of a priority at Barnard (whether they are serials or monographs). We prefer to have a wider variety of authors and, further, we do not deem the effort it would take to complete a run worth our time. Zines go out of print quickly; authors decide they hate an issue and do not want it distributed any more; they move and do not provide contact information, etc.

Although we prioritize our authors, we do not create authority records for them, which is a potential danger when authors change their names or publish under different ones, as they are wont to do. Barnard does not create authority records for any materials, though, so that is that.

In an effort to provide some catalog access to the hundreds of zines in our backlog, Elmore has allowed me to create brief records that provide basic information about each zine until he can catalog it for real. (See Table 4.)

Table 4

000   00267cas a22001213a 450
001   5951766
005   20061011154746.0
008   061011c xx u $ 0 0eng d
040     $a NNC $c NNC
100   1_ $a Kim, Patti.
245   10 $a Alternazone.
500   __ $a Zinebrief
500   __ $a A personal zine.
655   _0 $a Zines.
852   8_ $b bar $h In process. Ask for help at the Barnard Reference Desk.

Classification Scheme

At first Elmore attempted to accede to my wish that the zines be classed according to the Library of Congress system, but he found that it was too difficult to determine subject headings for the majority of the publications. Too many of them ended up in "general topics" and so were more or less going into Cutter order anyway until he convinced me to let go of the dream. This is one battle I do not feel too bad about losing. I agree with Julie Bartel's analysis in *From A to Zine* that zines are best served by being collocated by author.[6] Their subject content is not consistent enough to warrant LC or other subject shelving in our current collection. I think this will remain true even as the collection expands.

Conclusion

It seems to me that very often it is a reference librarian, or even a student or community member, who has the big idea to collect little zines at their library.[7] Because zine cataloging practice is still developing, it is not easy on catalogers. One of the people from whom I sought advice before I launched the collection, Jim Danky of the Wisconsin Historical Society,[8] recommended that I make sure that the zine collection not just be "Jenna's project."[9] I do not think I succeeded at that very well, and so many aspects of the collection — including cataloging — are more of a struggle now than they might have been, had I done more collaborating as I developed the project. I mention this because it is a mistake that radical leaders are notorious for making — assuming that others will join in the struggle just because it is so obvious to them that theirs is a just cause. Collecting and cataloging zines and other alternative materials is to me at the very heart of libraries' missions, but you still have to make the case to your colleagues. Check out the first three items in the American Library Association's Library Bill of Rights[10] for some help:

I. Books and other library resources should be provided for the interest, information, and enlightenment of all people of the community the library serves. Materials should not be excluded because of the origin, background, or views of those contributing to their creation.

Zines are usually written by people normally under- or not at all represented in library catalogs:

1. young people
2. poor people
3. people with ideas outside the mainstream
4. people who have bad spelling and grammar

These are some of the same people we are trying to serve and encourage to take better advantage of our collections. One way to do that is to make the collection better reflect the community it serves by including materials published by its members.

Because zine creators' motivation is generally altruistic, as I wrote earlier — a desire to contribute their knowledge or experience to their community — and they are unburdened by the need to sell a certain amount of copies or keep advertisers happy, zine content can be a lot more free and diverse than you find with mainstream and even small press publishers. At times, you find information in zines that you cannot find elsewhere because of its personal nature or its more flexible interpretation of what is legal or appropriate to print. Again, the ALA Library Bill of Rights:

> II. Libraries should provide materials and information presenting all points of view on current and historical issues. Materials should not be proscribed or removed because of partisan or doctrinal disapproval.

Zines provide some of the only print content on activist activities like marches and civil disobedience. It is libraries' responsibility to collect, maintain and preserve these records to help future generations understand our times.

Communicating it better than I can in her article about collecting "Unabomber" Ted Kaczynski's papers, Julie Herrada writes,

> In his article "Mind over Matter," Terry Cook reminds us that: "... it is thus important to remember the people who slip through the cracks of society. In western countries, for example, the democratic consensus is often a white, male, capitalist one, and marginalized groups not forming part of that consensus or empowered by it are reflected poorly (if at all) in the programmes of public institutions. The voice of such marginalized groups may only be heard (and thus documented)—aside from chance survival of scattered private papers—through their interaction with such institutions and hence the archivist must listen carefully to make sure these voices are heard" [Terry Cook, "Mind over Matter: Towards a New Theory of Archival Appraisal," *The Archival Imagination: Essays in Honour of Hugh A. Taylor*, ed. Barbara L. Craig (Ottawa: Association of Canadian Archivists, 1992)].[11]

Herrada says in the same article, "If we, as keepers of history, collect and protect only what is appealing, socially acceptable, or politically correct, we are hardly doing our jobs."[12]

The Library Bill of Rights continues:

> III. Libraries should challenge censorship in the fulfillment of their responsibility to provide information and enlightenment.

As librarians know, sometimes self-censorship is more dangerous than the overt banning of particular items. In the case of zines, the self-censorship is carried out to such a degree that we do not even consider the materials that we are de facto rejecting. The number of public and academic libraries that I know to be actively collecting zines—either with or without active engagement from an MLS librarian—is around 25. With an estimated 117,341 libraries of all kinds in the United States,[13] I think we can do better.

I wish I had made more of an effort from the very beginning to include my colleagues in the planning and implementation process of the zine collection at Barnard, so that it would be their mission, as well. As it is now, I believe that some of my colleagues see the zines as cute or even interesting, but that they are not much of a priority. I convinced my boss, Carol Falcione, Dean of Information Services, to let me start the collection by tying it to our women's studies collection, which is our strongest. I wrote a seven-page proposal making the connection between zines and women's studies and advocating on several other points. It would perhaps have been advisable to have wooed the other librarians with as much determination.

However, this lack of enthusiasm is partially a Barnard/Columbia culture issue. It seems to me that many of the librarians, particularly in public services, on both campuses, for reasons ranging from being overextended in their local work to being not especially interested in the intellectual life of librarianship, are not all that jazzed by projects like this one. The general focus is on serving our students and faculty, which can take more than all of our time. "More than all of our time" is no exaggeration. In order to maintain the zine collection, I read zines on the subway and catalog at lunch. For me, it is worth it.

Addendum

Almost immediately after turning this article in for publication, but without enough time to rewrite it to reflect changes that are not yet fully known, the full cataloging responsibility was shifted to the Zine Librarian. That is likely to mean that more zines will be assigned subject headings — and that catalog records will be a lot sloppier for the foreseeable future!

Links

LiveJournal <http://www.livejournal.com>
Zine Librarians <http://groups.yahoo.com/group/zinelibrarians/>
Zine Libraries <http://www.zinelibraries.info>
Zine Wiki <http://www.zinewiki.com>

Notes

1. <http://zinewiki.com/index.php?title=Beer_Frame>
2. <http://www.bamboogirl.com/>
3. <http://www.bust.com/>
4. Per the magazine, as it wasn't in Ulrich's.
5. "Library of Congress Subject Headings Weekly List 27 (July 6, 2005)." Available: <http://www.loc.gov/catdir/cpso/wls05/awls0527.html> (accessed February 7, 2007).
6. Julie Bartel, *From A to Zine: Building a Winning Zine Collection in Your Library.* Chicago: American Library Association, 2004, p. 87
7. The editor of this book says that this is because catalogers are not encouraged to do collection development and that such requests are taken more seriously when they come from public service librarians anyway.
8. Incidentally, it was also Danky's suggestion to collect two of each zine, thereby making an almost disposable stacks copy while maintaining a preservation copy.
9. James Danky, "Re: Modest suggestion?" August 13, 2004, 4:32 pm [personal e-mail].
10. Adopted June 18, 1948, by the ALA Council; amended February 2, 1961; January 23, 1980; inclusion of "age" reaffirmed January 23, 1996. Available: <http://www.ala.org/ala/oif/statementspols/statements if/librarybillofrights.pdf> (accessed February 1, 2007).
11. Julie Herrada, "Letters to the Unabomber: A Case Study and Some Reflections." *Archival Matters* 28, no. 1, 2003–04: 43–44
12. Ibid, 37.
13. American Library Association "Fact Sheet 1." Available: <http://www.ala.org/ala/alalibrary/library factsheet/alalibraryfactsheet1.htm> (accessed February 7, 2007).

CE-MARC: The Educator's Library "Receipt"

Tom Adamich

Curriculum-Enhanced MARC (CE-MARC) provides information on curriculum-enhanced (CE) cataloging and its daily use in today's K-12 standards-based classroom. CE-MARC is developed under the editorial supervision of Carolyn Karis, *Knowledge Quest* Associate Editor for Resources.

According to *The American Heritage Dictionary of the English Language,* the basic definition of the word *catalog* is, "To make an itemized list of; to classify according to a categorical system." People use "itemized, classified" lists everyday.

Everyone knows that the *receipt* we are given when we purchase something at the store is an "itemized, classified" listing of the item or items we purchased and includes a wealth of information, both general and specific.

The typical receipt contains important details about the store where we purchased the item or items (its name, the establishment's address, its phone number, the manager's name in some cases, etc.). Additionally, a receipt also lists detailed facts about the product or products we've purchased (the identification/inventory number(s), price(s), date/time of purchase, product category or categories). Finally, the receipt often provides special instructions or related information regarding the product(s) we've purchased (return policy, refund information, local events, future sales).

School libraries have created "itemized, classified" lists of the materials found in the library for years! This "receipt" has changed its look over time (from being presented on a series of cards to appearing in the form of a MARC (Machine Readable Cataloging) record and will continue to change as teacher-librarians learn more about "metadata cataloging" using markup languages, etc. Steven J. Miller's comprehensive overview of metadata cataloging is available online (Miller) and will be covered in future CE-MARC columns.

The challenge school libraries face, in the words of Sheila Intner in *Cataloging Correctly for Kids* (2006), is to "[show] how cataloging and classification standards designed with adult materials in mind [can be] applied equally well to materials for kids" (Intner, 2006 vii). As curriculum alignment and standards-based instruction become the norm in schools, a cataloging record which includes proof that the item's structure and content supports a particular set of objectives will undoubtedly influence an instructor's choice of resources and act as a type of educator's performance assessment portfolio.

In order to address this challenge, several key "education-specific elements" have been developed and added to the cataloging process. These elements — called "curriculum-enhanced MARC" (CE-MARC) — were originally developed by Roger Minier of the Northwest Ohio Educational Technology Foundation (NWOET) in 1993 to deal with the lack of child and education-specific cataloging in MARC records (Murphy, 1995). Minier's list originally included the following MARC field tags:

- 520 Summary, etc.
- 521 Target Audience Note
- 658 Index Term — Curriculum Objective

Since creating the original list, the following MARC field tags have been identified as having "child and education-specific" parts, and, thus, these tags are also used in CE-MARC cataloging (Knight, 1993):

- 505 Formatted Contents Note
- 526 Study Program Information Note
- 586 Awards Note
- 653 Index Term — Uncontrolled

Each of these field tags and their related child and education-specific parts can be viewed in basic structural form at the Library of Congress, Network Development and MARC Standards Office website: <http://www.loc.gov/marc/bibliographic/ecbdhome. html>. Let's look at each CE-MARC field tag in numerical order and greater detail, examining each tag's makeup and relationship to curriculum support.

505 Formatted Contents Note

This note contains listings of an item's contents (in the case of school library media center items, a 505 field tag could contain the listing of a book's table of contents, songs found on a music CD, footage segments of a DVD or videocassette, parts of a kit, elements of a cataloged website or database, etc.) The contents note can contain a complete listing, a partial listing, or an incomplete listing (in cases where the item has multiple parts that are not all available to the cataloger at the time of cataloging). Listed below are simple examples of each and their associated coding:

505 0_ $a pt. 1. Solids — pt. 2 — Liquids — pt. 3 Gases. [a book on elements]

505 2_ $a Honey pie — Cry baby cry — Birthday — Sexy Sadie. [partial contents of a music CD; can you guess the title of the album by a famous group from the 1960s?]

505 1_ $a 1 pack of 55 Slides — 3 microscope lenses —1 package of 5 tongs. [incomplete contents for a science kit that also may include the microscope and related text]

Contents notes can be helpful to teacher-librarians supporting curriculum by showing a teacher whether a particular topic being taught is contained in a book, a movie addresses a desired theme, or a kit has the necessary parts to teach a state standard.

520 Summary, Etc.

This note provides a general overview of the item and, in the case of CE-MARC, its scope and relationship to instruction and/or a particular instructional group. The contents of this field tag can take several forms: summary, abstract, annotation, review, phrase, or scope and content note. In addition, the 520 summary tag can include **URIs** (Uniform Resource Identifiers), which may include **URLs** (Uniform Resource Locators) or **URNs** (Uniform Resource Names); this information can provide direct Internet access to related summary information.

520 2_ $a Kit contains books, transparencies, and a video to be used in teaching phonetic awareness of consonant sounds to students classified as reluctant readers or reading below grade level. [example of a scope and content note]

520 3_ $u http://www.ojp.usdoj.gov/bjs/abstract/cchrie98.htm [examples of an abstract online and the use of a Uniform Resource Identifier for access]

Summary notes could include terminology used in a particular school's curriculum language (e.g. "service learning" or "memoir") while picture book notes might be written in language that is understandable by student of that reading level.

521 Target Audience Note

Target audience notes are usually composed of four main types: age level; grade level; interest level; and reading or lexile value. This field tag may also contain information describing an audience's "special characteristics" (for example, vision-impaired users). Movie ratings and reading levels can also be found in this area.

521 0_ $a 3.1. [a book with a third grade reading level]

521 1_ $a 7–10. [an item targeted for ages 7–10]

521 2_ $a Grades 7–12. [an item geared for use from grade seven up to and including grade twelve]

521 3_ $a Vision impaired $a fine motor skills impaired. [library material to be used by an audience with special needs and/or characteristics]

521 4_ $a Highly motivated. [example of interest level assignment]

521 8_ $a 660 $b Lexile. [coding for reading lexile value assignment]

Since target audience field tags are repeatable, a number of different target audience characteristics can be included in one MARC record.

526 Study Program Information Note

Typically, the study program information note tag includes information on reading management or motivation programs such as *Accelerated Reader*© and *Reading Counts*©. Useful education content such as the interest, reading, and point values associated with a particular program component, as well as program number information, are often included:

526 0_ $a Accelerated Reader $b grades 3–5 $c 4.4$d100 pts. $z No. 47191 [example of an *Accelerated Reader*© description including interest level, reading level, points, and test number information]

Many school libraries also use the $z in the 526 field tag to give special instructions to students and/or teachers about each test.

586 Awards Note

The awards note field tag provides information on the various children's, young adult, and adult book and other material awards programs. For school libraries, the most common are the Newbery Award Medal/Honor and the Caldecott Award Medal/Honor. Other popular youth-based award programs include the Coretta Scott King, Michael Prinz, Quill series (graphic novel, young adult, children's illustrated book), Edgar (children's and young adult), and the Audie:

586 $a Caldecott Medal, 1979

Note that the year the book won the award is included, as the inclusion of the date is helpful when compiling a list of award-winning books over a time period.

653 — Index Term, Uncontrolled

The index term, uncontrolled field tag is an excellent location for teacher-librarians to use when assigning terms that are not found in the *Library of Congress Subject Headings* or *Sears List of Subject Headings*. While these terms are unique to the school library activities of a particular school building, school district, or region, they provide useful information to local users. By placing these "uncontrolled" terms in the 653 MARC tag, the teacher-librarian is able to retain local information while still maintaining the standards and requirements of the MARC cataloging structure:

653 1_ $a fuel cells $a carbon compounds [terms that describe the main focus or subject content of the material]

653 $a honesty — character trait #2 [vocabulary describing the material's relationship to a school's character trait instruction program; no focus/content level provided]

658 Index Term-Curriculum Objective

This MARC field tag contains valuable standards-based index terminology, including curriculum standards, course of study objectives, correlation factors, and associated standards coding. An interesting study on the creation and application of a 658 mapping project has recently been completed by AcademicBenchmarks, an education support company. Details of this study and its impact on determining the alignment and/or correlation of library materials to state/national standards will be discussed in a future CE-MARC column.

658 $a Reading objective 1 (fictional) $b Understanding language, elements of plots, themes, motives, characters, setting by responding to the multiple-meaning word $c NRPO2–1991 $d Highly correlated. $2 ohco [example of an index term-curriculum objective tag which includes all of the tag's elements: the main curriculum objective ($a), the subordinate curriculum objective ($b), the curriculum code ($c), the correlation factor ($d), and the source of the developed tag ($2)]

Future widespread use of the 658 Index term-Curriculum Objective (when provided in a user-friendly format) might prove to have a dramatic effect on the school's ability to access current, credible standards/materials information.

Cataloging materials from a child-based and education-based perspective is an exciting, developing area of school librarianship. Future CE-MARC columns will help school librarians make sense of emerging forms of cataloging (e.g., metadata-based cataloging using Dublin Core, XML markup language) and other "metadata in education" topics.

Works Cited

Intner, Sheila S., Joanna F. Fountain, and Jane E. Gilchrist. (2006). *Cataloging Correctly for Kids.* Chicago: American Library Association, vii.

Knight, Lorraine. (1993). From MARC to metadata: the 658 story. MARC4Media series. Prepared for the National Curriculum-Enhanced MARC Conference, Bowling Green, Ohio, 1993. Available: <http://www.nmm.net/market_resources.shtml> (accessed April 19, 2006).

Library of Congress. Understanding MARC Bibliographic: Machine-Readable Cataloging. Available: <http://www.loc.gov/marc/umb/> (accessed May 7, 2006).

Library of Congress. Network Development and MARC Standards Office. MARC 21 Concise format for bibliographic data. Available: <http://www.loc.gov/marc/bibliographic/ecbdhome.html> (accessed March 21, 2006).

Miller, Steven J. Metadata and cataloging online resources. Available:<http://www.uwm.edu/~mll/resource.html> (accessed March 21, 2006).

Murphy, Catherine. (1995). Curriculum-enhanced MARC (CEMARC): a new cataloging format for school librarians. (ERIC document no. ED399952). Washington, DC: Educational Resource Information Center. Available: <http://eric.ed.gov/ERICWebPortal/Home.portal?_nfpb=true&_pageLabel=RecordDetails&ERICExtSearch_SearchValue_0=ED399952&ERICExtSearch_SearchType_0=eric_accno&objectId=0900000b80124b5e> (accessed March 21, 2006).

[Reprinted with permission from American Library Association and American Association of School Librarians. *Knowledge Quest* 35 (1), September/October 2006.]

Dr. Strangecataloger: Or, How I Learned to Stop Worrying and Love the Tag

Jennifer Erica Sweda

"Tags? Patron-supplied keywords, going right into the OPAC without being vetted by a cataloger?" I didn't even have to glance down to know my knuckles were turning white.

I'm the sole technical services librarian on a small task force of librarians and programmers who are creating a software product called PennTags, <http://www.tags.library. upenn.edu>, an academic version of a social bookmarking tool. Social bookmarking tools — think del.icio.us, Flickr, and so on — are web-based services that store, organize and share Internet links by employing user-created taxonomies, or "folksonomies." With Web 2.0's increased interconnectivity, social bookmarking tools aren't revolutionary, but our product marks a change from similar types of software. We've created the product for an academic audience who will, we hope, use it to bookmark, tag, and share and discover in both their research pursuits and their personal interests; additionally, we've also realized the value of being able to bookmark and tag items available in other library products and we've incorporated that functionality, which other products have not. PennTags, still in pre-release, offers unique development, implementation and research opportunities because it is one of the only such tools available specifically for an academic audience and is integrated with other Penn library products (Thomas and McDonald 2005; Lippincott 2005). Our tool allows users to bookmark things off the open Web, but they can also bookmark journal articles and library holdings in our catalogs. And our IT director added one new brilliant — and, for me, initially terrifying — feature: tags assigned to bookmarked items in the catalog appear directly in the bibliographic record in the OPAC.

"Who gave you permission to do *that*?" I asked, incredulous. "Permission?" the IT director answered. "I just *did* it!" Fair enough. It's always easier to ask forgiveness than permission, and IT people can be forgiven a lot.

Now, you have to understand something. I'm an old-school cataloger through and though. I took every cataloging course offered at my alma mater. I put myself through school as a copy cataloger. I can tell you how the ALA Cataloging Rules of 1949 differ from AACR1, and how AACR1 differs from AACR2. My library participates in

NACO/SACO/PCC and just about every other acronym we can find. I dream in ISBD punctuation and MARC coding. I see the value in an established subject thesaurus, syndetic structure and authorized headings. I understand the policies of literary warrant and specificity. I understand the history, consistency and integrity of my profession. My professional experience has taught me that cataloging is an essential library function and I advocate strongly for it. Sure, the many rules and formulae aren't the whole of cataloging. We catalogers know that there's as much, if not more, art as science in our work, but I do understand and appreciate that science.

And now, patron-supplied metadata, in the catalog? In *my* catalog? Oh, the humanity! What would this mean for the catalog, for its users, for its creators? Oh yes, it was a white-knuckle moment, all right. Many years ago, during an annual review, I had been instructed to "develop a broader imagination" when applying standard cataloging rules for print materials to an e-book project. Such a stickler for the Holy Writ!

Yet somehow, I have become very intrigued by the idea of including tags in the OPAC. This hasn't been done before, though I've read calls for this type of innovation in the blogosphere and the professional literature. And indeed, as soon as word of our product got out, the email messages and requests for information started to pour in. One student at the University of Washington contacted us for our thoughts on "'user-driven interpretation' or 'non-expert metadata gathering.'" Another at Oslo University College commented that my library "seem[s] to be the only library that has incorporated the [tagging in the OPAC] functionality. A functionality which is long overdue." A library team at one of the top schools in the country wondered how we'd arrived at the "radical idea of adding [tags] to the OPAC" and asked us to consider having them for a site visit. Since when has cataloging created a buzz anywhere other than cataloging departments? This old-school cataloger knew we were onto something.

But what is cataloging if not making information accessible to users? I think most us would agree that the catalog, for all the good work that goes into it, falls short of many of its aims and many of its patrons' needs. There are a tremendous number of improvements that could be (and are being) made, and many of those improvements are coming from the Web 2.0 world. Repurposing data that we have already created is not only smart and efficient, it's what librarians do best. Cataloging is the creation of metadata, and I think allowing patron-supplied tags to be visible in bibliographic records is an exciting and worthwhile application of Web 2.0 technology.

PennTags constitutes an experiment in tagging behavior, patron interaction with the library, and the research process. Only current members of the Penn community (students, faculty and staff) can post to PennTags, but anyone on the Internet can view PennTags. Users can organize posted resources by assigning tags, by adding annotations, and/or by grouping posted items into projects. PennTags is a set of Perl scripts combined with AJAX technologies for parts of the user interface, and an Oracle database for storage and retrieval. PennTags uses these elements to create a lightweight application framework that can ingest, retrieve and format records quickly using a simple and flexible record structure. The intersections of posts, tags, owners, dates and projects provide a rich matrix of metadata to describe, organize and relate posts made by our users (Winkler 2006).

PennTags allows for side-by-side architectures: users can tag items in our OPAC and the keywords used will be viewable along with authorized subject headings assigned by professional catalogers. Tags and users are hyperlinked in the OPAC so that users can investigate other resources sharing those terms and names, adding another layer of searching to the catalog and increasing its use as a discovery/recall tool (Voorhees and Harman 1999; Shirky 2005). The breadth and quality of patron-supplied metadata in the OPAC may encourage our library to consider offering co-searching of PennTags and our catalog or, in the case of a 0-hit OPAC search, the option for a redirect to PennTags content (in library resources or the open Web).

Including patron-created taxonomies (or "folksonomies") in the catalog is appealing to me because taggers have certain advantages over catalogers when organizing the subjects and items which inform their research and interests. The primary strength of established thesauri (Library of Congress Subject Headings, etc.) lies in the authority structure; the primary purpose is the syndetic (i.e., broader/narrower/related terms) structure, which maximizes the ability to find related topics. The primary strength of folksonomies lies in harnessing intersections of disparate topics and better capturing the synthesis between desired subjects. Taggers need not adhere to LCSH policy, which states that a work can not have a subject heading assigned to it unless that heading represents at least 20 percent of the work. Taggers can focus on postcoordination of terms to improve subject access in cases where no precoordinated LCSH heading exists. Likewise, taggers need not follow the LCSH policy of specificity, which prescribes that the most narrow subject term be assigned, but rarely in concert with a broader term. Finally, taggers can choose any terms that have personal relevance, whereas LCSHs are issued through the Library of Congress only for topics for which there is literary warrant. Combining tags and LCSH enhances both architectures and creates a horizontal, not vertical, arrangement.

The personal tagspace of one of our users, a Ph.D. candidate in music, provides a good example of the advantages of tagging when trying to research the overlap between two distinct topics. This user's stated goals for her annotated bibliography project are: "(1) historicize the Classical Hollywood orchestra, and (2) interrogate the cultural significations of the orchestral sound that Hollywood both deployed and helped to form" (Kelly 2006). She is looking at examples of orchestral/formal music, but as they appear in pop culture (Hollywood movies, Disney cartoons, etc.). Clearly, she is using tags similar to established musical subject headings, but she is also creating tags that highlight the intersections of *her* interests (e.g., "highbrow_lowbrow") in ways that LCSH cannot do well, if at all. This very specific research need then reinforces the OPAC, with this user's tagspace becoming a viable taxonomy of music in our catalog for her *particular* topic of interest. Because this project and others like it become stand-alone content-management systems, marked by assigned subject terms and the ability to be searched, they each function as a catalog of sorts.

PennTags supports a true patron-created folksonomy for describing library resources. While enabling fine-grained distinctions and original intersections, PennTags addresses the issue of "sloppy tags" (Guy and Tonkin 2006) by giving users the tools to leverage their own, or shared, taxonomies. The most recent incarnation of the posting page now offers "My recent tags" and "My favorite tags" options, so users can strive toward consistent personal folksonomies. Users may also execute a bulk change for specific personal tags by using the "Manage my tags" option in their own tagspace. A future release may include an "Other users have used..." feature to promote system-wide consistency. PennTags has the potential to provide a lensed view of both personal and research interests in the Penn-Tags community. On the PennTags entry page, a tag cloud of the most used tags offers information about the research and interests of our 500 early adopters. A planned "lensing" option, provided through a user-manipulated slider that controls a tag cloud, will dramatically and graphically show how folksonomies might be leveraged, allowing users to hone in quickly on topics in which they or other users are most interested.

The creation of PennTags marks a new opportunity for studying how patrons interact with library-owned and open-web resources. Libraries and researchers can see what interests patrons, what they collect, annotate, collate and winnow to create research projects (Thomas and McDonald 2005). PennTags also provides a mechanism to see the arc of the online research process and its final results, because many users post their completed projects publicly. Data yielded by PennTags may affect collection policies and library services. Finally, PennTags should enable further study into the creation and usefulness of patron folksonomies in describing library resources.

So, do I think librarians should stop cataloging materials? Of course not. Do I prefer the Amazoogle approach that some patrons request and that we keep reading everyone is demanding of us? No. Will I ever let go of authorized thesauri for folksonomies? Probably not. But the world has changed since I became a cataloger only twelve years ago, and I have never been a librarian who thinks that consistency and tradition, for consistency and tradition's sake, are reasons enough to continue doing something without investigating any methods of improvement. I don't feel like the "Catalogers against the world!" attitude that we sometimes take on (at times for good reason) is always appropriate. As a cataloger, I have often defined myself in opposition to new trends in information organization, and I've come to realize that I'm doing myself and my profession a disservice. In terms of subject access, subject cataloging and tagging do different things, and I can now see the validity of both. I'm excited that my institution is on the forefront of incorporating these concepts and this technology into our library products. I think the coexistence of established subject headings with user-created tags, authorized thesauri with folksonomies, isn't a radical idea — or rather, *it is*, but that's a good thing. I'm curious to see the tags users create for the materials to which I assign LCSH or MeSH — how the terms differ (terminology, granularity/specificity, scope) and what I think those differences might tell us about user needs and cataloging practice. It will be interesting for those at my library to see what our catalog looks like when it begins to take on more of the flavor, the research interests and pursuits, the social networks, of its parent library and university.

Catalogers have often argued we are technically adept professionals, that we do change with the times, and that's certainly true. But now I think it's time to step up and embrace the concepts that our technology can already accommodate, and that other tools are providing, right in our own OPACs. I think there *is* value in patron-supplied metadata. How we catalogers harvest that metadata and use it to improve access to our holdings and services, as well as allow for the creation of communities of users interested in using, sharing and discovering them, is up to us. If our library products can become ever more radical, then so should we catalogers.

References

Guy, M., and E. Tonkin. (2006). Folksonomies: tidying up tags? *D-LibMagazine* 12(1). Available: <http://www.dlib.org/dlib/january06/guy/01guy.html> (accessed September 8, 2006).

Kelly, D. (2006). Cinema and Orchestra Ann. Available: <http://tags.library.upenn.edu/project/5332> (accessed September 4, 2006).

Lippincott, J. (2005, March/April). Net generation students and libraries. *EDUCAUSE Review,* 56–66.

Shirky, C. (2005). Ontology is overrated: categories, links and tags. Available: <http://www.shirky.com/writings/ontology_overrated.html> (accessed September 5, 2006).

Thomas, C. F., and R. H. McDonald. (2005). Millennial Net value(s): disconnects between libraries and the information age mindset. In *Free Culture and the Digital Library Symposium Proceedings,* ed. M. Halbert, 93–105. Atlanta, GA: MetaScholar Initiative at Emory University.

Voorhees, E. M., and D. Harman. (1999). Overview of the Eighth Text Retrieval Conference (TREC-8). Available: <http://trec.nist.gov/pubs/trec8/papers/overview_8.pdf> (accessed September 4, 2006).

Winkler, M. (2006, October 16). Interview by author. Philadelphia, PA.

Drawing Reference Librarians into the Fold

Dana M. Caudle and *Cecilia M. Schmitz*

Even in the age of Google, the catalog is still important for finding materials owned by or accessible to an individual library or consortium. To perform this vital function, catalogs must be accurate. Librarians should also continually strive to make catalogs easier for patrons to use, or they will go to Google. All librarians, whether they are in public services or technical services, want the catalog to be as accurate and useable as possible. Reference librarians work directly with patrons and know first-hand what problems they experience and what types of information the catalog needs to provide. However, they lack the skills — and, in many cases, the authorization — to fix the catalog. Catalogers know how catalogs function and perform the necessary tasks to keep them functioning well, but they are not likely to encounter specific problems in the course of their work. This is particularly true in an integrated library system like Voyager, because the catalogers are working in a technical services interface separate from what the public sees. What is correct on the technical services side sometimes fails to display in a meaningful manner in the public catalog. It is critical to the library's mission for reference librarians and catalogers to pool their knowledge and cooperate on solving specific problems in the catalog and making it stronger and more useable. Sadly, in some libraries, relations between catalogers and reference librarians are weak or adversarial, and the patrons are the ones who suffer. However, catalogers can change that by finding ways to build or strengthen coalitions with reference librarians, and to let them know their input is valued. Therefore, it is advantageous for catalogers to get reference librarians involved in catalog maintenance and improvement.

In 2001, the Auburn University Libraries Cataloging Department, as part of a continuous quality improvement initiative, set out to improve relations with the Reference Department. Cataloging librarians and staff volunteered to serve on the reference and information desks. The Chair of the Cataloging Department, in addition to working on the reference desk, began to attend Reference Department meetings. This involvement opened up lines of communication between Reference and Cataloging. Initially, the Reference Department was reluctant to report problems, because the reference librarians did not want to be perceived as criticizing or offending the librarians and staff in Cataloging. After Cataloging made it easier to report problems, the reference librarians became comfortable reporting them and began to make broader suggestions. It became apparent that the Reference Department often did not ask for things because the librarians didn't understand the technology, and therefore thought their requests were impossible. The Cataloging Department tried to project the idea that it was open to suggestions and that nothing was too outrageous to consider, even though it may be technically impossible. The catalogers presented explanations on the workings of the Voyager catalog to the reference librarians, either at the weekly Reference Department meetings, or through e-mail conversations between reference librarians and librarians and staff from the Cataloging, Acquisitions, and Systems Departments. These explanations covered why things work the way they do in Voyager and what was possible, in terms of both the cataloging rules and the technology, using language regular people could understand. For example, the catalogers tried to minimize excessive references to specific MARC tag numbers and other cataloging or computer jargon because these things just confused the reference librarians. The catalogers also showed a willingness to tweak the system by adding information not otherwise found on cataloging records and bending a few rules to make the catalog more understandable to patrons.

Overall, the catalogers learned what concerned the reference librarians, and devised ways for Cataloging to make their lives easier. Perhaps the biggest example of this is the treatment of journals in the catalog. The consensus at Auburn is that having all holdings — whether print, microform, or electronic full-text — on a single record is less confusing for patrons than separate records. To accomplish this, the catalogers load a single bibliographic record for each individual journal in Voyager, and attach separate holdings records for each format. The reference librarians particularly wanted records in the catalog for the individual electronic journals in the aggregator databases; patrons often have citations with the journal name, but they don't know which aggregator database might contain their desired article. Patrons may also not remember which aggregator they used to find their citation. Reference librarians can now search for the journal title in the catalog and check the coverage for print, microforms, and full-text electronic resources in one place. In the case of full-text electronic resources, they can also click on the link(s) for each resource to go directly to the resource.[1] In the case of aggregator databases, each link on the record displays the name of the aggregator. Ideally, the URL for each aggregator links directly to the journal, or as close to the journal's articles as the package will allow. If that's not possible, the link pulls up the aggregator's search page.

Another way Cataloging improved relations with the reference librarians was to establish an e-mail distribution list called "Lib_cathelp" which goes to those members of Cataloging who deal with catalog maintenance, electronic journals, and print journals. Reference librarians had trouble remembering which person in Cataloging was responsible for fixing their particular problem. This had resulted in much confusion when they went to a person who could not immediately help them. Now instead of having to remember which person in Cataloging does what, they e-mail Lib_cathelp and their message goes to everyone on the list. The appropriate person on the Lib_cathelp list takes responsibility for handling the problem and e-mails a response back to the reference librarian thanking them. This response takes one of three forms: what was done to solve the problem; the long-term strategy for solving the problem if it cannot be done immediately; or why the problem cannot be solved. At first Lib_cathelp only included people in Cataloging; it later expanded to include librarians and staff from other Technical Services departments, such as Acquisitions and Systems.

Currently, all reference librarians are using the system. The number of requests varies from month to month. Some problems, such as misspellings, are easy to fix, and some take a bit more effort. Reference librarians report broken URLs in the catalog. The requests that go to the Acquisitions Department often involve license restrictions. Many of the requests provide information about electronic journals, such as whether the electronic journal once had full text but now does not, and vice versa. There are frequent requests to catalog or add holdings for free electronic resources. Other problems concern print volumes and holdings. One request pointed out that a set record listed the holdings as being in closed stacks (where, in fact, they were), but the analytic records for the individual volumes listed them as being on the fourth floor. The cataloger corrected the analytic records indicating the volumes were indeed in closed stacks. Here is an actual request received on the Lib_cathelp list, which illustrates the sort of problems that can occur:

> It looks like the holdings are wrong on this record. It's the Proceedings of the Royal Society of London, Series A, Containing Papers of a Mathematical and Physical Character. The AubieCat record says it has issues from 1934–1990, but it's really 1905–1934. I think there may be other problems, but from the reference desk, I can't figure them out.[2]

The response from the catalog maintenance unit:

> This is one of those messy cases where the online provider calls something a title change and we do not. If you search AubieCat for ti: Proceedings of the Royal Society of London. Series A, the third hit, the one with the date range 1905–1990, is the title in question. Apparently in 1934 the section title changed and JSTOR has the ranges 1905–1934 and 1934–1990 available in different places on their site. I just now added another holding to our record so that now all years are linked from our one record. Thanks for letting us know about this.[3]

As you can see from the question and response, the cataloger was able to clarify the holdings and straighten out the problem. This example is but one of the wide varieties of problems the Cataloging Department has been able to fix by getting the Reference Department involved.

Having open lines of communication with the reference librarians also makes it possible to come up with enhancements to the catalog that they find useful. It was not possible to limit a search to government documents until one of the librarians requested this. Cataloging and Systems eventually accomplished this by adjusting the location-based search limits provided within Voyager. Similarly, patrons frequently come to the reference desk because they have a hard time identifying media in a search across the full catalog. Cataloging is currently working on a solution similar to the government documents problem by setting up searches limited to certain other subsets of records within Voyager, particularly the videos, DVDs, music and audiobook CDs, and vinyl albums. Reference librarians also took exception to the "no hits" message patrons received when a catalog search failed. With the help of the Systems Department, the default "no hits" message on Voyager now includes a list of options for the patron to get help if he or she cannot find the desired material. These options are: asking for help in person at the main or branch libraries' reference desks; calling the AU Libraries using the local or toll free numbers listed on the page; and links to "Chat with a librarian," which sets up an instant messaging session with a reference librarian, or to "Ask a librarian," which sends an email to the Reference Department.[3] The Cataloging Department would also like to present suggestions of different searches for patrons to try when they get no hits similar to those offered by Google and other search engines, but neither Cataloging nor Systems have figured out a way to do this in Voyager yet.

Catalog maintenance and improvement should be the function of all librarians. Patrons need catalogs that accurately reflect the holdings and resources of the library. Catalogs can be difficult to use for many patrons, and librarians should do everything they can to make them easier to use. Although catalogers are very conscientious about catalog maintenance, the chances are that they will not be able to find every problem. Reference librarians who work with patrons and the catalog on a daily basis are better positioned to spot problems catalogers will never find. Because they must use the catalog extensively, reference librarians are also able to suggest improvements to it. By getting reference librarians to notify the Cataloging Department of problems and to request catalog improvements, the result is a stronger, more useable catalog. Catalogers are able to do a better job of maintenance and reference librarians' lives are easier. Ultimately, however, the patrons benefit the most from this cooperation.

References

1. See "MARC: It's Not Just for Cataloging Anymore" in this book for technical details on how we do this.
2. Liza Weisbrod, "Proceedings of the Royal Society of London," 5 May 2006, distribution list (12 May 2006).
3. Jack Fitzpatrick, "Re: Proceedings of the Royal Society of London," 9 May 2006, distribution list (12 May 2006).
4. Auburn University Libraries, *AUBIECat WebVoyage* [2006]. Available: <http://aubiecat.auburn.edu/> (accessed 30 November 2006). The URL is for our Voyager OPAC main page. To see the actual "no hits" message with the list of options, use this URL, then type "gone with wind" (don't include the word "the") in the "Quick Search" box on the page. Or go to the AU Libraries home page at <http://www.lib.auburn.edu/> and type the same search in the "Search Catalog" box located directly under the banner.

MARC: It's Not Just for Cataloging Anymore

Dana M. Caudle and *Cecilia M. Schmitz*

As all catalogers know, MARC stands for machine-readable cataloging. The MARC record formats provide a standard way to encode bibliographic information so that libraries can share and manipulate it electronically. The Library of Congress initially developed MARC to share the information on catalog cards with other libraries. Since then, MARC records have become the basic building blocks of online library catalogs. The delineated fields in MARC records identify and characterize bibliographic data, making it easy to search, retrieve, and display data elements. In addition to the MARC format for bibliographic records, there is also a MARC format for holdings records, allowing libraries to encode information about their holdings. In recent years, some people have called for switching to other, more modern schemes for encoding bibliographic data, such as XML. OCLC's WorldCat database, the largest collection of bibliographic records, contains over 73 million MARC records as of 2006, which represents a significant commitment of the library community to the MARC format over the decades.[1] The sheer number of records to be converted is one of the key arguments against scrapping MARC in favor of some other scheme. One of the claims for XML is that it is more flexible. However, MARC can be quite flexible for those willing to think outside the box. The Anglo-American Cataloguing Rules (AACR2), and other systems of rules, classification, and thesauri determine the specific content of MARC fields, but it is important to note that the MARC format is separate and distinct from these content sources. Since the MARC formats are coding schemes independent of content, it is possible to use MARC for more functions than traditional cataloging. This chapter will discuss the ways in which the Auburn University Libraries have solved particular problems by exploiting the functionality of MARC for purposes never envisioned by its designers. Auburn did not plan these ad hoc solutions, which have evolved in unforeseen ways over time. Taken together, the solutions allow us to better perform catalog maintenance and to manage our electronic resources through the Endeavor Voyager catalog. Auburn has automated the generation of the electronic journal and database lists on the library's website based upon data in Voyager. The following sections will discuss marking records in Voyager, which has all kinds of uses, and our home-grown electronic resource management system.

Using MARC to Mark Records

One of the hardest parts about maintaining large sets of records is being able to identify them as a group; therefore, it is useful to find some way of marking or identifying these records for retrieval. The 440/830 fields can identify materials in series, and sometimes the cataloger can identify sets of records with an artificial series title, assuming she can come up with a plausible title. Thanks to Auburn's innovative use of the 710, 773, and 910 fields, we can pull up a list of related records for any special project, set of materials, or all electronic journals in a database package with relative ease. The IT staff in the IT and Online Resources Unit of the Cataloging Department use MS Access to retrieve the records from our Voyager catalog and generate a report for the set. A catalog search in Voyager for the appropriate code or phrase located in the 710, 773, or 910 fields will also pull up a list of records. Being able to generate reports and pull up a list of all the records in any of these groups with a simple catalog search makes catalog maintenance much easier, and serves all kinds of useful purposes. For instance, we mark records in our Voyager catalog to identify those serials which are standing orders and those which originate from memberships, which helps both the Acquisitions Department and the subject specialists with collection development. We also mark records to identify gift collections, such as the Schwabe or McLeod collections. When a donor gives a large collection of materials to the library, the cataloger can use a 710 02 field to give the collection a name. Searching this name will pull up all records in the donated collection. We don't physically house the items together, but the simple name search allows the donor to "see" his or her donation as a virtual collection in Voyager. We also mark records to identify special collections of specific items, such as honors theses or blueprints, and as part of minimal level cataloging projects or large inventory projects such as the Microform Inventory Project. Because we've tagged them, we can quickly produce lists for maintenance purposes. To maintain access to our electronic resources, we mark individual records for the electronic journals, databases, and conferences in packages such as JSTOR, Academic Search Premier, and IEEE. Finally, we mark records we get through PromptCat and other sources of cataloging in order to identify all records from a particular source so that we can better manage our outsourcing. Thus, marking the records allows us to do many different things.

The practice of marking records originally grew out of Auburn's need to identify standing orders, and began long before we used Voyager. The Serials Department decided to use the 710 02 field to identify first standing orders, then later serials to be cut during our first major serials cut. We used the code QQZ for standing orders and the code QQZCX for those which were canceled. We chose the 710 field because a simple author search would retrieve all the records in title order and in a single list. We simply used the QQZ code identifier as our author. We chose first indicator 0 because it was a pre–AACR2 indicator and therefore easy to co-opt. We chose second indicator 2, which indicates the item is an analytic, because it seemed logical to think of the individual titles as analytics in series, with the "series" being the standing order. To avoid patron confusion over weird in-house codes in the public catalog, we configured first NOTIS, and then Voyager, to omit the 710 02 field from the display configuration, so that the field is suppressed from public view but still indexed. We chose to start the codes with QQ to minimize the chance that patrons would pull up these records as false hits in other author searches. Later we created additional special Q codes for other types of serials, such as those from memberships.

The Cataloging Department adopted this idea and began to use the 710 02 field to identify records for special collections coming from a particular donor and to identify particular materials such as blueprints, honors theses, CD-ROMs, and Geographical Information System (GIS) materials. Those catalogers who were responsible for cataloging regular theses used the 710 02 field to identify which departments the theses originated from. Over time, the Cataloging Department took on major inventory and retrospective conversion projects, such as the Microform Inventory Project and the Micro-Card Recon Project. The catalogers marked the records used in these projects with the 710 02 field for easy identification. When the Cataloging Department began to experiment with other types of cataloging, such as minimal level and Dublin Core records, they also marked these records for later revision. The Special Collections and Archives Department, which has done its own cataloging in the past, marks their records with AMC Archives. Here are samples of some 710 02 fields used by Auburn:

710 02 McLeod Collection (a donor collection)
710 02 Schwabe Collection (a donor collection)
710 02 Blueprint
710 02 QCD-ROM
710 02 QGIS
710 02 US newspapers
710 02 Auburn University — Theses — Biological Sciences
710 02 Auburn University — Theses — Religion
710 02 Microform inventory project
710 02 AMC Archives

The Cataloging Department also wanted to be able to identify the source of the records obtained through various cataloging outsourcing projects. We use the 910 field for this purpose. It is not part of the standard MARC record, and is for user-designated content. At the time that the contracts were drawn up, the cataloger who set up each outsourcing project designated a 910 field to identify the vendor; this field would be added to all outsourced records upon being batch-loaded in Voyager. For example, all records received through OCLC PromptCat have the following field added: 910 Promptcat. This allows the administrator of the project to readily determine who produced the record, so that they can work with the vendor to make any necessary adjustments to the program. It is possible to run a keyword search using the phrase in the 910 field to pull up all records received through a particular outsourcing contract. We can also use Microsoft Access to create a report listing the records.

The consensus at Auburn is that having all holdings — whether print, microform, or electronic full-text — on a single catalog record is less confusing for patrons than using separate records for each format. We made this decision at the request of the Reference Department (see "Drawing Reference Librarians into the Fold"). Patrons come to the reference desk with citations to specific journals, and often do not remember which aggregator database they used, or should use, to find the article. In order for reference librarians and patrons to be able to search for a journal and find all holdings and links to the electronic versions in one place, Auburn catalogs its electronic journals and databases at the level of the individual journal or database, and uses a single record for all electronic and print versions. Voyager allows multiple holdings records for a bibliographic record, each of which will generate a holdings statement in the OPAC. The catalogers put the URL and coverage of each aggregator containing that journal on a separate holdings record attached to the bibliographic record for the journal, along with other holdings records for print and microforms. Auburn also maintains records for its aggregator packages as a whole, and catalogs selected websites at the request of the subject specialists. To aid in maintenance of all of our electronic resources, the Cataloging and Acquisitions Departments created special codes to identify them. Because aggregators frequently add and delete journals from their packages, we use the codes to call up the bibliographic records for all the journals in a package, so that we easily can add or remove the holdings record for that package from the individual journal records. Having searchable codes also comes in handy when an entire database or package has to be canceled. For example, we might lose access to Project Muse; using the code, a simple search calls up all affected journals, allowing us to quickly delete the holdings record with the link to the canceled package. The bibliographic record for the journal remains in the catalog with all other holdings being unaffected by the change. This way of maintaining our electronic journals is labor intensive, although we've found a way to automate part of it. Maintenance would be extremely difficult to do without marking the records so that we can find the proper ones easily. However, both reference librarians and catalogers feel that this treatment of journals is in the best interest of our patrons.

At first, the Cataloging Department assigned a code in the 710 02 field to each individual electronic journal or database in a given package. Auburn is not the only library to use the 710 field for identification purposes, but we are unique in using special codes and suppressing them in the public catalog. Using Q codes for electronic resources grew naturally out of the practice of using QQZ for standing orders. Each code starts with QEJ if it is for an electronic journal; QEM if it is for an electronic monograph; QER if it is for another type of electronic resource such as a web site; or QR if it is for a related electronic resource. We add a final letter or letters to designate the acquisition method: C for current print subscription; F for free; FC for free with current print subscription; G for free print version also; K for part of a package; and a few other designations. Thus the code QEMK added to a record for an IEEE conference proceeding accessed through IEEE Xplore means that it is an electronic monograph and part of a larger package. The 710 subfield $b contains a second code which identifies the specific package. Originally, we manually entered all these 710 fields on each journal record and performed catalog maintenance of our journal packages by hand. Now we do it automatically.

After we had been using the Q codes for a while, the 773 field, a legal field for host item, became the standard field for identifying the aggregator containing the journal. We decided to gradually begin making the switch to the more accepted 773 field, instead of continuing to use a code in the 710 field. It was also becoming difficult and unwieldy to maintain the various code lists identifying the electronic journal and database packages.

The 773 is also indexed and searchable, retaining the benefit of being able to call up all marked resources with a simple search. It also allows us to replace the codes for our packages with the full title of the package. This change makes it easier to identify the package at a glance, and dispenses with the need to create a new code every time we acquire a new package. If the electronic resource is a journal or database in a package, it gets a 773 field containing the package's title and publication information. For example, all the electronic journals in Business Source Premier have a 773 for Business Source Premier. Each electronic resource also receives a 773 field containing one or more Q codes for the type of resource it is. These Q codes are important because the reference librarians want to be able to search for lists of electronic resources by type. For example, the journals in Business Source Premier carry a 773 field with the codes qqee, qqpp, and http, indicating that it is an electronic resource, a periodical, and available as a remote resource, respectively. We use a 773 18 field for the Q codes with the indicators 1 and 8. First indicator 1 tells the system not to display a note and second indicator 8 tells the system not to generate a display constant. Voyager implements these indicators as designed, so the fields do not display in the public catalog. The following Q codes are used in the 773 field as appropriate:

    qqee = electronic resource
    qqss = serial
    qqmm = monograph
    qqpp = periodical
    qqnn = newspaper
    qdatabase = index and database pages
    qgovper = government periodicals eList

We have automated catalog maintenance of our electronic packages using the 773 field. We originally used the 710 02 Q code to call up a list of journals to be changed. We now search the 773 field to identify the journal records. We harvest the Voyager bibliographic numbers for every affected journal record. The IT staff then prepares a file containing this Voyager bibliographic record number, the package name, the serial's URL, and the coverage. Next, we run Visual Basic scripts that use the Voyager bibliographic record number as a match point between the file and the catalog. The scripts automatically delete the old information from each matching record and add the new information from the file in its place. At the same time the scripts also add the appropriate 710 and 773 fields.

Marking our electronic records has other benefits as well. Auburn also uses the 710 field to generate its A–Z list of electronic journals located on our library web site. The method Auburn uses for generating the database lists will be discussed in the next section. The A–Z list is an alternate way to provide access to our electronic journals in addition to the catalog and in fact is created directly from information in the catalog. A Perl script identifies the electronic journal records by looking for every instance of the QEJ code in the Voyager tables; it extracts the package name, URL, coverage, and any special notes from the attached holdings record, and uses that information to automatically create the list of journal links and place it on the web site. A programmer in the Systems

Department wrote the script using standard Perl programming with functions and operations specific to MARC. It is a chronological job set to run automatically each morning, generating a fresh list incorporating any changes made in the catalog the previous day. The only requirement for the Perl script to work is that the codes be in an indexed field. The Catalog Department's IT and Online Resources Unit has programmers who work with the programmers in the Systems Department to make in-house Voyager innovations, such as this Perl script, possible. Since the Perl script as presently written works with the QER code in the 710 field, we did not eliminate the 710 field when we decided to use the 773 field and records now carry both. Eventually we will reprogram the Perl script to use the 773 field and phase out the use of 710 fields.

The Q codes for electronic resources and the 710 02 fields for collections are very useful to the Reference Department and it is the responsibility of those people in the Cataloging Department who work on the reference and service desks, as well as attend reference meetings, to publicize them. A special master record in the catalog lists the 773 field Q codes. Catalogers maintain separate lists in MS Access for the 710 02 field phrases. The Cataloging Department IT and Online Resources Unit maintains a list of the 710 02 field Q codes on the Cataloging Department's web site as some of these are still in use.

No single way of marking will fit all sets, as the reasons for marking various sets of records differ. This is why Auburn uses the 710, 773, and 910 MARC fields with a variety of phrases and codes tailored to the particular project to mark our records. Auburn's system has evolved over time as projects have changed. To be most effective, the exact mark (i.e., the MARC field and the identifying code or phrase to be used) should be thought out carefully before the start of a project, and applied from the beginning as each record in the group is added. After the records are in the system, it becomes extremely difficult to identify all of them if they were not marked from the beginning. Sometimes the initial method of marking records creates problems that cannot be foreseen at the start, or a better method for identification is found and it is necessary to change marks midstream. As discussed above, such reasons triggered Auburn's change from using the 710 field to using both the 710 field and the 773 field to mark our electronic resources. This is not necessarily a problem, as the original marking makes it easy to find the records and change the mark. Marking should be dynamic, not set in stone.

We hope this section has demonstrated that marking records can be a powerful tool for catalog maintenance of large sets of materials, and that it also can serve other purposes, such as generating a dynamic list of electronic resources for a library's website; aiding collection development; managing outsourcing projects; and building goodwill with donors of large collections. Regardless of the purpose for marking groups of records, the key idea is being able to quickly and easily identify the records involved. By using distinctive codes and phrases in certain MARC fields, it is possible to either pull the records up in Voyager with a simple catalog search or pull reports from Voyager using MS Access. When one of the authors gave a paper in 2003 and mentioned our methods of marking our records, the response of one listener was, "I wish we'd thought to mark our records."

ERMS: Taming the Chaos of Electronic Resource Management

In the first section, we discussed the ways in which Auburn manages its electronic resources at the journal level. In this section, we will describe the different treatment Auburn uses for its database packages, which allows us to not only generate the database lists on our website, but also to perform digital rights management. Voyager has an electronic resources management module, but it does not link to the catalog and does not meet all of our needs. The Acquisitions Department could not use the Voyager acquisitions module for digital rights metadata such as access restrictions because they found retrieving it to be nearly impossible. We were using an Excel file for this metadata, but it was becoming unwieldy, and the reference librarians had to call Acquisitions when they needed information such as the number of simultaneous users for a database. A Perl script looking for a code in the 710 field would be able to generate a list of databases by title on the website similar to the list for electronic journals, but we also needed a way to list our databases by subject. This required a different approach. Working together, the Cataloging Department's IT and Online Resources Unit, the Acquisitions Department, and the Systems Department collaborated to design a system that would both generate lists and track digital rights metadata.

We catalog and mark our database packages as a whole package in addition to cataloging the individual journals. Unfortunately, the MARC bibliographic record has no real place for digital rights metadata, so we created an electronic resource management system (ERMS) based on 9xx fields added to the MARC holdings record for each database we catalog. Using the MARC holdings record has several advantages: it is less constrained and more configurable for non-bibliographic information; it is machine-readable, giving us the same functionality as the bibliographic record; it is invisible to the public so we don't have to suppress our in-house information in the public catalog; and the holdings record and its information are not wiped out when it is necessary to overlay the attached bibliographic record. The 9xx fields in the MARC holdings format are user-defined, making them a good choice for containing all the information we need to generate the database lists and store the digital rights metadata.

We chose to use the 924, 952, and 965 fields to record the information for generating the database lists. The IT and Online Resources Unit maintains the information in these fields. The 924 field contains the name of the database. The 952 field contains a summary about the database which is visible to the public. To generate the database title list and associated summary list, we use another Perl script, written by a programmer in the Systems Department, which searches the Voyager holdings records for the presence of a 924 field. When the script finds a holdings record with this field, it pulls the name from the 924 field and the URL from the 856 field to create a link on the title list, then pulls the text of the summary from the 952 field placing it on a separate summary list. An About button next to each database title links it to its summary, and every summary has a link to return to the title list. When patrons click on the About button, they see the text of the summary from the 952 field for that database. For example, the Perl script finds a 924 field on the holdings record for the JSTOR package. It takes the name JSTOR from the 924 field and combines it with the URL from the 856 field, so that clicking on the name will take the patron to the JSTOR package. Then it places the name from the 924 field and the summary text about JSTOR from the 952 field on the summary list and creates links between both lists. The entries for JSTOR look like this:

Database Title List:
<ABOUT> JSTOR[2] [from 924 field; includes URL link to JSTOR; clicking on ABOUT leads to database summary list]
Database Summary List:
JSTOR [from 924 field]
JSTOR provides access to several collections of backfiles of scholarly publications covering the social sciences, humanities, and sciences. JSTOR includes the full runs of each journal, generally up to 1–7 years from the present. Note: Auburn University subscribes to the Arts & Sciences I & II Collections and the Health & General Science Collection. [from 952 field]
Return to list.[3] [Takes patron back to title in database title list.]

Another Perl script, also written by a programmer in the Systems Department, generates the list of databases by subject on the website from the 924 and 965 fields. The 965 field contains a list of subjects. Each subject corresponds to a subject heading on the database subject list. We add a three-digit ranking number at the front of each subject name. The Perl script adds the database name from the 924 field under each subject heading listed in the 965 field. It uses the ranking number attached to the subject heading to place the database in the desired order on the list. The reference librarians decide the order in which databases will be ranked and programmers in the IT and Online Resources Unit place the appropriate ranking number with each subject heading. For example, the 965 field on the JSTOR holdings record contains the heading 400 Biological Sciences, among others. The Perl script places a link for JSTOR under the subject heading Biological Sciences. The 400 tells the Perl script to put JSTOR toward the bottom of the list:

Biological Sciences[4] [heading from 965 field on holdings records]
Biological Abstracts
Zoological Record
PubMed
MEDLINE
CAB Abstracts (1910–present)
AGRICOLA
ASFA: Aquatic Sciences & Fisheries
Oceanic Abstracts
Environmental Sciences & Pollution Management
TOXLINE
Web of Science
Current Contents/Science Edition
JSTOR
BioOne [names from the 924 fields on holdings records]

The other subject headings for JSTOR contain different ranking numbers, so that JSTOR appears in different place on those lists.

The digital rights metadata goes into the 977, 990, 995, and 997 fields on the holdings record. The Acquisitions Department maintains all digital rights metadata. The 977 field contains a code for the type of database. The 990 states whether the database is full text. The 995 field has defined subfields for the Voyager bibliographic record number; the title; the source of acquisition; the cancellation policy; the archive policy; notes about confidentiality; and when the subscription ends. The 997 field has defined subfields that give the date the subscription began; access restrictions such as the number of simultaneous users and whether off-campus access is allowed; the course packs that have access; the effect on print subscriptions; and classroom logins for use in bibliographic instruction sessions. Not all of these fields are present on every database holdings record. For example, the JSTOR holdings record has all four fields, but the holdings record for Academic Search Premier only contains the 990 field. Just as not all fields may be present, not all of the subfields in the 995 and 997 have information. We have configured Voyager to display information from certain subfields in the 997 field in the public catalog because the reference librarians find it useful to have this information in the catalog where they can easily locate it. Subfields displayed include when the subscription began; number of simultaneous users; off-campus access; and classroom logins.

In conclusion, electronic resources bring a magnitude of problems for libraries. The debate on the best ways to handle them is ongoing. Some libraries choose not to put their electronic resources in the catalog, preferring to maintain separate lists for them on their websites. Some choose to use vendor packages like TDNet to manage their electronic resources. Auburn maintains lists of our electronic resources on our website, which patrons find to be convenient and useful, but we also feel strongly that patrons should be able to find electronic resources in the catalog, too. Philosophically, we think that the catalog should include all the library's resources. Our patrons are not served by having to look in different places just because the resources they want are in different formats. This commitment to "one-stop shopping" is also why we put all formats on a single record. At Auburn, we decided we wanted to provide the fullest access possible for our electronic resources, but we didn't want the work of maintaining both the catalog and separate lists of electronic resources on the website. We found ways to accomplish these objectives using the catalog, by trying to think outside the box and see just how much we can do with it. Some solutions, such as running Perl scripts against the catalog to create our electronic resources lists, take advantage of the fact that Voyager is a Windows-based application that will work with outside software. We realize that the solutions we've described in this paper may not work for all libraries. With the Endeavor/Ex Libris merger, it is possible Auburn will have to migrate to Ex Libris. We may have to rethink some of our practices based on limitations in Ex Libris that we do not have in Voyager. However, whatever system we use, we will continue to believe that the catalog exists to make information retrieval easy for the patron. If we keep this purpose in mind and continue to find innovative uses for the catalog, it will remain dynamic and will continue to successfully coexist with Google and the like.

Acknowledgments

The authors would like to thank Jack Fitzpatrick of the IT and Online Resources Unit and Henry McCurley, Head of the Cataloging Department, for their invaluable explanations of both technical details and reasons behind Auburn's innovative uses of MARC.

References

1. OCLC Online Computer Library Center, WorldCat Facts and Statistics, 2006. Available: <http://www.oclc.org/worldcat/statistics/default.asp> (accessed 8 December 2006).
2. Auburn University Libraries, Indexes and Databases by Title, 2006. Available: <http://www.lib.auburn.edu/find/bytitle.html#J> (accessed 9 December 2006).
3. Auburn University Libraries, Indexes and Databases by Title, 2006. Available: <http://www.lib.auburn.edu/find/bytitle.html#147> (accessed 9 December 2006).
4. Auburn University Libraries, Indexes and Databases by Subject, 2006. Available: <http://www.lib.auburn.edu/find/bysubject.html#7> (accessed 9 December 2006).

"Respect My Authoritah": Eric Cartman and Enhanced Subject Access

Daniel CannCasciato

Introduction

For over a hundred years, it's been widely accepted that one of the aims of the library catalog is to help the patron find what the library has on a particular subject: a simple enough concept. I have found, though, that the tools at our disposal for achieving this aim are occasionally obstacles to fulfilling that goal. Academic library catalogers in the United States predominately utilize the *Library of Congress Subject Headings* and its user's manual, *Subject Cataloging Manual: Subject Headings,* to provide subject access to our materials. The problem with this can be twofold: (1) The Library of Congress has a primary constituency of the United States government; and (2) no one has enough time and staffing. One of the unavoidable outcomes of this situation is that my cataloging priorities and needs are not being met by the Library of Congress. I suspect theirs are not being met by what I do, either. From a very selfish outlook, though, I want to focus only on my unmet needs and how I attempt to get them met.

My unmet needs are not personal, generally. In the professional context of my daily work, my unmet needs are what I can infer are those of my users. These folks are trying to find some information on subjects and I have a declared mission to help them find those materials if we have them. I review patron search logs from our library catalog and try to adjust the subject structure to help meet the needs those logs indicate. Thus, on some level, I've begun to adopt one of the characteristics of a fictional (and poorly animated) eight-year-old boy, Eric Cartman[1]. Eric does not allow his needs to go unmet — not without a fight, at least. In fact, Eric will go to any length to get his needs met. Is this good behavior for a cataloger? Well, as with most librarians, I'm somewhat more conservative in behavior than is Eric, which has kept me both employed and out of jail, and is a behavior I will continue to follow. However, for subject cataloging and authority work, Eric can be a good model in the sense that whenever he has a chance to grab the reins of power, he does so tenaciously. Whenever possible, he says to the other characters in the land of *South Park,* "Respect my authoritah!" Here's how that helps a cataloger doing subject authority work.

"Respect My Authoritah"

Let's say your patron wanted to find some materials (information resources) regarding the subject of Maritime Indians. Well, in general, they would look for information by using the term Maritime Indians. There's a reason for this: authors write about the Maritime Indians. Here's an example from 1968: *Someone Before Us: Our Maritime Indians.*[2] As a cataloger, I'd like my patrons to find these materials, but the Library of Congress folks have decided using such a term is not acceptable. If you look for these types of terms as subject access points to assign to works about American Indians from geographic locations, you will not find much help. Yet authors, heedless of this practice, continue to use these terms in their works. "California Indians," "Washington Indians," and "Oregon Indians" are all terms used by authors. Eric Cartman would not stand for this. As he is my now more frequently channeled alter ego, neither will I. (My previous alter ego would make a change to a name authority record and declare the reason was, "Because I said so." That stood me well for almost a decade, until I met up with Eric Cartman. There can be some overlap, of course, between my old and new mottos.)

As Eric generally does, I first started with the authorities. I proposed to the Library of Congress, through the Subject Authorities Cooperative (SACO) Program, to have the term "Maritime Indians" created as a "see" reference. It was rejected because of the time involved to create many references of a similar type. That is, there's not enough time and staffing. That certainly doesn't meet my needs. It doesn't help my patrons. And Eric doesn't take rejection, so why would I? In response and defiance, I've created a reference locally for our patrons. Now, if one searches on *Maritime Indians*, he or she is directed to Indians of North America—Maritime Provinces. The impact for the Maritime Indians is not an overwhelming concern, of course, because they are, after all, in what is now called Canada. But what of the patron interested in California Indians? In Eric Cartman fashion, I've done more. I've created a number of references of this type, even though the authority (LC) did not. "Respect my authoritah," I say to myself. So now our patrons, locally at least, have access from terms such as California Indians, Washington Indians, Oregon Indians, Pacific Northwest Indians, and so on.

What I'm suggesting here is that all catalogers doing subject authority work should channel Eric Cartman a little more. After one rejection, Eric might decide to obliterate an entire power structure, which is clearly beyond my own commitment and the bounds of common sense and remaining employed. (Also, I happen to like the folks I correspond with at LC.) However, I'm perfectly happy to create a couple of hundred "see" references so that heading of the type [place] $x History $ y [date] can be browsed chronologically. If LC doesn't want to meet my needs, well, I do.[3] I think doing so helps my patrons.

As little Eric Cartman would on his three-wheeler, I go around looking for ways to enforce my newfound authoritah. I made "see" references for the countries of Central, South, and North America. Now, when our patrons search our catalog for South America, they are also directed to the 13 individual countries on the South American continent:

1. —> See also narrower term ARGENTINA
2. —> See also narrower term BOLIVIA
3. —> See also narrower term BRAZIL
4. —> See also narrower term CHILE
5. —> See also narrower term COLOMBIA
6. —> See also narrower term ECUADOR
7. —> See also narrower term FRENCH GUIANA
8. —> See also narrower term GUYANA
9. —> See also narrower term PARAGUAY
10. —> See also narrower term PERU
11. —> See also narrower term SURINAME
12. —> See also narrower term URUGUAY
13. —> See also narrower term VENEZUELA

What the heck? I'm working on a project for Europe and Africa as well. Once you begin making things right in the world, it's hard to stop.

Reform?

One thing that infuriates Eric no end is being rejected. I have some difficulties taking "no" for an answer as well. And I'm not always rejected. (Unlike Eric, if most of my proposals were rejected by LC, I'd wonder about *my* proposals, not LC's rejection of them.) Many times, though, the Library of Congress folks have respected my authoritah suggestions. Over the years, I've contributed many new headings through the SACO program.[4] A little success breeds less tolerance for rejection. While Eric takes it too far, clearly, he is on the right track sometimes. Sometimes we, as catalogers, cannot and should not accept no for an answer. I believe we are, in fact, obligated not to follow along. A good example of not following is two recently rejected headings: CAMPAIGN FINANCE REFORM and ELECTION REFORM.

In the Orbis union catalog from the Northwest, the term "election reform" is used in titles 65 times. In OhioLINK, it is used 56 times. Yet if you look in the LC authority file, you do not find that term as an authorized heading. You don't find it as a "see" reference, either. LC's rationale, which was pretty good, is that the term is ambiguous. It could mean various aspects of either topic. No argument there. Yet it's still a topic that our patrons need access to, just as they did with Maritime Indians. While LC has opted not to provide direction for patrons on this vague topic, I have. For the time being, I've opted to use the terms themselves rather than redirect the patron to somewhat more convoluted headings. For example, does ELECTION REFORM involve works about ELECTIONS—CORRUPT PRACTICES or does it refer to ELECTION LAW? I've decided it doesn't matter. For now, search that term, get both types of works. Then the patrons can select what fits their needs. CAMPAIGN FINANCE REFORM is usually about CAMPAIGN FUNDS—LAW AND LEGISLATION, but not always. Sometimes it's broadly concerned with just CAMPAIGN FUNDS, sometimes it's concerned with ADVERTISING, POLITICAL. So, once again, I've decided to wield my power and simply use the term itself.

"Damn Hippies"

Eric is basically a conservative libertarian type, and he uses terminology for groups of people that many consider inappropriate. Eric would probably find some companionship with the members of the Klu Klux Klan — not that he interacts with the Klu Klux Klan, being a fictional character from Colorado. I'm just suggesting that he has some decidedly similar characteristics as to the righteousness of his views. I could see Eric at a Klu Klux Klan rally (but only as a leader) and even see him suggesting the use of the nuculure bomb to help right the world.

Okay, anyone reading that previous paragraph is probably going crazy at my ignorance. "Klu Klux Klan?" "*Klu?*" It's Ku Klux Klan. And it's not "nuculure"; it's nuclear. I knew both those things. (Really!) However, in our catalog you can search under *Klu* and get led back to the correct heading. You cannot search under *nuculure*, though, and get to nuclear. I have decided on a Cartman-like one-person policy for these matters. I think we can and should make references from mistaken understandings, but not from those that are generated by simple mistakes or typos. I saw enough examples in our search logs for the Klu Klux Klan that I added it as a reference to two authority records. Done.

Because I said so.

Respect my authoritah!

Notes

1. Eric Cartman is one of the four main child characters on the *South Park* television show (<http://www.comedycentral.com/shows/south_park/index.jhtml>). He makes Bart Simpson look like a choirboy. He is a selfish and sociopathic little boy. As a role model, he is useful only in a very limited sense. He rides around on his three-wheeler, sometimes dressed as a police officer, and commands the others to "Respect my authoritah!" whenever he can. Only in this sense do I find him a useful role model.

2. George F. Clarke, *Someone Before Us: Our Maritime Indians.* Fredericton, NB: Brunswick Press, 1968

3. For example, in our catalog you can browse GREAT BRITAIN—HISTORY and get chronological information of the type:

Great Britain History 1307–1327, Edward II — See Great Britain History Edward II, 1307–1327
Great Britain History 1327–1377, Edward III — See Great Britain History Edward III, 1327–1377
Great Britain History 1377–1399, Richard II — See Great Britain History Richard II, 1377–1399
Great Britain History 1399–1413, Henry IV — See Great Britain History Henry IV, 1399–1413
Great Britain History 1399–1461, House of Lancaster — See Great Britain History House of Lancaster, 1399–1461
Great Britain History 1399–1485, Lancaster and York — See Great Britain History Lancaster and York, 1399–1485
Great Britain History 1413–1422, Henry V — See Great Britain History Henry V, 1413–1422

This is much better than the usual, LC authorized sequence of

Great Britain History Richard II 1377 1399
Great Britain History Richard III 1483 1485
Great Britain History Roman Period 55 B.C.–A.D. 449
Great Britain History Stephen 1135 1154

4. Recently approved headings include: GLASS CEILING (EMPLOYMENT DISCRIMINATION), NIGHT CYCLING, NATURALNESS (ENVIRONMENTAL SCIENCES), NUTRIENT TRADING, INCA ICE MAIDEN (ICE MUMMY), ADAPTIVE NATURAL RESOURCE MANAGEMENT, ADAPTIVE HARVEST MANAGEMENT, VERY LOW-CALORIE DIET, WET MEADOWS, ROPES COURSES, and NOBEL PRIZE WINNERS.

High-Speed Cataloging Without Sacrificing Subject Access or Authority Control: A Case Study

Carrie Preston

Numerous publications have addressed the topic of efficiency in cataloging (e.g., Mastraccio 2004; Fischer, Lugg and Boese 2004). Such publications recommend the use of workflow analysis techniques, as well as optimal use of technology, to increase the number of items cataloged without sacrificing important components of record quality. Often, these publications take a broad view, describing the reorganization of an entire cataloging or technical services department to increase efficiency.

This paper is intended to demonstrate the application of efficiency-increasing techniques on a much smaller scale: a specific cataloging project performed by a single cataloger within a cataloging department that was not, at that time, engaged in a systematic process of overall transformation. We hope the techniques utilized in cataloging National Bureau of Economic Research online working papers at Ohio University's Alden Library may be applied by other institutions who wish to refine the cataloging process, either in order to complete specific projects or to increase overall cataloging efficiency while stopping short of total organizational redesign. Limitations of these techniques and possible future developments will be addressed in the final section of this chapter.

Background

The Ohio University Libraries comprise Alden Library, the main library of the University's Athens, Ohio campus; the Music/Dance Library, Southeast Regional Depository, and other smaller establishments located on the Athens Campus; and libraries located on the university's five regional campuses (Ohio University Libraries 2005). As of this writing, the libraries hold over 2 million volumes. The Ohio University Libraries are a member of OhioLINK, a statewide consortium of academic libraries that provides access to a vast number of electronic journals, electronic books, and other online resources (Ohio-

LINK 2006). The Ohio University Libraries also acquire and provide access to a wide variety of online resources above and beyond those provided by the consortium.

As of this writing, Alden's Technical Services Department includes two cataloging-focused sub-departments, Monograph Cataloging and Serials & Non-Print Cataloging, as well as sub-departments devoted to library acquisitions and physical processing of materials. The two cataloging sub-departments together employ four professional catalogers and five paraprofessionals who perform at least some cataloging work (in addition to other duties). These staff members catalog materials in all formats acquired by Alden Library, including online formats. At the time when the project described in this paper was initiated, only one professional cataloger (myself) and no paraprofessionals were engaged in the cataloging of online resources on any significant scale. Alden Library catalogs materials in MARC format, utilizing OCLC cataloging software and contributing bibliographic records to OCLC's WorldCat database, and applying Library of Congress classification and subject headings.

The Problem

Since 1992, Alden Library had received print copies of working papers published by the National Bureau of Economic Research (NBER) in Cambridge, Massachusetts. However, Alden had ceased to receive print copies of working papers issued after February 2001. Thereafter, the library had access to the new working papers via the NBER web site (National Bureau of Economic Research 2006), but papers published after February 2001 were not represented in the library catalog. Public service staff were concerned that patrons be able to find and utilize these publications, which tend to provide quick dissemination of research relevant to a wide variety of academic subjects. In autumn 2004, a reference librarian approached me with the request that an individual catalog record be created for each of the online working papers.

The task appeared quite daunting on initial examination. Since Alden Library had ceased to receive print copies, NBER had posted over 2,000 additional working papers to its web site. Some had been cataloged as electronic reproductions by other OCLC member libraries, and therefore had bibliographic records available in OCLC's database for immediate download, but many of the most recent papers had not yet been so treated. Furthermore, NBER continued to add working papers on a weekly basis, averaging 22 new papers per week in 2005. When the request to catalog the NBER working papers was made, I was responsible for the vast majority of electronic resources cataloging at Ohio University Libraries, as well as being primarily responsible for the cataloging of print serials and periodicals, audiovisual materials, and microforms. Clearly, if I was going to catalog each new NBER working paper shortly after its date of issue and still fulfill my other job duties, I was going to have to maximize the efficiency with which I performed the task.

Ultimately, my approach to the problem involved three major components:

1. The use of technology, principally OCLC's Connexion Client cataloging software and OCLC Macro Language programming;

2. Strategic streamlining of the MARC record; and
3. Workflow analysis and (self)-management practices that increased efficiency, while allowing me to focus on the most intellectually challenging, value-adding aspects of the cataloging process.

Building the Streamlined MARC Record

OCLC's Connexion cataloging software can be programmed using a sophisticated macro language, allowing the software to perform such tasks as creating a new MARC record and adding various fields to it without the intervention of the human cataloger (OCLC 2003). Using OhioLINK's standards for cataloging electronic resources (OhioLINK 2004) as a starting point, I examined the various components of the MARC record for an NBER working paper. I found that these components could be divided into three categories:

1. Those that the software can provide without human intervention. These include any component of the description that is identical for all NBER working papers. For example, all NBER working papers are PDF documents requiring the use of Adobe Acrobat Reader; the software can be instructed to automatically endow each MARC record with a note field containing this information.
2. Those that require human input, but not on a particularly high intellectual level. For example, it takes relatively little skill to determine the sequence of Roman and Arabic numerals used to number the pages of each working paper, but the cataloging software available to me could not determine this pagination information on its own.
3. Those that require human input on a high intellectual level, such as the application of authority-controlled subject headings and name entries.

Category 1 and 2 components make poor use of professional catalogers' education and experience, and therefore of their time and effort. Computers can handle many of these components as well as, if not better than, catalogers (a computer is guaranteed to type simple descriptive fields in the same manner every time, with no chance of typographical errors and no need for proofreading). However, the computer programs available to the average cataloger today are not able to perform the complex intellectual tasks of category 3. Therefore, my goal was to spend as large a percentage of my effort as possible on category 3 components.

First, I created a macro (a programmed script) for the OCLC Connexion Client cataloging software, which automatically created a skeletal MARC record and inserted all category 1 components. Then, category 2 components were carefully evaluated, their usefulness weighed against the amount of cataloger time and effort required to include them in the MARC record.

1. Where possible, category 2 components were simplified in order to shift them to category 1. For example, a physical description statement (MARC field 300) with detailed information about pagination and illustrations was replaced by the simple,

universal statement "1 v." Since all or nearly all NBER working papers seem to have bibliographical references, a note (MARC field 504) stating that such references are present was included in the record, but the page numbers on which the references appear (which require human intervention to determine) were omitted.

2. In other cases, category 2 components were simply eliminated. For example, coding of the Illustrations fixed field, which is specified as optional in OCLC's Bibliographic Formats and Standards document (OCLC 2003), was eschewed in order to eliminate the need to visually scan each working paper for illustrations.

Ultimately, the aspects of each working paper requiring human attention were reduced to its issue number, title, authors, and subject matter. The issue number is a component of each paper's uniform resource locator (MARC field 856), as well of its series title (MARC field 440/490/830). Cataloger effort devoted to the issue number was minimized by having the cataloger enter it into a text box at the beginning of record creation, after which the software automatically inserts it into the relevant MARC fields. This left only the title statement (MARC field 245), authority-controlled author names (MARC field 100/700), and authority-controlled subject headings (MARC field 6xx) to require the cataloger's personal attention. See Figure 1 for a summary of the MARC fields ultimately included in the bibliographic record for an NBER working paper, and Figure 2 for an example of such a record.

Figure 1. MARC fields in the streamlined bibliographic record for National Bureau of Economic Research working papers

Handled by Cataloger
- Title and statement of responsibility (MARC field 245)
- Author's names, authority controlled (100/700)
- Subject headings, authority controlled (6xx)

Handled by Software
- Required fixed fields (008 and 006)
- Basic codes for physical characteristics (007)
- Series call number (090)
- Publication details (260)
- Basic physical description (300: "1 v.")
- Series title (490/830)
- Basic bibliographical references note (504)
- Electronic reproduction note (533)
- Basic technical notes (538)
- Corporate author (710)
- URL (856)

Eliminated from Record
- Optional fixed fields (e.g., Cont, Ills)
- Detailed physical description (300)
- Pagination of bibliography (504)
- Detailed technical notes (e.g., file size)

Members of cataloging email lists have recently had lively discussions about the usefulness or necessity of various components of the traditional MARC record, such as the pagination of whole books and of their bibliographies (see, for example, the discussions regarding "MARC simplification" and related topics on the AUTOCAT email list, AUTOCAT 2006). In eliminating physical description details and similar information from the MARC records for NBER working papers, I am not claiming that this information has no value. Rather, I work under the assumption that, if limits on available cataloger time

Figure 2. Bibliographic record for a National Bureau of Economic Research working paper published in 2006. Only the italicized portions vary for each bibliographic record

Type: a	ELvl: K	Srce: d	Audn	Ctrl	Lang: eng
BLvl: m	Form: s	Conf: 0	Biog	MRec	Ctry: mau
	Cont: b	GPub	LitF: 0	Indx: 0	
Desc: a	Ills	Fest: 0	DtSt: s	Dates: 2006,	
006		m　　d			
007		c $b r $d u $e n			
090		H11 $b .N2434x no.*(paper number)*			
100	1	*(First Author's Name)*			
245	1	x	*(Title)* $h [electronic resource] / $c *(statement of responsibility).*		
260		Cambridge, Mass.: $b National Bureau of Economic Research, $c 2006.			
300		1 v.			
490	1	NBER working paper series ; $v no. *(paper number)*			
504		Includes bibliographical references.			
533		Electronic book. $b Cambridge, Mass. : $c National Bureau of Economic Research. $n Mode of access: World Wide Web; may require Adobe Acrobat Reader.			
6xx		0	*(Library of Congress Subject Headings)*		
700	1	*(Second Author's Name)*			
700	1	*(Third Author's Name)*			
710	2	National Bureau of Economic Research.			
830	0	Working paper series (National Bureau of Economic Research) ; $v no. *(paper number)*			
856	4	$u http://papers.nber.org/papers/*(paper number)*			

and effort make it necessary to eliminate *something,* eliminating descriptive details that are not required for retrieval does the least amount of harm to the smallest number of patrons. This is especially true in the case of online resources, where details like the pagination of the bibliography are literally a click away.

Focusing Cataloger Effort

The next challenge was to empower the cataloger to perform category 3 tasks in as efficient a manner as possible. Informal "time and motion study" observation of my own and other catalogers' work revealed much room for improvement in this area. Many catalogers I had worked with had a tendency to take unnecessary actions, such as using the mouse or arrow keys to move the cursor to the "correct" line in the MARC record before typing a new field, even when that field would be automatically put in its place by the cataloging software upon completion of the record.

These behaviors may have been especially characteristic of Alden Library's catalogers, who at that time had not yet made systematic efforts to learn about and exploit the advanced features of OCLC's cataloging software. However, such behaviors may also be characteristic of catalogers in general, who are drawn to the work — and excel at it — due to their highly detail-oriented personalities. Furthermore, catalogers whose careers predate the advent of modern cataloging software may simply be in the habit of performing actions that once required human attention, but can now be automated. The challenge was to harness catalogers' tendencies in a way that allowed them to concentrate on the tasks most worthy of their skills and talents. Therefore, I sought a way to focus the cataloger's attention (and keystrokes, mouse movements, etc.) in a way that would maximize efficiency (and presumably minimize carpal tunnel syndrome).

Ultimately, the instructions given to a cataloger first learning to catalog NBER working papers become something along the lines of:

1. Press the keyboard shortcut for the NBER record-building macro.
2. Enter the paper number in the text box, then allow the macro to build the record.
3. Type the title and statement of responsibility in the empty 245 field provided by the macro.
4. Press the enter key and add a 100 field containing the first author's name. Control the author's name using F11 [the OCLC keyboard command that searches for a heading in the authority file and allows the cataloger to view the resulting authority records, confirming a match if one is available].
5. If necessary, press enter again and add 700 field(s) containing the second and third author's names. Control the names using F11.
6. Press enter again, then add 6xx fields containing subject headings, controlling them using F11 or Shift-F11 [a command used to confirm the presence of multiple headings in the authority file at one time].
7. Proofread field 245 *only*, then update the record [the command that officially adds it to OCLC's database] and export it into the library's catalog.

The training includes specific emphasis on performing only the necessary actions. For example, the trainee would be specifically instructed *not* to move the cursor around in order to insert fields into a specific part of the bibliographic record screen, when the cataloging software was perfectly capable of assuring the correct placement of such fields on its own.

At first glance, these instructions may seem unduly restrictive, treating catalogers like robots forced to perform a set sequence of actions. However, keep in mind that the goal is to allow the cataloger to spend the maximum amount of time and effort on the most intellectually challenging, least robotic aspects of the job: authority work and subject analysis.

I have had the opportunity to train one other cataloger in this specific procedure for NBER working papers, as well as to train other library staff in similar procedures developed for other cataloging projects. Naturally, catalogers unfamiliar with the use of these sorts of computer programs can be skeptical about their utility, or feel the need to confirm that the computer really does things right each time it builds a record. When training catalogers to follow a procedure of this sort, it is vital to emphasize the goal of minimizing the drudgery in the cataloger's job while maximizing the interest and satisfaction derived from tasks like subject analysis. In my experience, catalogers who give streamlined cataloging procedures an honest chance soon come to see the value of the approach, especially when it appears as a light at the end of a seemingly hopeless backlog tunnel.

Limitations and Future Directions

In devising my scheme for cataloging the NBER working papers, I worked within various limitations, including the following:

1. My library's online catalog was designed to handle traditional MARC records, not other types of metadata. Furthermore, my library's cataloging department had a strong tradition of creating MARC records using OCLC's cataloging software, rather than using other formats or utilities.
2. I was proficient in cataloging and in the use of OCLC cataloging software, including some simple programming of the latter. However, I was not trained in the sort of computer programming that would allow me to do sophisticated maneuvers in which, for example, data is shared between the cataloging software and other programs.
3. My library's culture currently emphasizes including as many resources as possible in the library catalog (rather than, for example, creating different databases to store metadata about different types of resources, or depending on outside mechanisms such as web search engines).

Because of these limitations, I did not really consider trying to "catalog" the working papers in a format other than MARC, or creating a computer program to transform whatever metadata was embedded into the PDF document into MARC. Nor did I attempt to persuade the public service librarian who brought the papers to my attention that the working papers did not need to be included in the library catalog, since patrons could find the working papers by using the search engine on NBER's web site or a general search engine such as Google. In the terms used by business writers such as Hammer and Champy (2005), I did not "reengineer" the process of providing access to the NBER working papers, but merely increased the efficiency of the existing process without altering its fundamental nature. Though I successfully created a procedure for the quick production of traditional MARC records using familiar cataloging software, thinking outside of these particular boxes might have led to an even more effective solution.

A simple innovation, offering little challenge to traditional notions of cataloging, might be a computer program that reads each working paper's title and author names from its web page and pastes them into a correctly cased and punctuated 245 field in the MARC record, so that catalogers would be spared yet another less-than-intellectually-challenging aspect of record creation. At the other end of the spectrum might be software that could not only assemble a descriptive record but supply some form of subject analysis as well (maybe in the form of authority-controlled headings, maybe not). A computer program that can reliably apply Library of Congress Subject Headings without human assistance may be far in the future, but simple metadata harvesting mechanisms are possible now, and it behooves catalogers to learn the technological skills necessary to create and utilize such mechanisms.

Another type of innovative thinking might question Alden Library's (and probably many other libraries') belief that all resources of value should be made discoverable via the library catalog, rather than relying on patron discovery through freely available search engines or other mechanisms. Since some research suggests that college students are more likely to start their information searches with search engines than with the library catalog (e.g., OCLC 2005), a reexamination of Alden Library's catalog-centric philosophy might lead to the dismissal of the entire idea of cataloging NBER working papers. The time currently devoted to cataloging the NBER working papers might be spent providing access to other materials, such as unique, uncataloged physical materials held by Alden Library, which currently cannot be discovered via either the library catalog or Google.

Such fundamental changes in cataloging practice — or, more broadly defined, the process of creating metadata to describe and provide access to information resources — may well take place in the not-too-distant future. However, the many entrenched and interconnecting standards and systems currently utilized by catalogers make such change slow to happen, while many libraries are faced with the need to increase cataloging efficiency immediately. Ultimately, I hope the process described in this paper might serve as an example of how catalogers can improve efficiency within their current systems, while preparing for greater change in the future.

References

AUTOCAT. (2006). Search the AUTOCAT archives. Available: <http://listserv.buffalo.edu/cgi-bin/wa?S1=autocat>.

Fischer, Ruth, Rick Lugg, and Kent C. Boese. (2004). Cataloging: how to take a business approach. *Bottom Line* 17 (2) :50–54.

Hammer, Michael, and James Champy. (2005). *Reengineering the Corporation: A Manifesto for Business Revolution.* New York: HarperCollins.

Mastraccio, Mary L. (2004). "Quality cataloging with less: alternative and innovative methods." In *Innovative Redesign and Reorganization of Library Technical Services,* edited by Bradford Lee Eden, 79–118. Westport, CT: Libraries Unlimited.

National Bureau of Economic Research. (2006). NBER working papers. Available: <http://papers.nber.org/>.

OCLC. (2003). Basics: use macros. Available: <http://www.oclc.org/support/documentation/connexion/client/basics/macros/>.

OCLC. 2005. *College Students' Perceptions of Libraries and Information Resources: A Report to the OCLC Membership.* Dublin, OH: OCLC.

OhioLINK. (2004). Standards for cataloging electronic resources. Available: <http://platinum.ohiolink.edu/dms/ercatstandards.htm>.

OhioLINK. (2006). About OhioLINK. Available: <http://www.ohiolink.edu/about/>.

Ohio University Libraries. (2005). Just the facts. Available: <http://www.library.ohiou.edu/info/facts.html>.

Monographic Collections Structure and Layout Revisions: Or, How to Tweak LC Call Numbers for the Good of Your Users

Brian R. Thompson

How many different types of gardens are there? A lot, according to the Library of Congress Classification Schedules.

A garden can be notable (SB465 — 466), it can be formal (SB461), and it can be botanical (QK71—73). It can be Japanese (SB458) or Victorian (SB458.7), a rock garden (SB459) or a community garden (SB457.3). Arboretums (QK479 — 480) are a type of garden. Parks and reserves (SB481— 485) frequently include gardens.

I wrestle with these call number options — and many others — on a daily basis in my role as Curator of Horticultural Literature at the Elisabeth C. Miller Library of the University of Washington Botanic Gardens (UWBG) in Seattle. As the largest horticultural library in the Pacific Northwest, we hold a collection of 15,000 books. It spans very few LC classes and subclasses, requiring close attention to details particularly of SB (Plant Culture) and QK (Botany).

But these are more than just cataloging questions. As the Internet provides more knowledge sources, and our users' expectations for greater service and easier access grows, I believe these decisions are essential to how the library will thrive, or even survive in an increasingly competitive environment for information resources and services.

Elisabeth C. Miller Library

The Miller Library is a university library, yet unlike most campus libraries it is independent of the University of Washington Libraries system. This has disadvantages — there is no central support for many operations and services — but also advantages. Chief amongst these is the ability to respond to immediate needs without the often time-consuming process of review by a larger bureaucracy.

Instead, the immediate administrative environment of the Miller Library is the

UWBG, a recently formed body that creates an umbrella over several institutions and their related operations, including

- a major arboretum
- a restored wetland and shoreline
- display gardens
- an herbarium
- research greenhouses
- outreach and education programs
- meeting space for local plant societies

These facilities and programs are used by University of Washington students and faculty, but also other colleges and high schools, horticultural professionals, the general gardening public, and anyone who enjoys visiting the 320 acres for strolling the gardens, viewing the birds, or attending private events in the rental spaces.

Miller Library in the Bigger Picture

The Miller Library was created by a donation to the University from Pendleton and Elisabeth Carey Miller, a keen gardener and plant and book collector, in the early 1980s. The Millers had an innovative vision of creating a library that not only served its host academic community but also the needs of avid and beginning home gardeners, and the many professionals in horticulture and related fields in the area, including training programs at local community colleges and high schools.

The Miller Library was successful in balancing these three major constituents until 2001 when an arson fire destroyed Merrill Hall, the home of the library. Fortunately the majority of collections were saved or restored, but the library was closed for seven months, and after that operated out of a limited, interim space with the majority of collections in storage, and very little work space for library patrons.

The positive side of this disaster was the ability to start with new space. The library staff was closely involved with the architects in designing a new home that promoted and supported a diverse community of users and that would accommodate many nontraditional uses of a library. The result was the showpiece of Merrill Hall, when it reopened in early 2005.

However, in the four years of restricted space and accessibility to collections, much had changed in the outer world. The Internet had become the major research tool for students, researchers, teachers, professionals and even for many technophobes amongst home gardeners. A library that thrived on in-person usage needed to create incentive for those users to return.

Two significant staff changes occurred in 2005, too. David J. Mabberley was hired as the director of the yet-to-be-named UWBG, with a mandate to create a cohesive entity that promoted cross-support between the various units. Foremost of his energies was for the organization to develop a sense of its "Pacific Northwestness," to celebrate and promote the plants and ecological communities of our region.

A few months later, Karen Preuss was hired as the new Library Manager. Fresh from many years in public libraries, she brought considerable knowledge and experience in making a library vibrant to a diverse audience and at promoting the public use of library collections.

The Problems — and the Solution

When the dust had settled from the move and the new management was in place, a period of assessment and brainstorming followed. From informal surveys of library users, input based on the experience of the long-term staff, and new ideas from Mabberley and Preuss, three major areas of change were determined:

1. Develop a Pacific Northwest focus for the library's collections. This not only would promote "Pacific Northwestness," it would also support the master plan of the Washington Park Arboretum, the largest single unit in UWBG. This plan calls for the creation of Pacific Connections, a series of gardens that will display plant communities from temperate regions of the Pacific Rim including the Pacific Northwest.
2. Make a significant majority of the Miller Library collection available for circulation. Miller was established as a strictly non-lending library, but this policy had gradually eased so that by early 2005 a small section of second copies, about 10 percent of the collection, was set aside in a special lending collection. To truly serve the public, it was determined that closer to 90 percent of post–1950 titles needed to have at least one circulating copy.
3. Make it easier for library patrons to find things. Users seem less willing to make extensive searches in the on-line catalog, preferring instead to find one or two relevant books and then browse the adjacent shelves. Analysis determined that for most subjects useful books could be found in at least six different places, and in some cases more. Patrons were missing many titles of interest unless given extensive help by library reference staff.

The solution — really many solutions in one — led to a whirlwind of activity that involved closing the library for two days and moving every one of the some 15,000 books in the publicly accessible collection. All this less took place than a year after moving those same books into the new building.

The Run–Around

Previously the Miller Library had three main collection divisions:

- A reference collection of key titles for ready reference never left the facility, about 10 percent of the total.
- A separate Lending Collection, another 10 percent, was shelved along one wall. It included mostly second copies and was available to circulate to the general public after a simple and free registration procedure.

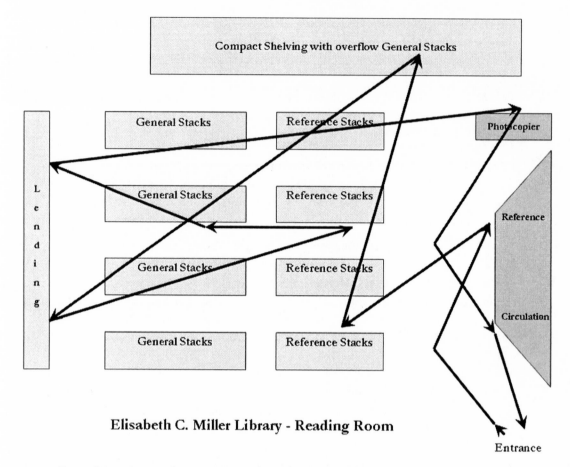

Elisabeth C. Miller Library - Reading Room

- Everything else was kept in General Stacks, a generally noncirculating collection located in central tall stacks, with some spillover into mobile compact shelving. These books were available for checkout by the immediate staff, faculty and students of the UWBG.

The distinction between botanical and horticultural books, as dictated by the Library of Congress classifications (LCC), created further divisions, as will be discussed below in "The Great Divide."

To illustrate the problem, let us imagine a patron's search for books on, say, maples. Beginning at the reference desk, this search could look something like this:

1. Reference stacks: a book on maples throughout the world
2. General stacks (in compact shelving): a book on the maples of Europe
3. Lending collection: to check out a book on maples of the United States
4. Reference stacks: to learn what maples are good for growing in northwest gardens
5. General stacks: to learn how to grow a sugar maple
6. Lending collection: to check out a book cultivating Japanese maples
7. Photocopier: to copy information from books you can't check out
8. Reference desk: to check out the books you can
9. The door: to get out as quickly as possible!

To begin solving this problem, we looked to a model developed by many bookstores that offer both used and new books. Recognizing their customers' priorities, these stores shelve first by subject. Used and new books are interfiled. The distinction is not that significant to the buyer. More important is finding everything available on the subject of interest.

Similarly, we observed that library patrons were not concerned with the staff's distinctions between the Reference, Lending or General collections. As with book buyers, finding everything on the subject of interest was of most importance. Only when this goal was achieved was the question of circulation raised.

This parallel between bookstore shoppers and library patrons led to the — aha! — realization that our library could adapt the bookstore model. Shelve everything first by subject, then choose some distinctive labeling to indicate if a book is available to circulate or is for library use only. Reference and Lending as separate collections could become things of the past.

This initially caused some concern amongst the library's reference staff, but after discussions and analysis of what books were used most extensively for reference, a small ready-reference collection of some 50 books was established at the reference desk, separate from the public access collection. Easing concerns, too, was the relatively small size of the overall collection and stacks, as no reference work would be located very far away.

The Great Divide, or, How to Make Library of Congress User-Friendly

As befits our academic setting, the Miller Library has used LCC only since its opening in 1985. With my oversight of cataloging, LCC schedules have been a constant in my ten years with the library. Early on I became quite frustrated with the hair-splitting decisions required for books that were a good subject fit for two or even more places. When providing reference help — a necessity for all staff in a small library — the run-around illustrated above only aggravated my cataloging frustrations. I've long been motivated to make some changes to fit our specific needs.

Discussions with friends who are full-time catalogers in academic settings eased my fears of "challenging" the LCC system. Being mindful of the necessity of maintaining consistency and clear documentation, I began making very minor changes. But I'd been itching to do much more and was very glad of having the administrative backing to do so!

As a plant science library, we also deal with the hierarchy of plant taxonomy. Comparing the two systems is instructive. The LCC hierarchy is finely diced, and if viewed from a taxonomic perspective, was clearly built by splitters, not lumpers. This approach, while logical within a large hierarchy, breaks down at the user level. Our informal analysis of current patron research techniques — or the lack of them, as discussed above — showed it consists primarily of finding the shelf of interest and browsing in the immediate vicinity. Even if the catalog is used for the initial identification of relevant works, browsing is still key for locating additional sources. There is an expectation that everything will be in one place.

For instance, a garden enthusiast planning a vacation to the Northeast won't likely recognize the following distinctions:

LCC	Subject	Example
QK71–73:	Botanical Gardens	New York Botanical Garden
QK479–480:	Arboretums	Arnold Arboretum
SB465–466:	Notable Gardens	Longwood Gardens
SB481:	Parks and Reserves	Central Park

Thus she will miss several books that would enhance the trip.

But the biggest divide in a small collection like ours is between botany (QK) and horticulture (SB).

Maples of the World	*Maples for Gardens*
By	By
D.M. van Gelderen	C.J. van Gelderen
P.C. de Jong	D.M. van Gelderen
H.J. Oterdoom	
QK495.A17	**SB413.M365**

Two books on a common subject, with one common author. The first reviews maple species from around the world. The second discusses the use of those same species in garden settings. Why should they be in two very different places in the library collection?

These are examples of a frequent dilemma facing the cataloger, especially with books about a single plant genus. Very few titles, especially amongst more recent publications, are exclusively about the botany or the horticulture of a plant. This is often true for the interests of the library patron, too.

The solution? Bring these disparate call numbers but similar subjects together in one place. But first an overall structure needed to be created.

The New Structure

A careful review of the classification schedules for QK (Botany) and SB (Plant Culture), and even QH (Natural History/Biology — General) finds many examples of parallel construction. For example:

- Natural History biography: QH26 (collective) and QH31 (individual)
- Botany biography: QK26 (collective) and QK31 (individual)
- Plant Culture biography: SB61 (collective) and SB63 (individual)

Within subclasses there is often repetition. Biology biographies are considered distinct from natural history and are found at QH429–429.2, while biographies of key figures working with Ornamental Plants are listed at SB404.8 and Landscape Architects' biographies from SB469.9–470.

These parallels can be found over broader ranges, too. QH101–198 and QK101–474.5 both delineate geographical distribution of general organisms (QH) and plant floras (QK) in much the same order, starting with North America, working through the regions and states, before systematically working around the world.

Finally, there is the example of QK495 and SB413, illustrated above. Throughout QK and SB there is much repetition from the perspectives of botany, agriculture, general horticulture, ornamental horticulture, gardening and gardening design.

While these levels of distinction are valuable for some purposes, the collective observations by the Miller staff showed that, at least for the patrons who use our library, this structure causes more confusion and obfuscation than help. If a researcher is interested in gardens, the distinction between formal or botanical, or a designation of arboretum or park, is in most cases unimportant.

Compiling this feedback and based on my own reference experiences, I set out to create a linear flow of call numbers that emphasized broader subject themes and less repetition. In designing this flow, there were several considerations:

- Trying to anticipate the needs of the majority of our end-users in finding all relevant resources
- Batching subjects horizontally, rather than according to a vertical hierarchy. This approach bridges the parallel, vertical constructions illustrated at the beginning of this section. Biographies, for example, are kept together, ignoring the minor professional distinctions between those noteworthy individuals working in Plant Culture, with Ornamental Plants, or even in Landscape Architecture
- Allowing some subject areas to be less specifically defined in order to allow other, closely related subjects to be interfiled. These subsumed areas typically have a small representation in the literature, or had distinctions that were determined insignificant to our users
- Eliminating orphan books — one or two books alone at a class number — and unused numbers in the schedules, folding the associated topics into broader subject areas
- Creating new call numbers from gaps unused by LCC if necessary to batch similar subjects
- Minimizing the number of changes that would be necessary within the existing collection

Is It QK495 or SB413?

The special case of QK495 and SB413 provides a good illustration of this process. QK495 lists over 300 first Cutter numbers that distinguish different families of angiosperms (flowering plants) in alphabetical order. For example, QK495.A17 is the Aceraceae or Maple family, while QK495.A67 is the Aquifoliaceae or Holly family. A similar, although much shorter, list of families are scheduled for the Gymnosperms (cone-bearing plants) at QK494.5.

The horticultural schedules are quite different. SB413 has its own A–Z list, but the first Cutter in this case designates the common name of plants, so that SB413.M365 designates maples, while SB413.H7 is for hollies.

The major problem with this system is the lack of consistency in the use of common plant names. Books about that favorite spring flower called daffodil by some, narcissus by others, and jonquil by yet others are all found at SB413.D12. In contrast, maple books can be found at SB413.M365, unless they're about Japanese maples. Those books are at SB413.J34.

This is further complicated by the special treatment given to orchids and roses. Probably because of popularity and the large number of books written about these two subjects, each has its own class: SB409 for orchids, SB411 for roses.

As Miller is principally a horticultural library, I decided that SB was the most appropriate place for all our books on a single plant, including those written from a strictly or primarily botanical perspective. This also would minimize the changes to this important group of books (some 5 percent of our collections). However I decided to use the organization by plant family found traditionally in QK495 as more logical than the common-name approach found in SB413. The results look like this:

> **SB409:** Remains as the designation for orchids with additional breakdown according to traditional schedules.
> **SB410:** A new designation for monocots (most flowering bulbs and grasses and including orchids, hence this position next to orchids), divided by families from A–Z. For example, *Narcissus* (the botanical name for narcissus, daffodils and jonquils) as a member of the amaryllis family can be found at SB410.A486, near its close relative the amaryllis (SB410.A481). SB410.9 and above, traditionally included with roses, is not used.
> **SB411:** Remains as the designation for roses with additional breakdown according to traditional schedules. SB411.9 and above is used for other members of the rose family (for example, plums at SB411.9.P78).
> **SB412:** A new designation for all dicots (the remaining flowering plants), divided by families from A–Z. All maples, including Japanese maples, are found at SB412.A17; all hollies at SB412.A67.
> **SB413:** To prevent confusion with other libraries, this designation was voided.
> **SB414:** A new designation for all gymnosperms (conifers), divided by families from A–Z. For examples, pines, formerly found at either QK494.5.P66 or SB413.P54, are now together at SB414.P666. The extra "6" distinguishes pines from other, closely related members of the pine family, including hemlocks and firs. (Note: SB414 is traditionally assigned to Forcing of Flowers, but these were lumped with SB127, Forcing as part of Plant Culture).

This was the most complicated section to revise, however similar principles were applied throughout the collection. Over 2,000 books, nearly 15 percent of the collection, were eventually given new call numbers. A complete list of the changes is included as an appendix to this chapter.

Pacific Northwest Connections

Foremost in all these changes was the creation of the Pacific Northwest Connections (PNWC) collection, a name chosen to emphasize both the library's support of the Pacific Connections gardens in the Washington Park Arboretum and the library's focus on regional authors writing about regional gardening, horticulture, floras or ecosystems. The PNWC collection immediately was seen as the new focal point of the library, to be housed in low stacks that previously held the reference collection, and prominent to visitors as they first enter.

Defining the collection was straightforward. Geographically, it would include the states of Washington, Oregon, Idaho, and Alaska, plus British Columbia and the Yukon Territory in Canada. After some discussion it was decided to include California, too, as particularly the northern part of the state shares a significant amount of the flora and horticultural concerns of our region.

The "connections" correspond to the proposed gardens in Pacific Connections: Chile, New Zealand, Australia, China, plus other key Pacific Rim floras and gardening traditions, such as those in Japan and Korea. In response to input from local horticultural experts, the floras and gardens of the northern Mediterranean and southern Africa were also identified as having extra significance for our region, and so books on these were also included in PNWC.

One key decision, which took considerable time and process to conclude, was the branding of these books to identify them as part of PNWC. Several mock-ups were tried and reviewed by staff and volunteers; input from the latter was critical because they are responsible for shelving and getting the books back to the right place. Rejected models included printed (with PNWC) spine labels; and adhesive colored dots attached to the call number label or elsewhere on the book spine.

A simple green stripe made with a 4mil polyester transparent label protector (1¼" × 3⅛") on the book spine, with no additional labeling, was decided as the most effective and reasonable way to identify a PNWC book. Previously, red stripes were chosen to identify a book as circulating.

Our patrons (and volunteers who shelve) now have a simple color pattern to remember:

> No stripes — General Collection, doesn't circulate
> Green stripe — PNWC Collection, doesn't circulate
> Red stripe — General Collection, circulates
> Red and green stripe — PNWC Collection, circulates

Making It Happen, or, How I Spent My Thanksgiving Vacation

When we began applying these administrative and theoretical issues to the books on the shelves, the scope of the project began to reveal itself:

- Identify and extract the PNWC books from three existing collections, a total of 1,900 books
- Interfile the PNWC books into a single A–Z run and label each with a green stripe
- Merge the remaining books from the three collections into a single A–Z run of General Stacks, leaving gaps for changes in the LC call numbers
- Update the individual catalog location record for 1,400 of the PNWC books (the others could be changed globally)
- Update the individual catalog location record for 750 of the General Stacks books
- Change the call number for over 2,000 books — both on the physical spine and in the catalog record — to reflect changes in LC

- Move these more than 2,000 books to their new locations, filling the reserved gaps but creating new ones where they previously were
- Tighten the collection to eliminate all remaining gaps

Ultimately, all 15,000 books in the public collection were moved at least once to a new physical location, with many moved twice or even three times.

The extraction and the interfiling of the PNWC collection, and the merging of the remaining books into the General Stacks, were accomplished while the library was closed on November 22–23, 2005, the two days before Thanksgiving. A dozen utility-size book carts were rented. The full staff plus several skilled volunteers put on jeans and worked very hard. By 6:00 on Thanksgiving Eve, the job was done.

To make the best use of time, the merging of the General Stacks was done from both the front and the back. Thank goodness, the two runs matched when they met, in the middle of the Bonsai books. The story of the first transcontinental railroad was our inspiration.

The remaining projects were completed as the daily tasks of running the library permitted, but dominated the technical staff's time through the spring. By April 2006, the "Extreme Makeover" of the Miller Library was complete.

Conclusions

Is it working? The anecdotal answer is a resounding Yes! Feedback from library users from all three constituencies (academic, professional, public) has been very positive. Comments have included:

- "You have twice as many iris books as I thought you had."
- "My previous research on maples missed several key resources."
- "This [PNWC] collection contains all the books recommended by [local horticultural expert] Dan Hinkley — that's great!"
- "This layout really makes a lot more sense." (Miller Library staff member)

Another measure is the response during general library tours and research methods classes. I have taught these for nearly 10 years and I find the new layout makes it much easier to orient first-time users, while the reduction of call number fragmentation allows me to introduce broad scopes of the collection without having to explain a lot of exceptions.

Library staff and long-time users have had the expected transition period of not finding titles at the old familiar call number or shelf. While learning new call numbers takes practice, the impact of searching for new physical locations was lessened by the short period of time in the new building. Perhaps the best measure of acceptance has been the sustained energy and dedication that the library staff — particularly the technicians and paraprofessionals — has given to making the conversions.

In May 2006, Karen Preuss and I presented all these changes as part of a panel for the Council on Botanical and Horticultural Libraries annual meeting in Los Angeles. The response was enthusiastic, with the revisions to LCC particularly resonating with this audience. The keen interest in all the details — I had prepared only a summary — was especially surprising. Clearly, I had not been alone in my frustrations with the status quo.

While all this is heartening, we are only now measuring and evaluating actual library usage, a process hampered by the lack of clear baseline because of the chaotic nature of library operations since 2001. Another factor curtailing statistics has been our manual circulation system. We plan to automate by the end of 2007, but actual use patterns won't become clear until after that new system has been up and running for a period of time.

At this point we can say only that these changes have provided a focus of interest for our library that has been sustained beyond the expected excitement over the completion of a new building. We are clearly saying to our users that we put their interests first and these changes are for their benefit. This attitude, if nothing else, continues to help build our community and provide incentive for the use and support of the Miller Library.

Appendix

Summary of Changes
Elisabeth C. Miller Library, University of Washington Botanic Gardens
November 2005–April 2006

Subjects	LCC	Former LCC	# Books
General Reference			
Atlases, Dictionaries, Directories, etc.	A–P		
General Science	Q		
Meteorology; Climatology	QC 981–995		
Geology/Physical Geography	QE 1–500		
Conservation, Ecology, Restoration			
Environmental sciences — general	QH 73*	TD 146–893.6	15
Conservation — general	QH 75–77		
Conservation — plants, plant communities	QH 75–77	QK 86–86.4	30
Invasive, noxious plants (not garden weeds)	QH 79*	SB 610–614.3	20
Ecology — general	QH 540–541		
Ecology — plants, plant communities	QH 540–541	QK 900–911	15
Habitat/Landscape Ecology	QH 541.15.L35		
Restoration Ecology	QH 541.15.R45		
Urban Ecology	QH 541.5.C6		
Wetland Ecology, Restoration, Management	QH 541.5.M3		
Botany			
Nomenclature, Terminology, Name Indexes	QK 9–13		
Classification	QK 9–13		
Nomenclature for Cultivated Plants	QK 13.1*	SB45.5	5
Systematics/Taxonomy — Principles/Methods	QK 14*	QK 91–97	15
Systematics/Taxonomy — Plant Families	QK 14.1*	QK 91–97, QK495.A1	25
Botanical, Biological Literature, Writing	QK 14.5–14.6*		
Botanical, Biological History	QK 21		
Biographies — Plant Collectors, Botanists	QK 26–31		
Biographies — Naturalists	QK 26–31	QH 26–31	10
Botany General Works	QK 41–47		
Botany Popular Works	QK 50		

Herbaria	QK 75–77		
Botanical Illustration	QK 98–98.3		
Plant and Landscape Photography	QK 98.35*	TR 1–1050	25
Useful Plants, Economic Botany	QK 98.4.A1	SB 107–108	10
Edible Plants, Food Plants, Agricultural Crops	QK 98.5.A1	SB 170–197, SB 295	10
Ethnobotany	QK 98.6*	E 78–98, GN476.73	20
Weaver Plants, Dye & Resin Plants	QK 98.7	SB 241–289	5
Medical Botany, Herbals	QK 99		
Poisonous Plants	QK 100		
Floras — North America	QK 108–144		
Floras — By state	QK 145–195		
Floras — North America, by state	QK 108–195	QH 102–181	55
Floras — The rest of the Americas	QK 201–275		
Floras — all others	QK 281–474.5		
Plant Anatomy	QK 640–707		
Plant Physiology	QK 710–899		
Plant Evolution, Genetics	QK 980–987		

Zoology

Insects, arthropods (Popular Works)	QL 434–599		
Birds (Popular Works, In Gardens)	QL 671–699		

Horticultural Basics

Horticultural Therapy	RM 735		
Permaculture	S 494.5.P47		
Soils	S 590–599		
Irrigation	S 619		
Fertilizers, Soil Improvements	S 631–667		
Horticultural Bibliography, Literature Guides	SB 14.5–15		
Horticultural Congresses	SB 16		
Horticultural Directories	SB 44		
Horticultural Encyclopedias, Dictionaries	SB 45		
Gardening Encyclopedias, Dictionaries	SB 45	SB 450.95	30
Plant & Seed Sources	SB 45.2*/ 45.3Xx*	SB 115, SB 118.486–8, SB 450.94	30
Horticultural Practices, Principles	SB 46	SB 51, 317–318	25
Horticultural Careers	SB 50		
Growing from seeds	SB 117–118.4		
Nursery Mngt.	SB 118.5	SB 319.4	5
Floriculture, Greenhouse Mngt.	SB 118.8*	SB 415 (some)	30
Propagation	SB 119–124		
Pruning	SB 125		
Forcing	SB 127		
Growth Regulators	SB 128		

Food Plants

Vegetables	SB 320–349		
Greens, Salad Greens	SB 339	SB 351.S25	5
Peppers	SB 344*	SB 351.P4	5
Tomatoes	SB 349		
Herbs	SB 351.H5		
Mushrooms	SB 352.85–353.5	QK 603–617	25
Fruit and fruit culture	SB 354–401		

Ornamental Plants — Monographs

Orchids	SB 409		
Monocots (arranged by family)	SB 410*	QK 495, SB 413	207
Roses, Rosaceae	SB 411, SB 411.9*	QK 495, SB 413	20

Dicots (arranged by family)	SB 412*	QK 495, SB 413	606
Conifers (arranged by family)	SB 414*	QK 494.5, SB 413	40
Specialized Growing Settings			
Home Greenhouses, Conservatories	SB 415		
Garden Rooms, Conservatories	SB 416		
Light Gardens	SB 416.5*	SB 126	10
Hydroponics	SB 416.7*	SB 126.5	10
Terraniums, Glass Cases, Cloches	SB 417		
Container Gardening	SB 418		
Indoor & Conservatory Plants	SB 419		
Roof Gardening, Green Roofs	SB 419.5		
Ornamental Plants — Groups			
Alpine and Rock Garden Plants	SB 421		
Rock Gardens	SB 421	SB 459	30
Annuals, Aquatic Plants, Bulbs	SB 422–425		
Carnivorous Plants	SB 425.5	SB 432.7, QK917	10
Climbing Plants, Vines	SB 427		
Ericaceous Plants	SB 427.9*	QK 495.E68, SB 413.E7	5
Ferns (horticulture)	SB 429–430*		
Ferns (botany)	SB 429–430*	QK 520–532	35
Foliage, Variegated Plants	SB 431–431.2		
Bamboo (horticulture)	SB 431.6*	SB 413.B2	20
Bamboo (botany)	SB 431.6*	QK 495.G74	15
Grasses, Ornamental Grass (horticulture)	SB 431.7		
Grasses, Ornamental Grass (botany)	SB 431.7	QK 495.G74	15
Groundcovers	SB 432		
Lawns and turf	SB 433–433.34		
Mosses, Lichens & Liverworts	SB 433.55	QK 532.5–589	30
Perennials	SB 434		
Trees & Shrubs (horticulture)	SB 435		
Trees & Shrubs (botany)	SB 435	QK 475–477, QK 481–488	25
Conifers, Evergreens	SB 435.1*	SB 428, QK 494	40
Arboriculture, Tree Pruning, Street Trees	SB 435.76–437		
Succulents, Cacti	SB 438		
Native Plants	SB 439–439.35	SB454.3.N38 (some)	5
Plant Display, Garden History			
Flower Exhibition, Arranging, Display	SB 441–450.7		
Garden & Garden Plants History	SB 451–451.36		
History of Horticulture	SB 451–451.36		
Ornamentals — History	SB 451.4/.42*	SB 404.5–404.6	10
Garden Culture, Selection			
Ornamentals — Selection	SB 452*/452.2*	SB 407	120
Plants for Problem Places	SB 452.4*	SB 408	
Garden Culture (general & by regions)	SB 453–453.3		
Organic Gardening	SB 453.5–453.6		
Special Topics & Types of Gardens			
Bonsai, Miniature Plant Gardening	SB 454.3.B6*	SB 433.5	90
Borders	SB 454.3.B7*	SB 424	15
Color in Gardening	SB 454.3.C64		
Cottage Gardening	SB 454.3.C68		
Cutting Gardens	SB 454.3.C8	SB 405	
Dry Gardens, Drought tolerant plants	SB 454.3.D7	SB 439.8	25
Exotic Gardens, Tropical, Semi-tropical plants	SB 454.3.E96		

Gardening Calendars	SB 454.3.F6		
Fragrant Gardens	SB 454.3.F7	SB 301	3
Mediterranean Gardening	SB 454.3.M43		
Natural Gardens, Wild Gardens	SB 454.3.N38	SB 439 (some)	5
Gardens — Spiritual Aspects, Sanctuary	SB 454.3.P45		
Shade Plants	SB 454.3.S4	SB 434.7	20
Woodland Gardens	SB 454.3.S4	SB 439.6	5
Small Gardens	SB 454.3.S53		
Gardening on Different Soil Types	SB 454.3.S65		
City Gardens	SB 454.3.U7		
Gardening and Weather	SB 454.3.W43		
Gardening with Wildlife	SB 454.3.W5		
Winter Gardens	SB 454.3.W6	SB 439.5	25
Gardening Tools	SB 454.8		
Literature, Lore			
Gardening Literature	SB 455		
Gardening Essays	SB 455	SB 455.3	10
Garden Ecology Literature	SB 455.4*	QH541.5.G37	5
Natural History Literature	SB 455.5*	QH 81	5
Plant Lore	SB 456*	QK 83	45
Plants of the Bible	SB 456.2*	QK 84	5
National Plants, Official Plants	SB 456.4*	QK 85	5
Garden Design, Construction			
Cultural Garden Styles (Japanese, etc.)	SB 457–458.7		
Policies, Practices for Arboreta, Botanic Gardens, Public Gardens, Parks, etc.	SB 464*	QK 71–73, 480, etc.	
Notable Gardens — General	SB 465		
Notable Gardens — Specific	SB 466		
Arboreta	SB 466	QK 480	20
Botanical Gardens	SB 466	QK 71–73	60
Parks	SB 466	SB 482	5
University of Washington Gardens	SB 466.5	Various	24
Biographies — Gardeners, Horticulturists	SB 469.9–470	SB 61–63	30
Biographies — Architects, Designers	SB 469.9–470		
Landscape Architecture	SB 470.5–472		
Home Landscaping, Design	SB 473		
Landscape Materials, Structures	SB 473.4–475.9		
Garden Problems, Solutions			
Pests, Diseases, Weeds; ID	SB 599–618, 950–985		
Plant Pathology	SB 621–795		
Pests, Diseases, Weeds; Control	SB 950–985		
	*New LCC	**Total:**	**2070**

Cataloging Heresy

A. Arro Smith

Cataloging is hard. It takes practice. It is like learning a whole new counter-intuitive language. The punctuation alone is enough to scare some library school students to the reference desk — and they never, ever venture into the technical services department again. After the horror of their mandatory "organization of materials" class, some even become children's librarians!

And then some of us love it. We revel in the secret handshake of the MARC fraternity. We pledge for life. We enjoy the power that comes from being able to create the perfect surrogate record. We relish our mastery over the arcane rules that bring order to the confusion and chaos of unprocessed acquisitions. Some of us never want to step outside the cloisters of our technical services department. It is safe, and we are in control — bibliographic control.

However, the cloister is not the real world. And although we have mastered a Byzantine world of rules in order to exercise bibliographic control, we should not let ourselves become its slaves.

Two Main Problems

Traditional catalogers often suffer from two main disabilities. The first is a lack of perspective. Huddled in the back rooms of their libraries, they rarely have much contact with the public who use their bibliographic surrogates. They falsely believe that they are entrusted with a noble quest to bring order to the uncataloged by rigorously applying the traditions and rules of the cataloging profession. But the truly noble quest is to serve the users of the library: to find out whom a library serves and how they search for materials to solve their information needs. No two libraries will serve the same population of users, so no two libraries' catalogs should be identical. In order to create metadata that library patrons will find useful, catalogers must know their users. They must spend time assisting patrons find their desired materials — at the reference desk, out in the stacks, or even by hovering around the OPACs and just being available to answer questions. To be a good cataloger, you must also be a good reference librarian.

Blind faith in the rules and traditions of our profession is the second disability many catalogers suffer from. Respect for and encyclopedic knowledge of AACR2, MARC, DDC, LC and LCSH are required to create bibliographic order from the chaos of life; and, as stated above, cataloging is difficult. But we need to use the tools of the trade to create bibliographic records for the patrons we serve. We need to consider the "rules" as guidelines. Most of us do not work at the Library of Congress: we work for the people who live in our own communities and use the public library, attend our schools and universities as students, or we might be cataloging materials for our coworkers at a special library. We must know the principles and rules that dictate each DLC and member record imported into our catalog; but we also must be courageous — and smart enough — to know when to modify these records so that *our* patrons will be able to find what they need in our collections.

Cataloging for Patrons

Each library's catalog is for its own patrons. With the exception of union catalogs, the Library of Congress, and large academic libraries or research libraries, the raison d'être for our catalogs is to assist non-professionals in finding information in our collections. The catalog is not created for catalogers, but for library patrons. With this in mind, catalogers should tailor their work to their specific users.

A well-developed collection generally reflects the sophistication of its users. A collection for a high school library will be more sophisticated than that of a middle school media lab. A public library may be designed to serve its community of school-age patrons and life-long learners; but its collection will not be as sophisticated as a university library supporting the research of its colleges and departments. A library's catalog should reflect the appropriate level of sophistication.

This is a personal story, so the author begs your pardon to allow him to use the first person.

I used to be an adherent of the orthodox notion that there was only one way to catalog a book: the right way. If a DLC record could not be found for a new accession, I worked hard to create a record that would pass muster at any research institution. I prayed that one day my humble, mid-sized public library would even contribute my records to OCLC, to be immortalized in cataloging heaven.

But my cataloging aspirations were tempered by my patrons' inability to understand the bibliographic surrogates they encountered in our OPAC. I discovered this when taking shifts at the reference desk. Instead of simply using my staff terminal to find requested material, I often walk the inquiring patron to a public OPAC station and demonstrate how to conduct a search. At first I took extraordinary pleasure in introducing unsuspecting patrons to the joys of subject tracings. But often these sophisticated DLC and contributed records only produced confusion in my public library patrons. There was just too much information: information that might very well be useful in a research library where the collection holds several linear feet of materials on a subject and the different subject subheadings guide the user to the exact title they need. But in my mid-sized public library, we might have only a handful of individual titles on a subject. All of the over-lapping subject tracings just add confusion. Here is an example from a single book on heart attacks:

MYOCARDIAL INFARCTION—PREVENTION
MYOCARDIAL INFARCTION—PSYCHOLOGICAL ASPECTS
MYOCARDIAL INFARCTION—RISK FACTORS
MYOCARDIAL INFARCTION—UNITED STATES—PATIENTS—BIOGRAPHY

When confronted with a list of subheadings in the results of a subject search such as this, my patrons often assume that each of these represent a separate title. They duti-fully record the call number for each of the records these subject headings point to — not realizing that they all point to the *same* title. For my mid-sized public library, a single subject heading, MYOCARDIAL INFARCTION, would serve the patron much better than the list presented here; but only if the "see" reference is properly coded from HEART ATTACK.

I spent years cataloging with a first-generation ILS (which will go unnamed) that provided "see" references only in the authority records for the main subject headings. The authority records for the subject headings with subheadings did not include the "see" ref-erences. So if a new accession came with a DLC record that included the list of MYOCAR-DIAL INFARCTION subject headings with subheadings listed above — but without the plain MYOCARDIAL INFARCTION general subject heading — there was never a "see" generated from HEART ATTACK. So only my patrons with advanced medical degrees were well served by the catalog in this instance.

This example illustrates two concepts that offer solutions to the problems of tradi-tional cataloging: parsimony and perspective.

Parsimony

My idea of parsimony in cataloging comes from the tradition of Occam's razor. It is also commonly known as the K.I.S.S. principle: "Keep it simple, stupid." The fourteenth century philosopher proposed using economy in logic. I advocate extending this concept to the catalog, as well.

When cataloging a new accession, the cataloger should be mindful of both the intel-lectual content of the item in hand and the contents of the collection it is joining. If the new item is the only work on that subject, then only use the most general subject head-ing — with no subheadings. If the new item is joining a small collection of similar items, consider whether the intended reader will appreciate multiple subheading listings to dis-tinguish the various titles, or whether the patron will favor a simple list of all of the var-ious takes on the subject returned in a single list. I use a "two-screens" rule when making a decision on the amount of parsimony to practice when editing subject headings: if the titles for a certain subject extends past two screens on the patron's OPAC, I begin to employ subheadings to distinguish the titles. Otherwise, I believe my patrons enjoy the ability to click once on a single subject without subheadings and view all of the available works.

Of course, I do not hesitate to make exceptions. If I believe my patrons would appreciate the subtlety that the subject subheadings included in a DLC record provide, I leave them in. My patrons are especially interested in material about Texas, so I always leave this geographic subheading. However, almost my entire collection deals with the United States, so I always edit out this geographic subheading. Likewise, the entirety of my nonfiction collection would be considered "popular works," so this subheading always gets nixed.

Keeping a minimum of relevant subject heading also makes authority control more efficient, especially when checking for accurate "see" references. And this leads to the second concept, perspective.

Perspective

A perfect ILS may exist, but my experience with two vendors has shown me that each system has its strengths — and its weaknesses. And in monitoring the comments on a popular cataloging email list, I have never found a cataloger who does not have at least a few complaints about his ILS vendor.

In both of the systems in which I have cataloged extensively, it is often not apparent from the cataloger's desk just what the patron will see at the OPAC. Simply because you have included MARC fields in a record does not necessarily mean they are going to be indexed and displayed for your patrons' use. So I encourage catalogers to use the patron interface of their systems as often as possible in order to include the user's perspective as part of your cataloging routine.

For years I scrupulously added "see" references to the series authorities in my first-generation ILS database, and they worked fine when I searched for them in the cataloging module. But one day I was assisting a young patron desiring books in the *American Girl* series. I had carefully cataloged each permutation of the *American Girl* books: *Molly, Samantha, Kit, History Mysteries*, etc. Yet none of them were showing up in the OPAC. Even though the "see" references were constructed according to MARC authority specifications, they were producing an error in the series index, and none of *American Girl* titles were being displayed.

My lesson: check the OPAC to make sure my cataloging intentions are benefiting the patrons. Sometimes a "work-around" needs to be invented. In this case each *American Girl* book required two series entries, one for the main series and another for the sub-series. Other issues might require an adjustment in the indexing protocols for the ILS. And occasionally the vendor needs to recode the software in the next upgrade. But if the cataloger is not using the public interface, these problems might never be discovered.

Most modern systems have updates and "fixes" to download every few months. It has been my experience that with every "fix" at least one unintended consequence follows. An example: Our ILS vendor had specified in its RFP response that its title indexing architecture would "skip" initial articles (such as *the, a* and *an*) if patrons entered them in a search. The RFP also included examples of common foreign language initial articles. Once installed, it became evident that Spanish and French language initial articles were not being "skipped" accurately. The vendor addressed this problem in a software upgrade.

But in a later upgrade, all of the initial article "skipping" disappeared. The following upgrade restored only the English language initial article indexing. It took repeated prodding to finally get all of initial article indexing architecture restored in yet another upgrade. Again, use your patron interface to monitor "upgrades."

The next sections include some best practices that I have developed to serve my patrons. Each addresses a specific problem that my patrons had accessing the collection of my library. They may or may not be appropriate for your particular library. They are not for the conservative or the orthodox.

Cataloging Heresy

My public library patrons read a great deal of series fiction. As sequels become trilogies, and then tetralogies, hexologies, ad nauseam, my patrons have a difficult time figuring out what to read next. Granted, often the series order will be prominently displayed near the title page of the book in question; but that is of little use when all of the books are checked out. Bibliographies of sequels are also updated annually, but most patrons would rather go to the dentist than find and use a bibliography. And then there is the series record in the OPAC. In my current ILS, the series tracing is displayed in the item's bibliographic record along with its number. However, when a series name is searched, it first returns a list of titles in alphabetical order without the series number. These can be sorted by publication date, but these dates often are misleading if both paperback and hardcover editions have been acquired within the series. To see where in the series a particular title falls, one must click on each individual title and locate the series tracing. This is not difficult, but it is time-consuming when a patron is looking for the sixth title in a particular series and does not know the name of the individual title. For example, "I need the sixth *Left Behind* book." There are (as of this writing) thirteen in that series. One would have to go through each title in the series until stumbling on the tracing for the sixth. (It is *Assassins*.) Helping a patron with this quest is part of good reader's-advisory work. But assisting the tenth or twentieth patron to find the next *Left Behind* book makes me apocalyptic.

To solve this problem, I have added a uniform title to each work in the series, with a subfield for the number (MARC 240 10 $a Left behind. $p #1). Now all of the *Left Behind* books are listed with their sequel numbers in the first title search display on the OPAC (e.g., Left behind. #1; Left behind. #2; etc.) My reference librarians and circulation clerks love this innovation. This is in addition to the orthodox series tracings. Ideally the series search would reveal the sequel numbers on the first screen, but my vendor does not provide this functionality.

Another similar example of the series fiction problem is with the *Harry Potter* books. This is a de facto series that does not have an official series title (and don't even get me started on the whole LC series authority abdication). Fortunately all of the books begin with the same two words: *Harry Potter*. Now each bibliographic record includes sequel information in the notes field; but again, finding the third in the series requires examining the notes field in each bibliographic record until the correct one is found.

To solve this problem, I altered the title entry (MARC 245) with the series information in brackets after the title. Our patron can scan the title list and locate *Harry Potter and the Prisoner of Azkaban [#3]* without hunting through each of the full bibliographic records for the note, "sequel to *Harry Potter and the Chamber of Secrets.*"

The act of weeding our collection has also taught me some valuable lessons about cataloging. Each year we print out a report of items that have not circulated well to be considered for de-accession. Sometimes there are surprises: books on a popular topic that were well-reviewed have simply sat on the shelf and collected dust. One specific category of books that had not circulated well in my library was handbooks and commentaries on popular fiction. For example, two books relating to the Harry Potter series: *The Science of Harry Potter: How Magic Really Works*, and *The Wisdom of Harry Potter: What Our Favorite Hero Teaches Us About Moral Choices*. With Harry Potter as the subject, you would think they would be a hit; however, neither title had circulated well.

Both of these books had full MARC records, including the subject heading POTTER, HARRY (FICTITIOUS CHARACTER). But the audience for these two books is not the library patron using the OPAC to look up the subject POTTER, HARRY. These readers do not even know nonfiction books *about* Harry Potter exist. To solve this problem, I added a uniform title entry to each record (MARC 240 10 $a Harry Potter). Now when patrons do a title search on Harry Potter, the first listing points them to two books *about* Harry Potter that they probably did not even know existed. And these titles now enjoy robust circulation. This is the very essence of what a cataloger should strive to do: make information accessible for their patrons, even information the patron did not know existed.

Classification Heresy

My experience is with a public library, so I am only addressing Dewey Decimal Classification issues here. And let me state for the record that I love the elegance and simplicity of DDC, but sometimes it is not intuitive for the user. And sometimes things can get lost in the depths of the nonfiction collection.

Let us return to the previous example involving the Harry Potter handbooks and commentaries. Many popular fiction authors have been honored with monographs that discuss their work. Again, if the books receive a good review, you think they will be a popular addition to your collection. But if the only access to these works is through the subject index, they might never be found because it may not occur to fiction readers to perform a *subject* search in the catalog to find information *about* their favorite authors.

In many public libraries, fiction is classified, not within the DDC scheme, but by the last name of the author. This makes for a very user-friendly browsing experience — if the books are properly shelved and the titles are in alphabetical order within author ranges. Many fiction readers consult the catalog only when they cannot first find their desired item on the shelf, and then they only execute a title or author search.

Nonfiction books *about* fiction are shelved in the Dewey 800s. Generally the only people executing subject searches for authors are students researching works from the

Western canon. (The only people actually browsing the 800s without the aid of the OPAC are retired English professors.)

During a weeding project, I found that a number of titles that should have enjoyed at least some popularity due to their subject matter — popular fiction authors — were languishing in the 800s. To find *The Tony Hillerman Companion*, the patron would have to execute a subject search on HILLERMAN, TONY—CRITICISM AND INTERPRETATION; and this reader would have to be savvy enough to know that such a thing might even exist.

To solve this problem, I manipulated the classification. In a bold move that drove many of my old-school shelving pages crazy, I reclassified works of popular fiction criticism so that they are shelved with the fiction they discuss. The spine label for books by Tony Hillerman has an *F* for fiction, and then the first six letters of the last name (F HILLER). For *The Tony Hillerman Companion: A Comprehensive Guide to His Life and Work*, edited by Martin Greenberg, I added a third line with the letter *Y* and the first letter of the author or editor's last name (F HILLER YG). This is a convention used in many Dewey libraries to denote literary criticism in the DDC 800s; but I have adapted it for the general fiction classed by author. (Why the *Y*? I think it is one of the ancient mysteries of library science.) So the popular criticism is now shelved with the fiction, and it falls at the end of that author's works. On the shelf after all of Patrick O'Brian's novels of nineteenth century life on the open seas rests *A Sea of Words: A Lexicon and Companion for Patrick O'Brian's Seafaring Tales*. And now it actually circulates.

I did this only to the "popular" fiction criticism. The "real" literary criticism is still in the 800s. When deciding where to classify a "handbook" or "companion," I consider the probable reader. Here are some of the authors whose criticism was reclassified: P. D. James, Stephen King, Tom Clancy, and Frank Herbert. Scholars and researchers will continue to find their books in the 800s, accessed through the OPAC. Popular readers can also access their materials through the OPAC, but now they can also discover commentaries about their favorite authors by serendipity.

Both students and adults often ask for poetry books at the reference desk. They usually do not have anything specific in mind: they just want to browse through some anthologies. The standard reference interview fails when we begin describing where the anthologies for American poetry are kept (811.008), and English poetry (821.008), or poetry from Spain, France, etc. The patron just wants to look through some poetry books, and they really do not care what country the poem is from as long as they can read it in English.

Poetry is a discrete collection that begged to be reclassified in order to make it user-friendly. Here I disregarded standard DDC practice to create a scheme that would bring all of the anthologies together. I reclassified all of the general poetry anthologies to one call number: 808.81 (which is traditionally reserved for collections from more than one non–English literature). I also reclassified a few specialized poetry anthologies that are often requested (and these are nonstandard numbers that I have adapted), as well as anthologies of other literature forms. Here is an outline of my broad categories:

808.81: General poetry anthologies
808.819287: Women's poetry anthologies
808.819354: Love poetry anthologies
808.819896: African-American and Black (Jamaican, African, etc.) poetry anthologies

808.81938: Religious poetry anthologies
808.82: Drama anthologies
808.83: Fiction anthologies (criticism)
808.84: Essay anthologies
808.85: Speeches
808.86: Letters
808.87: Humor anthologies

My patrons enjoy the "one-stop shopping" aspect of this scheme, and my reference librarians love the simplification. Even in a mid-sized public library, this aggregation of all the poetry anthologies makes for a very browsable collection.

The dog breed section of Dewey Decimal Classification was intuitive to neither our patrons nor our librarians. DDC assigns different call numbers to "non-sporting dogs," "working and herding dogs," "sporting dogs," and "toy dogs." My patrons did not care to decipher which category their miniature poodle belonged in while browsing for a book. (The miniature poodle officially belongs with the "non-sporting" dogs, not with the "toy" varieties.) So I uniformly classed all of the dog breeds into one number and then Cuttered each book by the common name for the breed. Now my shelves devoted to dog breeds look very similar to those in a bookstore, and my reference librarians are able to impress exasperated patrons looking for a book on their new charmingly destructive bull terrier puppy by rattling off "636.72 BUL" without even consulting the catalog.

Test preparation books presented a similar problem. General tests were grouped in the 370s, but specialized ones were classified within their subject: ASVAB was with military science, MCAT and LVN were with the medical books, postal exams were postal. It was my experience that patrons desiring these materials did not particularly want to browse for other books on the subject, and that the reference librarians had a hard time remembering where each specific test prep book was shelved. To add to the confusion, negotiating the catalog for these materials was always dubious because of the many permutations of the test preparation guides (Barron's, Kaplan, Princeton Review, etc.) and the fact that there were so many records with an "overdue-billed" status. Even if the catalog showed an ASVAB on the shelf, it was often missing (and presumed stolen).

My solution was to reclassify all of the test preparation books into a single arbitrarily chosen call number for standardized tests (378.1664) and Cutter them by the popular name of the test: ACT, AP, ASVAB, CLEP, etc. When a patron asks for a particular test prep book, we walk them over to one section of the stacks and see what we can find, just like a bookstore. In addition, I add a third line to the spine label noting the year of publication. This makes weeding old editions much more efficient. Both patrons and reference librarians love it.

Conclusion

Cataloging and classification is for library patrons. It is not for the cataloger. When standard cataloging practices do not return the most efficient results for your patrons, innovate and become a cataloging heretic. The only people who will know that you have deviated from standard practice are other catalogers — and how often are our catalogs audited by other catalogers? And who really cares what other catalogers think? If orthodox cataloging and classification does not make sense for your collection and your patrons, change it!

Some caveats: If your library is part of a consortium, consider the effects of your nonstandard practices on your partners. You may need to contribute a traditional record to the union catalog and OCLC, and then modify the record only displayed in your OPAC.

Document all of your nonstandard cataloging practices in a policy manual. None of us are going to live forever, and we do not want our legacies to be tarnished when the new cataloger spends her first six months on the job muttering "What the...?" Note each MARC, AACR2, DDC, LC, and LCSH policy deviation. Include notes about why each heresy works for your library collection. Print out a hard copy and put it in a binder that is clearly labeled. Make sure your staff knows where this binder is kept, and instruct them to find it in case you are hit by a bus or flee the country unexpectedly.

Finally, remember the cataloger strives to create order out of chaos. A large part of order comes from consistency and predictability. If orthodox cataloging and classification fail to bring order to your collection — order that your patrons can understand and use — innovate! It is your job to make your collection work. Take risks and experiment; but apply your innovations consistently throughout the collection.

Talkin' the Cataloging Blues:
The Poetry of Albert Huffstickler

Sylvia Manning

"So the big boss called me in,
favored me with his friendliest grin,
says, 'Another year has come and gone.
Now what did you say your name was, Son?'"
from *Talkin' PCL Blues No. 5* by A. Nonymous

For the seventeen years Albert Huffstickler worked in the cataloging division of the General Libraries, University of Texas at Austin, located in the Perry-Casteneda Library (the big one), random rants with comic rhyme came across his fellow employees' workstations from time to time. One of his retirement gifts from Auto-Cat would be a "Special Limited Edition" collection of these irregular, informal in-house publications, gathered from dozens of desk drawers. He hadn't been A. Nonymous at all.

"I always felt good when I got one of his PCL poems," says Margi Bienemenn. "And I always admired that he had the courage to speak up when something bothered him about the politics of the library."

For example, in *Talkin' PCL Blues No. 11*, Huff treats the politics of motivating workers to work harder, addressing supervisors:

...I have taken my own personal poll and you have my word
that most of the people in this building are not here for their health;
they could do without the companionship, the fraternity of kindred souls,
the entertaining conversation.
It may come as a surprise to some of you but there are people in this very building
who prefer massage parlors to libraries....
And they aren't making enough money and you want them to do more.
Doesn't that make you a little paranoid?

On the recurrent subject of a livable wage, from *No. 12*:

Well, I don't want to be the one to gripe
but my clerk typists are too weak to type.

"Malnutrition," one told me.
"Can't lift a finger." ...

All of which is just to say
here's a friendly reminder coming your way,
you all up there at the top,
that we're still here down at the bottom....

The problem isn't going away
and neither am I,   Nonymous, A.

Paulette Delahoussaye, retiring now from a long-held professional position with UT General Libraries, says she got out her *Talkin' PCL Blues* just last week. "Many job-related issues still apply." Asked if she thought it a good idea for libraries to hire poets, she replies, "Shouldn't turn 'em away, that's for sure."

Huffstickler got his library work done: he was given charge of Marking and Plating. One of his two assistants, Steve Bush, responded to Huff's death in 2002 exactly the way Huff had shown him to do. He wrote a poem. Here's a verse:

It's funny that I remember his backpack and shoes,
And his other creation: "Talkin' PCL Blues."
He'd write of job freezes and of merit pay
And would always sign it with "Nonymous, A."

Huffstickler thought we were each of us a poet — if we only knew, if we only looked up from the tedium, if we listened deeply. Margi remembers "the little poetry workshop out of his apartment that I attended for a while. He helped me hone my poetry into my own style."

Huff's basic instruction to all of us was to write a poem about anything on your mind. Write it any way you can, any way you like. Don't worry about whether it's good or bad poetry or poetry at all. Then write three more and send out the batch with a self-addressed stamped envelope, for publication in some little zine. Look in *The International Directory of Little Magazines and Small Presses, Dustbooks*, or look in the back pages of *Poets and Writers* magazine, or find an e-zine and save the stamps. Huff always had a list to share. He didn't submit online, but you can find some of his poetry on the Internet with just a name search.

We know Huff's job evaluations never mentioned A. Nonymous or *Talkin' PCL Blues* or his larger body of work, widely published. Fortunately, they're all preserved in his papers at Texas State University–San Marcos, in the Southwestern Writers Collection.

Also in these papers at the Southwestern Writers Collection is an essay published by *The Small Press Review*, 1988, entitled "The Poet's Sphere," in which he speaks directly to this idea of writing for those around you:

"I don't write just for journals or just for other poets: I write for this community and have come to learn just how it is that a poet functions within a community, how he can ritualize an event ... how his words can have a transforming effect on that person, that community's experience."

He mentions a poem for Darnell's losing her father, Mary Beth's having a baby, Linda's hospitalization, O.J.'s death, and "for Jim Kiecke recalling another time when the vision was strong in us both." He could have mentioned poems he wrote for coworkers just because he thought they needed one, like this one, for Loretta:

> Loretta
> I think you're a midnight river
> with lights along the shore
> playing over the water like silent music.
> Far above, the stars watch, giving nothing away.
> I think we've been on this planet for a long time
> and have forgotten where home is.
> But sometimes at night,
> watching the play of light on dark waters,
> we remember and grow still
> and everything we ever were
> comes back to us with a dark splendor
> like lights on the surface of a midnight river.

He could have mentioned his poems about the room itself:

> That room where we all banded against the uncertainty of the outside,
> each with his own fears that became part of the common fears,
> each with his own hopes that bound us in a common hope —
> a hope that time would pass us out of this room into a broader view
> or merely hold us here safe without too much change, too many disturbances.
> We were so vulnerable outside that room.
>
> (from "That Room")

In "The Legionnaires," he describes a dream in which the cataloging staff has become a foreign legion, though the catalogers lack the legionnaires' sense of escape through risk and have instead "That terrible sense of exile that hovered like a pall over our desks, cubicles." And yet,

> I miss it some days because, you see, there was something else going on,
> subtle, hard to define, a linking that carried us forward through our days.
> We took care of the sick ones, covered up for the lame and lazy, and
>   soldiered on.
> The face of the human condition is seldom glamorous.
> Glamor is ephemeral, evanescent.
> We were determined to last — though we weren't sure why — and did.
> We were plain, utilitarian, enduring and, in short, what it's all about:
> mankind or unkind stumbling along, the most foreign of God's legions,
> not certain where he's going but carrying on, serving out his time,
> here and here to stay.

"The job is not that great," he said in his essay. "What I do every day is pretty mundane and unexciting. And still, I wouldn't take anything for what I've learned from working and writing poetry in the library community.... I might never have come to believe what I believe now totally: that the artist (the poet) is not separate and different. He is a functional and necessary part of a community whether that community is as small as the library community at the University of Texas at Austin or as large as the world."

UT–Austin flew its flag at half-mast the day Huff died, though he'd retired ten years earlier. Steve Bush wrote his poem. Margi Bienemann, who had held on to her *Talkin' PCL Blues #1*, could have read aloud for the library community and for the whole world to hear,

> When I'm dead, don't bury me.
> Just shelve me in the library —
> under D for Dead or G for Gone
>   or you might just say
> I'm out on loan —
>   in the dead file,
> where the retrieval system
> can't retrieve me,
> believe me. Percented.
> RE-classified.

Key words, Dead and Gone. Here's another one, Abandonment, written three months after he left the job:

> Abandonment
> Key word.
> We're all abandoned.
> That's how we got here.
> Who abandoned us?
> We abandoned ourselves
> to the vicissitudes
> of mortality and individuation.
> Sylvia says
> there's no word in the English Language
> for birthing yourself.
> Well, that's because we've forgotten.
> Easier to deny responsibility
> when you've made a mess of things.
> No one wants to feel abandoned
> but there's no escape
> if you deny that you chose to come here.
> So here we sit
> with our hair in our eyes
> abandoned
> while above and beyond us
> the stars range
> infinite in number
> and each pursuing
> its chosen course.

About the Contributors

Tom Adamich has been a certified teacher-librarian since 2000 and a librarian since 1991. A graduate of the Kent State University (Ohio) School of Library/Information Science and KSU College of Education (school library media certification), Tom has been a teacher-librarian and consultant for the Indian Valley Local Schools (Ohio) since 1999 and president of the Visiting Librarian Service, a contract librarian firm he has operated on a full or part-time basis since 1993. Currently, Tom also serves as the head, Cataloging Department at Robert Morris University in Pittsburgh, Pennsylvania, and has been involved in K-12 cataloging research and its connection to critical thinking skill development and standards-based education since 1998.

Wendy Baia is head of Serials Cataloging at the University of Colorado at Boulder. She has specialized in serials cataloging at three U.S. academic libraries for more than 30 years. "Save the time of the user" is her favorite cataloging motto, and she's never regretted a decision that followed this principle.

Jeffrey Beall is a cataloger at Auraria Library, University of Colorado at Denver. His articles have appeared in *American Libraries*, *Library Journal*, *Library Hi Tech News*, *Cataloging & Classification Quarterly*, *Library Resources & Technical Services*, and many others. His current research and writing examines the strengths and weaknesses of keyword searching and metadata-enabled searching.

Joan M. Benedetti worked for five years as a librarian-cataloger at the Los Angeles County Museum of Art until she retired in 2002. Previously she was the museum librarian at the Craft and Folk Art Museum for 21 years. She has written extensively on solo librarianship, art museum librarianship, and folk art terminology.

Susannah Benedetti received her master of library and information studies degree from the University of Wisconsin–Madison. She is currently coordinator of Cataloging Services at William M. Randall Library at the University of North Carolina–Wilmington. She has published in *Library Resources & Technical Services*, *Technical Services Quarterly*, and *Collections: A Journal for Museum and Archives Professionals*.

Sanford Berman, former head cataloger at Hennepin County Library (Minnesota), is an honorary member of the American Library Association and contributing editor for *The U*N*A*B*A*S*H*E*D Librarian*.

Daniel CannCasciato has been contributing SACO headings since 1993 and watching *South Park* since the late 1990s. He's been a cataloger since 1991 and thinks it's a terrific profession to be involved with. Currently, he's head of Cataloging at the Central Washington University Brooks Library.

Dana M. Caudle received her master of library and information science degree from the University of Texas at Austin in 1990. She worked briefly at Texas A&M Galveston, NASA Johnson Space Center and NASA Lunar and Planetary Institute before becoming a cataloging librarian at Auburn University Libraries in 1992.

tatiana de la tierra is a writer and librarian whose research interests center on Latina lesbian cultural productions. She is director of Hispanic Services at Inglewood Public Library in California and can be reached at tatiana@delatierra.net.

Bradley Dilger (Ph.D., University of Florida, 2003) is an assistant professor of English at Western Illinois University. His research focuses on the role ease (making it easy) plays in cultural constructions of technology in American society, but he also works extensively with new media, network theory, and web accessibility.

Chris Dodge was formerly a cataloger at Hennepin County Library in Minnesota and librarian at *Utne Reader* magazine. He now writes, edits, and indexes on a freelance basis in rural Montana.

Ann Doyle is the branch librarian (and was, for some years, the only librarian) at the First Nations House of Learning Xwi7xwa Library, which has recently become part of the University of British Columbia Library. She served as chair of the Canadian Library Association Native Peoples Interest Group (2003–2005), and is an active member of the BC Library Association First Nations Interest Group (1992–present). Due to a startling failure in judgment in 2004 she began a doctoral degree and is now writing her comprehensive exams. The working title of her is research is "Naming and Reclaiming Indigenous Knowledge: Towards Principles of Knowledge Organization for Sovereignty." She is grateful to be part of the circle of Indigenous librarians and their allies.

Emily Drabinski is a reference and instruction librarian at Sarah Lawrence College. Her research and practical interests focus on critical pedagogy as it relates to library instruction. She lives in Brooklyn, New York.

Michelle Emanuel is a cataloger at the University of Mississippi, working with videos and foreign language materials. She is also the bibliographer for Modern Languages, and is responsible for material selection and bibliographic instruction for that subject area. Since 2005, she has been a co-director of the Oxford Film Festival.

Frank Exner, Little Bear is a Squamish Indian originally from British Columbia, Canada. He has a master of information science degree and master of library science degree from North Carolina Central University's School of Library and Information Sciences. He also has a doctoral degree (DPhil [information science]) from South Africa's University of Pretoria Department of Information Science. His thesis is named *The Impact of Naming Practices among North American Indians on Name Authority Control.*

Robin Fay is a database librarian, a metadata freelance agent, web editor, artist, and a wearer of many hats. She occasionally blogs about various library issues at <http://robin-news.blogspot.com/> and dreams of the day when she will have a housecleaning robot.

Jenna Freedman developed the zine collection at Barnard College in New York City, about which she speaks and writes fairly often. She founded a zine librarians' discussion list (<http://groups.yahoo.com/group/zinelibrarians>) that also meets unofficially at ALA. Her hobbies include creating and contributing to zines and participating in Radical Reference (<http://www.radicalreference.info>).

Tina Gross is a librarian, activist and poet originally from Minnesota. Her favorite authority record is the one for Edward Gorey.

Brian Hasenstab is assistant technical services librarian at Regis University. He is a Wanda Coleman fan.

Matt Johnson received his MLS from Queens College (CUNY) and has published on a variety of topics in queer studies. A former museum library cataloger and information retrieval thesaurus consultant, he currently works as a taxonomy analyst at a web search engine and volunteers with the Leather Archives & Museum.

Thomas Mann, Ph.D., a member of AFSCME 2910, is the author of *The Oxford Guide to Library Research*, third edition (Oxford University Press, 2005) and *Library Research Models* (Oxford University Press, 1993).

Sylvia Manning worked as NEA cataloger at University of Texas–Austin with a workstation near Huffstickler's Marking and Plating, where she'd worked while in school. His close friend since 1967, Sylvia received Huffstickler's papers in 2002 to prepare for the Southwestern Writers Collection at Texas State University, San Marcos, and for the Center for American History at UT Austin. A poet and playwright, Sylvia also has a home book repair service, Save the Book.

Tracy Nectoux lives in Champaign, Illinois, and has recently completed her MLIS from the Graduate School of Library and Information Science at the University of Illinois at Urbana-Champaign. She is a member of ALA, SRRT, GLBTRT, and the Progressive Librarians Guild. She is not a member of any cults, unless the ALA counts as such.

Carrie Preston is the head of Serials and Non-Print Cataloging at Ohio University Libraries. She is a graduate of the University of Michigan School of Information.

Carol Reid is a cataloger at the New York State Library in Albany. She has written extensively on the subject of censorship and is former editor of the NYLA Intellectual Freedom Roundtable newsletter, *Pressure Point*, and ALA's *SRRT Newsletter*. Her "library limericks" can be found in the 2006 book *Library Juice Concentrate*.

K. R. Roberto is the co-editor, with Jessamyn West, of *Revolting Librarians Redux: Radical Librarians Speak Out* (McFarland, 2003) and is currently the serials/electronic resources librarian at the University of Denver.

John Sandstrom is an academic cataloger who got hijacked into public library collection development about 20 years ago. His past also includes brief interludes of working for various vendors and even being a consultant. He is currently at El Paso Public Library (El Paso, TX) as the manager of Collection Development and Acquisitions and acting manager of Cataloging and Processing.

Cecilia M. Schmitz received her master of library science from the University of Arizona in 1986. She worked at Texas A&M University before taking her current position as a cataloging librarian at Auburn University Libraries in 1988.

A. Arro Smith is the Technical Services manager for the San Marcos Public Library and a doctoral student at the University of Texas at Austin School of Information. Most recently he appears as "Mr. June" in the Men of TLA calendar, a fundraiser for the Texas Library Association's Disaster Relief Fund. His email is arro@ischool.utexas.edu.

Michael Summers was awarded the MA (distinction) in library and information studies by University College London in 2005. His dissertation was called *Pop Music in British Libraries*. He now works in the library of the Royal Academy of Music, London; before that he was on the editorial staff of the *New Grove Dictionary of Music and Musicians*, second edition.

Jennifer Erica Sweda practices the dark art of social sciences cataloging at a major Ivy League university library. She received her MS, LIS from the University of Illinois at Urbana–Champaign and her MLA from the University of Pennsylvania. In her spare time, she acts as an academic writing tutor, freelance editor, jewelry designer and (bad) potter. She continues to work toward unclenching — which, for a cataloger, is no small feat.

Brian R. Thompson is curator of horticultural literature at the Elisabeth C. Miller Library of the University of Washington Botanic Gardens in Seattle. He has an MLS from the University of Washington and a BA in mathematics and astronomy from Whitman College in Walla Walla, Washington.

William Thompson is a reference librarian at Western Illinois University.

Beth Thornton spends her workweek overanalyzing serial bibliographic and holdings problems at the University of Georgia, where she is head of Serials Cataloging.

Christopher H. Walker is the serials cataloging librarian at the Pennsylvania State University. He sees no incompatibility between adhering to national cataloging conventions and agitating for national conventions that make a little more sense.

Kelly Webster has been a cataloger for 10 years. She is a member of the Oneida Tribe of Indians of Wisconsin, past president of the American Indian Library Association, and compiler of the bibliography *Library Services to Indigenous Populations*. She enjoys rock and roll, Dr Pepper, and driving.

Bella Hass Weinberg is professor, Division of Library and Information Science, St. John's University, New York. She organized the conference entitled *Cataloging Heresy: Challenging the Standard Bibliographic Product*, and edited its proceedings. Dr. Weinberg consulted on the development of RLIN's Hebrew capability. She has radical ideas on non–Roman cataloging.

Jen Wolfe worked as a rock 'n' roll cataloger at Seattle's Experience Music Project museum, then relocated to Iowa, where her current position is metadata librarian for Digital Library Services, University of Iowa Libraries. Her electronic surrogate can be found at <http://www.jenw.org>.

Jennifer Young is a serials cataloger at a large university in the Midwest. In her spare time, she enjoys reading/watching science fiction, music, puzzles/games and being a gadfly.

Index